Dream Cultures

Dream Cultures

Explorations in the Comparative History of Dreaming

EDITED BY
David Shulman
and
Guy G. Stroumsa

New York Oxford
Oxford University Press
1999

Oxford University Press

Oxford New York
Athens Auckland Bangkok Bogotá Buenos Aires Calcutta
Cape Town Chennai Dar es Salaam Delhi Florence Hong Kong Istanbul
Karachi Kuala Lumpur Madrid Melbourne Mexico City Mumbai
Nairobi Paris São Paulo Singapore Taipei Tokyo Toronto Warsaw

and associated companies in
Berlin Ibadan

Published by Oxford University Press, Inc.
198 Madison Avenue, New York, New York 10016

Library of Congress Cataloging-in-Publication Data

Dream cultures : explorations in the comparative history of dreaming / edited by
David Shulman and Guy G. Stroumsa.
p. cm.
Papers originally presented at a workshop held at the Jagdschloss
Hubertusstock, in Markt Brandenburg, in September 1995.
Includes bibliographical references.
ISBN 0-19-512336-0
1. Dreams—Cross-cultural studies—Congresses. 2. Dreams—
History—Congresses. 3. Dream interpretation—Cross-cultural
studies—Congresses. 4. Dream interpretation—History—Congresses.
I. Shulman, David Dean, 1949– . II. Stroumsa, Gedaliahu A. G.
BF1091.D68 1999
135′.3—dc21 98-17107

1 3 5 7 9 8 6 4 2

Printed in the United States of America
on acid-free paper

For our friend Charles Malamoud
and in memory of Catherine Malamoud

Contents

Contributors

Aleida Assmann is Professor of English and Comparative Literature at the University of Konstanz and an authority on English Renaissance works. Among her books are the edited volumes *Schrift und Gedächtnis* (with Jan Assmann and Christof Hardmeier, 1983), *Kanon und Zensur* (with Jan Assmann, 1987), and *Weisheit* (1990).

Hubert Cancik is Professor of Classics at Eberhard-Karls University in Tübingen. His main fields of research are the cultural history of antiquity, the history of ancient religions, and the history of classical scholarship. Among his books are *Mythische und historische Wahrheit: Interpretationen zu Texten der hethitischen, biblischen und griechischen Historiographie* (1970), *Dioniso in Germania* (1989), *Nietzches Antike* (1995), and *Antik-Modern* (1997).

Wendy Doniger is Mircea Eliade Professor of the History of Religions at the University of Chicago. By training a dancer and Indologist, she is the author of *Asceticism and Eroticism in the Mythology of Śiva* (1973), *The Origins of Evil in Indian Mythology* (1976), *Dreams, Illusion and Other Realities* (1984), *Other People's Myths* (1987), and many other books and essays. She is currently completing an encyclopedic study of sexual doubling in world literature.

Cristiano Grottanelli is Professor of the History of Religion at the University of Pisa. His special interest is in religion and mythology of the ancient Near East and classical Greece. His most recent book is *Kings and Prophets* (1998).

Galit Hasan-Rokem is Max and Margarete Grunwald Professor of Folklore at the Hebrew University, Jerusalem. A poet and translator in Hebrew, she is also the author of *Proverbs in Israeli Folk Narrative: A Structural Semantic Analysis* (1982), a book on Georgian proverbs in Israel, and *The Web of Life: Folklore in Rabbinic Literature* (1996, Hebrew).

Moshe Idel is Max Cooper Professor of Jewish Thought at the Hebrew University, Jerusalem. Among his many works are *Kabbalah: New Perspectives* (1987), *The Mystical Experience in Abraham Abulafia* (1987), *Golem: Jewish Magical and Mystical Traditions on the Artificial Anthropoid* (1990), and *Hasidism: Between Ecstasy and Magic* (1995).

Stéphane Moses is Professor Emeritus of German and Comparative Literature at the Hebrew University, Jerusalem, and Founding Director of the Franz Rosenzweig Research Center for German-Jewish Literature and Cultural History there. Among his publications are *Une affinité litteraire: le "Titan" de Jean-Paul et le "Docteur Faustus" de Thomas Mann* (1972), *Système et Revelation: La philosophie de Franz Rosenzweig* (1982), *Spuren der Schrift: Von Goethe des Celan* (1987), *L'Ange de l'histoire: Rosenzweig, Benjamin, Scholem* (1992), and numerous essays on Goethe, Büchner, Nietzsche, Freud, Kafka, Benjamin, Celan, Jabes, Levinas, and Jewish philosophy.

Jean-Claude Schmitt is Directeur d'Etudes at the Ecole des Hautes Etudes en Sciences Sociales, Paris. He is a historian of the European Middle Ages working on the relations between folk and ecclesiastical culture and the historical anthropology of this period. Among his works are *Mort d'une hérésie* (1978), *Le saint lévrier* (1979; English translation, 1983), and *Les revenants* (1994; English translation, 1998).

David Shulman is Professor of Indian Studies and Comparative Religion at the Hebrew University, Jerusalem. He has published translations into Hebrew and English from classical Indian poetry and several books on the literatures and religion of medieval south India. His works include *Tamil Temple Myths* (1980), *The King and the Clown in South Indian Myth and Poetry* (1985), *The Hungry God* (1993), and (with Don Handelman) *God Inside Out: Śiva's Game of Dice* (1997).

Guy G. Stroumsa is Martin Buber Professor of Comparative Religion at the Hebrew University, Jerusalem, specializing in the history of early Christianity, Gnosticism, Manichaeism, and the religious and intellectual life of late antiquity. Among his works are *Another Seed: Studies in Gnostic Mythology* (1984), *Savoir et salut* (1992), *Hidden Wisdom: Esoteric Traditions and the Roots of Christian Mysticism* (1996), and *Barbarian Philosophy: the Religious Revolution of Early Christianity* (1999).

Sara Sviri holds the Catherine Lewis Lectureship in Medieval Jewish Studies at University College, London. Her main area of interest is the formative period of Islamic mysticism, in particular the imprint of late antique systems on its ascetic and doctrinal aspects. She has been also studying points of contact between Islamic and Jewish spiritual systems in Spain of the pre-Kabbalistic era. She is the author of *The Taste of Hidden Things: Images on the Sufi Path* (1997).

Barbara Tedlock is Professor of Anthropology at the State University of New York at Buffalo. She has worked extensively in Mesoamerica. She edited the volume *Dreaming: Anthropological and Psychological Interpretations* (1987).

Dennis Tedlock is McNulty Professor of English at the State University of New York at Buffalo and a leading scholar in the areas of mythology, ethnopoetics, and Native American studies. Among his books is a translation of the *Popol Vuh: The Mayan Book of the Dawn of Life* (1995), which won the PEN Translation Award.

Wai-yee Li is Professor of Chinese Literature at Princeton University and the author of *Enchantment and Disenchantment: Love and Illusion in Chinese Literature* (1993). She is now working on a study of historiographical modes in medieval Chinese sources.

Christine Walde teaches Classics at the University of Basle. She is the author of *Herculeus Labor: Studien zum pseudosenecanischen Hercules Oetaeus* (1992). From 1990 to 1993 she was a research fellow at the Sigmund Freud Institute, Frankfurt, working on the classical heritage in Freud's *Interpretation of Dreams* and in psychoanalytical dream research. She has recently received support from the Deutsche Forschungsgemeinschaft for a project on the representation of dreams in ancient poetry from Homer to Silius Italicus.

Dream Cultures

1

Introduction

David Shulman and Guy G. Stroumsa

1

This volume attempts to draw out some elements of a comparative, cross-cultural history of dreams. We treat dreaming as a cultural act, for while we by no means assume that we can make direct contact with the dream itself, in any of our texts, there is no doubt that the dream report and all subsequent interpretation and decoding are expressive of culturally specific themes, patterns, tensions, and meanings. Every dream culture articulates issues and makes assumptions, implicitly or otherwise, about the relatively private or public nature of dreams; the conditions in which dreams may reveal the future (or the past); the boundaries between the individual and society; the composition of the dreaming subject; and so on. To tell one's dream—first, perhaps, to oneself, then to another (perhaps a professional interpreter), and finally to still wider circles—is *always* an overdetermined act or statement, at once situating the self in relation to a rich universe of cultural meanings and implied metaphysical intuitions and creating, or re-creating, that same universe from within.

The essays included in this volume were initially presented at a workshop held at the Jagdschloss Hubertusstock in Markt Brandenburg in September, 1995, under the auspices of the Einstein Forum in Potsdam and the Institute for Advanced Studies of the Hebrew University of Jerusalem. The workshop was held exactly one hundred years after Freud finished the redaction of his *Traumdeutung* (although the book appeared only in 1900). Yet as *Kulturforscher*, we sought to understand the significance of dreams in different religious contexts in a way rather alien to the psychoanalytical tradition. Our primary assumption—that the place and role of dreams, and the very status of dreaming, are strongly influenced by cultural traditions and religious attitudes—led us to search for conspicuous differences in cross-cultural patterns of dreaming and of dream interpretation, rather than for their universal elements. The modern assumption that dreaming is the most private and personal of modes is not shared by many of the cultures represented here, which sometimes see dreams as highly objectified, even capable of appearing in the consciousness of disparate subjects. We make no commitment to either of these views; our efforts have focused on the dream as witnessed, transmitted linguistically, framed as text, and interpreted, always in a culturally specific context. Such a context inevitably situates dreaming within an organized ecology of cultural forms and assigns its value. Some cultures (for example, the Maya peoples of Central America) make dreaming one of the most central and powerful of all expressive and ontic domains, while others may relegate dreaming to the periphery of the truly real. Theories of dream-communication—the modes of encoding, decoding, and interpretation—are always keyed to the semantics of such articulated cultural space.

The chapters in this volume thus deal with the comparative cultures of dreaming. As such, they build upon earlier cross-cultural and interdisciplinary studies, and reflect certain assumptions and emphases that we shall attempt to make explicit here. Various collective efforts have been devoted in recent years to the place of dreams in different cultures. There have been excellent studies by anthropologists and medievalists, for example, and several important collections have been published. We wish to mention the volumes edited by Barbara Tedlock and Tulio Gregory.[1] Most recently we have *Il sogno raccontato*, a rich volume of essays on the various literary expressions of dreams in Western culture.[2]

Perhaps the most influential collective enterprise in this domain remains that of Roger Caillois and Gustav von Grunebaum, which appeared a generation ago.[3] The authors attempted a wide-ranging analysis of dreams within various cultures, but the focus of their essays is not on the differentiated, culture-specific (or religion-specific) perception of dreams in a comparative mode. Islam is well treated, with six essays, but relatively little attention is devoted to other religious traditions. The main methodological assumption of the volume, it seems, was the recognition that in the age of modernity ushered in by Descartes, "We have less need of our dreams," in von Grunebaum's lapidary formulation.[4]

We do not intend to discuss this assumption. Our approach is at once less broad and more encompassing. On one hand, we did not seek to be as interdisciplinary as Caillois and von Grunebaum, and did not attempt to include here any contemporary physiological or psychological studies of dreaming. On the other hand, we have sought to cover as varied a cultural and religious ground as possible. We have not forged a single approach, nor have we concentrated on any single civilization; and this is not, by any means, an encyclopedic effort. Obviously, our collection of articles is far from being exhaustive. We have three papers on India, for instance, but Africa remains a missing continent.

We cannot pretend that our collective investigation has led us to any clear-cut conclusions—nor to generalizations free of context, of universal implication.

It may be possible, however, to point to some problems that we felt could be formulated more sharply, or more intensely, through our common endeavor.

Since we approached the comparative history of dreams from the perspective of the history of religions, the first question to be asked is whether we can draw a taxonomy of dreams established upon the different types of religions. (Of course, the relation between concepts such as "culture" and "religion" is not always constant: in China, for example, we find several competing religions within a single overriding cultural frame, in contrast to the situation in medieval Christian Europe.) Can we perceive a clear difference between the nature, importance, and role of dreams within religions established upon revelation and those, as in Greece, where such a single revelation, emerging from a precise moment and locus, does not play a role? Prima facie, it would seem that while in polytheistic systems contact flows rather freely between the divine realm and the human world, no place is left for an infinite series of private revelations in a revealed religion, where the borders are much more closely guarded. In a monotheistic system, moreover, significant dreams can come either from the divine world or from the realm of Satan. We do not mean to imply that all so-called polytheistic systems attribute the same degree of religious significance to dreaming. As Hubert Cancik shows in his chapter, public Roman religion almost ignores dreaming, in striking contrast to the central importance of dreams in Greek myth and cult.

Still, the evidence shows that dreams retain a major place in cultures formed under the impact of monotheistic, revelatory religions. Although we can detect a clear shrinking of the *poiesis* expressed in dreams in the transition from late-classical to Christian culture, dreams retain a crucial, although new role in the latter. As for Islam, there is no need to repeat, after the various studies in *The Dream in Human Societies*, that dreaming and dream interpretation play remarkably rich and differentiated roles in various Islamic cultures. What this shows, at the least, is that even in revelatory religions, the gates of revelation can never become hermetically closed. Here dreams play a central role. It should be emphasized that since dreaming is usually, in some sense, a personal phenomenon, the individual can develop a direct link to the divinity through dreams—hence the great danger of dreams for religious hierarchies and orthodoxies. Dreams are often the direct path to heresy. Indeed, the hallmark of a heretic is often the revelatory dreams which, as in the case of Mani, he experiences already in his childhood, and which set him apart from the traditional religious hierarchy. It is in this context that we can understand the constant shying away from—indeed, often fierce opposition to—dreams on the part of religious authorities, who are motivated by a wish to contain, as much as possible, the power of divination. In the pervasive religious system of medieval Europe, as we learn from the essay by Jean-Claude Schmitt, we find both a remarkable efflorescence of popular dream culture and a consistent effort on the part of the ecclesiastic authorities to take control of this potentially subversive domain.

We have looked for new ways of understanding the role of dreams in cultures shaped by different religious worldviews. Dreams are not only directly connected to divination; they also reflect on other segments of culture. It is here that the core of our analysis should be focused. By their very liminality, dreams are at the confluence of theology, cosmology, and anthropology. In a sense, they permit, where other media fail, a way of intracultural communication of great flexibility. In particular, dreams offer a constant balance between the private world of latent images, fears, and hopes, and outside reality, cosmic as well as social. Dreams present the means to reestablish the constantly shattered equilibrium between these two realms. They accomplish this essential task in different ways, always directly related to the individual religious cultures. Such, at least, is the assumption underlining our work.

An important key—by no means the only one—for understanding the parameters through which this equilibrium is established and broken is the nature of the subject and its boundaries. Religious traditions with a predominant view of the person as a well-defined entity, set in opposition to the outside world, will encourage a dream culture of a certain nature. A religious tradition for which the self is not real in the deepest ontological sense, or is ultimately to be dissolved, or is thoroughly interpenetrated with nonself elements, will undoubtedly produce a dream culture of a rather different nature. Different dreams will be noticed, emphasized as significant, described, memorized, singled out in the literary tradition, and presented as models. In a crude way, dreams can be perceived as coming from "outside" or from "inside"—and this choice has far-reaching cultural implications. The relationship between dreams and myths, although too complex an issue to be treated in passing, might be mentioned as an analogous problem for differential, comparative analysis. Dennis Tedlock discusses a highly unusual pattern of dreams reported within myths in Mayan texts.

Although one should be careful not to draw direct analogies between linguistic patterns and religious perceptions, variation in the ontological status of dreams is also reflected in language. *Blepô oneiron* ("I see a dream," Greek), *ḥalamti ḥalom* ("I dreamt a dream," Hebrew), *es träumt mir/ich traume, je rève*: these are very different ways, chosen almost at random, of referring to the simple act of dreaming. Does the Greek way of speaking of dreams, with its insistence upon vision, reflect a universal pattern? It is hard to imagine a dream culture in which vision would not play a central role, but one should also mention the importance of *hearing* in dreams (particularly emphasized by Dennis Tedlock with reference to the Mayan corpus). It might be interesting to check whether voice and sound are more prominent in a certain kind of religious culture, for instance in those that stem from aniconic religions. But we tread here on very thin ground, and historical reality is too complex to allow for any easy categorization. We can, at least, state that dreams reflect the fundamental diglossia of humans. The thought expressed in dreams, or more precisely in the representation of dreams, is figurative rather than abstract, and here too, it complements diurnal ways of relating to the outside world and organizing it.

When we speak of the outside world and of the cosmos, we also refer to the temporal dimension. Do dreams suppress or create time? Do they prolong or shorten it? Dreams can refer to the past, either real or mythical. They can also refer to the future, either as divination (which usually means the immediate future, which can be predicted and often also manipulated) or as Utopia, the dream of an ideal future, parallel in a sense to the original ideal time, the *Urzeit* or mythical beginnings of history. The notion of utopia also reflects the passage from dreaming *stricto sensu*, that is, fundamentally a personal activity, to the metaphorical use of the term, which refers to collective representations. Do different cultures relate these two areas differently? How does dreaming, in the utopian mode, but also in other respects, link with specific eschatologies?

2

Dreaming is a language—like all language, more or less displaced; like all language, both over- and underdetermined. To read the dream, or to hear it, or to know it, or to understand it, is to address oneself to the existence of one or more active codes. There is, perhaps, a near-universal experience of dreaming as communication, a more or less enigmatic presentation of meaningful messages to the self (and *from* the self, or from some profound dimension of reality, or from God). This experience, however, reaches us only in modes pregnant with the axiology and anxieties of a given, usually complex, usually multivocal cultural world.

None of this is new: earlier studies have departed from the same point; comparative typologies of dreams, as culturally perceived and interpreted, have been offered; illuminating parallels and divergences among dream cultures have been noted. We have tried to go a step farther by addressing, above all, primary issues of integration—that is, the integration of dream culture, and the peculiar expressivity of dreams, into the wider arenas where major cultural themes, obsessions, and choices are always present; then, the integration of dream interpretation into the culture's ontological and semiotic maps; and finally, the integration of dream theory into the culturally specific economies of consciousness and the notions of personality, so that dreaming can be seen in the context of an implicit or explicit anthropology and metapsychology. We seek, in short, to explore where dreaming belongs within a given cognitive and expressive universe; within a given metaphysical range; and within a given understanding of the dreaming subject. Can the dream dream the dreamer? Is the dream internal to the dreamer, or to his god?

These areas are closely correlated. Let us take an example. A South Indian folktale tells us of a king who dreams of an amazing silver tree, its leaves of emerald, with ruby fruits; an emerald parrot is perched, singing, on a golden swing hanging from its branches. The king, in his dream, casts a serpent jewel at the parrot, and the vision vanishes. As in so many Indian stories, the king, on awaking, has one overriding wish—he wants to see this tree in waking reality. He sends his three sons in search of it. The elder two soon give up the quest, but the youngest persists. Aided by advice from an old woman, he finds the tree of his father's dream inside a fortress that has no gates. He steals a jewel from a serpent who lives near the fortress, and watches as the serpent kills himself in rage; then, with the aid of the jewel, he enters the fortress and sees the tree turn into four lovely princesses, who ask him to marry them. He agrees—but first he must seek the emerald parrot, who is "really" the sister of these princesses; she is kept captive on a lotus in a lake across the seven seas. The prince makes his way across the water, shines the jewel on the sleeping princess, and wakes her. Now they can rejoin her sisters and, together, return to the prince's home. But the king, seeing his son surrounded by five radiant women, is still dissatisfied; he had sent him, after all, to find his dream. The prince stands the five princesses in a row and, to everyone's horror, beheads them all with a single stroke of his sword. Suddenly, right there in the palace, the dream is reenacted: the miraculous tree stands, with emerald leaves, ruby fruits, the golden swing, the parrot, in his father's presence. The prince casts the serpent jewel at the parrot, and the apparition disappears, leaving in its place the five women who will become his wives, as he assumes the kingship.[5]

The basic pattern of this story is well represented in Indian literature. The dream is an objective "fact" that can be found or recovered in the outer world, and that makes itself present in consciousness through mechanisms, say, of karmic memory or intersubjective sensitivity. Thus the king in effect is dreaming for his son—a dream of sexual and psychological maturation that entails the quest, its various acts of violence and faith, and the final reintegration of the prince and his new brides into his father's reality. The dream establishes an ambiguous channel of communication, not so much between parts of the father's self or selves (as we might expect in a Western ontology) as between the father and his child, and between both these figures and a tantalizing but accessible, visionary world outside them. In this sense, above all others, the dream speaks a powerful truth. If we think in terms of the three domains outlined above, we would say: this story uses the dream, as a heavily determined trope or expressive device, to articulate a pattern of generational conflict and psychic growth; it fixes the dream firmly at the center of a fluid ontological continuum, where an internal experience demands external reexperiencing, confirmation, or conditional concretization—or where it may even be impossible to locate a clear innerness as opposed to a clearly differentiated outside; and it emerges from an understanding of subject or self as deeply involved in negotiating precisely this slippery boundary, in which the objectified dream in some sense repeatedly forms or shapes the dreamer and his or her evolving and expanding selves. There is also the fascinating problem, implicit in the structure of this tale, of the status of the dream narrative in relation to the wider narrative frame. The father makes his dream into a story that actualizes itself, in unexpected ways, in the story the son tells of himself, or, we may assume, *to* himself. Here full maturation into an adult mode of being—marriage, mature sexuality, the assumption of power and a public role—requires the son to live out (and also, perhaps, ultimately to uproot) his father's dream.

Even in this slight example we note a standard feature from the domain of encoding: the striking dream image is opaque, a veil for the human reality of falling in love and marrying. This image has to be destroyed, within the story itself (in fact, within the dream itself), before the underlying process can be complete. In most dream cultures, dreaming is a language that, like other languages, needs deciphering. The following chapters offer differing examples of this process which, taken together, suggest a rough typology: there are dreams that present the dreamer with a clear-cut message, seemingly entirely transparent (e.g., the materials relating to Alemano, al-Tirmidhi, and pseudo-Maimonides, discussed by Moshe Idel and Sara Sviri); others present encoded messages of varying levels of ambiguity (e.g., the Roman examples set out in Hubert Cancik's chapter).

In certain cultures, the encoded dream can be unambiguously decoded, leaving us again with a clear-cut message; in others, a residue of ambiguity is a structural feature of dreaming per se. Contextual features, relating in particular to the identity and existential situation of the dreamer, may be decisive in decoding, as we can see in Artemidorus and the other Greek materials discussed by Cristiano Grottanelli. Coded dreams include the false messages sent by the devil (as Guy G. Stroumsa and Jean-Claude Schmitt show in many Christian materials)—although we might also allow for the possibility that true messages could come from this demonic source. And within this wide range of encoded dream communications, there is a variation in the role of the interpreter. Galit Hasan-Rokem shows that in Midrashic materials the dream follows the interpretation (so that the responsibility of the decoder is enormous, literally one of life and death); in other cases, the message exists *only* within its interpretation, the two domains being so interpenetrated that the linguistic formation of the dream could almost be said to preexist, to antedate its imagery and its narrativized report. Language enters into this process at different points in different cultures: at the very beginning, or even before the beginning, in many Indian dream materials; very late, after the fact of dreaming and its remembrance, in Talmudic dream culture; somewhere between these two poles in Artemidorus, or the Mesoamerican materials, or, perhaps, in Freud (see the chapter by Christine Walde).

There is also a third possibility in terms of coding and decoding, alongside the options of transparent and opaque messages embedded in the dream. There are dreams with no message, in any "real," semantically weighty sense—dreams that, rather than communicate contents, represent existential states or transformations. At least one set of Chinese dreams presented by Wai-yee Li seems to fit this category, as do most of the Indian materials studied in this volume. Vasavadatta's dream, discussed by Wendy Doniger, is a concrete waking experience encoded only in the sense that all perception is subject to disguise. The dream of the parrot-messenger, from Kerala in south India, discussed by Shulman, seems primarily aimed at effecting the rare coincidence of selves, or of language and identity, that is perhaps most possible in the dream domain. Here a dream of lovers' separation ends by a realignment, a tautology of existence that finds expression in the repeated trope called *śleṣa*, literally an "embrace," a superimposition. The trope encapsulates and triggers the shift in state inherent in the process unfolding through the dream.

Dream tropes of this sort require attention. Many of the authors have isolated and defined such figures, which constitute, in specific dream cultures, the peculiar language of both dreaming and interpretation. In this area of culturally specific figuration, we feel we have progressed beyond Freud's original definition of four major forms of dream symbolism (condensation, displacement, considerations of representability, and secondary revision; see Aleida Assmann's presentation of still earlier syntheses in Chapter 15). A notion of overdetermination remains in a remarkable number of cases. The dream-message is reinforced internally by a series of potential markers, by the characteristic tropes or figures, by verbal and visual images strongly keyed to individual dream cultures. As in all linguistic forms, principles of selection operate powerfully to express the genre broadly defined as "dream," and to clue the listener or interpreter about the boundaries and peculiar intensities and textures of the dream text. We have also suggested that more attention needs to be paid, in general, to issues of "marking"—poetic, syntactic, or generally linguistic—with relation to dream texts; Barbara Tedlock's explication of evidentials in dream reports shows just how critical, and informative, this area can be. Evidentials, like other elements in the linguistic texturing of dreams, also speak to ontic issues: the dream's "as-if" quality is set off by such markers, which may also have an impact on the recurrent question of where, if the dream is "subjunctive," the indicative or objective reality forms are to be sought. Both Freud and the Talmudic tractate *Berachot* suggest, for example, that the key to this problem lies in the payment offered the interpreter—the rock-bottom reality that ensures a link between dream and world.

Typologies, in themselves, and especially in cross-cultural contexts, may be barren. At best, they may suggest lines of force that require study in a given case. The simple division we have presented in the above forms of dream expressivity, in relation to encoding, may be correlated to other domains—for example, that of the dream's ontological status, which varies from fully objectified externality to pure subjective fantasy ("it was *only* a dream"), with a third possibility, that of dreaming as an act of linguistic creativity, mediating between the two poles. Dreams with no message, our third category above, seem most closely linked to the third ontic option. Even more fertile, perhaps, is an attempt to correlate the dream communication with theories of self-organization or self-presentation, as we find in Moshe Idel's chapter on astral dreams. Idel distinguishes between the loosely organized "centrifugal" personality and a much more severely delimited and controlled "centripetal" structure. It would appear, in general, that the centrifugal type is broadly aligned with the relatively more objectified (and transparent) dream, while a centripetal vision of self and person puts dreaming further along the continuum toward the subjective pole. And in both cases—indeed in most dream cultures—one finds a latent or implied division within the self, which reproduces itself in the strange forms of self-conscious doubling that we find in so many reported dreams. The dreamer dreams, and watches himself dreaming. Often a series of embedded frames is present, the dreamer knowing within the dream that he is dreaming—although such cases of what is called "lucid dreaming" seem to require a paradoxical kind of knowing, knowledge that is itself a dream. In the more intense and sophisticated dream cultures, such as in Mesoamerica, these forms of lucid dreaming may reach almost unimaginable complexity, with multiple dreams within dreams within dreams. (These patterns are discussed by Barbara and Dennis Tedlock.) But lucid dreaming also seems to be a universal phenomenon, differently conceived and understood within the varying civilizational contexts.

Everywhere, dreaming speaks to the composition, or decomposition, of the self. Markers, tropes, frames, and ontic presuppositions are all relevant to any analysis of this domain, which offers tremendous potential for unlocking the hidden metaphysic of cultural intuitions, perhaps too deeply buried to be formulated explicitly from within. From an analytical, external perspective, we can see very striking contours: for example, the deep division in the self that seems to find expression in late antiquity, and especially in Christian dream-culture—and that continues right up through Freud, as Stephane Moses shows in his nuanced essay. This splitting illuminates, by way of contrast, the subtle and striking problem of internal doubling that we see, for example, in the Indian materials (in the chapters by Wendy Doniger and David Shulman). There are further aspects open to comparative analysis—to mention only one more, the role of time and memory relative to dreaming. Thus we find an evolving, future-oriented (divinatory) dream culture in the Midrashic materials, and in Artemidorus, in contrast with a retrospective trend evident in the Christian materials; the same division, broadly stated, seems present in India between the future-oriented Hindu dreams and the eerily retrospective Buddhist ones of the Tamil *Maṇimekalai.* These distinctions have meaning and, at times, a rich resonance and—such is our hope—give color and purpose to intercultural comparisons.

Such comparisons emerge partly through intertextual resonances in these essays. We have referred above to the common theme of lucid dreaming, where the dreamer's awareness of the dream is embedded within the dream itself. In one way or another, every system of dream interpretation faces this issue of the dream's frame and the transitions it makes possible, within the totality of consciousness, from nondream to dream states and back again, or from one dream level to another. Several of the essays attempt to characterize the dream frame and its markers, and to formulate the relation between this frame and other ontic realities recognized by the culture (see Wai-yee Li, Shulman, Barbara and Dennis Tedlock, Assmann). Indeed, there is reason to argue that the articulation of the frame for dream narrative and dream interpretation is the central diagnostic key for a differential typology of dream cultures. The frame not only enables and structures the transition to and from dreaming; it also shapes the contours of time, space, and consciousness within which the dream can be said, or felt, to exist. When the frame is strongly embedded within the dream, as in various types of lucid dreaming, a restless inner movement, leading toward transformation, tends to emerge, sometimes overwhelming the subject and catapulting her or him to new forms of awareness. When the frame is relatively rigid, or implanted firmly in the waking world, the impact of the dream may be partly neutralized (both in individual and social terms), and the dreamer rendered relatively passive, a spectator at an idiosyncratic internal drama.

More porous or malleable frames may allow for startling effects, as when the future, for example, infiltrates the present in a backward movement—time flowing, as it were, upstream.

Such frames, which determine how the dream is molded into cultural form, might even, for all we know, determine how the dream is dreamt, as an act of cultural creativity. And each such frame has a spatial aspect capable of analytical formulation: we can sometimes distinguish dreams dreamt at the outer margin of the subject, as if split away from his or her inner core, from those in which the subject is poised at the margins of the dream, seen as an overriding reality from outside the bounds of the individual. Such spatial configurations are always contingent and colored by social meaning. Moreover, the cultural framing of the dream always and inevitably evokes the cultural framing of consciousness itself—its structure, internal dynamics, and situation vis-à-vis the subject and all forms of reality that this subject confronts. These two frames—of dream and consciousness—may overlap, to the point of isomorphism, or one may cut across the other in various unusual and surprising ways. Usually, however they may intersect, they tend to replicate one another in terms of their organizing principles of composition, which are always cultural creations, laden with axiological and metaphysical concerns.

It is this fact of consistent intracultural replication that allows us to conceive of a differentiated, comparative, nonuniversal syntax of dreaming, and of dream interpretation. Only such a syntax can make sense of the discrete morphologies of dream contents, of symbols, markers, and the lineaments of interpretation, all of these elements being integrated in unique expressive patterns flowing out of each specific frame. The essays gathered here may be seen as steps toward the future elaboration of such a context-sensitive, historicized syntax, or as examples of what such a syntax might look like in the case of particular dream cultures.

Dream interpreters also frequently echo one another: The uncanny connection between Artemidorus and Freud is well known, even explicitly affirmed by Freud himself; but the essays by Walde, Grottanelli, and Moses highlight the differing internal organization of these respective dream cultures and their distinct axiological bases. We might also note an implicit parameter of richness in dealing with these distinct traditions, and its potentially paradoxical dimension. Thus it appears that Artemidorus applies a remarkably rich interpretative spectrum to a relatively limited or even impoverished corpus of dream texts, in contrast to the luxuriance of modern dream texts together with the relative marginalization of dream interpretation in the modern West. For Freud, as for modern Western civilization as a whole, the dream has been fully subjectivized: it no longer refers to another world, outside the individual, nor has it any legitimate location within the public sphere. Even notions such as that of a shared dream—between husband and wife, for example, as we find in the examples of Al-Tirmidhi and his wife and Milton's Adam and Eve (cited by Sviri and Assmann, respectively), or in many parallel examples from India[6]—have become attenuated in the extreme and now appear rather exotic (as in the case of the analyst who dreams counter-transferentially of his patient). Nevertheless, the underlying, fundamental problem of the relation between existential realms, and the role of the dream as a tissue of potential connectivity, remain common to all the dream cultures discussed in this volume. The variation in articulating or conceptualizing this linkage is enormous; the following essays are meant to exemplify specific cases and, by their juxtaposition and intertextuality, to suggest a common problematic.

Certain basic, relatively simple questions arise naturally as we move through the dreams of one civilization after another. If dreams are perceived, almost universally, as inherently communicative (though not necessarily in referential ways), then we need to ask in each case: when do people tell their dreams, and where, and to whom? How is the telling structured? How does the dream content relate to narration, and to the social and cultural context? What images of authority reside in the act of interpretation, or of narrating the dream? Where is the dream situated in relation to the entire ecology of cultural forms? And, again: who is it who dreams, or is dreamed, or who dreams within the dream? What claims does that person make for the dream, the self, the world? How are these claims organized within the available domains of language, thought, and feeling?

Such questions informed the discussions that formed the essays included here. They are not meant to be exhaustive; but it is our hope that they trace, however fleetingly, a new agenda for the study of dream cultures, and of the dream of culture.

Notes

1. Tedlock: 1987; Gregory: 1985. Also see Kruger: 1992.
2. Merola and Verbaro: 1995.
3. Caillois and von Grunebaum: 1966.
4. See also the collection of essays, Caillois and von Grunebaum: 1959, which deals with a multiplicity of non-Western cultures.
5. Kannada story recorded by A. K. Ramanujan: 1997.
6. See O'Flaherty: 1984.

References

Caillois, R. and G. von Grunebaum (eds.). 1959. *Les songes et leur interprétation*. Paris.

——— (eds.). 1966. *The Dream and Human Societies*. Berkeley and Los Angeles.

Gregory, T. (ed.). 1985. *Il sogni nel medioevo*. Rome.

Kruger, S. F. 1992. *Dreaming in the Middle Ages*. Cambridge.

Merola N. and C. Verbaro (eds.). 1995. *Il sogno raccontato: Atti del convegno internazionale di Rende (12–14 novembre 1992)*. Vibo Valentia.

O'Flaherty, W. D. 1984. *Dreams, Illusion, and Other Realities*. Chicago.

Ramanujan, A. K. 1997. *A Flowering Tree*. Berkeley.

Tedlock, B. (ed.). 1987. *Dreaming: Anthropological and Psychological Interpretations*. Cambridge.

I

China and India

2

Dreams of Interpretation in Early Chinese Historical and Philosophical Writings

Wai-yee Li

The Readability of the World

In the *Zuo zhuan*[1] (*Zuo Commentary Tradition*, ca. fifth to fourth centuries B.C.?), the earliest narrative history in China, the representation of dreams emerges as one way to structure events and to impose order on human experience. Dreams establish causality—on the symbolic level, as a sign that is fulfilled, unravelled, or betrayed; on the literal level, as advice or warning heeded or defied. The representation of dreams is motivated by the need to interpret and define causes and consequences. In this sense it asserts or questions the "readability" of the world and shapes our understanding of causality, human agency, and possible "reason in history" (be it a moral scheme rewarding good and punishing evil, or a certain vision of order or teleology). I suggest that themes of control and order, or lack thereof, are dominant. Thus with dreams that realize ritual disorder or improper relations between the human world and the realm of the spirits, interpretation restores ritual equilibrium. Even when the message of the dream, often about the dreamer's death, is implacable, the struggle of control over its meaning is evident in the dream itself and/or its interpretation. Arbitrary injunctions in dreams and equivocal dreams that invite different decoding augur moments of loss of control, which are often overcome with interpretive ingenuity, but which nevertheless lead us to consider the scope and meaning of skepticism.

The interpretation of dreams in the *Zuo zhuan* thus tells of dreams of interpretation. It points to the following partly overlapping questions: Why interpret? What are the grounds of interpretation? How do interpretive structures evolve and disintegrate? What are the possibilities and limits of historical knowledge, or, put differently, the scope and meaning of skepticism? Why and how are interpretive acts represented? The interpretation of dreams is one aspect of a ubiquitous phenomenon in this text: the reading of signs, which structures events, defines narrative units, and abstracts patterns and meanings from the chronological flow. The *Zuo zhuan*'s commitment to chronology[2] forces on the reader a certain sense of totality, fluidity, and contingency, a feeling that multifarious events have no definite beginnings and endings, that everything is indeed connected to everything else. The reading of signs is what saves us from the sense of raw juxtapositions in the text.

On one level dreams do not diverge much from other signs in the *Zuo zhuan* such as results of divination, encounters with gods, ghosts, and spirits, riddles, astronomical phenomena, natural anomalies or observed details of a person's attire, speech, behavior, gestures, or movements in rituals. All are readable signs that yield prophetic or retrospective judgments. Whereas human signs, such as a gesture or a comment that captures the essence of a person and thereby explains character and destiny,[3] augment moral explanations and human agency in history, signs from the numinous realm may sometimes seem random and arbitrary and convey a determinist mood. In the dense symbolic universe of the *Zuo zhuan*, dreams function as both human and numinous signs. Decoded both in terms of the dreamer's motivations, hopes, and fears, and of a more general, "objectified" system of correspondence, dreams exemplify two parallel concerns in the *Zuo zhuan*: moral explanation, predicated on the human capacity to choose; and pansignification, whereby every human or nonhuman sign and action leads to consequences that may exceed human comprehension and control. There are tensions between these two concerns but both presume analogical thinking. Moral action implies correspondence to ritual, sociopolitical, and cosmic order, while pan-signification implies mysterious, universal correspondences.

Dreams and their interpretation often have a public and externalized dimension in the *Zuo zhuan*. Shared dreams (*tongmeng*) are sometimes presented as proof of the objective veracity of dreams. The interpretability of dreams is thus in part a function of the dream's nature as public spectacle. Thus the Jin minister Xun Yan's dream of his own decapitation is decoded by his codreamer:

> Zhongxing Xianzi (Xun Yan) was about to launch a military expedition against Qi. He dreamed of engaging in a legal disputation with Duke Li.[4] He did not win. The duke hit him with a halberd, and his head fell in front of him. He knelt down and put it back on, holding it while running. He saw shaman Gao of Gengyang. A few days later, he saw [shaman Gao] on the road. He spoke to Gao, who [it turned out] had had the same dream. The shaman said, "This year my lord will certainly die. As for affairs in the east,[5] your wish will be fulfilled." Xianzi assented. (*ZZ* Xiang 18.3)

Shaman Gao's authority as interpreter is based both on his presence in Xun Yan's dream and his status as codreamer. Xun Yan's dream acquires objectified validity because the shaman's role as spectator persists through Xun's dream and the shaman's own dream. There is no deliberation on the moral meaning of the dream: Is Xun Yan going to die as retribution for murdering his former ruler Duke Li (*ZZ* Cheng 18.1)? Does Duke Li's original intent to eliminate Xun's clan absolve Xun Yan (*ZZ* Cheng 17.10)? Can murder of a benighted ruler be justified? The legal disputation (*song*) suggests that Xun's guilt is debatable.[6] Does Xun Yan's replacement of his head suggest vindication? Instead of dwelling on past events, however, the shaman gives a matter-of-fact prediction of future developments. Notwithstanding the horror of decapitation, shaman Gao reads in Xun Yan's dream the portent of victory in his military expedition against Qi before his death. It is not clear whether the shaman, sensing Xun Yan's imminent death, is merely encouraging him in his final effort.[7] In any case, Xun Yan accepts the predictions with dignity, which are duly fulfilled (*ZZ* Xiang 18.3, 18.4, 19.1).

A certain opacity remains. The narrative answers the question of how and why Xun Yan dies by asserting without specifying the connection between his past and his final achievement and death. The account here is not concerned with Xun Yan's pschology or the evaluation of his character. Instead, shared dreams in the *Zuo zhuan* function as public spectacle that defines choices and actions shaping the fate of the polity. In another example, Kangshu, ancestor of Wei, appears in dreams to two Wei ministers and instructs them to support "Yuan" (Duke Xiang of Wei's second son by a concubine) as ruler (*ZZ* Zhao 7.15). Subsequent debates surround the ambiguous meanings of "Yuan": does it designate a proper name or does it mean "the eldest" (i.e., Yuan's older brother Mengzhi)? (The root meaning of "Yuan" is "primary.") In this case, an injunction repeated in two dreams establishes Yuan as legitimate successor to the throne. (It is quite likely that the whole account is fabricated to establish just that.) In contrast to the public and objectified nature of shared dreams in the *Zuo zhuan*, the motif is often used in literature to affirm perfect communion and the power of subjective projection.

The public dimension of dreaming is augmented by the sense of historical continuity in the grounds of interpretation. As example we can consider Duke Zhao of Lu's dream. When he is about to visit Chu, he dreams of his father Duke Xiang sacrificing to the god of the road. (The visit implies recognition of Chu hegemony by Lu. This is significant because Chu is usually designated [against all archaeological evidence] by the heartland states as semibarbarian, whereas Lu is a state steeped in the Zhou tradition.) The Lu ministers debate the meaning of the dream. Zishen argues that Duke Zhao should not go because Duke Xiang went to Chu only upon dreaming of the Duke of Zhou, sage advisor to the early Zhou kings and ancestor of Lu, sacrificing to the god of the road.[8] In other words, none but a sage such as the Duke of Zhou can sanction a trip to Chu. In addition, the Duke of Zhou's trip to Chu supposedly demonstrated Zhou authority over Chu[9] and would allay fears that a Lu ruler's journey to Chu might indicate Lu subordination. Zifu Huibo maintains that Duke Xiang in effect takes the place of the Duke of Zhou: having once visited Chu he can sacrifice to the god of the road and lead his son (*ZZ* Zhao 7.3). Duke Xiang's authority might in turn have been derived from his ritual competence during the visit to Chu. King Kang of Chu died while Duke Xiang was on his way, and Duke Xiang arrived only to attend his funeral. Chu officials wanted to have Duke Xiang place King Kang's clothes on his coffin, a ceremony appropriate for envoys rather than rulers from other states. Acting on the advice of Shusun Zhaozi, Duke Xiang saved Lu from humiliation by having shamans perform purification rites over the coffin with peach branches and reeds, which is due procedure when a ruler attends the funeral of a minister from another state (*ZZ* Xiang 29.1). The appeal to competing precedents, the authority of the figure in the dream, and the principle of substitution all establish the continuity, albeit construed in different ways, between past and present in defining grounds of interpretation.

The debate over the meaning of Duke Zhao's dream also shows how the dream is the locus of ritual uncertainty. But there is little doubt that the correct interpretation restores ritual equilibrium. Events in the *Zuo zhuan* that offend the modern rationalist bias are often represented with this interpretive confidence. It is scarcely surprising, therefore, that the Zheng minister Zichan, often depicted as a rationalist and a skeptic in modern accounts,[10] should also interpret dreams and explain the existence of spirits. He is merely extending reason and logic to realms receding from human consciousness and understanding. When Zichan is envoy in Jin, the Jin minister Han Xuanzi asks him how the illness of the Jin ruler may be related to his dream of a yellow bear entering through his bedroom door. Zichan explains that the yellow bear is no evil spirit, but the spirit of Gun, the mythical flood controller who failed.

> Formerly Yao [ancient sage-ruler] executed Gun at the Feather Mountain [for his failure to control the deluge]. Gun's spirit was transformed into a yellow bear, and it entered the Feather Abyss. Xia actually worshipped it, and the Three Dynasties offered sacrifices to it. Jin is the leader of the Alliance [and as such should perform the ritual role of the kings of the Xia, Shang, and Zhou dynasties]. Perhaps it has not yet offered sacrifices to it. (*ZZ* Zhao 7.7)

The sacrifices are duly performed and the Jin ruler recovers. Here the interpretation of an enigmatic dream image, based on historical knowledge, also restores ritual order.

In a similar vein, Zichan expounds on how he placates the vengeful ghost of Boyou, a Zheng nobleman murdered in a power struggle between different clans. Boyou appears in the dreams of the Zheng people vowing to kill his enemies, and his threats come true. Zichan reinstates Boyou's son, who is then in a position to offer sacrifices to his father. He explains, "When ghosts have a place to return to,[11] it will not become an evil spirit. I provide the ghost with a place to return to" (*ZZ* Zhao 7.9). The dream is the locus where ghosts and spirits can manifest their discontent; it is a moment of ritual disorder marked by uneasy tension between the realm of spirits and the human world. Dreams can be suppressed, however, because all things, including ghosts, can be assigned their proper place and mollified through the performance of sacrifice. Again we have the motif of control and order.

The restoration of ritual equilibrium suggests the potential continuum between dreaming and wakeful states, analogous to the fluid boundaries between the realm of the spirits and the human world. Zichan explains why Boyou can be a powerful ghost: his clan was in charge of government for three generations, and the things they used were abundant, elaborate, and refined (*ZZ* Zhao 7.9). The potency of ghosts, including the power to manifest themselves in dreams, thus depends on their family history and the material conditions of their previous existence. The readability of dreams in the *Zuo zhuan* is a function of continuities between past and present, dreaming and waking states; hence the insistent appeal to ancestors and beginnings. In admonitory dreams, advice or warning are usually given by a dead father or ancestor. Dreams portending endings (for example, the end of a ruling house) often invoke beginnings or have to be explained with reference to beginnings. In one example, a man from Cao dreams of a group of noblemen discussing the demise of Cao. The ancestor of Cao asks other Cao dignitaries to wait for one Gongsun Qiang. The dreamer's son leaves Cao, following his father's advice, when Gongsun Qiang becomes minister. The dream is told as retrospective explanation in the year before the fall of the Cao house (*ZZ* Ai 7.5).

The warning of the Cao ancestor is clearly told in a dream, but even cryptic dream images can be confidently decoded because of the presumed applicability of the symbols of wakeful life to dream interpretation. In one example, spatial positions and directions, a major concern in ritual texts, determine the meaning of a dream. "De dreamed that Qi, with his head to the north, was sleeping outside the Lu Gate, and that he himself was a crow perching above Qi, with his beak resting on the South Gate and his tail resting on the Tong Gate. He said, 'My dream was good. I will succeed to the throne'" (*ZZ* Ai 26.2). De and Qi, both adopted sons of Duke Jing of Song, become rival claimants to the throne upon Duke Jing's death. De eventually wins out. According to ritual texts contemporaneous with and later than the *Zuo zhuan*,[12] the southward-facing position signifies life, exalted position, and rulership, whereas the northward-facing position indicates subjugation and death. In somewhat later lore, the crow is associated with fire and the sun and is regarded as an auspicious bird: a red crow with three feet is the sign heralding Zhou conquest of Shang. The validity of interpretation here depends on the sway of underlying cultural codes. In another example, told during the Battle of Yanling between Jin and Chu, a Jin warrior, Lu Qi, dreams of shooting an arrow at the moon and hitting it. The arrow then falls into the mud. Divination unravels the meaning of these enigmatic images. "The surname Ji is signifed by the sun; other surnames, the moon. Here it must mean the King of Chu. To shoot and hit the target, and then to fall into the mud: he [the archer] must die also" (*ZZ* Cheng 16.5). Lu Qi duly shoots King Gong of Chu in the eye and is himself shot dead. Ji is the surname of the Zhou royal house and of some enfeoffed lords, such as the Jin house, which had original clan ties with the Zhou house. The diviner's interpretation is premised on the acceptance of the hierarchy of the Jis and rulers "of other surnames," analogous to the relations between the sun and the moon. The rules of reading here thus assume Zhou authority and the subservient allegiance of the feudatory states. It is conceivable that for both De and Lu Qi, dreams are told for propaganda purposes, to legitimize De's rulership and Jin superiority over Chu, respectively. But while the cultural meanings of positions and directions remain relatively stable during the period covered by the *Zuo zhuan*, the proper relations between the Zhou king and the feudal lords, and those between Ji-surnamed states and other states, are questioned and debated. Apparently effortless correspondences may thus be used to stake out contested positions.

Stable correspondences become more troubled when contending forces in the context are articulated in the dream and its interpretation. This sometimes happens with the dream message of death—especially the dreamer's own death—which may issue in a struggle of control over its meaning and prophetic power. (This is not true when narrative concern is not centered on the dreamer. In the examples of Xun Yan and Lu Qi discussed earlier, the focus is on the impending and ongoing battles and the fate of the states involved.) Dreams about death and loss of self lend urgency to the act of interpretation, as if the struggle for mastery in the dream should be reenacted in interpretation. One vivid example is Duke Jing of Jin's dream of a vengeful spirit, the ancestor of the Zhao clan that he eliminated. The ultimately implacable prediction of death, which confirms the power of the vengeful spirit over the Jin ruler, may be yet another example of the role of Jin ministerial families, in this case the Zhao clan, in shaping the narratives of the *Zuo zhuan*.

> The Duke of Jin dreamed of a vengeful spirit of immense proportions, with its hair hanging to the ground, beating its chest and leaping. It said, "For you to murder my progeny was not righteous. I have already gained permission for revenge from the high gods!" Destroying the great door and the bedroom door, it made its entry. The duke was terrified, and entered the inner chamber, and the spirit destroyed its door also. The duke woke up and summoned the shaman of Mulberry Fields. What the shaman described corresponded exactly to the dream. The duke said, "What will happen?" He replied, "You will not [live to] eat the grain of the new harvest!" The duke fell ill and sought doctors from Qin. The Qin ruler sent a doctor named Huan to treat the duke. Before he arrived, the duke dreamed of his illness assuming the form of two boys and saying to each other, "He is a skilled doctor, I fear he will harm us, where can we escape?" One of them said, "We will reside above the area between the heart and the diaphram, and beneath the fat at the tip of the heart—what can he do to us?" The doctor arrived and said, "There is nothing to be done about the illness. It is above the area between the heart and the diaphram, and beneath the fat at the tip of the heart—where it can neither be attacked [with heat treatment], nor reached [through acupuncture]. Medicine will not get to it. There is nothing to be done." The duke said, "[He is] a good doctor." He gave him handsome gifts and sent him back. In the sixth month, on the *bingwu* day, the Duke of Jin wanted to taste the new grain. He had the official in charge present it and the cook prepare it. He summoned the shaman of Mulberry Fields, showed him [the new grain] and had him killed. When he was about to eat, he felt swollen, went to the privy, fell in, and died. A eunuch had dreamed in the morning of carrying

> the duke and ascending to heaven. At midday, he carried the Duke of Jin out of the privy; thereupon he was killed to attend the duke in death. (*ZZ* Cheng 10.4)

The correspondences between the Jin ruler's dreams and the accounts of the shaman and the doctor, and that constructed between his death and the eunuch's dream, establish the public dimension of dreams and their interpretation. The duke's two dreams are in some ways symmetrical opposites. One involves the sound and fury of vengeance, the other surreptitious deliberation on self-preservation. The vengeful spirit breaks one barrier after another, progressively invading the space the duke considers his own. The direction of the movement is inward. The two boys, on the other hand, are external manifestations of the duke's illness. They move outward from inner space. Hiding in recesses inside him that cannot be reached, they are nevertheless part of him. The dream of destructive agents emanating from within the boundaries of the body is then more acceptable than that of destruction by an outside force. There is a residual sense of control, of owning one's illness and possibly death. Asserting this autonomy, the duke tries to defy the threat of the spirit and the shaman's divination, but accepts the doctor's diagnosis. This concern with human agency is echoed in the dream of the eunuch. The duke, who tries to escape his dream, ends up having his grotesque death dreamed by another.

The interpretation of dreams dramatizes the passage from private to public meanings basic to all interpretive acts in the *Zuo zhuan*. Once translated into words of judgment, the meaning or message of a dream becomes implacable. Thus the Lu dignitary Shengbo tries to control the meaning of his dream, which seems to portend death, but fails as soon as he dares to seek divination. The story is told in the year of his death:

> Earlier, Shengbo dreamed of crossing the Huan River. Someone gave him agate pieces as food. He wept, and his tears became agate pieces that filled his arms. Following [these events] he sang this song: "I crossed the Huan River, / And was given agate pieces. / Return! Return! / Agate pieces filled my arms!" He was fearful and did not dare divine [the dream's meaning]. When he returned from Zheng, in the year *renshen*, he reached Lizhen and sought divination for the dream, saying: "I was afraid of death, that was why I dare not seek divination. Now a multitude of people have been following me for three years, there is no harm [in divination]." He spoke [i.e., divined] about his dream, and died by the evening. (*ZZ* Cheng 17.8)

Shengbo fears that his dream portends death, because agate pieces are put in the mouth of the dead. After three years during which the number of his followers grow, he decides that the dream is already fulfilled in his increasing following (i.e., the agate pieces symbolize his followers). In pursuing this logic, he is trying to control the meaning of his dream. The moment he is confident of mastery, however, destiny mocks him. Once Shengbo seeks divination, the meaning of his dream as death is concretized in words; it becomes public and inescapable.

Interpretation and concomitant ideas of control and order are at risk with equivocal dreams that highlight disjunctions between different conceptions of ritual propriety. Apparently authoritative figures may give ritually improper commands in a dream.

> Wei moved its capital to Diqiu. The divination said, "Three hundred years."[13] Duke Cheng of Wei dreamed of Kangshu [ancestor of Wei] saying, "Xiang has taken over my sacrificial offerings." The duke gave orders to offer sacrifices to Xiang. Ning Wuzi opposed this, saying, "Ghosts and spirits cannot partake of sacrificial offerings not from those of the same kin. What is the matter with Qi and Kuai? Xiang has not received sacrifices here for a long time—Wei is not to blame. You should not interfere with sacrifices prescribed by King Cheng and the Duke of Zhou. Please change your decree on sacrifices." (*ZZ* Xiang 31.5)

Xiang is the grandson of the founder of the Xia dynasty. His former residence in Diqiu, now the Wei capital, raises the question of whether he is entitled to sacrificial offerings from Wei. Ning Wuzi maintains that only states descended from the Xia (Qi and Kuai) are responsible for sacrifices to Xiang. At issue is whether the sovereignty of spirits and ancestors is determined by lineages or territorial shifts. Both options localize their power and leave room for debate—hence the uncertain authority of Kangshu's dream injunction.

In some cases the misleading dream seems to underline human agency and responsibility. The Jin minister Zhao Ying commits adultery with his nephew's wife Zhao Zhuangji. His brothers, Zhao Tong and Zhao Kuo, want to exile him to Qi. Zhao Ying maintains that despite personal failings he alone can protect the Zhao clan from the attacks by other clans.

> Zhao Ying dreamed of a messenger from heaven saying to him, "Offer sacrifices to me, and I shall bless you." He asked Shi Zhenbo about this. Shi Zhenbo said, "I do not know," but afterward he told his disciples, "The gods bless the good and send calamities to the licentious. Licentiousness unpunished is already a blessing. With sacrifices, perhaps he will go into exile." He offered sacrifices and was driven into exile the next day. (*ZZ* Cheng 5.1)

The account sustains two interpretations. Either it shows how a person's conduct is the ultimate determinant of his fate, so promises of blessings from heaven are irrelevant, or it demonstrates the equivocation of the message from heaven. The word "blessings" (*fu*) may be construed to mean exile, because it amounts to escape from more severe punishment. The fact that misconduct is punished seems to point to a higher justice delivered through a dream message that is either irrelevant or equivocal. (The more disturbing irony of Zhao Ying's story is its broader context. Zhao Ying's prediction comes to pass. His erstwhile lover Zhao Zhuangi accuses Zhao Tong and Zhao Kuo of planning a rebellion, and the Zhao clan is almost totally eliminated [*ZZ* Cheng 8.6].)

The equivocal dream is more disturbing when it betrays a righteous man.

Shusun Bao, wise minister of Lu, is destroyed by his dream. The story is told retrospectively in the year of his death.

> In the beginning, Muzi [Shusun Bao] left the Shusun clan, reached Geng Zong, and met a woman. He asked her privately to bring food and passed the night with her. She asked about his trip, and he told her. She cried and sent him off. He went to Qi, and married a woman from the Guo clan, who gave birth to Mengbing and Zhongren. He dreamed of being crushed by heaven. Failing to hold out, he turned around and saw a person, dark and hunched, with deep-set eyes and a sow-like mouth. He cried out, 'Niu [bovine], help me!' Thereupon he held out [and won]. In the morning he summoned his followers, but there was no such person. He said to them, 'Mark this!'" [His description of the figure in the dream.] Then Xuanbo [Shusun Qiaoru, Bao's brother] fled to Qi,[14] and Shusun Bao sent him food. Xuanbo said, "Lu, because of our ancestors, will preserve our line. They will certainly summon you. What will you do if they summon you?" He replied, "That has been my wish for long." (*ZZ* Zhao 4.8)

Shusun Bao returns to Lu, and the woman of Geng Zong presents him with a son whom he identifies as the dream figure. "Before asking his name, he called him 'Niu,' and he answered, 'Yes'" (*ZZ* Zhao 4.8). Niu, the illegitimate son, eventually plots the death of Mengbing and the exile of Zhongren, and kills Shusun Bao by denying him sustenance in his illness. Instead of being his helper, the dream figure turns out to be his destroyer.

Yet even here the misleading dream establishes a new causality, for it is based on an interpretive intent, an attempt to explain the downfall of a good and wise man. Elsewhere in the *Zuo zhuan* Shusun Bao is known for his moral integrity, learning, and perspicacious judgment. One may also reconstruct the moral intent of the dream by referring to its context. Is Shusun Bao being punished for his illicit liaison with the woman of Geng Zong? But the consequences of this one licentious act seem especially disproportionate when Shusun Bao is compared to his elder brother Xuanbo. References to Xuanbo frame the dream: Shusun Bao leaves his clan in Lu because he foresees the baleful consequences of Xuanbo's liaison with Mujiang, mother of the Lu ruler Duke Cheng. Shusun Bao returns to Lu to take his brother's place and continue the line. He also leaves Qi without notifying Xuanbo, apparently disapproving of the latter's new liaison with Sheng Mengzi, mother of Duke Ling of Qi.

The equivocal dream thus represents both hermeneutic limits and the perceived need to explain. Shusun Bao's lapse of judgment is unaccountable without the dream. To bring the equivocal dream into the narrative is at once to explain yet not explain. On one level the dream explains Shusun Bao's misplaced trust in his illegitimate son, but this "explanation" also turns a flaw of character (lack of judgment) into something explained by an external cause (the dream), which may in turn be justified in a moral scheme (as punishment for a licentious liaison), albeit an inconsistent one (considering the fact that his much more licentious brother, references to whom frame the account of the dream, continues to enjoy success and honor with impunity).

The narrative, told in the year of Shusun Bao's death, begins with the retrospective and explanatory time marker "in the beginning" (*chu*). After Niu is defeated and order is restored, the word *chu* is used again to introduce prophecies about Shusun Bao told at the time of his birth; divinations based on the *Zhouyi* are all borne out by later events (*ZZ* Zhao 5.1). Even as Shusun Bao tries to control the meaning of his dream by seeking out and naming Niu, the divination shows that the word itself is but part of a sign determining his fate at the moment of birth.[15]

By pointing to mysterious correspondences withheld from human understanding, the misleading dream suggests an arbitrary determinism, whereby humans are mere playthings of the gods. Paradoxically, by inviting or allowing different decoding, the equivocal dream also demonstrates how causality, signification, and interpretation can be manipulated by human beings. The equivocal sign thus sustains two extremes in the conception of human agency. The manipulation of signs is most evident in the rise of Jin to hegemony. In 632 B.C. (*ZZ* Xi 28.3), Jin and Chu fought at Chengpu, in one of the decisive battles of the Spring and Autumn era. Jin won, and Duke Wen of Jin emerged as leader of the feudal lords, while Chu was halted in its northward and eastward expansion.

The account of the battle is framed by two dreams. On the eve of battle, Duke Wen of Jin dreams that he is struggling with the Chu ruler, and the latter forces him to lie down while sucking out his brain matter. The dream terrifies him, but his minister Hu Yan offers a favorable interpretation: "Auspicious! Our side received heaven, while Chu bent face down as if accepting punishment. We have, in addition, softened him!" (*ZZ* Xi 28.3). Commentators cite early medical texts that define brain matter as *yin* substance with softening properties.[16] The "softening" of the Chu ruler's teeth by the Duke of Jin's brain matter thus signifies the triumph of guile and diplomacy over brute strength. The trick of apparently yielding in order to overcome an aggressive opponent is a commonplace both in writings on the art of war (*bingfa*) and Daoist texts. Moreover, the predator, by virtue of his face-down position, seems to be punished for some crime, whereas the victim, facing heaven, seems to be also receiving its favor. (There is evidence that in ancient Chinese burial rites the face-up position sometimes marked superior status.[17]) The dream apparently portends disaster but is interpreted as boding the opposite. The discrepancy between surface and meaning here defines human agency in history. Told before the battle, the dream's bearing on subsequent events implies determinism. Yet the conflicting interpretations surreptitiously restore choice and the sense of open possibilities.

After the battle is over, we are told about another dream, that of Ziyu, the Chu commander and prime minister.

> In the beginning, Ziyu of Chu had fashioned for his horses agate-ornamented caps and jade-adorned martingales, but had not used them. Before the battle, he dreamed of the god of the river saying to him, "Give them to me! I will bestow

> on you the marshes of Mengzhu."[18] He did not hand them over. Daxin [Ziyu's son] and Zixi [Ziyu's clansman] asked Rong Huang to remonstrate with Ziyu, but he [still] did not listen. Rong Huang said, "One would brave even death if it were to benefit the country, let alone give up agate and jade! These things are mere dirt and dung! If you can bring success to the army, why regret losing them?" Ziyu did not listen. Rong Huang came out and told Daxin and Zixi: "It will not be the gods who defeat the prime minister. He takes no pains over the affairs of the people. Indeed he is defeating himself!" (*ZZ* Xi 28.4)

Although both dreams supposedly occur before the battle, their placement in narrative time defines different hermeneutic perspectives. Duke Wen of Jin's dream is an indeterminate sign, an enigmatic riddle based on the rift between surface and meaning. Because the reader is still at the threshold of action, such tensions suggest open possibilities and alternatives. It is not clear whether the dream "actually" portends Jin's victory, or whether Hu Yan's interpretation emboldens Duke Wen and influences the outcome of battle. The dream of the Chu commander Ziyu, on the other hand, is told after the conclusion of the battle as retrospective explanation for what transpired. It serves the function of closure.

In some ways the two dreams are symmetrical opposites. The interpretation of Duke Wen's dream emphasizes human agency and shows how signification may be manipulated; Ziyu's dream, with a god's clear but arbitrary injunction that is not obeyed, seems to define humans as passive victims of divine whims. If Ziyu's refusal indeed accounts for his defeat, we are faced with a random determinism. This is not acceptable to the *Zuo zhuan* author-editor(s)—hence Rong Huang's attempt to link his defiance to a general hubris and disregard for the people.[19] The simple structure of command and disobedience in Ziyu's dream is a fitting finale for this man, whose single-minded pursuit of his goals creates the illusion of freedom and power untempered by any awareness of forces beyond his control. He is described as "hard and devoid of ritual propriety" (*gang er wuli*). Ziyu refuses to heed signs; with him intention and execution are one. By contrast, the careers of Duke Wen and his followers are dominated by the theme of doubling—we recall that Confucius describes Duke Wen as "crafty and not upright" (*jue er buzheng*)[20]—and by their skill in manipulating signs.

Duke Wen and his coterie turn problematic signification into the basis of opportune and morally justifiable action. They manipulate the double lives of words and signs to achieve their goals and claim the moral high ground. Hu Yan's interpretation of Duke Wen's dream is thus concerned with the moral definition of the situation. The sequence in the text suggests a protopsychological explanation for the dream: the dream is preceded by a riddle (in the form of a popular rhyme) that fills Duke Wen with doubt, "Fields in fallow, lush and abundant, / Discarding the old and planning the new" (*ZZ* Xi 28.3). The riddle is not interpreted in the text, but it may be taken to mean that Jin is turning against old allies (Duke Wen was granted refuge in Chu during his exile) and revelling in its new power. Hence Duke Wen's question: "What about Chu's benevolence?" To which Luan Zhi, a Jin minister, replies, "All the kingdoms with the surname of Ji north of the Han

River have been eliminated by Chu. This is to think back on small benevolence and forget great shame—we had better engage in battle!" (*ZZ* Xi 28.3). Coming in the wake of such discussions, Duke Wen's dream points to the moral ambiguity of the confrontation. Jin is turning against a former benefactor, and the dream has to be made to indicate not merely Jin victory but also its moral superiority: it is "receiving heaven" (*detian*), while Chu seems to be acknowledging its guilt in its face-down position. The hegemonic enterprise—the struggle for supremacy among the feudal lords—thus depends on the power to manipulate and control significatory processes, to turn contingent words and events into omens. Through such interpretive ingenuity, the contingent, random, and arbitrary aspects of human action and calculations based on concerns of power fall into order, system, and dictates of ritual propriety (*li*), and also acquire the force of necessity.

If Hu Yan's interpretation of Duke Wen's dream shows how omens of legitimation and victory are constructed instead of being simply received, the capricious (and covetous?) god of the river in Ziyu's dream points to the problematic authority of some dream figures and dream messengers.[21] In a world populated by spirits and gods of uncertain hierarchy, it is not always clear why a god's command, delivered in a dream, should be obeyed. (Hence Ziyu's disobedience alone does not explain his downfall; Rong Huang has to turn to his flaws as a leader.) Elsewhere in the *Zuo zhuan*, gods are sometimes partial and inconstant, betray their promises, issue contradictory commands that violate ritual propriety, and ignore the conduct of the supplicant. Both arbitrary injunctions in dreams and ambiguous dreams amenable to different decodings lead us to consider the scope and meaning of skepticism in the *Zuo zhuan*. Such skepticism pertains not to dreaming as symbolic process but to the problematic political implications of dream interpretation in a world of values in flux and constant struggle for power.

While in most examples in the *Zuo zhuan* the "transparency" of dreams unravels causes and consequences and yields systems of order, there is a parallel fascination with opaque, equivocal, and arbitrary dreams, whose interpretation explores the space between cosmic order and random determinism, the "Way of Heaven" (whatever higher destiny that enfolds) and human endeavor. The act of interpretation itself thus embodies the struggle for control over meaning. Put differently, the familiar formulation of determinism versus human agency applies to both action and interpretation in the *Zuo zhuan*. The authority of interpretation derives either from preexistent analogies (yellow bear refers to the spirit of Gun; ingestion of agate pieces means death, etc.) that contribute to ritual and cosmic order, or from correspondences manipulated in the interest of moral justification and political advantage (as in Hu Yan's interpretation of Duke Wen's dream). Different modes and assumptions of decoding may well point to divergent sources or strata of the text. The concern with ritual propriety and with power may represent the concerns of Confucian, or more broadly, traditionalist schools and of protolegalist thought (if I may risk such an anachronistic usage[22]), respectively. In this sense the *Zuo zhuan* is a kind of contesting ground for different schools of political thought in the fifth and fourth centuries B.C. The fissures and tensions in the text result from the copresence of, and struggle between, different ways of understanding and using the past, different conceptions of language and rhetoric and, most urgently, different solutions to the crisis of instability and disintegration as represented by the events of those 255 years.

The Dreamability of the World

The concerns underlying the representation of dreams in the *Zuo zhuan*—the necessity and hazards of interpretation, the construction of order and system, the meaning of human agency in history—find their logical opposites in the treatment of dreams in the Daoist classic *Zhuangzi* (ca. fourth century?),[23] whose "inner chapters" (the first seven chapters) are roughly contemporaneous with, or possibly written about a century later than, the *Zuo zhuan*. In the *Zhuangzi*, the dreamer, instead of regarding dreams as signs to be decoded and objects of knowledge, dwells instead on the transition between dreaming and waking states, the experience of dreaming, and the meaning of awakening. He asks not whether the world may be read, but whether it may be dreamed; not how he can know and act, but whether knowledge and action are possible. While the idea of dreams of interpretation in the *Zuo zhuan* signifies the longing for readability, order, and system, in the *Zhuangzi* interpretation is embedded in the paradoxes associated with the dream experience, being at the same time elusive and palpable, opaque and transparent, a token of both freedom and determinism.

Paradoxically, the centrality of dreams in the *Zhuangzi* is defined through the valorization of the dreamless state. In Chapter 6, "The Great Ancestral Teacher" (*Da Zongshi*), Zhuangzi describes the "True Being of ancient times" (*gu zhi zhenren*):

> Sleeping he did not dream, awake he did not worry, eating he was indifferent to fine tastes, breathing he did from his deepest depth. . . . The True Being of ancient times did not know about taking pleasure in life, and did not know about abhorring death. Coming forth he was not glad, retreating he was not reluctant. Briskly he came, briskly he left, and that was all. He neither forgot his beginning, nor sought his end. He was glad to receive, and forgetting, would return [what he received]. This is called not using the mind to harm the Way, not using what is human to assist what is of heaven. This is called the True Being.[24] (*ZhZ* 6/48)

The dreamless state of the True Being is a consequence of his ultimate detachment. He is able to regard life as contingent, a mere phase in a process of constant transformation. In another passage from this chapter, Confucius[25] uses the certainty within a dream to question the sense of self and to affirm the detachment that rises above the distinctions between dreaming and waking states.

> Yan Hui[26] asked Zhongni [Confucius], "When Mengsun Cai's mother died, he wailed with no tears. His heart had no grief, and in mourning he had no sorrow.

> Without these three, he is yet known all over Lu as a good mourner. Is this not a case of not having the reality and yet obtaining the name! I find this most strange." Zhongni said, "For Mengsun has done everything and has advanced into the realm of knowledge. The inability to simplify some things [such as the emotions of life and death] means that some other [essential] things are simplified. Mengsun does not know what determines his coming into being, or what determines his death. He does not know about advancing, he does not know about falling behind. It is as if he is transformed into one thing waiting for transformations he does not know—is that not all?! Moreover, soon to be transformed, how can he know about not being transformed! Soon to be untransformed, how can he know about having been already transformed! Is it only you and I who have not begun to awake from our dream? . . . Mengsun alone is awakened. People wail, and he wails also, and that is simply the way it is. Moreover, this 'I' is no more than what we use with one another. How does one know what is this 'I' that I call 'I'? You dream of being a bird soaring in the sky, you dream of being a fish sinking into deep water. I do not know if what I am saying now are the words of the awakened or the dreamer. Reaching for ease is not as good as laughter, being adept at laughing is not as good as shoving aside and moving along. Rest content in shoving aside and moving along and leave behind transformations, then you enter into the oneness of the empty sky." (*ZhZ* 6/58)

The idea of transformation (*hua*) is burdened with the certainty of death ("His shape is transformed, and his mind is destroyed along with it. Is this not a great sorrow?" [*ZhZ* 2/11]) and the impossibility of certain knowledge ("For knowledge has to depend on something in order to be appropriate, and that which it depends on is never fixed" [*ZhZ* 6/47]). Constant transformations render the notion of "sincerity" implied in Yan Hui's question irrelevant. Simultaneously real and illusory, the dream experience feeds both skepticism and the impetus for transcendence. For it is by accepting emotions, beliefs, and sense of self as transitory, insubstantial, and dreamlike that one may be reconciled with the ultimate transformation, death. "The Great Ancestral Teacher" contains many references to detachment, forgetting (*wang*), and "abstinence of the mind" (*xinzhai*), yet its lively narratives also describe the requisite mental somersaults for creating imaginary realms that will lead to the attainment of such states. The idea of transformation may be divested of its negative echoes through active participation in a process:

> One happens upon the human form, yet one delights in it. As for the human form, there are ten thousand transformations which do not begin to have a limit; the joy therein is, then, uncountable! The sage therefore roams in the realm from which nothing can escape and where all is preserved. . . . "If my left arm is gradually transformed into a rooster, I will ask of it the hours of night; if my right arm is gradually transformed into a pellet, I will use it to get an owl for roasting. If my buttocks are transformed into wheels, I will let my spirit be a horse, and so I will ride—what need would I have for a carriage? For to gain something is a matter of timing, to lose something, a matter of following the flow of things. Rest in the right timing, be situated to follow the flow, and one will not be invaded by sadness and joy. This is what of old was called 'letting loose of the bonds.' . . . Now when a great smith casts metal, if the metal jumps

> and says, 'I have to be made into the Moye sword!'—the great smith will certainly regard this as inauspicious metal. Now if one by chance happens upon the human shape, and says, 'Human! Human!' the maker of transformations will certainly regard this as an inauspicious person. Now if one regards heaven and earth as a great foundry, and the maker of transformations as the great smith, where would I go and not agree? Suddenly asleep, in a trice I wake up." (*ZhZ* 6/51, 54–55)

Ultimate transcendence may be dreamless, but it too has to be attained through the ability to dream a world, or through mental acts of transformation crossing the boundaries between dreaming and waking states.

In the *Zhuangzi* the "dreamability" of the world issues in two notions of the self: the inconstant, arbitrary self, and the self transcending either-or, having attained higher consciousness through "loss of self"; two modes of reasoning and expression, one emphasizing division and fragmentation, the other, unity and flux; two kinds of language, one relative, partial, judgmental, the other, a new philosophical language celebrating play and polysemy.

These questions are explored in the butterfly dream at the end of Chapter 2, "On Seeing Things as Equal" (*Qiwu lun*), arguably the best-known dream in the entire Chinese cultural tradition:

> Zhuang Zhou once dreamed he was a butterfly—joyous and carefree in being a butterfly. His heart's desires were fulfilled, and he did not know about [Zhuang] Zhou. All of a sudden he woke up; there he was, palpably and irrevocably [Zhuang] Zhou. He did not know whether he was [Zhuang] Zhou dreaming of a butterfly, or a butterfly dreaming of being [Zhuang] Zhou. Between being [Zhuang] Zhou and being a butterfly there must be a difference. This is called the Transformation of Things. (*ZhZ* 2/23)

The dream is totally removed from the context of messages and morals defining dreams in the *Zuo zhuan*. The dream does not simply assert the sameness of life and death, waking and dreaming states, or the relativity of judgment. The final statement defining the experience as "the Transformation of Things" is itself medial, aspiring not to the stasis of sameness but to a flux encompassing opposites, always straining to transcend itself. The tone modulates between celebration of freedom for the spirit and the anguish of skepticism and mortality. The dream experience is nondifferentiation and sublime forgetfulness; "joyous and carefree in being a butterfly," Zhuang Zhou seems unencumbered by consciousness of the self and thereby attains union with the Dao. But it is also a kind of death ("he did not know about [Zhuang] Zhou"). The idea that the dreamer may be dreamed by another ("He did not know whether he was [Zhuang] Zhou dreaming of being a buttefly, or a butterfly dreaming of being [Zhuang] Zhou") mocks knowledge and the sense of freedom as illusory.

The doubleness of the butterfly dream echoes two notions of the self developed throughout the chapter: one demolished as inconstant and arbitrary, the other exalted as transcending either-or. In order to undermine the self, Zhuangzi breaks it up into composite, competing parts. He uses the metaphor of "music coming out of emptiness" (*ZhZ* 2/10) to demonstrate the unaccountable, capricious transformations of the human heart. "Without them [mental states] there is no I, without me they have nothing to draw from" (*ZhZ* 2/10). The mutual dependence of self and other (*bi*, i.e., mental states) undermines the integrity of both. It is not certain that the self is prior to ever-changing mental states. The self has no center, because there is no way to establish which organ or faculty should be held more dearly, which should be regarded as the "true lord" (*zhenjun*) or "true controller" (*zhenzai*). Its sources are unknown. Its inevitable fate is unfreedom, death, and degeneration.

Yet earlier, in the beginning of the chapter, Zhuangzi uses the same metaphor of "music coming out of emptiness" to celebrate spontaneous generation and heightened perception-consciousness. In that passage, one of the most remarkable descriptions of noise in early Chinese literature, Nanguo Ziqi dwells on the piping of humans, piping of earth, and piping of heaven. The piping of earth, the myriad noises made by wind blowing through bends, holes, and hollows of various shapes and sizes, is described with such sound and fury that we sometimes forget the supposed detachment of the speaker, Nanguo Ziqi. He is privy to such music because he has "lost himself": his body is like withered wood, his heart like dead ashes. Even as music comes out of emptiness (rows of tubes, the myriad hollows and apertures of the human heart and head), Nanguo Ziqi can listen because he is emptied of his self and has attained a higher level of perception-consciousness. The extended description of the piping of earth is followed by a cryptic definition of the piping of heaven: "For that which blows the ten thousand different voices makes each come into its own, as each of itself takes from it [according to its nature]. This animator—who is it?" (*ZhZ* 2/8). There are at least three ways of interpreting the piping of heaven: as the spontaneous self-generation and self-functioning of the piping of earth and of humans;[27] the generative force or principle that fashions the piping of earth and of humans;[28] or the balance between "self-engendering" (*ziji*) and the actualizing energy, between "self-choosing" (*ziqu*) and the impelling force. In all three interpretations the listener plays a transformative role. In the words of the Qing commentator Yao Nai: "To him who has lost himself, the myriad hollows and rows of tubes are all piping of heaven" (*ZhZ* 2/9). Listening is thus not merely passive reception of the sensual immediacy of sounds but also active engagement in philosophical understanding.

The proposition that loss of self heightens perception-consciousness is a paradox that brings out other paradoxes in the *Zhuangzi*. Expression and creation depend as much on the procreative void as on acts of choice, transformation, and interpretation. Loss of self is dramatized through performance in front of an audience. Nanguo Ziqi, for all his obliviousness, indifference, and self-forgetfulness, is quick to respond to his interlocutor Yancheng Ziyou. His state of being is quietistic, but his language is elliptical, dramatic, performative, provocative. He can treat the myriad voices as equal because all partake of, or are translatable into, the piping of heaven, but in order to see things as equal he has to rise above them by appealing to the category of the piping of heaven. The idea of loss of self is in part a response to this contradiction. But it also coexists with the sense of higher consciousness. All noises can be seen as equal, but Nanguo Ziqi's own voice deliberating on the nature of, and relationship between, the piping of men, earth, and heaven carries more authority.

There is, then, a symmetry to the beginning and ending of the chapter. Even as Nanguo Ziqi embarks on performative ruminations after his moment of oblivion and self-forgetfulness, Zhuangzi, after experiencing loss of self as the butterfly in the dream, ponders and gives a name to the transition between dreaming and waking states. The apparent moral of the butterfly dream is that Zhuangzi and the butterfly, self-consciousness and its negation, are equally valid manifestations of the Dao. By the same token, the moment when a lucid intelligence expounds on the Transformation of Things (*wuhua*) is no less transcendent than the moment of undifferentiation and intuitive union with the Dao. The Transformation of Things, by virtue of its mediatory function, transcends the logic of either-or. Nevertheless, there is a certain asymmetry between the two states of being in the parable. The butterfly is completely at one with itself; it does not ask whether it is Zhuangzi dreaming of being a butterfly or a butterfly dreaming of being Zhuangzi. It is upon waking that Zhuangzi poses the question, affirms the difference between the two states of being, and asserts that the difference defines two poles of a process of transformation, itself part of the great flux of all things. Zhuangzi is keenly aware of the irony implicit in this asymmetry. Transcendence is a form of forgetting, but philosophical reflection and language are rooted in remembering. The telling of the butterfly dream is thus itself a playful acceptance of the differentiating edge of philosophy and language.

Such acceptance is premised on a distinction between two modes of reasoning and expression, one emphasizing unity and flux, the other, division and fragmentation. Claiming the former for himself, Zhuangzi thus develops two parallel lines of thinking in this chapter. One establishes all knowledge, judgment, and argument as relative, partial, and based on the perspective of division and fragmentation. The other differentiates the argument at hand from other arguments by exploring the possibility of a new philosophical language. These two positions are in turn augmented by the two notions of the self discussed earlier: the inconstant, arbitrary self, and the self transcending either-or, having attained higher consciousness through loss of self.

In this chapter, "On Seeing Things as Equal," metaphors transcending the logic of either-or include "the treasury of heaven" (*tianfu*), the potter's wheel of heaven (*tianjun*), the whetstone of heaven (*tianni*), "proceeding on two alternatives [or walking on two roads]" (*liangheng*), the axis of the Dao (*Daoxu*), and illumination (*ming*). The treasury of heaven is knowledge of "the wordless disputation, the untold way" and thus transcends the opposition of language and silence. Both the potter's wheel of heaven and the whetstone of heaven are images for harmonizing and mediating competing versions of truth. The axis of the Dao is located where no position can find its opposite. All are metaphors of flux, inclusivity, and mediation. Translated into stylistic terms, metaphors transcending either-or become premises constantly revised, extended, overturned—statements that cast sidelong glances at their opposites, and incorporate, play with, and argue against them. In this sense the new philosophical language that Zhuangzi strives for is always dialogic, even when he is speaking in his own voice. He is always responding to an imaginary interlocutor. Hence his frequent use of the dialogue form, by which he can encompass different voices and challenge his own conceptions. The context of interlocution also establishes speech as a playful concession, silence presumably being preferred.

The presentation of dreaming and waking states as infinite regress, which may be arrested only with the Great Awakening (*dajue*), takes place within a dialogue, which functions as a bracketing device.

> Qu Quezi asked Chang Wuzi, "I have heard from the Master, 'The sage does not apply himself to any affairs. He neither hankers after profit nor avoids harm. He takes no pleasure in acquisition and follows no path. Not saying anything, he says something; saying something, he does not say anything, and he roams beyonds dust and grime.' The Master regarded these as wild words, but I consider them the Working of the Subtle Way." Chang Wuzi said, "This is what would confound even the Yellow Emperor, why would Qiu [Confucius] understand it? But you, too, are calculating too far in advance. You see the egg and seek the rooster, you see the slingshot and seek the roasted bird. I shall speak for you reckless words, you should listen recklessly. How about that? . . . " (*ZhZ* 2/20–21)

Contexts of quotation and interlocution here establish a kind of competition. Qu Quezi claims to be quoting Confucius, at the same time he congratulates himself on having surpassed Confucius, who does not seem to appreciate or understand his own description of the Daoist sage. What obtains is a rather tame summary of Daoist attributes, although for Confucius these are already "wild words" (*menglang zhi yan*). Chang Wuzi claims that Qu Quezi anticipates conclusions too readily; in doing so he turns Daoist transcendence into final, conclusive stasis. By contrast Chang Wuzi dramatizes the transcendence of opposites as the Daoist thought process, with all its pathos, anguish, and playfulness. He begins with an invitation to hypothesis: "I shall speak for you reckless words, you should listen recklessly. How about that?"

Chang Wuzi's "reckless words" move from declamatory splendor to profound skepticism. He gives his version of the Daoist sage: "Going by the side of the sun and the moon, holding under his arms space and time, merging with all things, leaving aside all uncertainties, respecting the common run of humanity. The crowd is toiling and anxious, the sage is foolish and oblivious, sees through the ten thousand ages to form One Purity, affirms the myriad things and lets them enfold each other." But this authoritative account is immediately followed by unresolvable questions premised on the certainty of death and the impossibility of knowledge. He seeks to treat life and death, waking and dreaming states, as reversible doubles, but prefaces his comparisons with "How would I know . . . "

> How would I know that to love life is not a delusion? How would I know that to hate death is not like someone who, having lost his home as a youth, knows not the way of return? . . . How would I know that the dead does not regret his initial longing for life? Those who dream of drinking wine cry and weep in the morning; those who dream of crying and weeping go hunting in the morning. While we are dreaming we do not know that we are dreaming. In our dreams we try to use divination to interpret our dreams [within dreams]. Only upon waking do we know that we have been dreaming. And it is upon the Great Awakening that we know this is our Great Dream. Yet the foolish ones think of themselves as awake, furtively certain of their knowing. Ruler? Herdsman? How limited! Confucius and you are both dreaming. I who call you dreaming am also dreaming. As for these words, their name is Supreme Paradox. If after ten thousand ages there is one meeting with the Great Sage who knows how to explain this, it would have been like waiting between morning and evening. (*ZhZ* 2/21)

There is such urgency in confronting mortality and the uncertainty of knowledge that Chang Wuzi can only appeal to an Archimedean point ("the Great Awakening," the meeting with the Great Sage) and an infinitely precious and precarious language ("the Supreme Paradox," *diaogui*)—all within the framework of "reckless words listened to recklessly."

The movement between the first and second sections of Chang Wuzi's speech (that is, the initial account of the Daoist sage and the series of questions on life and death, dreaming and waking) enacts the dialogic process postulated earlier. A declamatory statement with an aura of finality, often itself radical and akin to what we think of as "Daoist," is bracketed and (implicitly) questioned. This is a recurrent ploy in the *Zhuangzi*. We can see the same process, for example, in these often-quoted lines from the chapter: "Heaven and earth exist along with me, the myriad things and I are one." By translating the idea of "seeing things as equal" into striking metaphors, Zhuangzi apparently reconciles opposites, abolishes differences, and redefines linguistic reference. But as A. C. Graham points out, this statement, which has often been singled out as summarizing an essential aspect of Zhuangzi's thought, actually functions as one reference point in an argumentative process. For Zhuangzi follows the proclamation of oneness by questioning its validity: "Since oneness is achieved, shouldn't there be words for it? Since oneness has been called such, how can there be no words for it? Oneness and the word make two, two and one make three." The idea of oneness depends on language, yet language inevitably destroys it. Instead of simply asserting oneness, Zhuangzi emphasizes the need to see differences in oneness, and oneness in differences.

Chang Wuzi's questions on dreaming and waking states, life and death thus dramatize the flux and tensions inherent in processes of thought and expression. The reversibility of these opposites is not the message to be distilled. But this commitment to process and the striving to go beyond the outermost limits is deeply unsettling: we can in fact never be certain that we are not dreaming. The same logic and pathos characterize Zhuangzi's earlier discussions of beginnings and being. "There is a beginning. There is not yet beginning to be a beginning. There is not yet beginning to be a not yet beginning to be a beginning" (*ZhZ* 2/16). The two antecedent stages to "there is a beginning" can only be imagined verbally. Words acquire a new kind of independence from reference. The same exercise is repeated with different emphasis in the case of the opposites "being" and "nonbeing." "There is being. There is nonbeing. There is not yet having begun to be nonbeing. There is not yet having begun to not yet having begun to be nonbeing. Suddenly there is nonbeing, and I do not know whether 'there is nonbeing' acutally means 'there being' or 'there not being.' I have referred to something, and I do not know whether what I have referred to actually refers to something or does not refer to anything" (*ZhZ* 2/16–17). What begins as meditation on the idea of infinite past, which undermines all notions of origins, turns into a sudden confrontation with a logical contradiction and ends in a statement on skepticism. "Suddenly there is nonbeing": this is the language of immediate experience and half-involuntary mental engagement; the mind cannot cope with infinite regress, and has to seize on something as a provisional starting point. But the statement "there is nonbeing" balances precariously between "there being" and "there not being." Hence the final note of skepticism on the possibility of reference in language.

Like the statement "suddenly there is nonbeing," the references to Great Awakening and the meeting with the all-comprehending Great Sage in Chang Wuzi's speech function to arrest infinite regress. They represent a logical and psychological necessity. Conversely, the reversibility of dreaming and waking states and the hypothetical impossibility of going beyond dreams create and challenge this necessity. By calling the language referring to such matters "Supreme Paradox," Zhuangzi is again claiming for himself a new philosophical language that celebrates play and polysemy. The idea that the world may be dreamed can lead to anguish and skepticism; Zhuangzi confronts it with a new philosophical language and a new conception of subjectivity, turning it into a token of human freedom, marked not only by sublime self-forgetfulness of the dream—Zhuangzi is "joyous and carefree in being a butterfly"—but also by the "Transformation of Things" enacting mediatory movement between dreaming and waking, life and death, language and silence.

The radical, dialectical ramifications of the idea of the dreamability of the world in the *Zhuangzi* may be better appreciated when we compare it with the "dream chapter" (Chapter 3, "Zhou Muwang" ["King Mu of Zhou"]) in a later Daoist text, the *Liezi* (ca. A.D. third to fourth century?).[29] There are obvious parallels: the concern with the process of dreaming rather than the content of dreams; the association of dreams with power and creation; the reversibility of dreaming and waking states. In the *Liezi*,[30] however, there is a greater emphasis on resolution of contradictions. Hence the normative injunctions on restraint and detachment. This is evident in the opening story of King Mu of Zhou. King Mu is transported to realms of fantastic splendor through the aid of a Daoist magician (*huaren*, literally, "the person who transforms"). Upon King Mu's return to his earthly palace, his attendants tell him that his physical self has just been "lost in absorption" (*muocun*). The magician then explains that the king has taken his journey in spirit and that the realm of magical splendor he beheld in his dream vision (or hallucination) is actually no different from the palaces and parks that surround him every day. Greatly pleased, the king no longer pays attention to affairs of state and indulges instead in "distant wanderings" (*yuanyou*). His peregrinations take him to the ends of the world and the realms of immortals, until at the feast of the Queen Mother of the West he has a change of heart and decides to turn back. "Alas! Instead of perfecting and accumulating my virtue, I, the lone one,[31] have been indulging in music and pleasure. Posterity surely will judge me for my lapses!" (*LZ* 5/70). The power of subjectivity to create another world can thus yield both arguments for excess and "distant wanderings" (because worldly responsibilities and attachments would not matter) and for restraint (because the freedom to dream or imagine another world allows the acceptance of present constraints). The text presents both alternatives, but the latter is affirmed with the additional weight of imperatives from moral categories.

A dominant theme in this chapter is the reversibility of, and the problematic boundary between, dreaming and waking states. But whereas the *Zhuangzi* situates this in a matrix of opposed conceptions of self, language, knowledge, and experience, the *Liezi* presents this as a problem to be solved. One story tells how a rich man mistreats an old servant, who is nevertheless content because his daytime toils and tribulations are replaced by dreams of royal power and pleasures at night. The rich man, for his part, dreams of being an abused and overworked servant every night, and is therefore disturbed and ill. His friend chides him for trying to seek satisfaction in both waking and dreaming states, whereupon he alleviates the lot of his servant, and his own condition also improves. A potentially epistemological problem thus becomes a moral problem. The relativization of his wakeful state instills a sense of distance regarding his power, which he is consequently less inclined to abuse.

In another famous story, a woodcutter from Zheng comes across a deer, kills it, and has it hidden. He later fails to find it, and thinks the whole incident had been a dream. Someone who hears of his account follows the directions and finds the hidden deer. "He said to his wife, 'The woodcutter dreamed of getting a deer and knew not where it was, and now I have found it. He really dreamed it then.' His wife said, 'Maybe you dreamed about the woodcutter getting the deer. Perhaps the woodcutter does not exist. Now that you have found the deer, perhaps your dream has turned out to be real.' The husband said, 'I got the deer—why needs one know whether he dreamed or I dreamed?' The woodcutter never quite got over the deer. That night he dreamed of the place where he hid it, and of the person who found it." When the two claimants bring the case before the court, the judge decides to divide the deer between them. Hearing about this, the Zheng ruler exclaims, "He! Perhaps the judge dreamed of dividing a deer for people?" When consulted, the prime minister says, "Dreaming or not dreaming: your subject cannot distinguish that. If you wish to distinguish dreaming and waking [states], only the Yellow Emperor and Kong Qiu (Confucius) [would know how]. Now that the Yellow Emperor and Kong Qiu are gone, who can distinguish this? We would do well to follow the words of the judge" (*LZ* 5/75–76). Each new twist to this story develops because dreams are taken for wakeful events, and wakeful events for dreams. Final distinctions are possible only for ancient sages, now dead and gone. The judge's decision to divide the deer between the contending parties, who have both been deceived by dreaming as well as by waking states, thus undermines the viability of hierarchizing, or even differentiating between, dreaming and waking states. Insofar as the solution is presented as judicious, however, we reach the stasis of identity at the end of the story (comparable to the convergence of King Mu's hallucination with his actual abode), in contrast to the "Transformation of Things" in the butterfly dream, which suggests movement and mediation.

The normative bent in the *Liezi* is also traceable in the geography that charts the duration of dreams. In the far southwest is the kingdom of constant somnolence. Its inhabitants wake up only once in fifty days. They consider dreams reality, and reality, dreams. In the far northeast is the kingdom of constant wakefulness, whose inhabitants are harsh, aggressive, and competitive. The central kingdom is the land of variety, regularity, abundance, talents, and ritual propriety. Dreaming and waking in balanced measure, its inhabitants consider dreams dreams, and reality, reality. On one level this geographical account establishes and relativizes different perspectives on dreams and dreaming. But to the extent that the central kingdom is described most sympathetically, it is also upheld as the norm. Although the *Liezi* explores dreaming as symbolic process, its classification of dreams according to their genesis in certain emotions or objects contiguous to the dreamer is curiously pedestrian[32] (*LZ* 5/73). Whereas the *Zhuangzi* uses the idea of the dreamability of the world to question received categories of self, knowledge, and language, the *Liezi* posits it to underline the convergence or identity of different realms of experience. Once the dreamer recognizes this, subjective projection in dreams and illusion becomes the venue for restraint (*LZ* 5/70), detachment (*LZ* 5/78), or magical power (*LZ* 5/72).

Afterthoughts

In the history of Chinese literature, it is the idea of the dreamability of the world that has more important ramifications, but its urgency is derived from the imperative of interpretation and control implied in the idea of the readability of the world. The tension between the palpability of dreams and the urgency of message often define the literary representation of dreams. Daoist and Buddhist stories apparently urging renunciation tell of lives lived in a dream: the logic hinges on the dreamer's realization that if the passions and vicissitudes of life can be experienced in the brevity of a dream, they are then illusory or unreal and should be treated with detachment.

However, in contradistinction to the stated logic of such stories, enlightenment is of the moment, while the dream is represented as duration. The palpability of the dream as aesthetic illusion challenges the message of detachment. Moreover, it is much easier to empathize with attachment than with detachment—insofar as empathy is based on mental and emotional engagement, empathy with detachment is a contradiction in terms. The inherent contradictions in both the Buddhist idea of dispassionate compassion and the simultaneous fulfillment and transcendence of desire in the Daoist immortal often unfold in dream stories ending with Daoist or Buddhist enlightenment.

Later reworkings of the idea of "life as dream" or "passions lived in a dream" become increasingly focused on the contradictions of enlightenment and the ambiguous role of the aesthetic illusion itself. The eighteenth-century masterpiece, *The Story of the Stone* (*Shitouji*, also known as *The Dream of the Red Chamber* [*Honglou meng*]), is probably the most remarkable example of this dialectic of dream and reality, art and life, passion and enlightenment, nostalgia and knowledge. In some ways the insistent analogies between dreaming, imagining, remembering, and the activities of reading and writing still ring with echoes of the paradoxes of experience, knowledge, and language already embodied in the butterfly dream in the *Zhuangzi*.

Notes

1. The received text of the *Zuo zhuan* purports to be an exegetical commentary on the *Chunqiu* (*Spring and Autumn Annals*), attributed to Confucius. Materials are presented year by year, in a strictly chronological order. Liu Xin (50 B.C.–A.D. 23) seems to have beem the first to "use the text of the *Zuo Commentary Tradition* to interpret the *Classic* [i.e., *Chunqiu*]"; see Ban Gu (A.D. 32–92), *Han shu* (1983: 36.1970). It is almost certain that the *Zuo zhuan* and the *Chunqiu* were separate texts to begin with, and the decision of Du Yu (222–84), the great *Zuo zhuan* scholar and commentator, to collate the two texts resulted in *Zuo zhuan* narratives interrupted by the text of the *Chunqiu*. However, the presence of *Chunqiu*-style notations in the *Zuo zhuan* (some of which do not appear in *Chunqiu* itself) and the intrinsic logic of the chronological arrangement attest to a significant connection between the *Zuo zhuan* and *Chunqiu* or annalistic accounts in that style. For a complete English translation, see Legge 1872; for a more recent translation, see Watson 1989; a new complete translation is being prepared by Stephen Durrant, Wai-yee Li, and David Schaberg for the series "Chinese Classics in Translation," to be published by Yale University Press. Citations from *Zuo zhuan* refer to *Chunqiu Zuo zhuan zhu* (hereafter *ZZ*), Yang Bojun, ed. (1981). All translations in this essay are my own.

2. The strictly chronological arrangement means that episodes that belong to different narrative sequences are presented contiguously. To follow an event (for example, the rise or fall of a state, an intrigue, a rebellion, or a war) as it unfolds, the reader has to constantly refer to other sections or be already familiar with the text. The form of the present text may be a consequence of cutting up and reshaping existing materials into a commentary tradition of the *Chunqiu*, or the text might have developed from a need to elaborate and explain cryptic entries in annalistic traditions (which may include the *Chunqiu* as well as similar annals from other states).

3. To give one of numerous examples: Duke Hui of Jin is "slack and inattentive" (*duo*) when he receives the ceremonial jade signifying royal recognition (*ZZ* Xi 11.2). On the basis of this gesture Historian Guo predicts (correctly) that "the Lord of Jin will have no progeny" because the gesture signifies lack of respect for himself and for ritual.

4. Duke Li, the former ruler of Jin, was murdered by Xun Yan (*ZZ* Cheng 18.1). The guilt of Xun Yan is open to disputation because Duke Li had threatened to eliminate Xun Yan's clan, and Xun Yan was arguably acting in self-defense.

5. That is, the military expedition against Qi.

6. The word *song* may suggest legal uncertainty, but Xun Yan emerges as a more sympathetic character in this account. He seems more concerned with the fortunes of the state (i.e., the war against Qi) than with his own death, both in his prayer to the river god and as an unappeased spirit after death (*ZZ* Xiang 18.3, 19.1). Duke Li, on the other hand, is presented as ruthless and misguided in his attempt to establish a more centralized bureaucratic government by eliminating the powerful clans in Jin. The negative image of Duke Li is consistent with the emphasis on reciprocity in ruler-subject relations and, more specifically, the sympathetic treatment of ministerial dominance, especially in Jin, in the *Zuo zhuan*. Tong Shuye (1980: 59–61, 72, 270) gives an incisive discussion of this phenomenon.

7. See Du Yu's annotation in *Chunqiu Jingzhuan jijie* (1986: 943).

8. Duke Xiang's trip, but not the dream, is mentioned in *ZZ* Xiang 28.12.

9. Mencius mentions the Duke of Zhou's military expedition against Chu in his exegesis of temple hymns from Lu, but no such campaign is mentioned in the *Documents* (*Shang shu*). The *Yi Zhou shu* may be referring to Chu when it mentions campaigns agains the Xiong clans (Chapter 48, "Zuo Luo," see Zhu Youzeng ed., *Yi Zhou shu jixun jiaoshi*, in *Shixue congshu* 2/1 [Shijie shuju, n.p., n.d.], 127). Takezoe Teruo discusses these textual problems in *Saden Kaisen* (1961), Zhao 7/57.

10. This emphasis is obvious in many modern accounts of the Zheng statesman. When Zishen predicts fire in Song, Wei, Chen, and Zheng on the basis of astrological observations, Bei Zao asks Zichan to use jade utensils as sacrificial offerings to ward off disaster. Zichan refuses (*ZZ* Zhao 17.5). Fire breaks out in Zheng in the following year. Bei Zao makes the same request and Zichan refuses again with these oft-quoted words: "The way of heaven is far, the way of humans is near. How can one reach the other? How can one be known [through the other]?" Fire does not break out again (*ZZ* Zhao 18.3). During a great flood in Zheng, dragons fight (with one another) at the deeps of the Wei River outside the Shi gate. The people of Zheng ask Zichan to offer sacrifices to them. Zichan refuses, saying, "When we fight, the dragons do not watch us. When dragons fight, what is there for us to watch? As for sacrifices [urging departure], that place is their home. I have nothing to ask of the dragons, the dragons also have nothing to ask of me" (*ZZ* Zhao 19.10). In these instances, the agrument for noninterference in different spheres of phenomena and experience does not preclude the exercise of interpretive power whenever practicable.

11. According to Yang Bojun, the words "ghost" and "return" (both pronounced *gui* in modern Chinese, but in different tones) share the same rhyme and also sound similar in ancient Chinese (*ZZ*, 1292).

12. See *Zhou li* ("Xiaguan," "Sishi") and *Liji* ("Tangong xia," "Liyun," "Jiao te sheng") in *Liji Zheng zhu* (1981), pp. 30, 78, 89. In the cosmological system of the *Zhouyi* tradition, the south is associated with the sun, brightness (*ming*), the revelation of myriad things, and the rule of a sage king. See "Shuogua" in *Zhouyi Wang Han zhu*, Sibu beiyao edition (1985), 2a, and the image of hexagram thirty, *li* ䷝, in *Zhouyi Wang Han zhu*, j.3 11b–12a. These sources are cited in Fu Zhenggu (1993: 210).

13. Here we have one of the unfulfilled prophecies in the book. Wei lasts for another 420 years. This is sometimes adduced as one of the proofs that the *Zuo zhuan* decidedly predates the third century B.C., when Diqiu stops being the Wei capital with the fall of the Wei house.

14. Shusun Qiaoru has adulterous relations with the Lu ruler's mother Mujiang and

plots against the dominant Jisun clan. He flees to Qi when his conspiracies are exposed (*ZZ* Cheng 16.5, 16.11).

15. When Shusun Bao is born, his father obtains "*mingyi*䷣'s *qian*䷎" (*mingyi zhi qian*, i.e., the last line of the *mingyi* hexagram, which, if broken instead of whole, would have changed *mingyi* into *qian*) in divination. The diviner's interpretation enlarges on the images of drooping wings, starvation, and slander in the line statement of the last line of the *mingyi* hexagram. The *mingyi* hexagram is a combination of the *kun*☷ and *li*☲ trigrams, which are both associated with the sign of the bovine. For the translation of *zhi* as possessive, see Edward Shaughnessy (1983: 84–92) and Kidder Smith (1989: 425–426).

16. See comments by Zhao Xun and Du Yu in *ZZ*, 459. Takezoe Teruo cites medical texts which claim that animal brains can cause paralysis and refers to the "Neize" chapter of the *Liji*, which stipulates that pig brains be removed. Zheng Xuan's annotation points out its harmful effects (*Liji Zheng zhu* 1981: 98; see *Takezoe Teruo* 1961, Xi 28/20–21).

17. Yang Bojun observes that at the Banpo archaeological site, bodies on their backs were buried with accompanying items that indicated a higher status, while bodies facing downward had no such burial items (*ZZ*, 459).

18. The Marshes of Mengzhu are in Song, a nearby state that Chu is about to besiege.

19. For Ziyu's harshness as a commander, see *ZZ* Xi 27.4.

20. *Analects* 14.15. "Duke Wen of Jin was crafty and not upright; Duke Huan of Qi was upright and not crafty."

21. Recall Ning Wuzi's assertion that "ghosts and spirits cannot partake of sacrificial offerings from those not of the same kin" (*ZZ* Xi 31.5). This idea is echoed in other parts of the *Zuo zhuan*, where localized, particularized deities overseeing specific ancestral lines seem to be the rule. Thus people speak of becoming hungry ghosts when their progeny is eliminated (*ZZ* Xuan 4.3) or when they refuse to attend to sacrifices offered by their descendants (*ZZ* Xiang 20.7). When the Lu minister Zang Wenzhong offers sacrifices to seabirds that stop at the east gate of Lu, he incurs the criticism of Zhan Qin, who explains in a long speech how sacrifices should be determined by lineages and accomplishments (*Guoyu* Lu 1.9). See also the description of sacrificial distinctions for persons of different ranks in the *Liji*, "To offer sacrifices to whom one should not offer sacrifices is called licentious sacrifices [*yinsi*]. Licentious sacrifices bring no blessings" ("Quli xia," in *Liji Zheng zhu* 1981: 16); and *Analects* 2.24 (Confucius 1927), "To offer sacrifices to inappropriate spirits is to curry favor."

22. Xiao Gongquan (1982: 229–230) discusses the development of protolegalist thought in the Spring and Autumn era, especially in Jin and Zheng.

23. For a complete English translation, see (Watson 1968). Graham (1986) translates the first seven chapters, with illuminating critical essays on the *Zhuangzi*.

24. Citations refer to *Zhuangzi zuanjian* (hereafter *ZhZ*), Qian Mu, editor (1951).

25. In the *Zhuangzi*, Confucius functions either as a foil to, or an exponent of, Daoist attitudes.

26. Confucius's most esteemed disciple.

27. See comments by Guo Xiang and Cheng Yuanying, in Zhuangzi (1982: 1:50).

28. See Graham (1969–70: 150).

29. For the dating of the *Liezi*, see Graham 1986: 242–245.

30. Citations are from *Liezi yizhu* (hereafter *LZ*), Yan Beiming and Yan Jie, eds. (1986).

31. "I, the lone one" (*yu yiren*) is a conventional way for a ruler to refer to himself.

32. The distinction of six kinds of dreams is derived from the "Chunguan" chapter in the *Zhou li*.

References

Ban Gu. 1983. *Han shu* (History of Han). 12 vols. Beijing: Zhonghua shuju. Reprint of 1962 edition.

Confucius. 1927. *Lunyu* (Analects), in *Sishu jizhu* (*The Four Books*, with collected annotations and commentaries). Annotated by Zhu Xi. Shanghai: Zhonghua shuju.

Du Yu. 1986. *Chunqiu jingzhuan jijie* (Collected annotations and commentaries on the *Spring and Autumn Annals and Its Commentary Tradition*). Shanghai: Shanghai guji chubanshe.

Fu Zhenggu. 1993. *Zhongguo meng wenxue shi* (History of Chinese Dream Literature). Beijing: Guangming rubao chubanshe.

Graham, Angus C. 1969–70. "Chuang Tzu's Essay on Seeing Things as Equal," *History of Religions* 9.2–3.

———. 1986a. *Chuang Tzu: The Inner Chapters*. London: Unwin.

———. 1986b. *Studies in Chinese Philosophy and Philosophical Literature*. Singapore: Institute of East Asian Philosophies.

Legge, James. 1872. *The Ch'un Ts'ew with the Tso Chuen* (*The Chinese Classics*, vol. 5). Hong Kong.

Liji Zheng zhu 1981. (*The Record of Rites*). Annotated by Zheng Xuan. Taipei: Xinxing shuju.

Qian Mu, ed. 1951. *Zhuangzi zuanjian* (Annotations and commentaries on the *Zhuangzi*). Hong Kong: Dongnan yinwu chubanshe.

Shaughnessy, Edward L. 1983. The Composition of The *Zhouyi*. Ph.D. diss., Stanford University (Ann Arbor: University Microfilms International).

Smith, Kidder. 1989. "*Zhouyi Interpretation* from accounts in the *Zuo zhuan*," *Harvard Journal of Asiatic Studies* 49, 421–463.

Takezoe Teruo. 1961. *Saden Kaisen* (Collected annotations and commentaries on the *Zuo zhuan*). Taipei: Fenghuang chubanshe. Reprint of 1912 Tokyo edition.

Tong Shuye. 1980. *Chunqiu Zuo zhuan yanjiu* (Study of the *Zuo Commetary Tradition* of the *Spring and Autumn Annals*). Shanghai: Shanghai renmin chubanshe.

Watson, Burton. 1968. *The Complete Works of Chuang Tzu*. New York: Columbia University Press.

———. *The Tso Chuan: Selection from China's Oldest Narrative History*. New York: Columbia University Press.

Xiao Gongquan. 1982. *Zhongguo zhengzhi sixiangshi* (*History of Chinese Political Thought*). Taipei: Zhongguo wenhua daxue chubanshe.

Yan Beiming and Yan Jie, eds. 1986. *Liezi yizhu* (Annotations on the *Liezi*). Shanghai: Shanghai guji chubanshe.

Yang Bojun, ed. 1981. *Chunqiu Zuo zhuan zhu* (Annotations and Commentaries on the *Spring and Autumn Annals and the Zuo zhuan*). 4 vols. Beijing: Zhonghua shuju.

Zhouyi Wang Han zhu (*The Classic of Changes*). 1985. Annotated by Wang Bi and Han Kangbo. Sibu beiyao edition. Taipei: Zhonghua shuju.

Zhuangzi. 1985. *Zhuangzi jishi* (*Zhuangzi*, with collected annotations and commentaries). Compiled by Guo Qingfan. 4 vols. Beijing: Zhonghua shuju.

3

Dreaming the Self in South India

David Shulman

1

Once there was a city that was swallowed up by the sea. The disaster was not entirely unexpected, for a conditional curse had long before been laid upon the place, a curse connected to the dependable human potential for forgetting: if the king were ever to forget to celebrate the festival of the god Indra, the city would be flooded and destroyed. Close to the event, there were signs—dreamlike announcements and prophecies—that the condition was about to be fulfilled. But in the end it was, as usual, a matter of too much loving, and longing, and the inevitable sorrow that they entail.

The city was Pukār, also known as Kāverippūmpaṭṭiṉam, an ancient Tamil seaport on the shores of the Bay of Bengal. The king was the great Chola who fell in love with a woman from the nether world of the serpents—an impossible union, consuming in all ways. She left him to return to her mysterious domain, promising only to send him one day the son who would be born out of their love. And so she did: the baby was entrusted to a ship of merchants sailing the sea, but the ship was wrecked and the baby lost. When the king heard the tragic news, he was so overcome with grief—a double loss, doubly unbearable—that he forgot his duties, forgot to celebrate the festival. So Indra ordered the goddess Maṇimekhalā, deity of seafarers, to drown the city.

There is an important sequel to this story. Though Pukār was lost forever, the child was eventually washed ashore not far to the north, where he became the king of Kāñcipuram—one of the great historic centers of south Indian civilization and, in the middle of the first millenium A.D., an important site for Buddhist cult and learning. So the origin of kingship in Kāñcipuram was somehow bound up with the flooding of the older royal capital to the south, and with the notion of another king's passion and forgetting. Kāñcipuram was also, it seems, the place where the long Tamil narrative poem called *Maṇimekalai*, which will concern us here, was composed, perhaps in the sixth century, to tell the story of the flood and another, more complicated story as well, about a young courtesan who, in effect, dreams her way toward the Buddhist path.

Maṇimekalai is a book of dreams and dreamlike modes. It is attributed, almost certainly by expressive retrojection on the part of the Tamil tradition, to a poet named Kūlavāṇikaṉ Cāttaṉār, known to us from the ancient anthologies of shorter poems. We will have more to say about this attribution and the role played by the alleged author. It is also the only Tamil Buddhist work to survive, and one of the most lyrical and moving of all classical Tamil poems. In the background one senses, throughout, the impending destruction of Pukār, for the reason just described: this is both leitmotif and backdrop to the story of the heroine's unfolding. Since her story is so intricate, told in a strange forward-backward oscillation, filled with flashbacks to earlier lives—and since the dream logic it embodies is intelligible only in the context of this narrative—I will begin with a rough and much reduced summary of its major contours. The reader should bear in mind that the story also branches out continuously into various secondary and embedded narratives, some of them highly resonant with the central drama.

Maṇimekalai, the heroine, named after the same goddess of seafarers (Maṇimekhalā),[1] was the daughter of the courtesan Mātavi and her lover Kovalaṉ. Kovalaṉ had been killed, through tragic mistake, by the king of Maturai in the far south of the Tamil country; his wife, Kaṇṇaki, enraged at the loss of her husband, tore off her left breast and hurled it at the city of Maturai, burning it to ashes. Kaṇṇaki then became a goddess worshiped in a temple far to the west, in Vañci.[2] These events were known to the young, future courtesan Maṇimekalai as she was growing up in Pukār, and the vast sorrow they represented turned her heart away from the world, toward renunciation and the search for truth.

She was a beautiful woman, and her metaphysical bent was deeply disturbing to the courtesans, and others, in Pukār (especially to her grandmother Cittirāpati). Moreover, the Prince of Pukār, Utayakumaraṉ, was passionately in love with her. One day he pursued her into the public garden, where she had gone to pick flowers with her companion, Cutamati. To escape the attentions of the prince, Maṇimekalai took shelter in a crystal pavilion, where she could be seen but not touched. In despair, the prince went home. But that night the goddess Maṇimekhalā herself spirited the sleeping Maṇimekalai away to an island called Maṇipallavam in the middle of the sea. At the same time, the goddess appeared to the prince and urged him to renounce his passion for the girl. She also woke up Cutamati and informed her of Maṇimekalai's disappearance, explained that the time had come for Maṇimekalai to follow the Buddhist path, and promised that the young woman would return to Pukār in disguise. Later on this same night of eerie revelations, a painted pillar in the public hall began speaking, telling Cutamati the story of her former life.

On the island, Maṇimekalai discovered a Buddhist shrine; approaching it, she suddenly remembered all that had happened in her previous life. Soon the goddess Maṇimekhalā herself appeared and confirmed these memories; she also taught Maṇimekalai mantras that allowed her to fly through the air and to take on whatever form she wished. The guardian goddess of the island, Tīvatilakai, also materialized before Maṇimekalai; at her instruction, Maṇimekalai received from a pond in the shrine a magical bowl, Amuta-curapi, which produced inexhaustible supplies of food. This bowl had once belonged to a renegade Brahmin named Āputtiraṉ, who was abandoned by his mother and nursed by a cow. When Āputtiraṉ died, after many adventures, on Maṇipallavam Island, the bowl vanished into the pond. This same Āputtiraṉ was now reborn as the King of Cavakam (Java), with no memory of his past.

Maṇimekalai took the magic bowl back to Pukār with the aim of feeding all who were hungry. First to be fed was a divine woman named Kāyacaṇṭikai, who had been cursed with the disease of "elephant's hunger": no food could ever satisfy her craving. (She had tripped over, and unintentionally destroyed, a magical *nāval* fruit, which ripened only once every twelve years, and which a sage had set aside for his meal—also a once-in-twelve-years' event; in his anger, he cursed her to suffer a hunger equal to his own.) One mouthful from Maṇimekalai's bowl satisfied Kāyacaṇṭikai, and redeemed her. She flew off to rejoin her husband in the land of the Vidyādhara musicians, but on the way, she inadvertently flew over the mountain of the hungry goddess Durgā, who seized her shadow and used it to drag her down and devour her entirely.

Now that Kāyacaṇṭikai was gone, Maṇimekalai—still intent on avoiding the unwanted attentions of the lovelorn Prince Utayakumaraṉ—assumed Kāyacaṇṭikai's form (by means of the magical mantra) and went through the streets, giving food to the hungry from her bowl. She transformed the city of Pukār by her loving-kindness, and persuaded the king himself to turn the prison into a place of teaching and charity. But disaster was lurking: Kāyacaṇṭikai's husband, the Vidyādhara Kāñcaṉaṉ, unaware that his wife's curse had come to an end, came to Kāñci to look for her. He saw Maṇimekalai in Kāyacaṇṭikai's form, and watched as she spoke at length to the prince, whom she urged to renounce his passion; but the Vidyādhara wrongly assumed that he was seeing his wife in a romantic liaison with another man. He therefore hid himself in the public hall, at night, when Maṇimekalai returned there to sleep. When the prince also appeared, still intent on winning her love, Kāñcaṉaṉ emerged and killed him with his sword. No sooner had he done so than a painted pillar in the hall—a divinity locked in stone—spoke to Kāñcaṉaṉ and explained his terrible mistake; he also informed the unhappy husband that his wife had been swallowed by Durgā on her way home.

Now Maṇimekalai awoke and overheard this conversation, even as she saw the dead body of her would-be lover lying before her. She grieved over the prince, called out to him as her beloved. But again the pillar deity spoke, explaining to her that the prince had been her husband in many previous lives and had suffered his present fate because of an act of violence committed in his last human incarnation. The pillar also spoke of Maṇimekalai's future enlightenment through the words of the great Buddhist sage Aṟavaṇa Aṭikaḷ.

The queen, Utayakumaraṉ's mother, sought to have Maṇimekalai killed, since she had caused her son's death; but Maṇimekalai survived all attempts to harm her, and taught wisdom to the grieving queen. She then left Pukār to seek out the sage. On the way she found Puṇyarāja, the King of Cāvakam (and the original owner of the magical bowl). She took him to the Buddhist shrine on the island of Maṇipallavam, where he, too, remembered his former life and even exhumed his own former body, a buried skeleton, as final proof of this rediscovered story. The goddess of the island also revealed to the two pilgrims, Maṇimekalai and the Javanese king, that the city of Pukār had just been flooded and destroyed—for the Chola king, overcome by grief for his infant son lost at sea, had forgotten to celebrate Indra's festival, as had been foretold.

Maṇimekalai made her way to Kāñcipuram via the city of Vañci, where teachers of various sects and schools expounded their truths to her. At Kāñci she found Aṟavaṇa Aṭikaḷ and learned the ultimate wisdom of the Buddhist path. Here, too, she entrusted the magical bowl to a newly created shrine, where it continues to feed the hungry, to bring rain to the fields, and to heal all those in need.

Such is the story, unusual in Buddhist literature on several counts—the presence of a female protagonist who embodies the search for freedom; the eerie intricacies of remembering and forgetting that occupy nearly all the main characters; the lyrical and wistful portrait of human consciousness, in its various modes; and the striking connections between the metaphysics of self and self-knowledge and the external drama of destruction that involves the flooding of Pukār. But *Maṇimekalai*, for all its uniqueness, does not stand alone. It is, in fact, a twin. As even the above crude summary reveals, the Maṇimekalai story is closely intertwined with earlier events relating to Maṇimekalai's parents, Kovalaṉ and Mātavi, and to Kovalaṉ's properly wedded wife, Kaṇṇaki. These events are told in the famous Tamil narrative poem, *Cilappatikāram*, attributed to a Cera prince-poet, Iḷaṅkovaṭikaḷ. The *Cilappatikāram* is probably roughly contemporaneous with *Maṇimekalai* (and the attribution to the Cera prince is no more convincing than that of *Maṇimekalai* to the merchant Cāttaṉār). The two works echo one another repeatedly, to the point of sharing small textual segments, though for the most part we are dealing with a dense web of intertextual correspondences, as the Tamil tradition has always recognized. One should note that the *Cilappatikāram* also climaxes in a dreadful act of destruction, Kaṇṇaki's vengeful burning of the city of Maturai.

The tradition has its own way of asserting this linkage, tying the two texts intimately together. It tells us that the two poets actually composed their works initially for one another—an audience of one. This assertion serves to provide a frame within which the two poems can be situated, and which itself comments upon their meaning. We must take a moment, before turning to Maṇimekalai and her dreams, to address this traditional frame, which comes to us in the form of two *patikam* prefaces, apparently prefixed to the two works in the early medieval period. The *patikam* to *Maṇimekalai* tells us, rather simply, that Kūlavāṇikaṉ Cāttaṉ composed the thirty cantos of *Maṇimekalai-tuṟavu* ("Maṇimekalai's Renunciation," perhaps the original title of the work) for Iḷaṅko (lines 95–98). Rather more striking is the story offered by the preface to *Cilappatikāram*: here, when the Kuṟavar hill tribes came to Iḷaṅko with reports of an amazing vision of a goddess or woman (*tiru mā pattiṉi*) with only one breast, it is Cāttaṉ, Iḷaṅko's companion, who can explain what happened—by summarizing, in effect, the entire *Cilappatikāram* story, which Iḷaṅko will then embody in *his* thirty chapters. How does Cāttaṉ know this long, sorrowful sequence and, more important still, what it means in terms of karmic causality (*viṉai-viḷaivu*)? He knows because he was lying down—perhaps sleeping—in Śiva's temple in Maturai when the goddess of Maturai herself appeared there before Kaṇṇaki and informed her of her previous life and the tragic karmic preconditioning of her husband's death in *this* life (lines 39–54). Now we know, from the text of the *Cilappatikāram* itself, just when this revelation took place: it was right after Kaṇṇaki had torn her fiery breast from her body and cast it at the city of Maturai, which was consumed in the conflagration.

All of this has its own suggestive importance—even granting the assumption that the *patikam* is a later appendage to the text. In effect, the two prefaces recapitulate an "internal framing"[3] incorporated already into the *Cilappatikāram* itself: there, too, Cāttaṉ, "the great master of Tamil" (*taṇ ṭamiḻ ācāṉ cāttaṉ*), filled with a joyous and baffling sense of wonder and desire, explains Kaṇṇaki's story to King Cĕṅkuṭṭuvaṉ when the Kuṟavar hill people report a vision of this goddess with a single breast (25.65–66). But the prefaces also give the frame a special twist. They specify the first audience for each of the books, making these two single listeners, bound together in companionship, internal to what is really a single story in two installments—and also creating, by the same token, a certain disjunction between this internal hearing of the poems and *our* experience of them, *outside* the frame. This sets both works firmly in the *kāvya* mode of elaborate poetic narrative, as the tradition has always recognized;[4] despite current usage, neither *Cilappatikāram* nor *Maṇimekalai* is in any sense epic. On the other hand, it now transpires that Cāttaṉār's vision, whatever it was, precedes Iḷaṅko's education in the events he is soon to describe. Moreover, this vision is set in the stark and fearful night during which Maturai was burning. Our story—Maṇimekalai's story too—comes to us, then, via the visionary poet, amidst the flames.

Just what was the nature of Cāttaṉār's experience, as the *patikam* would like us to understand it? The verb is ambiguous: he was "lying" in the temple, in deep darkness (*nallirut kiṭanteṉ*, 41). Perhaps, in this state, he simply overheard the conversation between the city goddess and Kaṇṇaki. (Poetry, as A. K. Ramanujan used to say, is never heard, only overheard.) But Aṭiyārkkunallār, the medieval commentator, says that Cāttaṉār was asleep. In this case, the whole conversation—indeed the entire story of our two intertwined texts—would be a dream.[5] Of course, the two need not be mutually exclusive. Our poet could have overheard the goddess in a dream, and in any case, I am not sure that we need to resolve this question by opting for one unequivocal reading. What matters, in terms of the thematic drive I will emphasize below, is the tradition's sense of Cāttaṉār's initial experience, the penetrating illumination, on the edge of extinction, that gives birth to two great poems. It happens at night, in the dark, in the presence of startling visual and auditory images highly reminiscent of the dream state, and powerfully keyed to the dream textures that consistently inform our text. For the *Maṇimekalai* largely moves from one dream to another (sometimes one inside another), and it is not by chance that the literary culture around it classifies its composition as a dreamlike act. Such statements, an implicit literary criticism on the level of the living use of the classical texts, are never misleading.

2

So Cāttaṉār, in this perspective, has given us a kind of dream text originating in a moment of fiery destruction. Let us see how the poem itself supports this reading. In what follows, I will trace certain powerful, interlocking themes, integrated by a stable set of linguistic and poetic means and by a common affinity with dreaming, broadly understood. I assume, as a working hypothesis, that the domains of themes, figuration, narrative structure, framing, and poetic language are all, in some way, mutually reinforcing. We will thus look briefly at the textures and syntactic patterns that are so characteristic of this book and of its specific expressivity.

Let us begin with what could be considered a master trope, emblematic of the whole. Maṇimekalai has gone to the public garden with Cutamati, to pick flowers (for she has ruined the garlands she was weaving earlier by her tears, generated by hearing the story of her father's death). Utayakumaraṉ, the prince who loves her (although one wonders, already at the outset, whether this is really the right word), is out in the streets; he has just brought a wild elephant back under control. Now, as he passes the courtesans' houses, he sees through an open window a young man of the merchant class, standing beside his lover in a state of apparent bewilderment. One hand clutches a vīṇā, but the man is frozen into stillness, like a painted picture (*vaṭṭikaic cĕytiyiṉ varainta pāvai*, 4.57). The prince is interested, and asks the man what is wrong (*yātu nī yuṟṟa iṭukkaṇ*). The young merchant hastens to bow to the prince and to explain:

> Like a flower hidden in a vase,
> Maṇimekalai, Mātavi's daughter,
> her beauty fading,
> was on her way to the garden.
> I saw her pass, and the terrible sorrow
> that overtook her father, Kovalaṉ,
> overwhelmed me.
> My heart lost its center, my hand strayed

to the wrong string of the *vīṇā*.
A wrong note rang out: that is what distressed me. (4.65–71)

The prince, predictably, finds this story a cause for rejoicing: he now knows where to find Maṇimekalai. But if the force of the image is lost on him (as nearly everything he hears and sees throughout this story fails to touch him truly), it need not be on us. The lover has seen a disturbing vision of a striking young woman fading, her beauty hidden and denied; this vision calls up in him an empathic identification with her father's suffering, and the result is a strident, unconscious disharmony. The wrong string is unintentionally sounded, a false note disturbs the setting of love. This is enough to turn the young merchant to stone. We should observe the somewhat unusual, indeed oblique, causal nexus: vision connects to emotion, which decenters concentration and produces the false note, and the latter then freezes body and mind. Here causality—in a profound sense, always felt to be ultimately incoherent in a Buddhist metaphysics—has the same zigzag quality, the same slippery movement from conditioning frame to dependent result, that we find in so much Buddhist theory, for example in the analysis of "conditioned origins" (see below). In this sense, our slight example is entirely appropriate to its wider setting of primary perceptions. Moreover, once again in accordance with a major strand within this wider setting, the ultimate, contextualizing level—the level of potential resolution—is essentially an aesthetic one.[6] Imagine a world very delicately attuned, so much so that a single wrong note can inflict deep pain in the heart or mind, but also labile, emotionally vibrant, and, in particular, rich in the varieties of desire. Here sorrow, ignited suddenly by memory, produces an immediate displacement, a glaring gap in the superficially smooth texture of experience. The merchant-lover has remembered a story—in this case, someone else's story—and, for a single pregnant moment, his world has come to a halt. There is a sense in which this kind of opening—the unexpected displacement, or discontinuity, that is signalled by the jarring note and that is somehow connected to memory, to story, and to sorrow—is, for our poet, characteristic of consciousness per se.

As already stated, this is a book about the structure, the inner dynamics, and the potentialities of awareness. Moreover, the poignant image just examined recurs in a remarkable passage in Canto 7, which we might call, in our own shorthand, "Nightfall in Pukār"—perhaps the most powerful attempt we have in classical Tamil to find extended lyrical embodiment for the subtle textures of night (and this in a literature that was particularly fascinated with nocturnal images and themes). Here is the setting: Cutamati, Maṇimekalai's friend, has been visited, her sleep disturbed, by the goddess Maṇimekhalā, who has already spirited her namesake Maṇimekalai away to Maṇipallavam Island; now the goddess returns to inform Cutamati of her friend's disappearance and to send her with this news to Mātavi. All this transpires in the burning ground, with its gruesome sights and sounds. Cutamati, still half asleep, is appropriately fearful, lonely, bewildered, and the manifold sounds of the night only enhance her fears. The town is asleep, yet the night is alive with murmurs, movement, strange cries:

Dancing girls were sleeping soundly
beside their sleeping instruments.
Gentle fingers blindly stroked, in sleep,
the untuned strings, and false notes
filled the night. Wives whose husbands
had just returned from their mistresses
were still angry, unappeased, their eyes red
as they feigned sleep, but full of wanting, too,
embracing these false men as if from sleep.
Little children, worn out from play,
from pulling their toy chariots, slept
peacefully beside their sleeping nursemaids,
enveloped in incense of white mustard.
House pigeons and water birds and birds of the groves
slept deeply, their beaks enfolded in their bodies.
The whole city, full of the festival, had settled
into sleep. But still there were noises:
watchmen calling out the hours
according to the water-clock in the palace,
hungry elephants trumpeting from their stables,
drumbeats of the guards who were prowling lanes and alleys,
the drunken songs of the shipbuilders, too full of rice toddy,
women splashing in the dark ponds to purify themselves
after childbirth, as others wafted smoke of margosa and white mustard,
heroes fierce as tigers screaming "Victory to the King!"
as they cut off their heads in sacrifice to the ghoul at the crossroads,
spirit-charmers singing mantras as they offered animals to the demons
to protect new mothers and young children and pregnant women
from grief—and many other sounds, too, softly spreading
through the night. . . . (7.44–86)

First, again, is the dissonance of unconsciousness musicality, the false notes struck from the untuned vīṇā—and to these unsettling resonances are added the irregular growls and rustlings and cries that, together, make up this strange nocturnal symphony. The tenor of the night is mixed, and sometimes violent: there is hunger, there is intoxication, there are the death screams of self-sacrificing warriors (apparently a regular nocturnal experience, at least during festival days), there is ritual activity of various kinds. In many ways, as I can attest from my own experience, this description feels uncannily appropriate to the texture of midnight in any Tamil city, even today. What is more to the point, the texture is that of dreaming itself, and as such meaningful in the context of this first extended dream narration in the *Maṇimekalai*. "Nightfall in Pukār" is the background to the goddess's self-revelation to Cutamati, to the prince, and to Maṇimekalai's own disappearance, still asleep, from her home. We hear Pukār as the dreamers hear it, unaware, in sleep.

Can we characterize this texture more precisely? Thematically, we have already noted the element of unconscious disharmony. At the same time, we cannot but feel the luxuriant profusion of noise and image; dream texture is agglutinative, cumulative, uneven. It also includes, within its own internal pattern, the transition in state that is built into dreaming per se: existential domains are mingled, demons wander through the streets, warriors move from this world to the next. Morever, this haunting, daunting moment of potential transformation is suggestively coded, its images dark and hidden, reduced to invisible sound. Their internal links are gently, but also tenuously, marked by the standard syntactical device of classical Tamil poetic narratives, a seemingly endless sequence of nonfinite verbs occasionally interspersed with adverbial time markers. The sense is of a chain of contiguous elements, loosely related, discrete, yet cumulative in effect. Within this chain there is the constant recurrence of certain key units, for example, the repeated, explicit statement that "X" or "Y" or indeed "the whole city" is asleep. The repetition provides the assurance, perhaps the illusion, of coherence among a strangely discontinuous assortment of individual elements. There is a sense in which this syntax is molded precisely to generate the consciousness or, to use another term, the experiential textures, it seems to describe. It could almost be a lullaby, mesmerizing the listener into dreaming.

Let me repeat: the *Maṇimekalai* is a kind of dream book, its textures apparently close to a culturally specific sense of dream experience. The awareness at the center of this dark and moving work is also closely linked to dreaming. As A̱ravaṇa Aṭikaḷ tells Maṇimekalai in the concluding canto, where the Buddhist teaching is made explicit, *uṇarvu*—"consciousness," "awareness," "feeling"—is "the sleeper's state" (*uṇarv' ĕṉap paṭuvat' uṟaṅkuvor uṇarviṟ puriv' iṉṟ' ākip pulaṉ kŏlātatuve*, 30.83–84). Of course, *uṇarvu* is a technical term here, the third in the sequence of the *nidānas*, "links" in a theory of conditioned origins (*pratītya samutpāda*), the well-known Buddhist chain of psychocosmology which we examine below; we should be careful not to load it with any extrinsic significance. Still, I will argue that this Tamil translation of *vijñāna* is meaningful within the more general metaphysical system of this book, and I will assume that this system is present not only in the philosophical/logical conclusion of the final cantos but also throughout the interlocking narratives that make up most of the text. We are searching here for those intuited, deeply embedded perceptions that have given birth both to the amazing story and to the explanations it offers of itself.

We will return to the chain of conditioned origins and to the place of *uṇarvu* as dream. For now, let us notice only that, as the dream is dispelled—as day breaks in Pukār—a powerful doubling seeps into language (and, apparently, perception as well).

kāvalāḷar kaṇ ṭuyil kŏḷḷat
tū mĕṉ cekkait tuyil kaṇ viḻippa
valampuric caṅkam vaṟit' ĕḻuntārppa
pulam puric caṅkam pŏruḷoṭu mulaṅkap
pukar muka vāraṇam nĕṭun kū viḷippa
pŏṟi mayir vāraṇam kuṟuṅ kū viḷippa
paṇai nilaip puravi palav ĕḻunt' ālap

paṇai nilaip puḷḷum palav ĕl̲unt' ālap
pūm p̆o̲lil ārkaip puḷḷ ŏli cir̲appap
pūṅkŏṭiyār kaip puḷḷ ŏli cir̲appa. . . .

Now the watchmen could go to sleep,
but lovers in their soft beds would have to wake:
there were conches sounding, with no meaning,
and poets singing artful blessings,
elephants trumpeting,
cocks crowing,
horses restless in their stables,
birds crying on the branches as they shook off rest
so the groves were full of their wild music,
like the bracelets chiming on women's arms. . . . (7.111–120)

Translation can hardly reflect the *yamaka* chiming that forms the true substance of these lines: the poet plays on the double meanings of *vāraṇam* ("elephant" as well as "cock"), *paṇai* ("stables" and "branch"), and so on, deftly alliterating and reconfiguring the repeated phonematic series. In a way, it is "only" play, not to be overly burdened with interpretation. On another level, we have here another feature integral to our theme—a salient marker of the transition between dream and nondream. The dream state points in two directions and incorporates a strangely doubled code, which both superimposes and displaces its basic units of meaning.

Before concluding this section, I would like to look at one more image, which seems to me to lead us toward the deeper logic of this narrative and its dream modes. Canto 5—still very much part of the same sequence with which we have been dealing, Maṇimekalai's visit to the garden and its consequences—concludes with a lengthy description of evening. The two girls are still in the garden, the prince has temporarily given up his quest and gone home; soon both Maṇimekalai and Cutamati will be asleep. At this point the city of Pukār itself is portrayed in an extended, tragic metaphor as a newly bereaved widow leaving the battlefield and going back to her parents' house. Note the direction: the regression backward, or even, we might say, inward, into the home or womb out of which this woman had emerged. The *haṃsa* goose, however, surprisingly reverses the sense of entropic self-enfolding. When the female goose is caught within the lotus flower that is closing as evening comes, the male rushes in to tear open the lotus and free her.[7] Night is falling, dreamtime approaching: a process of closing inward, in destructive circles or spirals, is disrupted and blocked. This, in a word, is the promise of the dream.

3

This dream logic can be simply and abstractly stated. Imagine a large circle spiralling inward in concentric patterns. At its central point, if and when it is reached, there is an implosion: this is the point of self-destruction which, because the circle is infinite in scope, actually repeats itself without end. Individual lives, or the lives of cities, or of the cosmos, follow this course of inevitable and recurrent self-annihilation. The energy that fuels the dreadful process has a name. Call it "forgetting," here synonymous with "not knowing"—in short, our normal consciousness. Thus the grief-stricken Chola king forgets to celebrate Indra's festival—and Pukār is lost to the flood. On the individual level, the lethal cycle or spiral is that of conditioned origin, *pratītya samutpāda*, described by A͟ravaṇa Aṭikaḷ at the book's close. Here is the chain that produces a given life, or a world. First there is ignorance, *petaimai*—actually qualified by the participle *ma͟ranta*, that is, "the ignorance that is forgetting." Then there is activity or, more precisely, agency—*cĕyal* (*karma*). Agency, following upon forgetting, conditions awareness (*uṇarvu*, see above), followed by name and form (*aruvuru*), sensual activation (*vāyil, ū͟ru, nukarvu*), and then, of course, the truly destructive drives of craving (*veṭkai*) and attachment (*pa͟r͟ru*), which provide the necessary preconditions for becoming (*pavam*), birth (*to͟r͟ram*), sickness, old age, and death (*piṇi, mūppu, cāvu*). The list is nicely stated in 30.159–169, which also divides the stages into time categories: forgetting and agency belong to time past; awareness and subsequent stages, through becoming and birth, belong to time present; the future is the preserve of disease, old age, and death.

The spiral thus moves, inevitably, toward death, which is never a real ending but only the certain conclusion of each twisted whorl, each new birth, each act of forgetting. None of this is new or in any way unique to *Maṇimekalai*. It is a well-known Buddhist vision, congenially adapted into the Tamil mode. But the Tamil heroine of our work does manage to escape the spiral; as we have said, the primary thrust of the narrative is toward exploring the mechanism and modes of her achievement. In effect, the question is how to bring about a significant break or rupture within the circular system of self-destructive, entropic becoming. Where there is deadly continuity of dependent conditioning—the future clearly embedded, and indeed determined, within the present and the past—one seeks space and a countermovement, a transition not forward toward dying but backward, toward (and beyond) forgetting. In the present case, the essential instrument of this reverse movement is the dream, which becomes a mode of memory.

How does it work? There are actually several parallel possibilities that we need to examine briefly. The dream mode is, in a sense, merely emblematic of a larger category of mantic or anamnestic semiosis. Maṇimekalai is transported in her sleep to the island of Maṇipallavam, where she will learn of her former life. Is she dreaming or awake? Technically, the latter, but she herself is unsure. "Is this waking reality or a dream?" is the first question she asks herself upon awaking on the island beach (*na͟navo ka͟navo ĕ͟npatai a͟riye͟n*, 8.21). This quandary, intrinsic to the dream ontology, is later intensified by the expansion in identity she undergoes as her former life is revealed to her at the Buddhist shrine on the island. She discovers that in her previous incarnation she was Lakṣmī, the wife of Rāhula, who died of snakebite and was reborn as Utayakumara͟n—the same prince of Pukār who is, understandably now, still in love with this same woman. All of this is, of course, somewhat disturbing. Thus when the guardian goddess of the island, Tīvatilakai, comes to Maṇimekalai and asks the deceptively simple question, "Who are you?," Maṇimekalai—already irrevocably altered in her understanding of herself—can only answer, logically enough, "Which me do you mean?" (11.8–9).

This progression can be seen as paradigmatic for major figures in our text, although it may take other forms. King Āputtiraṉ/Puṇyarāja, for example, goes through the stages of self-recovery in a still more graphic way: brought to the same island under Maṇimekalai's tutelage, he is made to excavate, in shock and wonder, his own former body. Cutamati, Maṇimekalai's friend, learns of her previous birth from the eloquent and mysterious pillar image (*kantiṟ pāvai*) in the great public hall in Pukār known as Ulaka-aṟavi, to the east of the goddess shrine. The pillar image is divine, and he tends to speak at night, in a realm of consciousness somewhere between waking and sleeping. He is also suggestively described as capable of explaining causes surviving from the distant past. Maṇimekalai also has an important exchange with this divinity, in the course of which he tells her his own intriguing story:

> I am one of the many gods, Tuvatikaṉ by name.
> As of old, this pillar has been appointed as my place
> by Mayaṉ, the divine artisan. I never leave it.
> Listen to my story: human beings know
> what even gods don't know. I have a friend,
> Oviyacceṉaṉ, a close companion. Someone or other
> must have told them in this city, so they always paint us
> together, in all the places we play, as if we were as close
> as flower and fragrance—though it is me whom they praise
> until their tongues become exhausted. . . . (21.130–140)

The context of this self-revelation is suggestive, in several ways. The immediate preface is a general statement. In Pukār, so the pillar image tells Maṇimekalai, there are images everywhere, in public halls and meeting places, at the seaside, in groves and shrines, wherever some conceptualized or envisaged divinity could be captured and held in place by a painted form, on clay or stone or wood or wall (119–128). All these images are meant to offer protection (*kāval*); Tuvatikaṉ, perhaps the most articulate and prominent of them all, also presumably performs this function—although, no doubt like the rest as well, he seems to be concerned even more powerfully with removing amnesiac blockages in the awareness of those who come near him. Indeed, the entire series might be seen as inspired by the anxiety of forgetting, for reasons we are beginning to understand. Beyond this general context, however, is the specific, lurid moment in which the pillar speaks: the prince has just been cut down, because of a mistaken perception, by the Vidyādhara husband of Kāyacaṇṭikai, in whose form Maṇimekalai was disguised; Maṇimekalai awakens to discover a corpse at her feet; the dialogue with the pillar image ensues. We will return, in greater detail, to this scene (see section 4 below), but it is important to bear in mind that the revelation volunteered by this deity emerges out of yet another characteristic moment of destruction, informed by notions of dangerous forgetting and misperception.

The pillar image seems trapped, condemned to endless ages in the confines of a singular condensed space. Even more striking, especially since it appears superficially so unmotivated, is the strange doubling that Tuvatikaṉ finds necessary to stress as he tells his story. He has a friend, who is as close to him as the fragrance to the flower; the two are always depicted together in the profusion of images that seems the norm in Pukār. Everyone—at least everyone human—knows that these two are somehow one, two shadow-selves combined; yet the pillar alone is praised. Once again, there is a poignant quality to this self-awareness, a disturbing sense of the ambiguous link between self and shadowy other, especially in the context of the hidden knowledge that becomes available through this captive divinity's speech. Insofar as the pillar's disclosures replicate the structure of the dream revelations—and the two modes are structurally and functionally alike, both recurring regularly to the same effect—then we might imagine that this theme of doubling runs parallel to the strange doubling in language and perception that we have seen in the transition from dream to waking, and that is, more deeply, integral to dreaming itself.

There are other analogous examples. A painted picture in the goddess shrine speaks to the prince, warning him (after the fashion of an earlier nocturnal vision in which Maṇimekhalā herself had appeared to him, telling him to forget Maṇimekalai, 7.3–14). He finds both of these communications wondrous (*tippiyam* = *divya*), although he is unable to internalize their practical and personal implication. Indeed, the prince is, in this matter, less fortunate than other major actors in the book. His consciousness of himself never expands to include the distant past, and the result is the obvious and necessary one—a pathetic death. In general, however, throughout the *Maṇimekalai*, we encounter a world where fragmentary revelations of the lost past keep opening up to those who are attuned, or ripe, to hearing them. They have certain stable features: an anamnesis that both extends the bounds of personal identity and, by the same token, undermines the integrity of the present, ego-framed self; a retrospective orientation that moves the subject backward, thus away from the entropic point of future implosion; and a paradoxical perception of radical discontinuity in the present that is rooted in the experience of identity expansion backward through time, as if the subject were being simultaneously filled with and emptied of his or her various selves. In this semiotically charged universe, replete with hints and pieces of past existence, one is frequently bombarded by unexpected metamessages that speak to overriding questions: *Who* are you? *Where* are you? And—much more rarely—*Why* are you who you are (or seem to be)?[8] One's ability to piece together a coherent picture out of these queries and partial answers is always, in principle, in doubt. The total frame is never present; nothing stands complete in itself; there are jarring notes and disharmonies at every step; but there is also a dependable potential for internal movement out of the destructive spiral. If the latter is energized, above all, by forgetting, then escape must lie in various forms of remembering, forms such as dreaming and the knowing voices of divinities trapped in paint or pillar.

4

There is also, however, another essential component to this process, which we might call "emptiness" or "hunger," strikingly evident in the same narrative unit just discussed—the pillar's nocturnal speech, heard or overheard by Maṇimekalai in the public space where the prince lies dead. Let us draw in, briefly, the narrative contours. Maṇimekalai has returned to Pukār with the magic bowl that produces endless food. She uses the bowl to satisfy the "elephant hunger" (*tantit tī*) of Kāyacaṇṭikai, who had unintentionally tripped over a marvellous *nāval* fruit that ripens once every twelve years and that was meant to satisfy the hunger of a Brahmin sage. He cursed her to suffer from unappeasable hunger until the next such fruit ripened, for *his* next meal, twelve years later—and also to lose her ability to fly through the sky. The curse ends as Maṇimekalai feeds the grounded and insatiable Kāyacaṇṭikai who, now happily sated, flies away—only to make the terrible mistake of overflying the Vindhya Mountains, where the hungry goddess Vintakaṭikai/Durgā seizes travellers' shadows, pulls them in, and devours them.

Meanwhile, in Pukār, Maṇimekalai has assumed the form of Kāyacaṇṭikai in order to escape the still lovelorn prince. But the latter is not entirely taken in by this disguise. Seeing "Kāyacaṇṭikai" feeding the hungry with the miraculous bowl, he suspects that this is really his beloved in another form; this suspicion grows stronger as she speaks to him, trying to instruct him in the transience of beauty (especially female beauty) and to turn his heart away from desire. The prince both knows and fails to know that he is looking at and speaking to Maṇimekalai—or perhaps he fails to know that he knows. In any case, he briefly leaves to return to the palace, intending to resume his search late at night. But he has, unfortunately, been observed in this interchange with "Kāyacaṇṭikai" by the real Kāyacaṇṭikai's Vidyādhara husband, who has come to Pukār to find *his* wife; the husband draws the obvious but entirely incorrect conclusion that his wife is in love with this prince. He then decides to lie in wait, in the Ulaka-aṟavi hall, for the prince's return, "like a serpent in its anthill home" (20.80). When Utayakumaraṉ does, indeed, come back to the hall, in the middle of the night, the Vidyādhara cuts him down with his sword. At this point the pillar speaks, explaining to the Vidyādhara his dreadful error and also informing him that his wife, though relieved of her hunger and the curse, has already been swallowed up by the hungry goddess of the Vindhyas.

Now Maṇimekalai, who has been sleeping in the goddess shrine to the west of the Ulaka-aṟavi hall, wakes up. The prince lies dead before her; the Vidyādhara stands horrified at his deed; and she has somehow overheard—perhaps still in sleep—the long speech of the pillar, gruesome with the reality of all that has happened. She is overcome with grief for the man who was her husband in many previous births—as the pillar now proceeds to inform her, filling in the gaps in the knowledge she gained on Maṇipallavam Island. It is at this point that the pillar also tells Maṇimekalai his own story, cited and discussed above.

Clearly, this extended passage is, in many ways, the real core of the entire book. Everything builds up toward this tragedy, and the remaining cantos deal with its emotional and cognitive aftermath. This is the moment in which the entropic spiral is cut, irrevocably, for our heroine, just as her suitor and former husband is literally cut in two. He, as we know, is still lost in entropy and prospective self-destruction, emerging out of ignorance, that is, forgetting, presumably active in his next birth; but Maṇimekalai will go on to a deeper wisdom and enhanced freedom, purchased partly through experience (her continued difficulties in Pukār) and partly through long lectures on logic and metaphysics. (It is striking that even Buddhist logic becomes a major theme in this book of dreams: logic is not learned but dreamt.) In any case, the paradigm of anamnestic semiosis still holds good: it is midnight; perception is occluded; destruction lurks and unfolds; the heroine sleeps, wakes, overhears; a revelation occurs through the eerie medium of the painted pillar image, who takes his listeners backward, and then forward, through time.

This is not, of course, a dream. Maṇimekalai wakes, this time, to learn the truth, almost as if the waking reality (*naṉavu*) were, for once, privileged over the dream world (*kaṉavu*). A closer look, however, dispels this impression—for Maṇimekalai is still very much caught up in the midnight world of altered consciousness. She is, in effect, dependent upon, and transformed by, the pillar's mantic speech, including those parts that she only overhears, perhaps in sleep. This theme of overhearing is, as we know, significant. Recall the earlier instance of the poet Cāttaṉār's dreamy eavesdropping on the conversation between Kaṇṇaki and the goddess of Maturai, with the city burning outside. Indeed, in a formal sense the present narrative sequence, at the center of the book's reported events, reconstitutes the major features of the general frame within which our text situates itself—in the *patikam* preface as well as the associated passages from *Cilappatikāram*, as discussed above. Nocturnal destruction, mistaken identity, and consequent crime, a revelation half-dreamt and overheard—both the poet and his heroine experience precisely this configuration, to a similar lyrical-noetic effect.

Why overhear? The missing details—always there is yet another linkage waiting to be restored—emerge from the retrograde process of recovery, the antidote to forgetting. The aim, in theory, would be to reach the point of beginning. Alas, the zigzag chain of interdependence has no ultimate beginning. There are only momentary insights that can come from almost anywhere—dreams, pillars, voices—each of which constitutes a kind of as-if beginning, hence a significant break in the entropy. But each such moment is no less partial than it is precious: one can, in truth, only overhear the whispered truth, never hear it fully, never reach the end.

Another way to think about all this emerges from the strand of the story connected to Kāyacaṇṭikai, so intricately interwoven with Maṇimekalai's own story, to the point where these two women are given the same external form. Kāyacaṇṭikai embodies, literally, the problem of hunger, which we should probably see as an analogous extension of the problem of awareness—or, perhaps, both are variants of the same deeper issue relating to lack and discontinuity. If forgetting fuels the spiral of dying, hunger is its experiential content. Stated simply, the *Maṇimekalai* is a book *about* hunger and feeding; concomitant with the heroine's recovery of memory fragments is her acquisition of the magical bowl that will feed the world. She is, at base, always filling a hungry gap, within herself or in others. She saves Kāñcipuram from the drought that threatens to destroy it; she frees Kāyacaṇṭikai of the impossible hunger that has bound her to the earth; she continually feeds the prisoners, the ill, the weak, the ignorant. Hunger here is not simply the need to take in food; it is more akin to a state of mind (like nearly every other component and process in this metaphysic) in which the primary awareness is one of empty space. The heroine's entire effort seems aimed at overcoming the breaks in the world, its discontinuities and emptinesses, its jarring displacements, its aching spaces of pain and need. Escaping entropy means, in this case, bridging the inner space—backward, toward the receding beginning.

Yet even this movement is both ironic and dangerous in its own way, and it is a major part of the poet's achievement that this potentially lethal aspect of remembering, recovering, becoming full is also seen and explored. Kāyacaṇṭikai, the insatiable—all empty holes—does become full, at last, and capable of movement, only to be swallowed up herself, via her shadow, in a still bigger emptiness, the belly of the goddess. This is a bold and plaintive statement, also strangely resonant with the musical image of the false and painful note. There is clearly a sense in which satisfying hunger fully is no less deadly—indeed, it is more deadly—than staying hungry. To fill the gap to the full, in this Buddhist world of discrete and flowing phenomena, habitually misperceived, is to be swallowed up, to disappear. Similar, we must assume, is the mind in search of its beginnings, listening to its story. Could one close the gaps entirely, could one hear the story through, rolling it backward, as it were, to the place before forgetting, one would find oneself in the nowhere place of no-self, and no knowing. A no-place, really, and fully empty.

5

Somewhat surprisingly, we find ourselves in the ambiguous domain of a precarious but eagerly sought-after connectivity. The *Maṇimekalai*, as Paula Richman has shown so incisively, is a Buddhist work through and through, committed to exemplifying Buddhist values and understandings. Stability, here, is always false. Fullness never lasts. Discrete disjunctures are the stuff of experience. There is no substratum of continuous selfhood, and no self that is not disguised. All dharmas are fleeting and elusive. Living is lethal. One generally moves forward toward the waiting implosion. And yet, within this slippery world of oblique and incoherent causes, we observe, in passage after lyrical passage, the deep desire, the hunger, and the possibility of reconnection. This, after all, is what *nidāna* really means—a link, perhaps mysterious and hidden from normal seeing—and the *Maṇimekalai* closes with the long exposition of the *nidānas* in terms of the chain of dependent origins, *pratītya samutpāda*, as we saw above. Recall that awareness, *uṇarvu*—the critical third *nidāna* and the first movement in present time—is the sleeper's state, the state that ineluctably follows upon forgetting and action.

The dream mode we have been exploring thus must comprise, in certain specific ways, that tenuous tissue of connectivity with which the text is so powerfully concerned. Let me try, in conclusion, to restate the major features and the motivating logic of this theme. Its centrality should, by now, be clear. The point is nicely made by yet another remark, to Maṇimekalai, by the prescient pillar: in the course of her metaphysical wanderings from teacher to teacher in Vañci, she will, the pillar assures her, encounter a hard-core "realist/skeptic" (*bhūta-vādin*) who will try to convince her that all she has learned—that is, the precious recovery of knowledge about her former lives—is no more than a "deluding dream" (*āṅku niṟ koṇarnta arun tĕyvam mayakka . . . kaṉā mayakk' uṟṟaṉai*, 21.109–110). This arrogant and misleading view will not, however, persuade her. The pillar is certain that she will, instead, give due weight to the dream, obviously the locus of transformative truth (cf. 27.281–1287, where this prophecy comes true).

The dream, or any of its analogues, offers a way back. It is a subtle and ambiguous state, often encoded. It is, however, an "earlier" form of consciousness than waking, which is given to externalized and objectified fixations.[9] In this sense, one does not actually "wake up" to enlightenment, or even to relatively less profound forms of truth; one is more likely to move toward insight by releasing oneself into dream. The dream, generally, acts like memory—a memory lost and restored. Its basic direction is backward, toward a beginning. It expands identity, on the one hand, by literally dis-closing its rupture with earlier lives and forgotten experience, but also by loosening the tight grasping of present identity boundaries, on the other. It seems to fill up the porous and forgetful mind as food fills the hungry body or rain fills the fields. It thus also heals, at least in part, the dissonance of aesthetic displacement, as in the recurrent image of the vīṇā's false note.

But the dream route backward has its own complexities. There are advantages to wakefulness, as Cātuvaṉ hints to the Nāga king in the lovely branch tale of Canto 16.[10] Sometimes the "dream" instructs the dreamer to forget further—as when the goddess Maṇimekhalā comes to Utayakumaraṉ in the night and urges him to put aside his passion, to forget Maṇimekalai. Emerging from dream sometimes offers the wider view, the more encompassing revelation, as when Maṇimekalai awakes in the temple in the presence of the dead prince and the loquacious pillar. And very often the anamnestic vision or divine pronouncement focuses on yet another terrible loss, flowing out of an act of forgetting, past or impending. This certainly applies to the moments when Cittirāpati, Maṇimekalai's grandmother, predicts the destruction of Pukār, and when Maṇimekalai herself hears from the goddess in Maṇipallavam, not long thereafter, that the city has in fact been destroyed under these same foreseen circumstances (25.176–204). As stated earlier, this flooding of Pukār is, on one level, the ominous backdrop and narrative telos of the whole long poem. Distraction, grief, forgetting: as these intensify, reinforcing one another, the world of collective experience is imperiled, as is the individual who, flooded by forgetfulness, is borne along within the self through ever-widening gaps.

The dream, at best, thus offers a vulnerable linkage to appease the human craving for continuity. Its textures, as we have seen, are strangely discrete, sometimes jumbled, loosely cumulating in a haunting web of partly familiar sounds and voices. Nearly always there is a blending of the known and the entirely foreign, as former selves are brought to light and reclaimed. Indeed, the dream psychology of the *Maṇimekalai* could be said to be one of uneasy activation of lost or forgotten selves, or parts of self, within a metaphysic of nonperduring, never-cumulating selfhood. One never knows, in this unsettling world, when another retrospective expansion of identity will take place. A dream may force former personae into consciousness, or a painted picture on the wall, a carved pillar, may suddenly speak to you, telling you your own lost story. But identity as such remains a mode of displacement, a frayed and discontinuous thread; the harder one pulls at the thread, and the farther one stretches it, the more tenuous and frail it becomes. Thus each attempt to reestablish connection with the past, however compelling, will always be marked by the double-edged quality of dream knowledge, its duplicated and disguised or encoded nature. The pillar speaks openly of his hidden double; the poet slips naturally into *yamaka* chiming and double entendres at the boundary of sleep or dream. Indeed, the doubling inherent in dreaming may well be the secret of its power in the context of a cosmology in which nearly everything in life is doubled, and half of the double, perhaps the more important half, is always missing.

The dream looks in two directions—back toward a beginning, and forward to a destructive ending. Poised between these directions, it offers hope of rupturing the devolving spiral. But the dream is also not unlike the dark shadow self that allows the goddess of the Vindhyas to grab hold of passersby and to devour them. The dream moves the dreamer back toward disappearance. Subtler and more inner than waking, it replicates the paradox of continuity through kenosis: empty-full, full-empty. Usually consistent with itself and with parallel forms of self-revelation, it nonetheless is marked off from the outer world, where waking consciousness works according to its own delusive law. There is a gap between dream and externality, as one sees from the standard emotions—amazement, fear, disbelief—that accompany the transition from one domain to the other. Sometimes this gap is also internal to the dream itself; thus we find dreams embedded in other dreams (in a manner similar to what is sometimes called "lucid dreaming" in the West).[11] Here the dreamer knows he or she is asleep and may, in this state, make contact with another dream—usually, in our text, with *someone else's* dream. For example, Maṇimekhalā, speaking with Cutamati at night in the burning-ground, speaks of Mātavi's dream at the time of Maṇimekalai's birth, when the goddess informed the new mother that her daughter would eventually renounce the world (7.33–38).

The context of that dream was Kovalaṉ's insistence that his daughter be named Maṇimekalai, because of an ancestor of his who was saved by the goddess Maṇimekhalā from drowning. This dream had a clarity and certainty that were unmistakable; the goddess spoke to Mātavi from within a dream "that was like waking reality" (*naṉave polak kaṉavakatt' uraitteṉ*). Cutamati is now asked to go to Mātavi and remind her, if she has forgotten, of this dream. As it happens, we also know about this context—the naming of Maṇimekalai—from the *Cilappatikāram*, where it is connected to yet another dream, that of Kovalaṉ, with the same manifest content, that is, the proleptic knowledge that Maṇimekalai will one day renounce the world (*Cil.* 15.95–106).[12] The same configuration—Maṇimekalai's naming, Kovalaṉ's dream with its announcement of her future renunciation, and also the added and encompassing theme of the destruction of Pukār because of the Chola king's distraction—recurs yet another time, in Canto 29.1–336, when Aṟavaṇa Aṭikaḷ explains it, in much the same language, to Maṇimekalai herself. The striking element here, apart from the consistency of the components and their internal relations, is the stress on certainty: the embedded dream, it seems, is even more convincing and real than a simple, nonembedded one. It functions almost as an impersonal object that can be passed from hand to hand, or from mind to mind (in marked contrast with our modern notions of the dream as ultimately subjective); and it is suggestively linked, in all three contexts, with the heroine's identity, insofar as the latter is meaningfully associated with her name.

This is the last feature of Maṇimekalai's dream world that we wish to study here. Apparently, the more internal, the more deeply embedded, a narrative fragment is, the greater conviction it carries—and the more "true" it must be. The same principle applies, in our texts, to the story within a story, or to the play within a play. In this sense, an embedded narrative stands opposed to linear narration, from chronological or biographical beginning to consequent end. Linear tellings of this type belong to entropy; they unfold away from the initial impulse, the generative forgetting, and thus propel the spiral further in its consuming course. Thus the story actually embodies the whole process of forgetting, so that each subsequent episode in the linear sequence is, in fact, still more deeply missing or forgotten. Each time one tells it forward, in this logical manner, one loses it more. Linear narration is, in short, another delusive mortal mode.

As the dream is embedded in waking, so the lucid dream is embedded within dreaming; such encapsulation, for all its complexity, its doubling within consciousness, is the major mode of liberating insight. In this light, moreover, we can now understand the corresponding encapsulation of the text as a whole within the frame offered by the *patikam* preface. *Maṇimekalai* is the second, self-completing segment of the poet's encompassing dream. The whole story and, indeed, all gradations of reality present in it, are internal to Cāttaṉār's metadream, the overheard nocturnal revelation in the temple with which we began. The entire book is thus, in effect, a dream within a dream—and, as such, presents its claim to truth. Entering the story, releasing the self in dream, would thus be (not in any abstract sense, but through the poet's creative working upon a mind that is not cut off from cosmos, that generates cosmos, that *is* cosmos) a practical and immediate mode of dreaming oneself free.

Hunger and fullness, forgetting and recalling, waking and dreaming, drought and rain—these are the alternate, but interpenetrating, antinomies of Cāttaṉār's poem. In general, hunger, wakefulness, and forgetting seem to have the upper hand. At best, there are momentary victories, as when Maṇimekalai leaves her begging bowl in drought-stricken Kāñci, thus reversing the imminent disaster; but Pukār is still destroyed out of the king's forgetting. Deeper and unresolved are the issues relating to the nature of that existential connection that, under the best conditions, may come into play. Could one hear the story through to the beginning and not be swallowed up? Can one dream one's way back to a point before forgetting and not wake in the destructive regression toward present-future? Is there a way out of the disguise that unintentionally brings death to the forsaken lover? Questions such as these, implicit in the compositional logic of the narrative, point to a delicate sense of discrete linkages that somehow touch without touching, without ever constituting completeness or restoring continuity in experience. Not even the subtle, double-faced dream can fill an innerness that has "nothing" as its deepest truth. Nor can the ramified story, seeking restlessly for its point of origin, reach its own completion—especially when told in the wrong direction, from start to "finish," as if outside the dream.

6

I have tried to tease out the logic of dreaming, broadly defined, in one south Indian Buddhist text. The exercise assumes the existence of a Buddhist sensibility, accessible to us no less through narrative and poetry than in explicitly metaphysical works. To our surprise, this sensibility seems concerned, to some degree, with issues relating to discontinuity within the devolving self, with its unhappy habit of linear narration. Dreaming, in this slippery and mostly destructive world, is largely retrospective, and in this mode helps the fragmenting and linearized subject to achieve a tenuous, perhaps liberating continuity within an expanded range of remembered experience. By the same token, the dream can be said to repeat experience, no doubt in subtler forms of awareness, thus both undermining the subject's identification with his present, more limited persona and blocking the future implosion in being and selfhood that self-forgetting must inevitably produce.

Buddhism disappeared entirely in south India, for somewhat mysterious reasons, in the medieval period. The ascendant mainstream, which we now call Hindu, was largely motivated by a different set of deep intuitions, within which dreaming, once again, finds a meaningful and expressive place. I cannot even begin to address here the vast topic of Hindu dream culture, or even of south Indian Hindu dreaming and its implicit logic. All I can do is to point, by way of conclusion, at the seemingly quite different set of notions that emerge from two short texts, chosen for the suggestive centrality that they give to the dream within wider contexts of poetic creativity. The first is a single, remembered (orally circulated) verse attributed to the greatest of the medieval Tamil poets, Kampaṉ, and to his son; the second is a striking dream journey, vicariously conceived, from fourteenth-century Kerala. For present purposes, this tiny and not necessarily representative sample—from a literature of immense scope and richness—must suffice.

First, I allow myself to posit a few hypotheses of a more general cast, relating to Hindu dream culture throughout the subcontinent. In contrast to the Buddhist materials seen above, Hindu dreams seem to be mostly present- or future-oriented. Retrospection is not the favored mode. Dreaming finds an honored place in a lengthy series that includes divination, mantic prophecy, poetic knowledge, and similar expressive states. Within this series, dream interpretation and dreaming itself are frequently subjected to a kind of empirical verification: many stories insist on the dreamer's search for his dream in the world outside (where he or she invariably finds it). There is a sense in which dreaming has an ontic and epistemic advantage over other forms of consciousness, though for reasons distinct from those that apply in the Buddhist sphere; in another sense, dreaming is strangely devalued, though not as impoverished as wakefulness.

Now to Kampaṉ's poem. Like most such isolated stanzas (known as *taṉippāṭal* or *cāṭu*), orally circulated and integrated into a wider system of popular literary culture, this verse is contextualized by a story that motivates and explains its primary expressive features. One night the Chola king was prowling the streets of his city (as Tamil kings, curious and anxious, tend to do at night), when he came upon the temple of the gruesome goddess Kālī—presumably on the onskirts of the town, where Kālī usually lives. Peering through the door, he saw the demon servants of the goddess busy grating sandalwood on stone to make the cooling sandal paste with which she is adorned. Kālī is a hot and terrifying goddess, always in need of cooling. Somehow, by chance or forgetfulness, or perhaps in impudent self-confidence, one of these demons fingered the paste that was meant for the goddess, even lifting it to his nose to smell its strong fragrance. A fellow demon, working beside him, warned him not to do this, but it was too late—there was no way for him to hide the subtle fragrance that adhered to his fingers. What else could the companion do, intent on safeguarding the rights of the goddess, except to cut off the offending hand?

All this the king witnessed, and was amazed. But somehow the surrealistic midnight scene required corroboration, or articulation, such as only the poet could give. There is another dimension to the king's need, that of a test or trial: would the court poet Kampaṉ, the very epitome of the supremely gifted singer, be able to divine what had happened without being told? A poet should know everything from personal experience, or from an inner vision, or from the prompting of the god or goddess who speaks through him or her. So the king went straight to Kampaṉ's house and knocked on his door. First to answer was the poet's son, Ampikāpati, a poet in his own right. Sleepily—for the king had woken him—he sang the first half of a Tamil poem:

karaikku vaṭakk'irukkum kāḻikkā ḷammaikk'
araittu vaḻicāntai toṭṭ' appey—

In Kālī's temple, on the northern shore,
they were grinding sandalwood on stone
to a fine paste. A ghoul, tough and heedless,
touched it—

This was as far as Ampikāpati could go—a precise but rather prosaic account of what the king had seen. As so often in stanzas of this type, a break occurs in the middle, leaving the poem initially incomplete, dangling tensely in the air. The pressure to find completion, a linguistic and thematic closure, is immense; neither the mind nor the ear can endure a half-finished poem. Someone, another poet, another voice, simply must step in to extricate the listener from the limbo of the open gap, just as the demon's act of half-unconscious transgression requires a complementary and closing act to contain and complete it. The king waits, restless and unsure. At this point Kampaṉ, poet and father, awakes and groggily sings the final two lines, as if describing his own dream:

uraittum
maṟaikkav āriyā tavaṉpeyin kaiyaik
kuṟaikkumāṅ kūrkatti kōṇṭu

though he had been warned.
They cut off his hand: there was no
escaping. Could anyone hide
such fragrance?

The primary image deserves to be restated and emphasized: there is an act of touching, which produces violent amputation and yet leaves a subtle and powerful residue of the original, unsevered whole. This, in a way, is the ironic miracle that the king needed to hear in words, an experience of mangled continuity across a break. Needless to say, the poets have passed the test, recapitulating in words the vision that only the king had seen.

Did they speak from out of a dream? Or was the king himself dreaming as he wandered the midnight streets? Technically speaking, we must answer "no" on both counts. The king was, it seems, awake, though the nocturnal eye sees differently from the eye of day. (This is one reason the king always goes out on these investigatory missions at night.) The poets had emerged from sleep, although they are still so close to it as to establish the link between poetic and oneiric forms of knowing. It is not by chance that the story insists on the sleepful setting, the rude awakening, the words that flow through the uneven transition from sleep to waking.

Already we are in a different world from that of Maṇimekalai and her dream memories. A considerable part of the energy at work in both story and verse focuses on the correlation between an externalized reality and its internal reexperiencing by the poet, who then translates it into words. Indeed, this triangulation—objectified externality, internalization in dream or vision, and linguistic molding—might be said to structure the entire field of medieval south Indian dream culture. Within this field, the experiencing subject is conceived in terms quite different from the Buddhist case.

Yet here, too, the dream comprises a special kind of linkage that we can attempt to define analytically. Perhaps the organizing principle is one of concentric recapitulation and mutual encompassment: each vector of the triangle is seen to repeat and reconstitute the other two, so that what is true of one will always be true of the others as well. This formulation also applies to the direction and forms of encoding, central to all three areas—the objectified act of transgression and mutilation, its dreamlike reexperiencing on the part of more than one subject, and the way language works to hold it. Each of the vectors is necessary and privileged in its own way. If there is anxiety present in this context, as there seems to be, it is not that of linear narration with its destructive closure but rather of potential failure to tie the threads together, to substantiate the mutual reinforcement of a single reality repeated across the apparent, and apparently broken, space.

In this sense, the dream becomes a mode, or an arena, for a kind of creative, expansive, and only partly conscious tautology (or, better, tautidentity), in which the dynamic re-coincidence of levels, closing the gaps between them, becomes the major move. Or, put differently, we could say that the disparate levels seem to converge in the dream or in dreaming, which binds them together in symmetrical self-encapsulation, at a single point. There are reasons for the facility of the dream in this respect, not least among them the fact that it is inherently more internal, hence higher and more encompassing, than waking perception. (The same or similar effects can be achieved, by the way, in this Hindu cosmos, by staring in a mirror.) Also relevant are the components of holism and its fragmented encodings in the dream which, in its "lucid" and self-conscious mode, may clearly reveal the code (the dream within a dream). But these abstract formulations have taken us too far from Kampaṉ's slight text; to illustrate them at work, we have to look more closely at the way the poem is built.

There is, to begin with, the resonance in theme between the registers we have outlined. Something is left over—cut off, but still fragrant, impregnated with the original sign of transgression. The dream, too, cut harshly in the middle, might be seen as another fragrant residue—as might the poem. There is, in this case, a question as to what releases the fragrance. In the poem, it is the act of grinding sandalwood into paste. Oddly enough, this very act has its parallel in the domain of language, for the first word that Kampaṉ, the father and master poet, utters on being awakened is *uraittum*—literally "speaking" (or "warning"; that is, the words spoken to the transgressing demon by his companion), but also, overlapping with a homonymous root, "grinding" or "rubbing." The poet, then, through a paronomastic device inherent in his art and in his vision, is somehow imitating the subject of his poem. Paronomastic joinings of this type are called *śleṣa*[13] (Tamil *cileṭai*) and always involve the superimposition or interweaving of semantic levels, triggered by phonetic collapse; we have already seen the affinity that exists between such linguistic doubling and the dream. The specific homonymous play with the root *urai* recurs in other Tamil poems. I cite the following example from the devotional poet Cuntaramūrtti Nāyaṉār, who addresses the god Śiva:

Now the gray miseries of age
will be upon me:
intent upon ungrateful deeds,
I have worn myself thin,
seen fine-ground turmeric
grow stale.

Death frightens me.

Grating and grinding my way
    to your bright feet,[14]
I wheeze and sputter,
confused,
knowing nothing
of the life of feeling.

Show me in your mercy
some way to be saved,
father, lord
dwelling in Iṭaimarutu.

If we take the double entendre seriously, as the poet requires us to do, we would have to conclude that speaking is a kind of grinding, the transforming of a crude or raw substance into its more subtle and more powerful (and fragrant) form. The process is not, apparently, a very gentle one, nor is it lacking in painful breaks.

This much is clear also from the manner in which the poem—we have returned to Kampaṉ—is composed. One poet, the less experienced, speaks and falls silent: there is acute danger, at this point, that the coalescence in levels will not be reached, that subject and object will both remain suspended in a no-man's land of incompletion. The older poet then fills in the gap (with the act of speaking/grinding) and goes on to speak of a failure to hide the telltale sign, and of the consequences of this failure. By now the identification of poet and demon accelerates—this, it seems, is how the poet knows what he knows—so that the act of amputation becomes internal to the poem, with its acknowledged break. By the time Kampaṉ has finished and can go back to sleep, the royal listener in the story as well as we, the listeners outside it, can easily fill in the remaining contours. The poet, too, must touch upon some precious but forbidden substance, an offering to the goddess, and the price he pays for this will be part of the poem.

In effect, what has happened is that the king and poet now share the visionary dream. This is not surprising: the dream, being internal, is more, rather than less, real—it is a truth quite capable of being shared by more than one observer. Hindu dreams are not the stuff of subjective experience, in our sense of the word. Indeed, the poem itself shows us a remarkable ambiguity or confusion in the subjective personae that it presents. It is difficult to capture this in translation, but the reader should know that the place where Ampikāpati, the son, gets stuck—at the word *appey*, "that demon"—has no clear referent. At no place in the poem is the subject of the touching, warning/grinding, or cutting explicitly and simply stated. There is a demon, "that one," whoever he may be; one deduces the nature of the transaction through its unfolding, without ever entirely unraveling the actors' separate roles. The "self" that dreams, in this framework, includes all the dramatis personae of the dream as well as the poet who reconstructs or reports their action, which runs parallel to, or within, both poem and dream.

We could say more about this little verse, but we have come far enough to sum up, roughly, certain fundamental perceptions. There is the objectified nature of the dream vision, which exists outside but can be experienced internally as well, thanks to the correlative contours that tie together these domains. There is a somewhat slippery subject, who simultaneously dreams, acts, and sings poetry, and who shifts roles within each of these modes. There is the focus on very immediate, essentially present-oriented experience, which the dream or poem restates. And there is a critical doubling in language, which splits into two homonymous registers at precisely the point of bridging the open space, enabling this connection through a subtle encoding or superimposing of domains. Whatever has been broken or spoken—and each of the three vectors we have isolated reveals analogous discontinuities or ruptures in structure and process—survives in a bittersweet residual form, carrying over something of the initial fragrance.

Sometimes we can see the dream encoding set out for us with surprising precision; our final example addresses this issue more directly, and also points in the direction a more complete analysis might take. The *Śuka-sandeśa* of Lakṣmīdāsa, a Sanskrit poem of 164 ornate verses composed in Kerala, apparently in the thirteenth century, belongs to the class of "messenger poems" (*sandeśa-kāvya*) in which the protagonist/speaker sends someone or something with a message of love to his or her distant beloved. The classical prototype for the entire class is Kālidāsa's great work, *Megha-dūta* ("The Cloud Messenger"), in which, as the name indicates, the unlikely envoy is a cloud. Other candidates for such missions include various species of birds, bees, the moon, the Tamil language, the wind, and so on. There are ancient roots to the entire paradigm in both Sanskrit and Tamil, but the classical format, already fixed in Kālidāsa's work, requires certain stable features: the lover, frequently anonymous, fastens upon some potential messenger, whom he addresses mentally with the long lyrical exposition that constitutes the poem; he begs or demands that the messenger agree to the mission and then describes, in elaborate detail (and generally in a highly eroticized fantasy mode), the route to be taken across the subcontinent, with its rivers and sacred mountains and other shrines; he offers an imaginary scenario that the messenger will find upon arrival, and that will allow him to identify the beloved, always in a state of acute, nearly fatal lovesickness; he then specifies the exact message, inevitably including words of comfort and the promise of a speedy end to separation, that the messenger is to deliver. These final verses, comprising the wished-for, wholly imagined message, often provide a swelling crescendo, rich in pathos, to the entire lyrical progression. For obvious reasons, this genre offers some of the most useful descriptions we possess of the geography of medieval India, to say nothing of the wealth of incidental information about social formations, local rituals, language, and regional traditions. Some parts of India developed a particular vogue in *sandeśa-kāvyas*; Kerala was one of these, and the *Śuka-sandeśa* is the earliest example of the genre from this region. Here the messenger is a parrot, and the mission is framed by a dream.

It is a remarkable work, couched in striking language that is stretched to the point of saying things never said before, or thought before, in Sanskrit. Before we examine that aspect of the poem that is directly related to dreaming, we should note that this class of poems is, in general, the "as if" genre par excellence in the mirror world of Sanskrit court poetry. Here the self, in its loneliness, imagines an articulate messenger into existence, humanizes it or him along with the entire landscape (now permeated by human emotion), and then entrusts this messenger with an imaginary message and describes the imagined circumstances of its delivery to an internalized image of the distant beloved. On the face of it, this format allows one part of the self to send a message to another, split-off part, so that what we, as listeners and readers, overhear is a richly textured polyphonic monologue, sometimes apparently on the edge of madness, and in any case issuing from a state of heightened intensity and altered awareness. We could call this state "love"—in poetic self-presentation—and we can also begin to appreciate the logic of having it all transpire in a dream.

The dream framework is set out for us in the opening verse of Lakṣmīdāsa's text:

> Drenched in autumn moonlight
> on the stage of delight,
> on the open roof of a tall palace,
> they slept, exhausted
> by the games of love.
> Is there a door to lock out fate?
> For he was dreaming, and in his dream
> was driven far away from her. (1.1)

His beloved is a dancer, and the palace roof and bedroom is a stage, illuminated by the moon, a fitting setting for the histrionic adventure that is overtaking the hero in his mind. The messenger poems prefer anonymous and prototypical lovers—thus an unnamed "he" dreams of "her." As if to reinforce the dimension of a heavily aestheticized splitting within consciousness, the messenger dreamt up by the sleeping hero is the echo bird, a parrot (*śuka*) who can be relied upon to repeat, verbatim, the latter's address. The lover begins with a series of pathos-laden verses describing his unhappy state, relative to the remembered past:

Suffused by love, and uneasy in its flow,
we suffered agonies of separation
whenever either of us could not be seen,
if only for a moment.
Now whole oceans, rivers, cities
lie between us, as if forever. (1.8)

But as we, the listeners, know, the present agony of separation—*viśleṣa*, literally a disjoining—is actually caused only by the lover's dream. His beloved lies asleep beside him, though in his dream he is certain that she is far away, with a crowded continent between them. He cannot tolerate this dreadful disunion and seeks out a messenger to close the gap. For our purposes, it is important to see that it is the dream that splits the couple in two, or rather, that divides the lover's mind into two and removes him from the state of unbroken loving. Or is it really unbroken? Part of the eloquence of this dream sequence derives from the implication that separateness, explicit in the dream, inheres in the normative condition and experience of love-in-union. At the same time, we cannot escape the sense of doubling that emerges fully in dream.

The poem's progression will then be from an initial (dreamed, illusionary) disjunction to various forms of subsequent (dreamed) reconnection, via the parrot messenger. Naturally, there will be room for the poet to play with this fractured frame, so rich in echoes and reflections. Dreaming thus appears at times *within* the hero's message, that is, within his dream:

I see you over and over in my heart,
I see you sitting, slowly walking,
speaking, laughing, joyful—
and I am tortured a thousand times over
for every such image
that melts away when I open my eyes. (2.70)

He is visualizing her in his mind, in the dream, and also opening his eyes, still in the dream: waking-in-dream turns out to be a painful state, unlike the sweet comfort of the dream within a dream. As we saw earlier, the more deeply embedded mode is usually privileged in crucial ways, although the present instance is not, I think, a case of lucid dreaming.[15] To look for instances of this type, which expose the dream code in relation to its frame, we have to turn to moments in which the poet allows himself to play with figuration in consistent patterns. In lieu of a long discussion, one example will have to do, from the passage in which the hero is trying to help the parrot identify his beloved, at the end of the journey:

You will know her by her crystal teeth,
her lips of ruby, her sapphire hair,
her diamond lustre, her smile of white pearl.
God created her to be a jewel of a woman,
and that is what she is—not just because she is so beautiful,
but because, for once, words mean what they say. (2.29)

We can, perhaps, put aside the question of practicality: since all women in Sanskrit poetry have smiles of pearl and hair dark as sapphire, the parrot may still have some difficulty in making the identification. The point lies rather in the ironic literalization of the conventional metaphors (more precisely, in terms proper to this tradition, the teeth of crystal and lips of ruby are *rūpakas*, the superimposition of one form upon another without erasing the difference between them). This should, of course, be a series of similes, all too predictable. But the poet has twisted the technique to suit his purpose. What looks like little more than a linguistic habit, with no existential power behind it, becomes an identity statement on the level of denotation (*mukhya-vṛtti*, in the poet's usage here): words actually mean what they say. The beloved really is a jewel. This highly unusual eventuality effectively closes off the always open space in language between the verbal token (*vācaka*) and its referent (*vācya*)—the gap that recapitulates the broken structure of both external experience and internal vision, as we have seen with reference to Kampaṉ's poem.

Another way to formulate this, without overloading the verse beyond its expressive limit, is to observe the temporary collapse of the space between the subject and object of the simile (the *upameya* and *upamāna*, in the Sanskrit terminology). The figure has, as it were, folded in on itself, in a kind of downward drift toward the literal and the concrete. Our poet has a conspicuous fondness for this move, which sometimes involves the play of paronomasia (*śleṣa*) such as we saw in the Tamil verse.[16] We cannot pursue this theme to the end, but perhaps a formulation can be attempted in terms of the dream logic present in this work. The dream begins with disjunction—*viśleṣa*—which brings two operative levels into awareness: within himself, the dreaming protagonist marks a division and a lack. This splitting inheres in dreaming, as it does in language and all experienced reality. But within this split and doubled world, coded by familiar figures, there is a countervailing movement toward rejoining or superimposing the separated domains, toward *śleṣa*—literally, an "embrace" or "junction"—or a literalized and embodied metaphor (*rūpaka*), in which two levels are made to coincide. There is a sense in which the dream itself is the primary locus of *śleṣa*, a paronomastic superimposition and reintegration of disparate elements (or words, or things).[17] It is not so much that dreams are "tropes," as Patricia Cox-Miller has claimed for another tradition,[18] but that they encode the parallel discontinuities in language, vision, and experience in consistent patterns of figuration, tending "downward" or "backward" to the concrete and thus narrowing or even temporarily removing the ever-present gap.

Stated more simply, the dream is now, it seems, less of a message (from the past, from the gods, from an unrealized future) than a coded promise of self-coincidence, where words might even mean what they say, and visions could be as they seem.

Such coincidence spills over into the imagined—dreaming and speaking—self. What does the lover request the parrot to repeat to his beloved?

In our love, you're even more me
than I am, and people know
I'm more you than you.
There's no distinction.
Let my words, right or wrong,
born from the turbulence of separation,
swell to a sea deep with joy
for you. (2.88)

Separation (*viśleṣa*), with its turbulence, has produced the total coincidence (*śleṣa*) of personae, experienced and acknowledged in the dream (but only, it seems, in the dream). And it is, perhaps, telling that the final benediction, the wish that brings closure to both dream and poem, takes the form of litotes, a double negation that first articulates the gap or absence and then verbally abrogates it:

May the two of us never again be disjoined,
not even in a dream.

Think, then, of the doubly negated statement of the dream: a point of fusion, where the doubling and dislocation inherent in consciousness are momentarily collapsed in an objective inner mode; where the shifting worlds of experience, language, and visionary image are superimposed, pinned together in paronomasia or embodied metaphor, their contours allowed to coincide through the subtle power of figuration and a repeatedly embedded code. *Śleṣa*—re-coincidence, refiguration—is the primary dream figure, a promise of connection. Even more than language itself, dreaming suggests the momentary focus of the multiple and displaced self in a multiple and dislocated cosmos. "As leaves are stuck together on a pin, the worlds are held together by this syllable,"[19] this dream.

Notes

1. I distinguish throughout the goddess Maṇimekhalā (Sanskrit spelling) from her namesake Maṇimekalai (Tamil spelling). For the cult of Maṇimekhalā, attested in early Buddhist literature and still widespread in southeast Asia, see Levi 1937: 371–383.

2. Today she is worshipped at Kŏḍuṅgallūr in Kerala as Ŏṟṟaimulaicci, the Goddess with a Single Breast. This is the story of *Cilappatikāram*, the famous twin-composition to *Maṇimekalai*, attributed to Iḷaṅkovaṭikaḷ. The mythic history of Kaṇṇaki, and the great text that tells it, have been studied in detail from various perspectives; see, in particular, Obeyesekere 1984; also Shulman 1980: 200–210.

3. For this term, which I owe to Dmitri Segal, see Shulman 1993: 147.

4. See Shulman 1991: 9–17.

5. Against this, see discussion by Pŏ. Ve. Comacuntaraṉār in his commentary on this passage (Iḷaṅkovaṭikaḷ 1970: 15).

6. I wish to thank Dina Stein for insights that have contributed to this formulation.

7. *aṉṉac ceval ayarntu viḷaiyāṭiya/ taṉṉ uṟu pĕṭaiyait tamarai yaṭakkap/ pūmpoti citaiyak kiḻittup pĕṭai kŏṇṭ'/oṅk' irun tĕṅkiṉ uyar maṭal eṟa* [5.123–126].

8. I thank Don Handelman for remarks pertinent to this passage, and for discussion of the conceptual world of *Maṇimekalai*.

9. Here the Buddhist theory is close to Hindu notions of the primacy of the inner over the objectified and discontinuous outside. See Handelman and Shulman 1997.

10. "Dying and being born are like sleeping and awaking" (*piṟantavar cātalum iṟantavar irattalum/ uṟaṅkalum viḻittalum poṉṟat' uṇmaiyiṉ*, 16.86–87).

11. See Hunt 1989: 70–76, and the essays by Barbara Tedlock (Chapter 5) and Dennis Tedlock (Chapter 6) in this volume.

12. These two passages are closely intertwined, repeating the same formulas; Kovalaṉ, too, sees a dream that is as vivid as waking, *naṉavu*—and that foretells his death at Maturai.

13. Yigal Bronner is preparing a full study of *śleṣa* in Sanskrit poetry and theory.

14. *uraippaṉ nāṉ uṉ cevaṭi cera: Tevāram* of Cuntaramūrttināyaṉār 615.

15. In the following verse, he complains that he cannot see his beloved even in a dream, since he can no longer fall asleep—not because, as we know, he is already alseep, but because he is too lovesick.

16. For a striking example, see 2.82, where the hero teases his beloved, in a remembered vignette reported to the parrot, by a double entendre built around the phrase *bimbâdhara*—a woman whose lower lip is red as the *bimba* fruit, or the *bimba* tree itself, with its fruits hanging low. "Just as dear to me as you are is this *bimbâdhara*"—by this point in the sentence, the beloved is already weeping in rejection and jealousy, but the hero concludes—"to the parrot" (parrots love to peck at *bimba* fruits). Incidentally, this verse belongs to an unusual set of several instances in which an utterance is broken off, blocked, or distorted, and recognized as such.

17. We may note here another powerful dream text, Kaṭikai Muttuppulavar's eighteenth-century Tamil work, the *Camuttira-vilācam*, in which a love-crazed heroine speaks a hundred verses to the ocean, *all* of them in *śleṣa*.

18. Cox Miller 1994: 3.

19. *Jaiminīya Upaniṣad Brāhmaṇa* 1.10—with reference to *Om*.

References

Cīttalaiccāttaṉār. 1971. *Maṇimekalai*. Edited with commentary by Pŏ. Ve. Comacuntaraṉār. Madras.

Cox Miller, Patricia. 1994. *Dreams in Late Antiquity: Studies in the Imagination of a Culture*. Princeton.

Cuntaramūrttināyaṉār. 1964. *Tevāram*. Tarumapuram.

Handelman, Don and D. Shulman. 1997. *God Inside Out: Śiva's Game of Dice*. New York.

Hunt, Harry T. 1989. *The Multiplicity of Dreams: Memory, Imagination, and Consciousness*. New Haven and London.

Iḷaṅkovaṭikaḷ. 1970. *Cilappatikāram*. Edited with commentary by Pŏ. Ve. Comacuntaraṉār. Madras.

Jaiminīya Upaniṣad Brāhmaṇa. 1921. Calcutta.

Lakṣmīdāsa. 1984. *Śukasandeśa*. Edited by Geeta Pattabiraman. Madras.

Levi, Sylvain. 1937. "Maṇimekhalā, divinité de la mer." In P. Hartmann (ed.), *Mémorial Sylvain Levi*, Paris, 371–383.

Obeyesekere, Gananath. 1984. *The Cult of Pattini*. Chicago.
Shulman, David. 1980. *Tamil Temple Myths*. Princeton.
———. 1991. "Toward a Historical Poetics of the Sanskrit Epic." *International Folklore Review*, 9–17.
———. 1993. "Remaking a Purāṇa: The Rescue of Gajendra in Potana's *Mahābhāgavatamu*." In W. Doniger (ed.), *Purāṇa Perrenis: Reciprocity and Transformation in Hindu and Jaina Texts*, Albany.

4

The Dreams and Dramas of a Jealous Hindu Queen

Wendy Doniger

Dreams are a serious matter in classical Hinduism, indeed seriously material. This is a subject that I have treated elsewhere at some length,[1] but it might be useful to summarize some basic Hindu approaches to dreams before focusing on the particular group of texts I wish to discuss. The Hindu attitude to dreams is part of a more general Hindu attitude to illusion, called *maya*. The entire material world is regarded, theoretically at least, as an illusion wrought by God for His (or Her) pleasure, for the game, the sport (*lila*); in a very basic sense, the universe (including ourselves) is a dream dreamt by God. This does not necessarily mean that it, and we, are unreal, though certain idealistic forms of Indian religions, both Buddhist and Hindu, do take this tack. On the contrary, for most South Asians it means that our own dreams are, in a sense, synchronized with those of the author of the universe and hence one of the most reliable sources of insight into the reality of that universe.

Dreams, myths, and illusion are alike in many ways, but they are also different in many ways and each teaches us something about reality. Each deals with a form of mental transformation, and with the epistemological problems raised by those transformations. The overarching illusion (*maya*) that the cosmos (sometimes referred to as *brahma*) is real at all is seldom visible to us. We can sense it, sometimes, through the minor illusions or mistaken perceptions (*bhrama*) that Indian philosophers (such as Sankara) discuss at some length: the rope mistaken for a snake, the shell mistaken for silver. Dreams, too, are often retroactively recognized as mistaken perceptions, but ones that catapult the dreamers into new understandings of their waking life. One might say that *bhrama* is the key to *brahma*.

In this essay, I wish to discuss the ways in which dreams illuminate various other sorts of illusions and are illuminated by them. I wish to do this by focusing on a complex cycle of classical Sanskrit texts surrounding the mythical figures of King Udayana, his queen, Vasavadatta, and a series of co-wives. Three episodes are told in the *Ocean of Story* (*Kathasaritsagara*)—which may not have been recorded earlier than the versions in Sanskrit plays, but comes out of a simpler and earlier genre. One tells of a celestial magician (*vidyadhara*) who disguised himself as Udayana and seduced a woman whom Udayana had intended to take as his co-wife (text 1, in which the co-wife is Kalingasena); another tells us that Queen Vasavadatta magically disguised herself and served the woman whom the king intended to make his co-wife, until the king saw through the disguise by means of the art of garland making (text 2, the co-wife Padmavati); in a third, Udayana became unfaithful and inadvertently called Vasavadatta by the name of her rival and, later, secretly seduced—while the queen watched in hiding—yet another rival that she had tried in vain to conceal from him (text 3, Viracita). This cycle of stories was taken up in three Sanskrit dramas, one by Bhasa, who replaced the magic transformations and disguises with a dream sequence (text 4, Padmavati again), and two by King Harsa, who replaced them with a portrait of a co-wife (text 5, *Ratnavali*) and a play within a play (text 6, *Priyadarsika*). We may represent the basic plots of these six texts on a chart:

Genre	What Conceals	Who Is Disguised	What Reveals
1. narrative	magic	magician	sleep
2. narrative	magic	queen	garland/portrait
3. narrative	disguise	co-wife	slip of the tongue
4. play	disguise	queen	dream/portrait
5. play	disguise	co-wife	necklace/portrait
6. play	disguise	co-wife	play

A comparison of these texts does not particularly illuminate Indian attitudes to the *content* of dreams, but it does tell us a lot about the *function* of dreams in Hindu culture. How do these various forms of illusion—magic impersonation, magic disguise, art, portrait, play, slip of the tongue, and, above all, dream—work, each in its own way, as roads to the recognition of the true self, and the true beloved? What do they tell us about the relationship between dreams, theatre, and personal masquerade? Working with a method somewhat akin to the linguistic principle of minimal pairs (which establishes the equivalence of sounds or letters that change the meaning when they replace one another in a word), we may excavate a series of minimal pairs of illusions. And we may ask questions about them: What are the functional equivalents of the dream, and why? Does the fact that dreams can be replaced by magic, art, and so forth, further blur or clarify the always problematic blurred boundaries between dreams and secondary elaborations?

Let us begin with the first text:

Kalingasena and the Magician

King Udayana wanted to make an alliance with a king whose daughter, Kalingasena, came to Udayana's kingdom of Kausambi and asked him to marry her, which he agreed to do. But Udayana's prime minister, who did not want this marriage to happen because he had promised the king's first wife, Vasavadatta, that she would have no co-wife, intrigued with the astrologers to delay the date of the wedding for six months, during which Kalingasena lived in the kingdom. The prime minister mentally summoned a demon [*raksasa*] named Yogesvara and told him to watch over Kalingasena night and day in order to catch her doing something that would prove her unfit to wed the king. In particular, he advised, "If she were to have an affair with a celestial magician [*vidyadhara*] or someone like that, that would be very fortunate. And you must observe the divine lover when he is asleep, even if he comes in a different form, for divine beings assume their own forms when they fall asleep."[2]

Now, a celestial magician named Madanavega had fallen in love with Kalingasena; he used his magic to come to her room in the form of the king and seduce her. The demon found the magician in his own form, asleep on the bed of the sleeping Kalingasena; for he was a divine man and had lost his false form because his magic power to do this vanished when he was asleep.

The demon called the prime minister, who brought the king to Kalingasena's room; he saw her asleep and the magician asleep beside her in his own form. The king wanted to kill him, but just then the magician was awakened by his magic and he went out and flew away to the sky. In a moment, Kalingasena woke up too; she said to the king, "Why did you go away a moment ago and come back with your minister?" The minister explained to her, "Someone who took the form of the king magically deluded you and married you; it wasn't the king." And they left. The minister told everything to Vasavadatta, who thanked him.

Udayana kept thinking about Kalingasena's beauty, and one night when he was full of lust he went to her room alone, with a sword in his hand, and asked her to become his wife. But she rejected him, saying, "You should regard me as another man's wife." The king withdrew and eventually forgot about her. But the magician, who had overheard the conversation, praised his wife and continued to visit her, though he added, "Even though you are a virtuous woman, you have gotten the reputation of a whore." [3]

The magician is revealed in his postcoital repose, the sleep that both allows possession and reveals it. For the Hindus believe that a god or demon who masquerades as someone else in bed is compelled to take his own true form when he loses mental control and hence inadvertently turns off the current from the magic projector in his mind. This happens when he sleeps, gets drunk, dies, gets angry—or makes love, when sexual passion strips away the final illusion, the cursed disguise, and reveals the true identity.[4] But in this case the unmasking takes place after the damage has been done, and Kalingasena is punished, and calumniated, for not seeing through the trick sooner. Vasavadatta plays no active role; the prime minister, assisted by the demon and, inadvertently, the magician, intervenes to get rid of the feared co-wife—who must, even at the end, still defend herself from the lustful Udayana.

But Vasavadatta plays an active role in other episodes in the cycle about Udayana, which begin with the same premise as the story of Kalingasena: for political reasons, Udayana must take a second wife (or wives). Before the encounter with Kalingasena, Udayana had become involved with another woman, in the following story:

Padmavati, the Lady with the Lotus

King Udayana of Vatsa, married to Vasavadatta, daughter of the king of Avanti, was so in love with her that he neglected his royal duties. His ministers decided to save him from himself by getting the king of Magadha, their enemy, to give his daughter Padmavati ("The Lady with the Lotus") to the king and to make the king believe that Vasavadatta was dead. The ministers gave the queen a charm that enabled her to change her shape, and she disguised herelf as a Brahmin woman, under the name of Avantika ("The Woman from the City of Avanti," in Vasavadatta's kingdom), and went to serve Padmavati at the court of Magadha.

When the king of Magadha offered Padmavati to Udayana, he accepted her. Vasavadatta made garlands for Padmavati, using a special technique that the king had taught her. The bridal couple returned to Vatsa, and Vasavadatta followed in the rear. The king asked Padmavati where she had gotten the garlands; she said she had gotten them from Avantika, and then the king knew that Avantika must be Vasavadatta. The minister told the king all, and the king and his two wives lived happily together.[5]

Udayana recognizes Vasavadatta by recognizing himself in her—through the art of the garland that he had taught her.

But before Padmavati (and, therefore, before Kalingasena), there had been another, as told in this story:

Viracita and the Slip of the Tongue

King Udayana married Vasavadatta, but after a while, Udayana became unfaithful and made love with a woman in the harem named Viracita, with whom he had had an affair before. One day he called the queen by the wrong name, Viracita, and had to appease her by falling at her feet. Later, a beautiful princess named Bandhumati was sent as a present to the queen. The queen concealed her under the name of Manjulika, but the king saw her and secretly seduced her. Vasavadatta, who was hidden, witnessed this act; furious at first, she eventually relented and accepted Bandhumati, for she had a tender heart.[6]

The king mistakes one woman for another, mistaking not the person but the name; when the queen conceals first the rival and then herself, the king finds the secret woman and the queen watches the secret act. In the end, all is revealed and all is accepted.

Three Sanskrit dramas of Bhasa and Harsa take up the story of Udayana and Vasavadatta from the narratives and weave elaborate, rococo variations on the theme of sexual masquerade. Let us begin with Bhasa's *Svapnavasavadatta*, "The Drama of Vasavadatta (who meets her husband) in a Dream," which shares with the first text from the *Ocean of Story* the revealing sleep/dream; with the second, much of the plot and the names of the women; and, with the third, more of the plot and the slip of the tongue.

The Dream of Vasavadatta

King Udayana was married to Vasavadatta and loved her too much to take a second wife, but there was a prediction that for the good of the kingdom he should marry Padmavati. The king's minister spread the rumor that Vasavadatta was dead, but secretly he put Vasavadatta in the care of Padmavati, giving her the name of Avantika. Udayana married Padmavati, and Vasavadatta made a garland for her husband's bride.

Padmavati was stricken with a headache and lay down in a room different from her own room. The king and the clown went to her own room to conciliate her, but the clown, seeing the garland that Vasavadatta had made, mistook it for a cobra and fled. The king, finding that Padmavati was not in fact there, fell asleep in Padmavati's bed. Vasavadatta came in and, thinking that Padmavati was in the bed, sat on it and said, "I wonder why my heart rejoices so as I sit beside her. And by lying on one side of the bed she seems to invite me to embrace her. I will lie down there." And she lay down.

Then the king, dreaming, called out, "O Vasavadatta," and the queen stood up and said, "It's the king, not Padmavati! Has he seen me?" Again the king called out, "O, princess of Avanti!" and she realized, "Good, the king is just talking in his sleep. There's no one here, so I will stay here for a moment and satisfy my eyes and my heart."

Udayana (continuing in his sleep): My darling, answer me. Are you angry with me?

V: No, no, but I am unhappy.

U: Is it because you are remembering Viracika [*sic*]?

V (angrily): Go away; is Viracika here too?

U: Then let me ask you to forgive me for Viracika.

V: I've stayed here for a long time. Someone might see. I'd better go . . .

As soon as she had left, the king stood up and cried out, "Vasavadatta! Stay, stay!" Then, not sure if he had dreamt it or not, he said, "If it's a dream, it would have been good never to wake up. But if it is a delusion, let me keep it for a long time."

Messengers brought a portrait of Vasavadatta with Udayana, sent by Vasavadatta's mother. The identity of Vasavadatta was revealed, through the portrait, and everyone lived happily together.[7]

There are three masquerades in this play, or at least quasi-masquerades: Vasavadatta masquerades as the minister's sister; Vasavadatta at first mistakes the king for Padmavati in the bed; and the king mistakes the real Vasavadatta for the Vasavadatta in his dream. The content of the dream is most revealing. The king, asleep (innocently) in the rival's bed, remembers another occasion on which he was unfaithful to his wife and was revealed by the shameful slip of the tongue (a subconscious act, just like a dream, hence a kind of dream within a dream). This conversation within the dream is particularly noteworthy because the traditional dream books usually analyze only the visual images of dreams, not the words.[8]

In both of these stories about the co-wife Padmavati, the king loves Vasavadatta more than the other woman, and merely takes a second wife for political reasons. But in Harsa's plays, to which we now turn, the king prefers the second wife erotically as well as politically, and Vasavadatta's quandary is not merely political, nor is it so easily resolved. Significantly, these co-wives do not have political pseudonyms, as Vasavadatta does when she calls herself Avantika, but, rather, natural pseudonyms, like Padmavati ("The Lady with the Lotus"): they are called Sagarika and Aranyika, the ladies of the ocean and the forest. In Harsa's plays, moreover, as in the third narrative text, it is the identity of the co-wife, not of Vasavadatta, that is concealed for political reasons, and the co-wife therefore suffers much of the loss of status and identity that Vasavadatta suffers in the other versions. To this extent, our sympathy is with the co-wife; but we also empathize with Vasavadatta, who suffers the loss of the king's love.

Let us begin with Harsa's *Ratnavali*, which takes up the story after the events known from the versions of the story that we have seen (the prediction that Udayana must marry Ratnavali, the rumor of Vasavadatta's death) and a few more: while Ratnavali ("The [Lady with the] Jeweled Necklace"), the daughter of the king of Simhala, was sailing to Kausambi, the ship was wrecked and Ratnavali was fished out by a merchant and given to the minister, who recognized her by the jeweled necklace she always wore. He put her in Vasavadatta's service as a handmaid named Sagarika ("Oceanic"). This is where the play begins:

Ratnavali, the Lady with the Jeweled Necklace

Vasavadatta tried to keep the king from seeing Sagarika, who was very beautiful, but Sagarika saw him and fell in love with him. She painted a portrait of the king as Kama, the god of love, and her friend painted in, beside him, a portrait of Sagarika as Rati, Kama's wife. The king then found the portrait that Sagarika had made of him and declared his passionate love for the unknown maiden who had painted his portrait and hers. Vasavadatta saw the portrait and became suspicious; she bribed Sagarika's friend, by giving her some of her own clothes, to get her to guard Sagarika. This woman, however, dressed Sagarika in the queen's clothes and arranged for the King to meet Sagarika when Sagarika was disguised as Vasavadatta. But Vasavadatta's friend overheard Sagarika's friend talking about it, and the queen went to the place of assignation, the portrait gallery.

> The king mistook her for Sagarika and made love to her with words, addressing her as Sagarika. But when the king attempted to kiss "Sagarika," the queen threw off her veil, in fury, and said, "Your Majesty, I really am Sagarika. For you have projected Sagarika into your heart, so that you imagine that *everything* seems to be made of Sagarika." The king said, "Oh, no! This really is Queen Vasavadatta." The king begged her to forgive him, but the queen went away.
>
> Then Sagarika, in disguise as Vasavadatta, started to hang herself with a creeper, in shame that her secret love had been found out. The king, thinking that she was Vasavadatta trying to commit suicide because he had made love to another woman, embraced her. Sagarika, thinking that he knew that she was Sagarika, rejoiced, but when she said, "Let me go, Your Majesty; don't offend the queen," the king realized, with joy, that it was Sagarika, and embraced her again. Just then the queen came back to forgive her husband and accept his apologies. She heard his voice and decided to sneak up on him from behind and put her arms around his neck. But then she overheard Sagarika say to the king, "What is the use of this false, insincere lovemaking? For the queen is dearer to you than your very life." The king replied, "No, but the affection that I feel for you has more passion because it comes from violent love."
>
> As soon as he said that, Vasavadatta came forth and the king, looking at her in embarrassment and confusion, replied, "My queen! Don't accuse me with no cause. I thought that this woman was you; it was a natural mistake, because she was wearing clothes just like yours. So forgive me." He fell at her feet, but the queen had Sagarika imprisoned—until she was identified (through the necklace) as the princess Ratnavali. Then Vasavadatta adorned Ratnavali with her own ornaments, took her hand and joined it with the king's, and they all lived happily together.[9]

There are a number of disguises in this involuted plot. The princess Ratnavali is disguised as a servant, Sagarika; the princess disguised as a servant is then disguised as the queen; the queen, not disguised at all, is taken for (the princess disguised as) the servant disguised as the queen; and the princess disguised as the servant disguised as the queen is mistaken for the queen. Vasavadatta begins the masquerade inadvertently when she gives her own clothes to her rival's friend, but then the reins are taken out of her hands when the clothes are used to deceive her. When Vasavadatta unconsciously impersonates Sagarika impersonating Vasavadatta, as David Shulman remarks, "The queen, in being herself, is playing at being another who is as herself."[10] Due to the double-double-cross, in which the king mistakes his queen for the Other Woman, and the Other Woman for the queen, he actually makes love to his queen when she is undisguised, thinking she is someone else pretending to be herself. He calls her by the wrong name, "Sagarika," a fatal error. This is the situation in a sexual fantasy: a man is in bed with his wife, and imagines that she is someone else pretending to be her.

The *Priyadarsika*, by the same author, Harsa, rings further variations on the same themes. Believe it or not, the plot gets even more complicated, and now it is the man, not the woman, who is split up and impersonates himself—or, in David Shulman's words, "undergoes triplication":[11]

Priyadarsika, the Forest Girl

King Udayana, married to Queen Vasavadatta, was supposed to take as his second wife the Princess Priyadarsika, but before the wedding could take place, Priyadarsika's father (Vasavadatta's uncle) had been deposed, and in the ensuing chaos Priyadarsika went into hiding under the name of Aranyika ("The Forest Girl"). Vasavadatta, not knowing who she was, took her into her service, but the king fell in love with her. The queen, worried that she had lost the king's affections, decided to stage a play about herself and King Udayana.

Aranyika was to play the queen, while their friend Manorama was to play the king. But Manorama, without Aranyika's knowledge, colluded with the clown so that the king took Manorama's place and Aranyika and the king could make love right before the queen's eyes. Vasavadatta gave Aranyika the ornaments from her body, and she gave Manorama the ornaments that Vasavadatta's father had given the king at their marriage. The king met Manorama, who was dressed like him. She gave him his/her ornaments, including the ring. The king made his first speech, and the queen said, "Bravo to the king," rising suddenly to her feet. The king said to himself, "What! The queen has recognized me!" But the playwright said to the queen, "Calm down. It's just a play," and Vasavadatta replied, "What! It is Manorama! But I thought, 'It's the king.' Bravo, bravo, Manorama! Well acted!" The playwright said to Vasavadatta, "Your Majesty, truly Manorama made you mistake one for another. Look: the form, garments, gait, voice—this clever woman has presented the king to us before our very eyes." Vasavadatta suddenly stood up again, saying, "I can't bear to see another falsification." The playwright insisted, "But it's just a play, theater, spectacle. It's not proper to leave the theatre at the wrong time and break the mood."

Vasavadatta walked away and found the clown asleep at the door of the picture gallery. She thought to herself, "The king must be here, too. I'll wake up the clown and ask him." The clown awoke, and in his stupor blurted out, "Manorama, has the king finished acting yet?" Vasavadatta said (sadly), "What! Was it the king who acted?" She saw Manorama and said, "Bravo, bravo, Manorama. Well acted. Get up. I know all about the play about Aranyika." The king, seeing Vasavadatta and Manorama, said, "What! The queen has recognized me."

The queen imprisoned Aranyika but set her free when she discovered that Aranyika was Priyadarsika. She joined the hands of Aranyika and the king, saying, "Her father gave her to you long ago."[12]

Vasavadatta salvages her pride with that last line, implying that duty, not passion, is what motivates the king—or so she pretends to think. This is an inversion of the sentiment that the king expressed in *Ratnavali*, to the queen's distress: that it was just duty, not passion, that joined him to the queen herself.

The clown's sleep, which lets him reveal the truth to the queen, a key moment in the plot, is a transformation of the king's dream in "The Dream of Vasavadatta." The great innovation here is the play within the play in which the king impersonates Manorama impersonating him. This situation involves not only a double impersonation but a double change of gender, a double–cross-dress; as if this were not complex enough, it is further complicated when the play is produced by those many Indian traditions—perhaps alluded to in this very play—in which men play the parts of women, and others in which women play the parts of men. At such a moment, one could imagine a woman playing the part of the king playing the part of Manorama playing the part of the king (like a male actor playing Rosalind playing Ganymede playing Rosalind, in *As You Like It*). As in the earlier Harsa play, but this time on purpose, Vasavadatta begins the masquerade, casting her rival as herself, causing her rival to impersonate her. But, once again, Udayana does not follow the part that she has written for him: he takes over the casting, reversing the queen's intention (to bring him close to her) by using the queen's play to stage his own infidelity right before her eyes. The two fantasies intermingle, and the queen's plan backfires as his fantasy becomes hers, his vision overpowers hers, and she sees not what she wants to see (her straying husband making love to her as she was when he loved her) but what she fears to see, actually sees, and allows herself to be talked out of saying that she sees: her husband making love to her rival. She stages her dream, and the king stages her nightmare. The queen moves, and the king checkmates her.

Vasavadatta is the least deluded character in all of the plays. Only in the *Ocean of Story* does the king see through the trick. In Bhasa he is fooled; in the *Ratnavali* he thinks he is the trickster (disguising his mistress as his wife), but still he is the one who is fooled; and in the *Priyadarsika*, where he again engineers the trick (disguising himself as himself), the queen still sees through it. His ignorance and confusion torment her, but her poignant knowledge of what is going on torments her even more. Where most women in this situation find it hard enough to watch their men replace them with women who replicate them (often in the form they had when they were young), Vasavadatta must literally watch her role usurped by her younger rival. The metaphor of the understudy here becomes literalized.

It is interesting to read these plays with an eye to the different consequences of the triplication of the woman (Vasavadatta in the *Ratnavali*) and the triplication of the man (Udayana in the *Priyadarsika*). Where Shulman has asked questions about the fragmentation of the king, Doniger would ask questions about the fragmentation of the queen, both within herself and in her complex relationship with the other women loved by the man she loves. For instance, the fact that (in the *Priyadarsika*) Vasavadatta immediately recognizes the king when he is disguised, while Udayana (in the *Ratnavali*) wrongly takes Vasavadatta for Sagarika disguised as Vasavadatta, is typical of the literature of sexual masquerade, which generally depicts women as more often tricking, and less often tricked, than men.

Who is staging the dream? Who is in control? We might make a distinction between active dreams and passive nightmares, conscious and unconscious tricksters: the active masqueraders are the manipulators, like Queen Vasavadatta at first both in *Ratnavali* and in *Priyadarsika* and like Udayana later in that play, while the the passive, unconscious masqueraders would include bewitched and possessed characters in myths, but also people who discover that, without willing it, they have been masquerading as themselves, like Vasavadatta later in the *Ratnavali*. Yet even (or especially) the active masqueraders tend to get caught up in their own tricks and discover a frame outside (or inside) the one that they themselves construct to impersonate someone else,[13] a frame in which that someone else or they themselves may unknowingly be impersonating themselves. This is what happens, in different ways and in different texts, to both Udayana and Vasavadatta.

Let me conclude by returning to the relationship between magical illusion (used by Kalingasena's magician), art (the trick of garland making), the slip of the tongue, dreaming (experienced by King Udayana in the play by Bhasa), masquerading (by the women in the first Harsa play), and playacting (by the man in the second Harsa play). The first differs from the others in several ways: the illusory form of the magician lies, prevents rather than facilitates the union of the king and his mistress, and is ended, rather than created, by the suspension of rational thought. In all of the other variants, the illusory form tells the truth, brings about the ultimate union of the king and the mistress, and is created by the suspension of rational thought. The exception highlights, if it does not actually prove, the rule: one can dream by daylight, through masquerade and the theatre, and reach out to the same kind of emotional truth—often a painful truth—that we find in our dreams.

Notes

1. [Doniger] O'Flaherty 1984.
2. *Kathāsaritsāgara* 31. [6.5] 1–96, 32. [6.6] 1–30, esp. 24–30.
3. *Kathāsaritsāgara* 33 [6.7] .166–217, 34 [6.8].1–65.
4. See Doniger 1994, 1995, and 1996.
5. *Kathāsaritsāgara* 15–16 [3.1–2].
6. *Kathāsaritsāgara* 14 [2.60].64–75.
7. *Svapnavāsavadattā.*
8. O'Flaherty 1984.
9. *Ratnâvalī.*
10. Shulman, 1997: 79.
11. Ibid.
12. *Priyadarśikā.*
13. O'Flaherty 1984.

References

Bhāsa. *Svapnavāsavadattā*. Ed. C. R. Devadhar. 1946.

Doniger, Wendy, 1994. "Speaking in Tongues: Deceptive Stories about Sexual Deception." *Journal of Religion* 74:3 (July), 320–337.

———. 1995. "The Criteria of Identity in a Telugu Myth of Sexual Masquerade." In D. Shulman (ed.), *Syllables of Sky: Studies in South Indian Civilization, in Honour of Velcheru Narayana Rao*. Delhi, 103–132.

———. 1996. "Sexual Masquerades in Hindu Myths: Aspects of the Transmission of Knowledge in Ancient India." In Nigel Crook (ed.), *The Transmission of Knowledge in South Asia*. Delhi, 28–48.

Harṣa. *Priyadarśikā*. Ed. V. D. Gadre. 1884. Bombay.
Harṣa. *Ratnâvalī*. Ed. Ashokanath Bhattacharya. 1967. Calcutta.
O'Flaherty, Wendy Doniger. 1984. *Dreams, Illusion, and Other Realities*. Chicago.
Shulman, David. 1997. "Embracing the Subject: Harṣa's Play within a Play." *Journal of Indian Philosophy* 25, 69–89.
Somadeva. *Kathāsaritsāgara*. 1930. Bombay.

II

Amerindia

5

Sharing and Interpreting Dreams in Amerindian Nations

Barbara Tedlock

We can only know what another has dreamed or imagined through cultural forms such as narratives, chants, songs, dances, or visual images. Since sensory perception is mediated by its translation into interpretable forms, shared dreams and visions are by nature culturally variable expressive representations. For example, dreams often provide an arena where the living may contact the dead, but the nature and evaluation of this contact between ancestors and dreamers is variable not only between cultures, but also within a single culture. Thus, in the American Southwest, while most Zunis and Navajos express fear of contact with the dead, Zuni medicine women and men together with Navajo peyotists actively seek such contact during dreaming and trancing. The Xavante of Brazil describe and interpret the nature of their contact with the ancestors as depending upon a dreamer's gender and time of life. While women of all ages share their dreams by singing laments, men vary their dream representations discursively according to their age group. Adolescent boys learn to compose dream songs by observing their ancestors at a distance during their dreams. Old men, on the other hand, speak of directly interacting with their ancestors in dreams and even merging their identities with them. They share their dreams by narrating myth segments relating to each image.[1]

Other cultures have elaborated dream narratives into large public rituals and developed sophisticated metacommentaries about the processes and products of dreaming. The Aguaruna of northern Peru, for example, have created and cultivated formal dream-telling performances known as "dream declarations." Dreams are related by means of reiterated phrases and a highly compressed vocabulary. In an example of dream fashioning by a young man, he opens his dream testimony by chanting in a loud and rhythmic style, "This is about a vision which was seen while sleeping. Oh, I saw a powerful vision and felt its greatness."[2] Moving from a passive to an active construction, he now embodies the dream image by changes in his vocal register. Speaking with the boastful voice of a warrior who appeared in his dream, he says, "Where someone is always killing my relatives, right there I will kill in revenge, wiping out the tracks in his abandoned trail. Perhaps he is my relative. Taking that very one, I will perhaps actually choose a relative. I will change his trail into an abandoned trail. Forming a single file of the children, happily I will lead them to where I will condemn them. Giving each of them a sip of manioc soup, with great joy I will lead them single file, to where I will kill in revenge." Next, he shifts from the direct quotation of what he heard a dead warrior say aloud in his dream to a third-person description of the visual setting: "As he was saying this, the wind was blowing, '*tuppu, tuppu*,' over me again and again. He was standing in a whirlpool of dust and leaves, like smoke, over and over again making a sound like a dried skin [being folded back and forth] '*kikug, kikug.*'" The emotional power of this narration is built up from a combination of metaphors such as "wiping out tracks," and "abandoned trail," which imply the death of an enemy, together with ideophones suggesting blowing wind and drumbeats.

Behind the multiplicity of Amerindian dream representations are numerous theories and practices of dreaming. These diverse theories are not static, internally consistent grammars or sets of ideas disconnected from the activities of everyday life. Rather, they are linked to social action and interpreted, manipulated, and employed in distinct ways in various contexts by individuals. Dream communication involves a convergence in the passing theories of individuals who embrace ad hoc strategies to make sense of a particular utterance. As Richard Rorty put it, "a theory is 'passing' because it must constantly be corrected to allow for mumbles, stumbles, malapropisms, metaphors, tics, seizures, psychotic symptoms, egregious stupidity, strokes of genius, and the like."[3]

In conversations with a number of Rarámuri individuals living in northern Mexico, William Merrill learned that, while they generally agree among themselves that sleep and dreaming are produced by the activities of one's various souls, they disagree on the precise actions of these souls during sleep. One man theorized that people feel drowsy when their souls feel drowsy and that they fall asleep when their souls fall asleep inside their bodies. Dreaming occurs when the largest soul arises and leaves the body, then again when it returns to the body. People wake up only when all their souls awaken. Another, equally knowledgeable, man reported a different theory, one in which souls never sleep inside the body and dreaming takes place only when one or more large souls leave the body and encounter other souls during their wanderings.[4]

Among the Zuni of New Mexico I learned that dreaming is accomplished by a segment of a person's self that travels outside the body and has experiences in past, distant, or future times and places. Although this part of the dreaming code is shared by all Zunis, there are two conflicting theories concerning precisely which part of the dreamer is traveling. One common notion is that one's thoughts are wandering abroad in the night. The second idea is that one's life essence or breath is wandering. These two theories roughly correspond to a person's social and psychological status as either poor or valuable in terms of initiatory religious and psychological knowledge. The theory that one's thoughts wander is more likely to be stated by poor Zunis, especially highly acculturated Zunis, who, although they are aware of the other theory, subscribe to the materialist mind/body dual opposition. As a result they argue that if one's wind or breath, which resides inside one's body, actually left during sleep, then one would simply die. Nevertheless, those who hold this theory express anxiety about dying while dreaming. "Valuable" Zunis, on the other hand, express no fear of dying while dreaming, or at any other time, since their initiation involves the strengthening of their inner essence, composed of breath and heart. Unlike ordinary Zunis, these medicine society members and rain priests have intimate knowledge of various altered states of consciousness, whether medicine knowledge of what they say is "passed through to the other side" or priestly knowledge of "seeing ahead." They have little difficulty in imagining dreaming, fainting, trancing (including trances induced by jimsonweed ingestion), and possession trancing (behaving like bears during medicine society performances) as forms of death. But these deaths are imaginal and reversible, not literal and irreversible.

Again, in my research with K'iche' Mayans in Guatemala, I found two primary theories concerning what happens when a person dreams. One is that the dreamer's "luck" or "destiny" leaves the body as a free soul and goes about in the world, meeting the free souls of other people and animals. The other theory is that the gods or ancestors approach the sleeping dreamer's body and awaken the "lightning soul," which then struggles with these visitors until they give the dreamer a message or warning. While everyone has a free soul that wanders outside the body during dreaming, only a shaman's lightning soul can receive complex messages from the cosmos and the ancestors at any time, whether during dreaming or not, without ever leaving the body. During divinatory rituals, shamans readily fall into the trance state, receiving important messages from the gods and ancestors about past, present, or future events. They have no fear of dreaming or trancing, which they consider to be similar states.

Dreaming, for shamans and lay persons alike, is a nightly struggle between the dreamer's actively engaged free soul, which ought to be in search of knowledge, and the free souls of the deities and ancestors who have important messages concerning the future but seldom say exactly what they mean. As one K'iche' expressed it, "Dreams want to win and not to be remembered clearly. Instead, you must learn to fight in order to win them, to remember whatever they advise."[5] Since the dream messages from the gods and ancestors concern the future, which K'iche' individuals see as a projection of the good and evil here on earth in the past and still here now, there are both good dreams and bad dreams, the latter including vivid, emotionally charged nightmares. The art of learning to see, hear, and interpret the uncanny in dreams is taught during formal apprenticeship. At this time the novice learns that while a noninitiated person's dream of being chased by a horse or other large domestic animal means "the casket," which is to say death for the dreamer, the same dream for a shaman indicates a visit to an ancestral earth shrine. In both cases the connection is made by way of a box, but for ordinary dreamers it is a wooden casket and for shamans a small box-shaped shrine where offerings are made to one's ancestors. Thus, for lay persons this dream would be interpreted as a personal event, while in the case of daykeepers the same dream would be interpreted at a social level, indicating that religious rituals should be performed. For the K'iche', then, an identical unsought dream varies in interpretation depending upon the religious status of the dreamer.[6]

Important aspects of these theories are predictable on the basis of ontology and psychology; for example, for a knowledgeable Zuni, who has but one soul or coessence (breath), dreaming is a much more dangerous activity than for a K'iche', whose body always has its breath present during the dream wanderings of the free soul. This predictability in symbolic thinking is brought about by the rhetorical principle of entelechy, by which particular symbol systems implicate other symbol systems in the inherent unconscious movement of symbolic action toward finishedness.[7] Since dream speculation and classifications are, as it were, philosophically, emotionally, and socially rooted differently among the Rarámuri, Zuni, and K'iche', both their dreaming and their dream theories take different shapes.

The classification of dreams into what might be glossed as literal and metaphorical, or in semiotic terminology, indexical and iconic, is common to many Amerindian cultures. For the Kalapalo of Brazil, some dreams are interpreted literally in terms of events from the dreamer's recent past. But when dreams are understood as the wanderings of the dreamer's interactive self, they are interpreted by means of metaphorical analogies between images of the self in a future context and images of the self's active participation in dreaming. Here, as well as in other Native American societies, such dream experiences reveal emergent possibilities rather than accomplished facts.[8]

Some Native American societies, including the Ojibwa, Xavante, and Quechua, have not made dreaming and dream interpretation into objects of a socially organized system of beliefs. This does not mean that members of these societies never represent dreams or theorize about the nature of dreaming. Rather, it means that such activities and speculations are individual rather than social and, as a result, there exists no collective tradition concerning the meanings of dream images nor a developed metalanguage for the discussion of dreaming. Even so, individual theories and interpretations of dream symbolism are created through dialogues between exterior social realms and interior private dream experiences.[9]

In some Amerindian societies, the dream text is analyzed by breaking down the narrative into isolated elements that are then read as an allegory, an inversion, a wish, or else as a literal description of past, present, or future occurrences in the world. Hupdu Maku dreamers in Brazil, for example, reduce a dream to a symbol such as "cassava bread," or "shotgun," or else into an action such as "drinking honey," or "shooting a jaguar." These elements are then interpreted as either a reflection or a reversal of waking reality in terms of visual, auditory, or sensory analogies expressed as metaphors. Since cassava bread resembles the giant armadillo's armor and the long barrel of a shotgun resembles the long snout of an anteater, a dream image of cassava bread means that the dreamer will shoot an armadillo, while the image of a shotgun indicates that he will kill an anteater. The principle of reversal is displayed when the dream image of a pleasurable experience, such as drinking honey, indicates the unpleasant experience of crying at a kinsman's funeral. Shooting a jaguar (since jaguars are shamans) indicates that the dreamer is in fact being shot with illness by a sorcerer's dart.[10]

Dream interpretation by means of isolated elements proceeds intratextually, without reference to anything but a lexicon of symbols. It is most frequently used by the uninitiated in the self-analysis of their own dreams. While a purely intratextual analysis focuses on dream imagery, a contextual analysis focuses on the immediate social and personal environment of the dreamer. A third mode of interpretation is intertextual, combining the content of a specific dream and its immediate context with texts of other dreams and nondream texts in order to arrive at an interpretation. As practiced among the K'iche' Maya of Guatemala and the Mapuche of Chile, contextual dream analysis involves the examination of dreamers' personal situations, including events and circumstances of their lives.[11] In these societies dreams occurring during an illness are interpreted as giving information about both the cause and the cure of that illness. Likewise, dreams occurring in proximity to natural disasters (mudslides and earthquakes), political events (elections, coups, rebellions), business transactions, journeys, births, deaths, weddings, and initiations are interpreted in relationship to these events. Dreams in these same societies can also be interpreted intertextually, through comparison with previous dreams, the dreams of other family members, or nondream texts provided by divination and mythology.

Links between dream portents and the events they predict are often made by way of myths. Among the Kagwahiv of the Brazilian Amazon basin, an incestuous sexual dream predicts killing a tapir because a tapir was an adulterous lover in an important myth. For the Hupdu Maku to dream of a smoked-out armadillo indicates that a kinsman will die because of a myth in which a man lures his brother-in-law into an armadillo's hole and tries to kill him there. On the other hand, to dream of either leaf-cutter ants or else a white-lipped peccary in the house indicates that "other people will kill us," because there is a myth in which heroes kill their grandmother by transforming leaf-cutter ants into poisonous spiders and then create and destroy white-lipped peccaries with thunder sticks. Among the Lacandon Maya of Chiapas, Mexico, to dream of maggots indicates beans, since the Lord of Death, Kisin, daily eats maggots from dead bodies as his beans. Among the Sharanahua Indians of eastern Peru, when shamans elicit dream reports from their patients, they typically consist of single images (such as a peccary or the sun) that simultaneously echo myths and overlap with the shamans' categories of songs and symptoms.[12]

The nature of the cognitive and emotional linkage between myths and dreams can be studied by treating each as a separate cultural system, or organized conventional set of signs, articulated with other systems but with a degree of structural autonomy. In southern Peruvian Quechua dreaming and myth there is a fundamental difference between the way signs function in dream interpretation and in myth telling. When myths are transmitted they remain in a narrative context and thus are comparatively resistive to semantic change. But when dreams are transmitted, they are subjected to an interpretation system involving the codification of a dream experience in terms of a few pivotal signified-interpretant complexes drawn from a limited, conventional lexicon. As a result, Andean dream symbology over the past four centuries, unlike both myth and ritual symbology, underwent major changes.[13]

Evidentials

In Amerindian languages the epistemological status of dream narratives and other performances is marked grammatically. Franz Boas reported the use of a Kwakiutl suffix which, when it was affixed to a verb stem, indicated that the action of the verb occurred in a dream.[14] He also discussed at some length another key suffix meaning "apparently" or "it seems like," as well as "in a dream." Since these suffixes include adverbial and conjunctional ideas implying evaluation of the ideas expressed in the word to which they were attached, he placed them together in a single classification expressing the sources of subjective knowledge. As a grammatical category, these types of suffixes, indicating unwitnessed events known only indirectly, have more recently been termed "evidentials."[15]

There are several evidential categories, including quotatives, auditory and visual inferentials, tense particles, and adverbs, that require the speaker to adopt a particular stance toward the nature and truth value of an utterance. Quotatives do not indicate verbatim quotation, but rather mark content that was learned from someone else. Yucatec and Itzá Mayan evidentials include a quotative particle meaning "they say" or "it is said." It is specific to the relating of myths, visions, and other religious experiences. Tzotzil Mayans, when narrating their dreams, qualify the oneiric activity with an adverb meaning "it seems," and whenever they narrate myths or dreams they insert a particle which indicates that the action was not directly witnessed by the speaker. Among the Dene Tha of northwestern Alberta, an adverb meaning "probably" is used in the narration of prophetic dreams to indicate that they may not materialize. Lakotas, of both North and South Dakota, punctuate their accounts of myths, visions, and dreams with third-person singular and plural quotatives.[16]

K'iche' Mayans sometimes intersperse their dream narratives with a quotative meaning "he, she, it says," indicating that authority for the statement lies outside the quotidian conscious waking self of the dreamer. This is in accordance with the K'iche' belief that the actions and experiences in dreams are those of the detachable free soul rather than of the more intimate life or body soul. The quotative is also used when relating myths, narratives, or anecdotes that do not deal with personal experiences. Among the Mazatecs of Oaxaca, Mexico, shamanic healing discourse is marked by the use of a quotative at the end of each line. In a trance, María Sabina chanted:[17]

I am a woman who shouts, it says.
I am a woman who whistles, it says.
I am a woman who thunders, it says.
I am a woman who plays music, it says.
I am a spirit woman, it says.

Throughout an entire evening of chanting she ended virtually every line with the quotative. She explained that she was not speaking for herself but rather repeating what the hallucinogenic mushrooms authorized her to chant.

Evidentials are also employed in prophetic narrative contexts. In Wintu, a California language that lacks grammatical categories expressing past or future tense relative to speakers, revelations about the future that come from intuitions or dreams are linguistically marked by an evidential suffix. Similarly, among Kagwahiv speakers an evidential particle appears in the place of a tense marker in each sentence of a dream account. Some speakers also use an adverb of time otherwise meaning "temporarily," thus emphasizing the evanescent quality of dreaming. In Cuzco Quechua, a past-tense reportative suffix is used to mark narrated events, including both myths and dreams, to which the speaker cannot attest because they were not experienced directly but only known indirectly, through hearing from others, or else in an altered state of consciousness. Dreams and visions are sometimes treated by the Kashaya Pomo, of Northern California, in the same way as ordinary waking experiences, using an evidential indicating true personal experience, but they may also be treated as myths, using a quotative.[18]

The use of evidentials in prophetic, mythic, and ordinary discourse indicates key epistemological differences between various Amerindian traditions. They also provide a means of access to what people think about and what they think. For dream researchers evidentials often reveal the existence of separate dream interpretation codes for lay dreamers and professional dream interpreters within the same society. Thus, for example, among the K'iche' the quotative is used in various prophetic contexts, but only by men and women who have been trained and initiated as dream interpreters. In a number of Native American cultures report forms consisting of verbs as well as particles indicate that the preceding or following utterance is a representation of the speech of a deity, ancestor, or other supernatural. There is no distinction, as there is in English, between direct discourse which is faithful to the wording or indirect discourse which is faithful to the meaning.[19]

Because speakers of English and other Indo-European languages usually foreground referential language functions at the expense of pragmatic functions, there exists a tradition of reducing dreams to clearly delineated referential meanings. Subsequently these are recorded in dream dictionaries and then subjected to content analysis for the purposes of interpretation. These procedures underplay the role of indexical processes that depend upon the relationship between linguistic signs and their communicative contexts. It is important to remember that dream sharing is only possible due to the various passing theories of culturally grounded narrators and interpreters.

Lucid Dreaming

What has come to be known as "lucid dreaming" occurs when one is asleep and dreaming and then suddenly becomes aware that one is, indeed, dreaming.[20] This key moment of lucidity is the result of an interior dialogue, imaginal conversation, or better, an intersense translation conducted at the crossroads of modes of consciousness. The dreamer is simultaneously cognizant of being asleep and removed from the external world, and of being awake and receptive to the inner world. At this crossover point complex synesthesias—visual, auditory, and tactile—often occur as a new dream entity emerges. This new dream, which often interrupts the narrative flow of the previous dream and fuses dreamer to dream imagery, may be experienced simultaneously as fearful and joyful.

Since lucidity violates all attempts to define an essence for dreaming or trancing, it was dismissed for many years as merely a type of mental awakening during sleep or trance. Not until experimental laboratory research demonstrated that lucidity was accompanied by normal rapid eye movements (REMs), and lucid dreamers and trancers were trained to signal their awareness of lucidity by way of exaggerated eye movements, did researchers agree that it was a form of dreaming. Lucidity can range from quasi-lucid states of consciousness in which dreamers are aware of dreaming or trancing, but not able to control the content of their dreams or visions, to full lucidity in which they combine the dreaming mode of experience with waking cognitive abilities in such a way as to control the outcome of a particular dream or waking vision.[21]

Phenomenologically speaking, lucid dreaming tends toward sensory clarity, bodily presence, and an expansive emotional thrill or numinous religious feeling. This can be seen in some dreams Franz Boas collected from the Kwakiutl of British Columbia at the turn of the century. In one of these a man reports that he was out sealing, and that when he was butchering a particularly large seal he found a quartz crystal in its stomach.[22] He hid the crystal in the woods and then gave a feast. After the guests left he lay down and "Then I dreamed that I was asleep," which is to say that he became aware that he was asleep. A man came to him, sat down next to him, and said, "You must not lie down with your wife for four years or else you will be unlucky, for you have received your treasure, the quartz crystal from me." Upon awakening he decided that he ought to follow the instructions the unknown man gave him; the man became his guardian spirit and trained him as a shaman. Another man from the same community dreamed one night that he was paddling his canoe with his four children aboard. All of a sudden, "It became very thick and foggy, we were lost in the fog. I was just sitting still in our traveling canoe. Then I stopped paddling. In my dream we were drifting about on the water. Then it became night and I went to sleep." When he awoke it was still foggy and his canoe was being rolled against some rocks he was unfamiliar with. "Then it cleared up and I awoke." The kinesthetic sensation of drifting and floating, like that of flying, is a common experience in lucid dreaming.

In both of these cases the Kwakiutl dreamer became aware, while asleep, that he was dreaming but did not use this knowledge to further direct or change the course of his dreaming. Thus, these are examples of what researchers call quasi-lucid dreams. Such dreams often contain unusually vivid colors, strange physical sensations, or verbal messages resulting in strong emotional affect. Dreamers usually remember, cherish, and later imaginatively reexperience such dreams, perhaps all the more so because they are unsought. However, they can be dangerous. As an Ottawa man said, "I was told that when a man dreams that he is dreaming, it means that he has almost died."[23]

Lucid trancing involves verbal and motor automatisms in which a shaman displays two or more distinct personalities to an audience. Among the Inuit, trances are generally voluntary and shamans describe the possessing agency or agencies as second, third, or fourth personalities outside and even alien to their own egos. These personalities are distinct enough that during public performances, some shamans maintain the presence of mind to address explanatory comments to their audiences. Others may need assistance, as in the case of a man named Qagtaq who shamanized by wandering about half-naked in a snowstorm until he achieved a vision which he related, in the form of nearly incomprehensible riddles, to his friends and neighbors. His shrill falsetto oracular utterances, which were punctuated by animal howls and frightening screeches, were interpreted by an old woman who had a great deal of experience in shamanizing.[24]

Ruby Modesto, a Cahuilla shaman, reported to her biographer, Guy Mount, that when she was young she dreamed so deeply that she did not know how to return to waking consciousness. One morning her father tried to awaken her but was unable to. Finally her uncle, who was a well-known shaman, brought her out of her dream. When she awoke her father made her promise never again to dream in that way until she knew how to get back from the dream by herself. She opens her account saying, "When I was about ten years old I dreamed to the 13th level."[25] At this point she shifts to the second person, explaining to her interlocutor that "the way you do that is by remembering to tell yourself to go to sleep in your 1st level ordinary dream. You consciously tell yourself to lay down and go to sleep. Then you dream a second dream. This is the 2nd level and the prerequisite for real Dreaming. Uncle Charlie called this process 'setting up dreaming.' You can tell yourself ahead of time where you want to go, or what you want to see, or what you want to learn." But there is still more: "On the 3rd level you learn and see unusual things, not of this world. The hills and terrain are different." A bit later, she describes the split consciousness characteristic of lucid dreaming: "Once, before I knew how to dream and think simultaneously, I was dreaming on the 3rd level and wondering how I was going to return. Suddenly a giant bird appeared, like a pelican; it came along and I grabbed its neck. We flew way up in the sky, I saw the earth burning below and I sort of came out of it into the 2nd level dream. It's really hard to come out of those higher levels."

This is an example of fully developed lucid dreaming: a form as self-conscious as Tibetan Buddhist dream yoga and the Hindu practice of "dream witnessing" found in Transcendental Meditation. Within both of these Asian traditions initiates are taught techniques to enhance lucid dreaming as a form of meditation which is naturally available during sleep. Throughout the Americas shamans talk of experiencing conscious or lucid dreams in which they become aware of dreaming and then, while remaining in the dream state, direct the actions of their souls, shadows, selves, or doubles. Lucidity can also be achieved during waking visions. Thus, a man living on the northern Alaskan coast was out sealing on the ice when he was attacked by a bear who bit and clawed him. Upon realizing that he was hallucinating he said, "Stop, you hurt me too much," and the bear left him and went away. After the man returned home he became a shaman.[26] All over the Arctic, when individuals realized that they were experiencing visions, they overcame the fear by becoming external observers of these events. As an Inuit man stated it, "When it appeared I tried to flee, but then the thought came to me that I had summoned this magic bear deliberately and of my own free will, so I remained where I was."[27]

Yekuana shamans of Venezuela consciously free their souls or "dream doubles" in order to direct the course of their dreaming. Among the Dunne-za or Beaver Indians of British Columbia and Alberta, there exists a long-standing tradition of dreamers or prophets, both female and male, who are able to leave their bodies and fly like swans along a trail of song into the sky, to visit the deceased and return with new knowledge and songs to their bodies here on earth. At Hopi and Zuni pueblos there are a number of powerful medicine women who act with volition in their dreams to seek herbal and spiritual remedies. Among the Xavante, individuals actively concentrate on particular spirits they wish to commune with, who eventually appear in a dream. Members of one Xavante patrilineage use special cylinders of polished wood to communicate with their dead; a lineage leader hangs the cylinder over the grave of a dead kinsman, or over his own sleeping mat, and that same evening he himself either visits his kinsman in his dreams or else he receives a visitation from his dead kin.[28]

A Blackfeet medicine man, shortly after his wife died, experienced a lucid vision in which he entered his previous night's dream and saw the ridge where he had slept, his own dead body, and the spirits of many other dead people sitting in grave boxes. When he saw the spirits "getting up and shaking off their clothes, they walked behind a woman and a baby toward the camp and into a painted tipi. At this moment one of the dead persons took the baby and laid it down on a red neck cloth." A dead person said aloud, "We shall kill this young man with the baby." Now the dead danced around, and "I saw my own dead body." So, just as the dead left their corpses in their graves, the dreamer now leaves his own sleeping body. "Then one of the dead took the baby and swung it around three times, then threw it at my body. My body dodged. Each of the dead tried to hit my body with the baby, but none succeeded." This was a close call, since touching his sleeping body with the dead baby's spiritual body would have killed him. Now one of the dead said, "Well we shall have to let him go this time," and another said, "My son, we will give you a neck cloth which belonged to the baby. This will give power to cure cramps and rheumatism. It also has power to pick up red-hot stones and fire."[29]

This man's experience that he was temporarily separated from his own body is designated by researchers as an "out-of-body experience," or "astral flight." Such experiences are commonly connected with lucid dreaming. Tonik Nibak, a Tzotzil Mayan weaver and flower vender living in Zinacantán, Chiapas, Mexico, reported astral flight during lucidity. She opens her narrative with the striking image of washing her hair and seeing it all fall out.[30] Because dreaming of losing one's hair is interpreted in her culture as a warning of poverty, sickness, or death for oneself or a family member, she interrogates her dream image, asking, "Why would my hair fall out like that?" Brushing aside the negative portent, she boasts, "That's fine! It always has so many lice in it. Never mind, I'll cover myself with an old blanket." Next, picking up an old rag (another sign of poverty), she wraps it around her head, covers herself with a shawl, and goes outside to gather firewood. Although gathering firewood is an everyday female activity in her society, dreaming of gathering firewood indicates that the dreamer, or a close relative of the dreamer, will die.

At this point in her dream she finds a pine stump, digs up all its roots, strips off the rotten parts, binds them all together, and carries them home. "There I climbed over the fence and put it down next to a live oak tree and flew off." Zinacantecos say that flying while dreaming indicates shamanic ability, since it shows that one's soul (the part of the self that flies) is very knowledgeable. Flying also happens to be a universal marker of self-consciousness, or lucidity, while dreaming.[31] Continuing with her account, she says, "When I landed far away I was asked by someone why I had left my wood in a heap and flown off. I became concerned and flew back to get it." At this point she "wasn't flying anymore" and "woke up," she says, but she notes that she was actually still dreaming even though "it seemed as if it was already light and as if it was on the earth's surface." In other words, it seemed as though she were awake. Becoming self-reflective, she takes a critical attitude toward the apparent reality of her dream. "It didn't *seem* as if it were in my dream," she says. "My pine arrived safely. I sat down at home with my load. I made a tiny corral of my pine. I stacked it. I looked at it. I woke up."

The feeling of being outside of one's corporeal body often arises during vision questing. As a young man, the Shoshone Sun Dance Chief John Trehero went with two friends to fast on a mountaintop that had an important cave. When they entered, just as it was getting dark, lightning flashed and thunder clapped even though no storm was approaching. Two of the men became terrified and ran out of the cave. Trehero remained alone, spending three days there. "On the third day, I heard a bell, drum beat, singing, way down deep in the cave. It was all dark, but I kept hearing this bell ringing and a drumbeat, way back there, and wondered what it was." He became aware that he was dreaming when these auditory hallucinations stopped and a tiny man appeared before him. "He came from the middle of the mountain, where it was dark." His name was Seven Arrows, and he said, "I see you have the nerve to stay. I see you are sincere. Your friends have gone home. I would like to take you back in here, show you some things."

Without any further thought Trehero went deeper into the cave with the man. "We came to a place where some men were throwing a lance at a rolling hoop; it was a gambling game. Then we came into another big cavern, where people were gambling on horse racing, and we went on until we came to a hand game." His guide told him, "That's not good. Now you have seen that, let's go on further."

They went deeper into the hill and heard a drum beating. "As we came closer we saw a tipi that was rolled up halfway, to let in air, and saw an Indian doctoring session going on. The patient was practically skin and bones and the medicine man was singing songs for him." At this point in the narrative it becomes clear that he is being selected to become an apprentice shaman. Seven Arrows, who will be his spirit guide, says, "I know you are sincere and will use your powers only for what is good. I want you to go back now; go back, take up your fasting. You should not use what I am going to give you to do any of the other gambling things that you saw back there. Go back home now, and I will tell you later what things I want you to work with. You will be able to help people to get well when they are sick. Now take up your fast and go from the mountain down to the lake and wash up, take a swim."

Trehero says that while Seven Arrows was leading him back to the entrance of the cave, "I realized that there was a solid stone wall in front of us. As we reached it, we walked right through the wall, and I saw my body lying there on the ground. I realized then that my vision had not been in the physical world. When I reached my body, I felt as though I was lying down on top of myself, and then I was awake." The bizarreness of walking through a solid wall taught him that his experience was not "in the physical world," and it also awakened him from his dream.

Dream Incubation and Active Imagination

While lucid dreaming and vision questing are still common occurrences in many Native American societies, there are individuals who have lost the living connection with their elders and thus their aboriginal culture of dreaming. To regain their spiritual bonds, some indigenous people practice dream incubation and active imagination. Cree artist Shirley Cheechoo has undertaken several overnight pilgrimages to a magical place known as Dreamer's Rock on the White Fish Reserve in Ontario. She recently described a spiritual quest she undertook with two of her friends. They prayed, burned tobacco and sweetgrass, and then slept. "As the new day was to begin a hole in the sky appeared and started to form a circle." A strange beam of light came down upon them, "I could see the sparkles of light around me. I knew the spirits were there. I knew I had touched another level of existence."[32]

Gerard Rancourt Tsonakwa, an Eastern Abenaki sculptor and storyteller from Quebec, carves and paints his deceased father's spirit guides, Spider Woman and Caribou Man, in hopes of encountering them in his own dreams. In a catalogue for a recent exhibit of his own and his wife's sculptures at the San Diego Museum of Man, he shares one of his father's favorite lucid dreams. His father begins his account by saying, "In my dream, I awakened."[33] He noted the position of his body, and what he saw when he turned on his side was "the morning sun shining through a dew-covered spider web." He had a strong emotional response to the web: "So beautiful it was! It was filled with sparkling color, a million tiny lights in a hand's breadth." At this point he noticed that "a black and yellow spider was busy repairing a tear in the web from an insect that got away." When he noticed the spider it stopped weaving and talked to the dreamer in "a tiny little voice," saying, "This is a Dream Net, it only lets good dreams through. This hole was left by the dream you are dreaming now!"

The dreamer's calm attitude of receptive detachment and the glimmering of the mandala-like spider web as it moved into his awareness are key markers of lucidity. The visual image of an orb spider's web, which is spun anew each night in complete darkness by touch alone, nicely parallels our nightly spinning of dreams in the utter darkness. Native Americans have long associated spider webs with protective and healing powers. Webs painted on war shirts and shields are protective since, like the sticky spiral strands and long radiating support lines of a spider web, they cannot easily be destroyed by arrows or bullets, which pass through leaving but tiny holes. In treating puncture wounds, orb webs are placed directly on top of the injury to coagulate the blood. Since bad dreams, like arrows and bullets, can bring sickness and even death, especially to helpless infants, protective web designs are used on baby hoods and cradles to prevent bad dreams from penetrating the baby's open fontanel. Small webbed bead dangles, strung on sinew between rawhide thongs, are hung from the top back of the hood, and geometric web designs are woven into amulets tied to the top of cradle boards or sewn directly onto hide cradle hoods.[34]

Among the Northeastern nations "dream nets," also known as "dream catchers," are constructed from a supple willow or red dogwood branch bent into a circle, then woven with plant materials or sinew into a spiraling orb. Several tiny glass beads or semiprecious stones—garnet, turquoise, rose quartz, or malachite—are then attached to the web. Finally a larger bead and a feather from a wild turkey, cardinal, or bluebird are tied to the center of the web, representing a garden spider hanging suspended head downward from the center of the web. Now the dream catcher, which is lashed to the top of an infant's cradleboard, can filter all dreams approaching the baby and only let the good ones flow through the net's center opening into the fontanel and thus the consciousness of the baby. Today, all over

Native North America, dream nets are created for adults as well as for children and sold at intertribal powwows as a way of sharing dreams.

Notes

1. Tedlock 1992: 113–115; Aberle 1966: 217–220; Graham 1986, 1995.
2. Brown 1992: 164–165.
3. Rorty 1989: 14; see also Davidson 1986: 442; Stromberg 1993: 8–9.
4. Merrill 1988: 104–111.
5. Tedlock 1992: 116.
6. Tedlock 1981: 320–322.
7. Burke 1966: 69–70.
8. Basso 1992: 96–99.
9. Grim 1983: 103–106; Hallowell 1975: 164–168; Vecsey 1983: 124–125; Graham 1995; Reid 1978; Mannheim 1992.
10. Reid 1978.
11. Degarrod 1989: 50–55.
12. Kracke 1992: 33; Reid 1978: 20, 27; Bruce 1979: 322, 324–325; Siskind 1973: 32–33.
13. Mannheim 1992.
14. Boas 1911: 443, 448, 496; Boas 1947: 305, 371.
15. Jacobsen 1986.
16. Hanks 1993: 137; Hofling 1991: 6, 102, 104, 105, 113, 126, 127, 136, 140, 142, 144, 145, 154, 166, 173; Guiteras-Holmes 1961: 254; Laughlin 1976: 11; Watson and Goulet 1992: 218; Walker 1980: xxiv, 148–171.
17. Wasson et al. 1974: 233–234.
18. Schlichter 1986: 56; Kracke 1992; Mannheim 1992: 146; Oswalt 1986: 40–42; Du Bois 1986: 325.
19. For a discussion of the grammar of reported speech in English see Rumsey 1990: 346–361.
20. The term "lucid dream" was coined by Frederick Van Eeden in 1969.
21. Hunt 1989: 118–127.
22. Boas 1930.
23. Radin 1936: 260.
24. Rasmussen 1931: 24–26.
25. Modesto and Mount 1980.
26. Spencer 1959: 316.
27. Merkur 1985: 195–196.
28. Guss 1980: 306; Ridington 1988; Geertz and Lomatuway'ma 1987: 130; Maybury-Lewis 1974: 287.
29. Lincoln 1932: 68.
30. Laughlin 1976: 163.
31. Price and Cohen 1988: 118.
32. Smith 1995: 31–32.
33. Hedges 1992: 12.
34. Vogel 1970: 224; Hail 1980: 144, 148, 149; Conn 1982: 65.

References

Aberle, David F. 1966. *The Peyote Religion Among the Navaho.* New York.

Basso, Ellen B. 1992. "The Implications of a Progressive Theory of Dreaming." In Barbara Tedlock (ed.), *Dreaming: Anthropological and Psychological Interpretations.* Santa Fe, NM, 86–104.

Boas, Franz. 1911. "Kwakiutl." In Franz Boas (ed.), *Handbook of American Indian Languages,* Washington, DC, 423–557.

———. 1930. *Religion of the Kwakiutl Indians.* New York.

———. 1947. "Kwakiutl Grammar with a Glossary of the Suffixes." In H. Boas Yampolsky and Z. S. Harris (eds.), *Transactions of the American Philosophical Society* 3. Philadelphia, 201–377.

Brown, Michael F. 1992. "Ropes of Sand: Order and Imagery in Aguaruna Dreams." In Barbara Tedlock (ed.), *Dreaming: Anthropological and Psychological Interpretations.* Santa Fe, NM, 154–170.

Bruce, Robert D. 1979. *Lacandon Dream Symbolism: Dictionary, Index, and Classifications of Dream Symbols.* Mexico.

Burke, Kenneth. 1966. *A Rhetoric of Motives.* New York.

Conn, Richard. 1982. *Circles of the World: Traditional Art of the Plains Indians.* Denver, CO.

Davidson, D. 1986. "A Nice Derangement of Epitaphs." In E. LePore (ed.), *Inquiries into Truth and Interpretation: Perspectives on the Philosophy of Donald Davidson.* Oxford, 433–446.

Degarrod, Lydia Nakashima. 1989. *Dream Interpretation Among the Mapuche Indians of Chile.* Ann Arbor, MI.

Du Bois, John W. 1986. "Self-Evidence and Ritual Speech." In Wallace Chafe and Johanna Nichols (eds.), *Evidentiality: The Linguistic Coding of Epistemology.* Norwood, 313–336.

Geertz, Armin W. and Michael Lomatuway'ma. 1987. *Children of Cottonwood: Piety and Ceremonialism in Hopi Indian Puppetry.* Lincoln, NE.

Graham, Laura R. 1986. "Three Modes of Shavante Vocal Expression: Wailing, Collective Singing, and Political Oratory." In J. Sherzer and G. Urban (eds.), *Native South American Discourse.* Berlin, 83–118.

———. 1995. *Performing Dreams: Discourses of Immortality Among the Xavante of Central Brazil.* Austin, TX.

Grim, John A. 1983. *The Shaman: Patterns of Religious Healing Among the Ojibway Indians.* Norman, OK.

Guiteras-Holmes, Calixta. 1961. *Perils of the Soul: The World View of a Tzotzil Indian.* New York.

Guss, David. 1980. "Steering for Dream: Dream Concepts of the Makiritare." *Journal of Latin American Lore* 6, 297–312.

Hail, Barbara A. 1980. *Hau, Kóla!: The Plains Indian Collection of the Haffenreffer Museum of Anthropology.* Providence, RI.

Hallowell, A. Irving. 1975. "Ojibwa Ontology, Behavior, and World View." In Dennis Tedlock and Barbara Tedlock (eds.), *Teachings from the American Earth: Indian Religion and Philosophy.* New York, 141–178.

Hanks, William F. 1993. "Metalanguage and the Pragmatics of Deixis." In J. A. Lucy (ed.), *Reflexive Language: Reported Speech and Metapragmatics.* Cambridge, 127–157.

Hedges, Ken. 1992. *Welcome the Caribou Man: Tsonakwa and Yolaikia.* San Diego, CA.

Hofling, Charles A. 1991. *Itzá Maya Texts with a Grammatical Overview.* Salt Lake City, UT.

Hunt, Harry T. 1989. *The Multiplicity of Dreams: Memory, Imagination and Consciousness*. New Haven, CT.

Jacobsen, William H. 1986. "The Heterogeneity of Evidentials in Makah." In Wallace Chafe and Johanna Nichols (eds.), *Evidentiality: The Linguistic Coding of Epistemology*. Norwood, 3–28.

Kracke, Waud. 1992. "Myths in Dreams, Thought in Images: An Amazonian Contribution to the Psychoanalytic Theory of Primary Process." In Barbara Tedlock (ed.), *Dreaming: Anthropological and Psychological Interpretations*. Santa Fe, NM, 31–54.

Laughlin, Robert M. 1976. *Of Wonders Wild and New: Dreams from Zinacantan*. Washington, DC.

Lincoln, Jackson Stewart. 1932. "Indian Dreams: Their Significance to the Native and Their Relation to the Culture Pattern." MA thesis, department of anthropology, University of California at Berkeley.

Mannheim, Bruce. 1992. "A Semiotic of Andean Dreams." In Barbara Tedlock (ed.), *Dreaming: Anthropological and Psychological Interpretations*. Santa Fe, NM, 132–153.

Maybury-Lewis, David. 1974. *Akwe-Shavante Society*. New York.

Merkur, David. 1985. *Becoming Half Hidden*. Stockholm.

Merrill, William. 1988. *Rarámuri Souls: Knowledge and Social Process in Northern Mexico*. Washington, DC.

Modesto, Ruby and Guy Mount. 1980. *Not for Innocent Ears*. Arcata.

Oswalt, Robert L. 1986. "The Evidential System of Kashaya." In Wallace Chafe and Johanna Nichols (eds.), *Evidentiality: The Linguistic Coding of Epistemology*. Norwood, 29–45.

Price, Robert F. and David B. Cohen. 1988. "Lucid Dream Induction: An Empirical Evaluation." In Jayne Gackenbach and Stephen LaBerge (eds.), *Conscious Mind, Sleeping Brain: Perspectives on Lucid Dreaming*. New York, 105–134.

Radin, Paul. 1936. "Ojibwa and Ottawa Puberty Dreams." In *Essays in Anthropology Presented to A. L. Kroeber*. Berkeley, CA, 233–264.

Rasmussen, Knud J. V. 1931. *The Netsilik Eskimos*. Copenhagen.

Reid, Howard. 1978. "Dreams and Their Interpretation Among the Hupdu Maku Indians of Brazil." *Cambridge Anthropology* 4, 1–28.

Ridington, Robin. 1988. *Trail to Heaven: Knowledge and Narrative in a Northern Native Community*. Vancouver, BC.

Rorty, Richard. 1989. *Contingency, Irony and Solidarity*. Cambridge.

Rumsey, A. 1990. "Wording, Meaning, and Linguistic Relativity." *American Anthropologist* 92, 346–361.

Schlichter, Alice. 1986. "The Origins and Deictic Nature of Wintu Evidentials." In Wallace Chafe and Johanna Nichols (eds.), *Evidentiality: The Linguistic Coding of Epistemology*. Norwood, 46–59.

Siskind, Janet. 1973. "Visions and Cures Among the Sharanahua." In M. J. Harner (ed.), *Hallucinogens and Shamanism*. London, 28–39.

Smith, Theresa S. 1995. *The Island of the Anishnaabeg: Thunderers and Water Monsters in the Traditional Ojibwe Life-World*. Moscow, ID.

Spencer, R. F. 1959. *The North Alaskan Eskimo*. New York.

Stromberg, Peter G. 1993. *Language and Self-Transformation: A Study of the Christian Conversion Narrative*. Cambridge.

Tedlock, Barbara. 1981. "Quiché Maya Dream Interpretation." *Ethos* 9, 313–330.

———. 1992. "Zuni and Quiché Dream Sharing and Interpreting." In Barbara Tedlock (ed.), *Dreaming: Anthropological and Psychological Interpretations*. Santa Fe, NM, 105–131.

Van Eeden, Frederick. 1969. "A Study of Dreams." In C. Tart (ed.), *Altered States of Consciousness*. New York, 147–161.

Vecsey, Christopher. 1983. *Traditional Ojibwa Religion and Its Historical Changes*. Philadelphia.

Vogel, Virgil J. 1970. *American Indian Medicine*. Norman, OK.

Walker, James R. 1980. *Lakota Belief and Ritual*. Lincoln, NE.

Wasson, R. Gordon, George Cowan, Florence Cowan, and Willard Rhodes. 1974. *Maria Sabina and Her Mazatec Mushroom Velada*. New York.

Watson, Graham and Jean-Guy Goulet. 1992. "Gold In; Gold Out: The Objectification of Dene Tha Accounts of Dreams and Visions." *Journal of Anthropological Research* 48, 215–230.

6

Mythic Dreams and Double Voicing

Dennis Tedlock

When we interpret the dreams of others, the process of interpretation has always already begun before we get there. At the simplest level, this means that we begin our interpretation when the dreamer has already formulated a narrative, one which may have been reformulated through successive retellings. But there is more to it than that. Before the narrative comes the rethinking of the dream by the awakening dreamer, and before the dream is even over comes the dreamer's interpretation of its ongoing events, an interpretation that may even include the realization that what is happening *is* a dream. But instead of treating prior interpretation as an obstacle to be overcome, I want to take it seriously as a phenomenon in its own right. And instead of trying to capture the dreams of others as they are told immediately afterward by the same individuals who dreamed them, as if to minimize prior interpretation, I want to attend to the ways in which others tell dreams that happened long ago to dreamers long gone.

Similarities between dream narratives and mythic narratives have often been remarked, but here we will be dealing with myths whose episodes *include* dreams. Among other things, such myths provide us with examples of dream reports that have been canonized by tradition. But we need to do more than simply extract these dreams from the stories in which they occur. By following closely the practices of the narrators, and especially the manner in which they weave dream episodes into longer narratives, we should be able to discern cultural differences in the construction of the boundary between the dreaming and waking worlds. At the same time we might catch a glimpse of the processes, usually hidden, whereby past dreams become mythologized and past myths offer themselves to future dreamers.

Waud Kracke observes that myth "as a series of vivid images depends on inner visualization for its communication and impact," so that "myths are constituted in a spatial-sensory modality like that of dreams."[1] I agree with this statement as far as it goes, but the emphasis on the visual domain may be culture-specific. It seems to me that we neglect the auditory domain in general and speech in particular, not only as tellers and interpreters of dream narratives, but even as dreamers. Our visual bias shows up as clearly in dream laboratories as anywhere else. Indeed, to "qualify as a dream, most workers agree," the report of an awakened sleeper must be "visually imagistic."[2] Such reports are most likely to be produced by REM (rapid eye movement) states, while non-REM states are more likely to produce reports that workers set aside as examples of "thinking" rather than "dreaming," or as "conceptual" rather than "perceptual."[3] There seems to be an unexamined assumption that the inner voices involved in thinking can be reported without ever having been perceived. As for the study of myths, a curious neglect of speech shows up there as well. In texts collected from oral traditions, quotations of dialogues among the characters typically take up half or more of the telling, but when Western analysts retell such myths they typically omit all quotations, as if the dialogues were something other than events.

Over wide areas of Native North America, there are oral traditions in which the experiences of the characters include dreams or visions that are either explicitly identified as such or strongly implied by contextual details. The actors appearing within these dreams may include gods or animals or spirits, but the dreamers are nearly always living human beings. Such stories are easiest to find among tribes in which ordinary people expect and even seek visionary experiences, and where such experiences may even be a marker of passage into adulthood. The result of a successful dream or vision is spiritual power that finds expression in a ritual, one whose performance may benefit not only the dreamer but others who may be ill or otherwise in need. But there are other tribes in which overtly marked dreams are rare or nonexistent among the events of stories, and dreamlike episodes are told as if they took place in waking life. Wherever this is the case, spiritual power is likely to be concentrated in the hands of secret societies, priestly guilds, or privileged kin groups, as on the Northwest Coast and in the pueblos of the Southwest. In such societies even autobiographical narration may require that dream episodes be encoded as waking experiences, if unusual ones.[4]

Among the openly vision-questing nations, there are some stories whose main purpose seems to be the presentation of a dream. In other stories dreams may occur even though they would seem to be unnecessary, given that the waking events are already thoroughly mythic. The characters who have the dreams live in a past that may be distant but in most cases is not at the distance of a prior world. One of the effects of openly narrating the dream as a dream is that it then becomes an experience of the kind a person of the present day might still have, rather than being confined to an age of miracles. At the same time, the interpretation of the meaning of the narrated dream is of a type that can still be applied, by analogy, in present-day life.

In the larger temporal scheme of a story with a dream in it, the dream itself is typically told at the time it happens rather than being held back until the awakened dreamer or returned visionary might tell it to the other characters. For the narrator, telling the dream as it happens involves something more than extending the reach of third-person omniscience into the world of someone else's dream. A dream may be told so much from the point of view of the dreamer that it almost seems as though the teller had been the dreamer, even though the narrative stays in the third person. This effect is partly produced through the "inner visualization" mentioned by Kracke, but it also requires inner audition. It is what literary critics call the free indirect style or double voicing, in which the voice of the narrator resembles the voice of a character without the use of direct quotation. Such voicing gives evidence of a process in the mind of a narrator that has a certain kinship with lucid dreaming. Both the double-voiced storyteller and the lucid dreamer must allow the simultaneous presence of two kinds of consciousness, one of them open to the flow of imagination and the other selective and even directive. The difference is that a storyteller whose imagination becomes too active may lose track of the plot, whereas a dreamer who becomes too purposeful may disrupt the flow of images and even wake up.[5]

The Dena'ina of Alaska are among the North American nations whose stories are sometimes centered on dream episodes. The example I quote from here, from Cook Inlet, was told by Peter Kalifornsky.[6] It concerns a hunter who is plagued by mice that keep ruining the meat he brings home. "At night when the man went to bed," we are told, "the mice ran all over him. Then when he finally went to sleep, the man had a dream." The important point here is not that the hunter goes to sleep despite the mice, but that sleeping in the presence of the mice will have an effect on his dream. "He dreamed about an open country: no ridges, no mountains, no trees as far as one could see." In other words, the hunter finds himself far from the place where he went to sleep. "There were all kinds of people all around. And there was a lady seated in front of him there." At this point the dreamer might continue as a spectator, treating all this as something he just happens to be watching, and remaining unaware that it is a dream until he wakes up. But in Native American terms such an outcome would merely demonstrate his incompetence as a dreamer, and that is not what dream stories are about. To be a successful dreamer he must move beyond the role of observer to the extent of realizing that the particular woman he finds in front of him should have an important message, one that is meant specifically for him and one that he must remember when he wakes up. This would seem to require a step beyond what dream researchers call quasi-lucidity, in which he could be aware that he is dreaming and yet remain a nonparticipant.

"I know you," the woman says to the dreamer. He remains inactive in the sense that he says nothing in reply to her, but just the occurrence of this "you," and his acceptance of its reference to himself, brings him to the threshold of participation in his dream. The narrator returns to describing the scene: "There were people there, but their faces were made differently than human faces. The woman was beautiful." In giving these and other details, such as the description of the treeless landscape, the narrator seems to be participating in the imaginal world of the dreamer. Indeed, if the dreamer were to give his own report of these aspects of the dream later on in the story, he could use the same words the narrator is using now.

The woman speaks to him again, addressing him in his role of hunter: "The way you are now is bad, and as a result you will have a very hard time. You have smashed the animals' bones and thrown them where the people walk on them. When the animals return here, they have difficulty turning back into animals." By the standards of ordinary Western dream experiences, this part of the dream seems doubly unusual: not only does the dream woman speak coherently and at some length, but she has begun turning the hunter's dream into a self-interpreting one. We may suspect that the narrator is speaking with a double voice again, this time combining a dream report with an interpretation someone might make after hearing the report, but it is difficult to know to what degree this might be the case. After all, we are dealing with a culture whose members are taught that figures appearing in dreams are to be understood as bearers of verbal messages. This suggests a cultural difference in the relative values placed on what dream researchers divide into REM and non-REM states. However that may be, there does seem to be a difference of values in the matter of lucidity. Laboratory researchers tend to celebrate lucid dreamers who take an active and even aggressive role in the dream world, whereas the dreamers celebrated in stories such as the present one are similar to a field researcher who has found the ideal informant.

The dreaming hunter continues his silence, but he also continues to pay attention to the messenger before him. To show him the results of his bad hunting practices, "she gestured, and the place turned into a different country. It was populated by horribly disfigured animals. There were people there who were tending to them." The sudden change of scene fits our own expectations of the dream experience, but the interpretation continues: "These are my children," says the woman. "Look what you did to them. You scorched off their skin with hot water." Then she changes what the hunter sees a second time: "Now look where you came from—the sunrise side," and he does so. The ability to shift the gaze is reported by lucid dreamers in our own culture,[7] but the directional mapping of the hunter's shift suggests a lucidity in which Native American cosmological consciousness is at work. We are dealing with a whole family of cultures in which noticing direction plays an integral role in the remembering and recounting of experience, and there is no obvious reason why lucid dreamers in these cultures should not pay attention to the orientation of dream events. In the case of the Dena'ina and many other North American nations, a dreamer's sense of orientation could be aided by the fact that the proper sleeping position is with the feet eastward. Assuming that the body of the sleeping hunter is properly oriented, the woman in his dream is not only turning his gaze back in the direction where his body lies, but aligning him with the axis of his body.

The dreamer now sees that the woman and himself "were at a land above the human land, which was below them to the east. And all kinds of people were coming up from the lower country, and they didn't have any clothes on. When they arrived, they put on clothes, and when they did, they turned back into all kinds of animals again." These transformations are the stuff of dreams again, but again the woman offers an interpretation: "The Campfire People," meaning human beings in the lower land, "take good care of us. They take our clothes for their use, and if the humans treat us with respect, we come here in good shape to turn into animals again," which is to say that the animal spirits, which have human form, put on animal clothes again. "We will be in good shape if the humans put our bones into the water or burn them in the fire."

Both the images and speeches of this dream are almost complete at this point, but there remains the narrative task of awakening the hunter. It is hard to imagine how this could be carried off any better than it is by the present storyteller: "As she was talking to him, the woman was standing behind him," which puts her west of him and means that she has been west of him the whole time, and that he turned his back to her when he looked eastward from his position in the land of the animals to the human land. Now, "when he turned to look at her, he saw a great big mouse sitting there. And the man got scared and startled, and he woke up." Seeing the dream woman as a mouse erases the boundary between dreaming and waking, and the man finds himself back in the place where he went to sleep while mice were running over him.

There is a kind of dream incubation in this story, if unintentional on the part of the dreamer, which depends on a notion that spirits are immanent in nonhuman beings, and that they are capable of representing themselves as humans. Similar incubations take place in stories told by the Arikara of North Dakota. In a story told by Alfred Morsette, the protagonist is a boy who is very ill because he hasn't been able to hold any food down for a long time.[8] A hunter in his family bags a wild boar, but the boy can do no more than look at the meat. "Later, after it got dark," we are told, "everyone went to bed. But the meat lay there. Everyone else had already eaten some of it." The narrator wants us to remember that the meat is still lying there in the dark while they all go to bed, including the one person who looked at it but did not eat. The presence of the meat, like the presence of the mice in the previous story, will have an effect on the course of events.

"And while this boy slept," the story continues, "he had a dream." Again the narrator tells the dream rather than waiting for the awakened dreamer to tell it. His first sentence is double voiced, in the sense that the awakened dreamer could have said the same thing: "A man came into the lodge." In the next sentence the narrator seems to tilt the balance toward the position of an omniscient observer: "Then the man came up to the boy where he lay on his bed, where he lay there sick." We could take this to mean that the narrator is claiming to observe the dream and the dreamer at one and the same time, but a more interesting possibility is that he is indirectly representing the boy as having a lucid dream. If this is correct, it means that it is the boy who is to be understood as doing two things at the same time. He sees a dream figure enter a dream lodge, but he recognizes this lodge as the same as the one in which he is sleeping, and he is conscious of the position of his real body in the lodge where the meat of the boar is also present.

What happens next is that the dream figure speaks to the dreamer, revealing himself as the spirit of the boar: "Now I have come. I want you to know. You were staring at me while they butchered me. But now it is my fate that you people must eat me, and you were wishing to eat some meat, but you were afraid to do it. Whenever you eat anything, you just vomit it up. Now I am going to doctor you." Again, as in the previous story, the dream figure speaks coherently and at length, turning the boy's dream into a self-explanatory one. And again, this could be a case of double voicing in which a dream report is combined with what would actually be a postreport interpretation. But the fact remains that a dreamer in this culture has been taught to treat the figures appearing in dreams and visions as messengers and bearers of gifts. The boy does not move from his place or say anything, so he is very much a dreamer, but he treats what the dream visitor says as addressed directly to him.

At this point the dream figure demonstrates a ritual for the boy. I describe the action as a demonstration because the boy, as a lucid dreamer in a seeking tradition, understands the figure's actions as something more than an accidental event he just happens to be witnessing and may not bother to remember. "And then this man who had come inside knelt down," the narrator tells us. "Then he brought out a wooden bowl. He put something in it, whatever it was." This last sentence seems to be a small concession to the fact that even a dream experience of this kind has its fuzzy areas or gaps. "He set it down. Then he put water in it. Then he stirred it. As he stirred it, it got foamy. It looked like soap suds." It is part of the boy's lucidity to understand these actions as something he himself should perform later on, in waking life. Other things could be going on in the dream, potential sources of distraction, but the dreamer is looking for actions that could be usefully repeated.

Here the man resumes speaking to the boy: "Now, I am going to pity you." This statement is a formulaic one, widely employed in accounts of dreams and visions in Plains Indian cultures. It is always followed by a gift of power to the dreamer. We might be tempted to assign it to the discourse of dream representations rather than of dreams, but its use is so consistent in the narratives Plains dreamers hear and tell all their lives that there seems no reason to doubt they could hear someone say it in a dream, when it would mark the events in progress as a dream while at the same time reminding the dreamer not to wake up just yet. In our own culture, one of the things lucid dreamers report as alerting them to the fact that they are dreaming is the recurrence of a visual cue that has become a marker of the dream world for them.[9] Here again we would seem to have a cultural difference, with a Western focus on the visual and a Native American attunement to the auditory.

Once the figure in the boy's dream has uttered the formula, he gets straight to the matter of his gift to the boy: "Now I want you to drink this. When you drink it, you'll have this song. Then there will be nothing the matter." So the gift is a method for curing the illness of not being able to hold down any food. "When you drink it, you'll begin singing this song. Now then there isn't going to be anything wrong with you—and you'll be well if you aren't afraid to do what I'm telling you to do." This will require a new kind of participation by the dreamer, but one that permits him to remain on the threshold of action. He has been listening to what was said to him and watching what was demonstrated for him, and now he will accept a drink. This will require him to get out of his prostrate body to the extent of sitting up, but not to leave his sick bed. As the experience of a lucid dreamer, it would seem to be a *half* out-of-body experience.

The narrator represents the boy as responding to the man's offer of a drink in his thoughts rather than as speaking out loud. The words he thinks to himself are double voiced in the sense that they could just as well have been spoken to the man: "It doesn't matter. I barely live from one day to the next. Well, I guess I'll drink it." When the boy has consumed the foam, the man says, "I'm the one you have drunk up here. I'm the one. It is nothing for me to eat anything. I don't know of any time when I ever threw something up. When I eat something, I eat it. Now you are going to be that way." Thus the dream figure gives a human voice to a boar, an animal that eats anything at all with impunity. "Now this song is the one you're going to sing. When you're about to eat, you'll sing this one in your mind." The words of the song go this way:

Now I'll be the one when you drink;
When you go around,
When you go around,
Then you'll drink me.

At the end of the story the narrator adds a detail that got left out here: "He was dancing while he was seated," moving in time to the song without getting out of bed. Here the dreamer, still only halfway out of his body, reaches his most active level of lucidity.

Having remembered to remember the song and the movement, the boy awakens. He calls for his mother and tells her, "Put water into a wooden bowl! You'll stir that tongue around in it." In specifying what should be put in the water he is engaging in an act of interpretation, since the man in the dream only "put something in it, whatever it was." The choice of the boar's tongue fits both the gift of the song and the goal of being able to eat anything and hold it down. "When it gets foamy, I'll drink it," says the boy, and when he drinks he sings the song to himself and dances while seated. In drinking what his mother has prepared and in dancing he acts in the waking social world, but in singing the song to himself he reenters the world of his dream. The inner voice he hears as he sings would be a double one, both his own and that of the spirit who sang, "Now I'll be the one when you drink." Here we would seem to be dealing with a waking dream, one that reverses the lucidity of the sleeping dream.

In another Arikara story told by Alfred Morsette, the protagonist is a young man whose wife has disappeared.[10] He tries to find tracks out on the prairie, an act that removes him from the social world even while he remains awake. Finally something happens: "While he was searching around, there lay something on the ground!" Notice the double voicing here, in which the narrator expresses the seeker's surprise without departing from the third person. "It was the remains of an elk that had apparently been there a long time," he goes on, speaking in a voice that could be that of the young man telling his own story. "The skull was there with the horns still on it." Next the narrator quotes the inner speech of the seeker: "They always say, 'Elk, you are holy.' Perhaps you might pity me." The wording is indirect, with the first sentence referring to any elk and the second softened with "perhaps," but it has the effect of a question addressed to this particular elk. The seeker is still awake, but like the dreaming boy who responded to the man who offered him a drink, he thinks these words rather than speaking them. He is, after all, communicating not with the elk's bones but with its spirit, just as the boy communicates with the boar's spirit. He also makes vocal sounds, but these are the nonverbal sounds of a person crying for a vision, "there where the elk's bones lay, going around them and crying." Like the boy who learned something while dreaming in the presence of the boar's meat, the young man hopes to learn something in the presence of the elk's bones.

This time the storyteller does not specify that his protagonist dreams, perhaps because the crying is sufficient to set the stage. The transition goes this way: "Oh, finally he was satisfied. He lay down and slept. A man touched him." This sounds a little like a hypnagogic hallucination at sleep onset, which can be terrifying. But if this dreamer wakes up, he does so only in the sense of entering into lucidity. He has after all been seeking a visitation, and he expects that the man who has touched him will have a message meant for him. Like the spirit of the boar in the boy's dream, the spirit of the elk addresses him directly: "Now, I've come to tell you. I know what you are seeking. You're seeking your wife. Your wife is not lost." Then he reveals the existence of an abductor: "Why, now he's overstepped his limits. A black bear is the one. He took your woman." At this point, instead of demonstrating what the young man should do, the spirit helper describes the steps he must take to liberate his wife and other women taken by the bear. The key item he needs for his quest, the equivalent of the sick boy's combination of a song and a boar's tongue, is revealed as follows: "You should ask your father to make you an elk whistle, one that imitates the sound of an elk." Then the dream ends with even less of a transition than it began: "'Now do these things quickly! Hurry!' Then this young man started out." The narrator never does state that he awakens from the sleep mentioned earlier, perhaps because his adventure will carry him into a thoroughly mythic space, one where he will take the form of an elk and gore the bear. The closest thing to an awakening is his return to his village with his liberated wife, there to resume a normal life.

A different handling of the passage from waking into dreaming can be found in a story told among the Mandan, neighbors of the Arikara. The version quoted here was narrated by Mrs. Good Bear, and it concerns a young woman named

Corn Silk.[11] Because her parents scold her for remaining single too long, she sulks. "When night came, she went outside and lay on top of the doorway of the earth lodge to sleep and would not go into the lodge that night. She went to sleep." This is the point at which someone touched the young man in the previous story, but what happens to Corn Silk is this: "When she awoke, someone was carrying her on his shoulders, and she knew that someone had her in his power. She couldn't get away." Leaving aside the statement that Corn Silk awoke, she is like the dreaming Arikara boy, aware of her body but unable to do much more than pay attention. If we interpret her awakening accordingly, it is not her exit from sleep but rather the onset of her lucidity. Instead of staying with her physical body except for sitting up, like the boy, she is having a fully out-of-body experience.

Corn Silk continues her quiescent awareness of her captor: "They went along until they came to his lodge. He put her in a bed, thinking she was asleep, but she knew everything that happened." In this dream world, so far, it is the dreamer who takes the role of the spirit immanent in a body, but she has not yet revealed herself. As Mrs. Good Bear continues the story, she doubles her voice with that of the observing dreamer: "Then there was another woman, an owl, and a large grizzly bear in the lodge." It is at this moment that Corn Silk realizes for the first time that a grizzly bear is her captor. Just how she senses this is hard to judge, since both characters in the lodge seem to be ambiguous in form: one of them is "a woman, an owl," and will later be called "Owl Woman," while the other is "large," as indeed grizzly bears are, but will later be referred to as "the man." Perhaps she is understood to have had an experience like that of the Dena'ina hunter, who saw for himself that spirits with human form can have animal bodies.

What happens next draws Corn Silk toward greater participation in her dream: "The man asked Owl Woman to cook something for Corn Silk, and she began to prepare food." At this point the dreamer is merely overhearing a reference to herself, but then Owl Woman says, "Corn Silk, you should get up and eat." Like the dreamers who heard the word "you" in the other stories, she accepts its reference to herself, here backed up by her very name. She has been awake, or rather lucid, the whole time, but her participation in her dream increases in the manner of someone who has been awakened from sleep and is getting her day started: "Owl Woman brought water for her to wash with, and then she ate." After this comes a whole series of horrifying adventures in which Corn Silk leaves this dream lodge and slowly finds her way back to her own, acquiring various powers from animal spirits along the way. On her return she does not search for her physical body and reenter it, as out-of-body dreamers (Native Americans among them) sometimes do, but is rather represented as walking home in her own body. If we were to insist on reconciling this event with what happened early in the story, we could interpret the awakening that took place as she was being carried away from her lodge as a real one, though her experience is described as that of a lucid dreamer. In fact it is her second awakening, when Owl Woman fixes breakfast for her, that sounds like a real one, but this is the one that is described as false. Such is the trickery whereby a storyteller may evoke dream phenomena to open a path into a mythic realm, but then, after keeping a character in that realm far longer than any dream could last—for days or years, even—substitutes a homecoming after a long journey for an awakening from a dream.

The story doesn't end with Corn Silk's return. People start disappearing from the village each night, and a young man decides to do something about it. He leaves the village, saying, "I will fast on the hills and see if I can find out what it is all about," which is to say he is seeking a vision. "He cried all day," Mrs. Good Bear tells us, "and a snowstorm and blizzard came up toward evening." She goes on to say what he saw and heard from his hilltop, but without letting us know whether or when he might have slept or awakened: "In the night during the storm twelve buffalo bulls came along under the hill walking in the snow." So far, he could be seeing actual buffalo, or he could be having a waking vision of buffalo in the snowy darkness, or he could be having a lucid dream in which he sees (and counts) buffalo while remaining aware of the position of his body. In any case the voicing is double, with the narrator using the same words the seeker could have used in reporting such an experience. "They were walking toward the village," she says next, which brings us (and the young man) to the realization that these buffalo are the reason the villagers have been disappearing each night. Then we (and he) get a closer look at them: "Each had a flat board about two feet long with hoofs, lungs, and a heart tied to the handle." Now they have become buffalo dancers who carry wands in their hands, and the young man, being a competent dreamer, is taking note of details that could be usefully reproduced.

Here the narrator increases her distance a little: "They stopped at the foot of the hill near the young man, circled around, and sang their song." Of course he remembers what he sees and hears, later instituting a dance that marks the end of the disappearances. Only toward the end of the story does the narrator refer back to his experience on the hilltop as a "dream." Perhaps this is simply because she has already stated that he was fasting in hopes of such an experience, but it does alert us to the possibility that storytellers in traditions such as hers might sometimes be aware of dream episodes in stories but let them remain implicit. She says nothing about whether the young man was asleep or awake when he witnessed the buffalo performance, but Native Americans in general place no particular value on the distinction we cling to by contrasting "dreams" with "visions." The point is rather to try to understand something even before the experience is over, and remember to remember.

In the myths of the Northwest Coast it is sometimes stated that a character has a dream, but in such cases the dream itself is not narrated. Conversely, when a fully narrated episode has the earmarks of a dream, there is no explicit reference to dreaming. In a Kwakiutl story from British Columbia, told by George Hunt,[12] the pretext for such an episode is not sleep but a near-death experience, and the darkness of a cave substitutes for the darkness of night. It is a cave used by harbor seals, at a place called Hollow Point, and the only way a hunter can get inside is through a hole in the ceiling. He needs a partner to lower him into the cave with a rope, haul out the seals he kills, and let the rope down one last time to haul him out. But when a man named Day Hunter is ready to come out of the cave, his jealous younger brother Night Hunter hauls him partway up and then cuts the rope. In the words of the narrator, "Day Hunter fell on the rocks of the beach inside the seals' sleeping cave. Day Hunter knew that his belly had split open, because his intestines were scattered over the rocks. But his mind remained steady." The hunter's fall into a cave with no way out is very much like a nightmare, but instead of escaping by means of a literal awakening he follows a path some of our own researchers have found to be therapeutic for nightmare sufferers,[13] entering into a lucid state. His awareness of his body and its location in the dreamscape resembles that of dreamers in the Arikara and Mandan stories.

Next we are told, "He lay as if dead where he had fallen." This doubles the narrative voice with the perspective of the seals, who think they are looking at a corpse, but the "as if" keeps the conscious subjectivity of Day Hunter in play as a third element. He turns out to be like Corn Silk, who observed Owl Woman and her grizzly bear husband in their home by pretending to be asleep, only he pretends to be dead. "He heard many men speaking to each other, talking about how he had dropped down. All the men were glad that someone they called Keeps Us Sleepless had died from a fall, so said the voices he heard. Many men gathered around him." These, of course, are the seals in their spirit form. In the Northwest the spirits of sea mammals have their own names for human individuals, and this dreamer has already won a great gift by overhearing the name the seals have given him. Now he hears someone shouting from a distance, "What are you crowding around over there?" Someone beside him replies, "Keeps Us Sleepless fell down into our house. Now he is dead over here." Then the distant voice comes back, "It serves him right that he is dead." Note that this sequence locates the dreamer in space but is entirely auditory.

In reaction to the conversation among the seals, "the heart of Day Hunter became strong, so that he stood up quickly on the rocks." Thus he becomes an actor in his dream, but only after gathering useful information. The quickness of his act gives him a glimpse of transformations: "Some of the seals had no time to dress in their sealskins. Many of them had time to dress." But the dreamer takes no further action: "Day Hunter just stood there waiting for the men to speak to him or kill him." Like the dreamers in the other stories, he expects that the figures before him might say something for his benefit, even though his dream started off as a nightmare and continues to be dangerous. In keeping with the formalities of the highly stratified societies of the Northwest, the immediate seal response to his new status as a live visitor is an indirect one. The local chief, whose name is Seal Face and who has a round quartz crystal on the nape of his neck, makes a speech: "Oh, people of my village, we have been profaned by our friend Keeps Us Sleepless, because now he has seen that we are people like him. Go on, ask him! Does he not want us to set him right?" In effect this is an offer of a cure, like the cure given to the Arikara boy by the spirit of the boar.

Like the sick boy, the injured Day Hunter remains an inactive dreamer in the sense that he thinks his response rather than speaking out loud. But instead of quoting the dreamer's thoughts, as the Arikara narrator does, this Kwakiutl narrator now quotes a seal man who reads the dreamer's thoughts. The man in question, "who had wonderfully good hearing," is in the crowd standing around Day Hunter. In reply to Seal Face's question about whether the injured hunter wants to be cured, the mind hearer says, "It is his desire that you do so, chief." Another man now fills a feast dish with the "water-of-life," from a pool near the corner house posts. "The man sprinkled it over Day Hunter's body. Day Hunter was put right. His wounds healed up." Here, then, is the cure, but there is more to be gained. The seal men, like the buffalo dancers seen by the Mandan dreamer, possess powerful objects, but instead of studying them with the intent of making copies, Day Hunter will be portrayed as taking an object with him when he leaves the cave. Here is a case of mythologization, and yet the part of the story that takes place inside the cave is realistically dreamlike (if one can say such a thing) in its details.

The chief speaks again: "What does our friend want for his spirit treasure? Will he not take the property grower?" Day Hunter, still unable to speak out loud, "thought that he did not want it," and the mind hearer conveys his thought. Next the chief asks, "Will he not take the carved house posts and that pool of water-of-life in the corner?" This time the narrator quotes both Day Hunter and the hearer, one of them thinking, "What is the use of it?" and the other saying, "What is the use of it?" The chief, becoming annoyed, makes his third and final offer: "Does our friend want the death-bringing wand?" Day Hunter thinks, "That is what I want, a death bringer," and this time his spokesman, expanding his role to that of a psychoanalyst, says, "That is what our friend chooses, the death-bringing wand, so he can take revenge on his younger brother." In holding out for a greater and greater gift, Day Hunter is playing the power game as it is often played in North American myths of questing heroes, but many such myths lack the obvious trappings of dreaming that this one carries. Unlike heroes who are portrayed as fully awake and ready for action, Day Hunter makes no threats but simply stands his ground as a desirous dreamer.

Like Corn Silk, Day Hunter acquires some additional powers on his way back to his village and arrives in the flesh. It is when he is standing in a canoe offshore, about to demonstrate the death-bringing wand to the villagers, that we learn he was given a song to go with it. By waiting for this moment to sing it the narrator puts his audience (and us as his readers) in the position of the villagers, whom Day Hunter addresses as "commoners." I will not quote the song, but will only say that when Day Hunter finished singing, the villagers saw him point the wand at four different mountains, each of which burst into flames. Thus his achievement as a returned dreamer went beyond the mere establishment of a new ritual. This ending is consonant with the political purpose of the story, which is to claim great power for the hereditary chieftainship of which Day Hunter is the founder. Among other things, the story has the effect of giving his descendants property rights to power dreams involving harbor seals and the cave at Hollow Point.

In a Yana myth from the mountains of Northern California, as told by Sam Batwi, a dreamer brings his entire dream into the waking world and affects everyone who lives there.[14] In stories of this kind, rare outside of California, a dream takes place in a previous world, one whose inhabitants are not the same as present-day human beings. This Yana example is exceptional in another way as well: the dream is not told by the narrator at the time it happens, but is rather told afterward in the quoted words of the character who dreamed it. His name is Wildcat, and he lives in an era when today's animals had human bodies and animal spirits, the reverse of their present situation. One day he goes out in the woods with his wife and their baby to gather pine nuts. Climbing a pine tree to knock down the cones, "he shouted back down to his wife from above, 'Are they big nuts?' Said the woman, 'Yes! Knock them all down!'" In this exchange he and his wife are in a one-to-one waking relationship, and it continues for a bit longer: "He threw down pine cones. 'There!' He threw them down again. 'There!' 'Yes!' the woman said." But then something odd happens: "In his heart, they say, Little Wildcat spoke to her, calling down to her from up above." He is still thinking of himself as "calling down to her," but now he does this "in his heart," using an inner voice, and "the woman's not answering." He has put himself in the position of a dreamer who can think words but not speak them, but his wife is not reading his mind.

"Hey-hey!" thinks Wildcat. "What could be happening to me that my sleep is so bad?" A bad dream is what he has on his mind, but for the moment he goes on knocking down pine cones and using his audible voice only to say "There!" each time they fall. Meanwhile, with his inner voice he says, "I dreamed during the night while I was sleeping: I dreamed about tearing myself down in pieces. I threw down my shoulder, I threw down my other shoulder, I threw down my thigh, I threw down my other thigh." This story comes from a culture in which the best way to prevent a bad dream from coming true is to tell it to other people,[15] but Wildcat goes on keeping his dream to himself. Meanwhile his wife busies herself pounding the fallen pine cones to get the nuts out of them, with the baby lying nearby in its cradle. "I dreamed about throwing down my backbone. I dreamed that I ran all over as nothing but my skull. I dreamed about it." Here is an out-of-body experience that takes on the shape of a horror story, and it is about to come true.

Finally the woman looks toward Wildcat: "Blood was dripping down from the pitch-pine tree. The woman was afraid. The woman ran away home. Wildcat hopped around by himself up above, nothing but a skull. The woman ran off without her child." From this moment on, Wildcat's bad dream becomes everyone else's. His skull, a human one, comes down to devour the child and then rolls and bounces all over the world with the sound of a high wind, killing everyone who crosses its path. Finally Coyote, disguised as an old woman, stops it. This woman is the first person ever to ask Wildcat (or his skull) why he acts the way he does, and for the first time he tells his dream out loud. She then claims she once had a patient with the same problem, and that she "helped him to be a person again." Describing her curing procedure, she says such things as, "I gathered some wood" and "I made a fire down in the fire pit." But then she starts using the second person, saying such things as, "Next, I put you down in the fire pit." The skull, being highly suggestible, says, "Let's see you do it to me!"

Now, were it not for the fact that Wildcat is already a dream incarnate, so to speak, and were it not for the fact that the old woman is really Coyote in disguise, the scene before us would be the kind in which a dream figure imparts a gift of curing knowledge. What Coyote does, of course, is to burn the skull, making the future world safe from Wildcat in his person as an actual human skull. But Coyote's trickery isn't quite as bad for Wildcat as it sounds. The narrator doesn't bother to say what would be obvious to his Yana audience, but the situation with animal bones is the same here as among the Dena'ina, where we started. Wildcat will never regain the fleshly human form he had before he dreamed himself into his future, but in the next era, when wildcats have animal bodies and hunters burn their bones, their spirits will be able to put on wildcat clothes again. Still, a human dreamer might be confronted with the spirit of the original mutilated Wildcat, the rushing skull. When such a nightmare happens, the best course is to remember the story. Instead of waking up one should ask the skull, in one's thoughts, what it has to say.

The dreaming that takes place in these Native American stories has visual and kinesthetic features of the kinds we ourselves associate with dreaming. But all these dreams also have an essential auditory dimension, one that includes speech or song or both. Moreover, what is said in these dreams often goes a long way toward making them self-explanatory. We cannot know, finally, to what extent this is a result of the processes involved in the mental storing and retrieving of dreams, or in the formulation and transmission of the longer narrative sequences in which dream episodes occur. But what we do have, staring us in the face (or ringing in our ears), is dreaming constituted as a cultural project that is very different from ours. In the laboratory version of our project, readers of dream reports give high marks to vivid images. It may indeed be the case that somehow, at bottom, human dreaming in general really is as overwhelmingly visual as so many researchers believe it to be. In that case we could say that Native American dreamers have set themselves the cultural task of thinking their way upstream in a biological current, altering the dream experience by means of lucidity—or, better, a "wonderfully good hearing" for which we have no name. Another possibility is that our very definition of the dreaming experience, neurological and otherwise, has been culturally shaped all along, and that Native Americans are talking about an overlapping but somewhat different array of experiences. These are visual, yes, but they also partake of sound and speech.

Here I am left with the image the wakeful Coyote saw when he confronted the skull of Wildcat, the dreamer gone wrong. "He's just lying there, big-eyed," says the narrator, doubling his voice with the inner voice of Coyote. "He just sat there as nothing but his eyes."

Notes

1. Kracke 1992: 32.
2. Webb and Cartwright 1978: 238.

3. Ibid.: 239.

4. It may be that one way to disguise dream experiences is to narrate them as waking omens; for possible examples see Tedlock 1995: 140.

5. On the effects of excessive control on lucid dreaming, see Hunt 1989: 120.

6. Kari 1994: 116–117.

7. LaBerge 1985: 62.

8. Parks 1991: 319–323.

9. LaBerge 1985: 113.

10. Parks 1991: 270–275.

11. Bowers 1950: 319–323.

12. Berman 1994.

13. LaBerge 1985: 162–166.

14. Luthin 1994: 728–736.

15. For other Native American examples of this practice see Kracke 1992: 33; Tedlock 1992: 118.

References

Berman, Judith. 1994. "Night Hunter and Day Hunter." In Brian Swann (ed.), *Coming to Light: Contemporary Translations of the Native Literatures of North America.* New York, 250–272.

Bowers, Alfred W. 1950. *Mandan Social and Ceremonial Organization.* Chicago.

Hunt, Harry T. 1989. *The Multiplicity of Dreams: Memory, Imagination, and the Unconscious.* New Haven, CT.

Kari, James. 1994. "Six Selections from Peter Kalifornsky's *A Dena'ina Legacy.*" In Brian Swann (ed.), *Coming to Light: Contemporary Translations of the Native Literatures of North America.* New York, 110–123.

Kracke, Waud. 1992. "Myths in Dreams, Thought in Images: An Amazonian Contribution to the Psychoanalytic Theory of Primary Process." In Barbara Tedlock (ed.), *Dreaming: Anthropological and Psychological Interpretations.* Santa Fe, NM, 31–54.

LaBerge, Stephen. 1985. *Lucid Dreaming: The Power of Being Awake and Aware in Your Dreams.* Los Angeles.

Luthin, Herbert W. 1994. "Two Stories from the Yana." In Brian Swann (ed.), *Coming to Light: Contemporary Translations of the Native Literatures of North America.* New York, 717–736.

Parks, Douglas R. 1991. *Traditional Narratives of the Arikara Indians: Stories of Alfred Morsette: English Translations,* vol. 3. Lincoln, NE.

Tedlock, Barbara. 1992. "Zuni and Quiché Dream Sharing and Interpreting." In Barbara Tedlock (ed.), *Dreaming: Anthropological and Psychological Interpretations.* Santa Fe, NM, 105–131.

———. 1995. "La Cultura del Sueño en las Américas." In J. J. Klor de Alva, G. H. Gossen, M. León-Portilla, and M. Gutiérrez Estévez (eds.), *De la palabra y obra en el Nuevo Mundo,* vol. 4, *Tramas de la identidad.* Madrid, 127–170.

Webb, Wilse B. and Rosalind D. Cartwright. 1978. "Sleep and Dreams." *Annual Review of Psychology* 29, 223–252.

III

Mediterranean

Classical and Late Antiquity

7

Dream Interpretation in a Prosperous Age?

Artemidorus, the Greek Interpreter of Dreams

Christine Walde

> I think that in general it is a good plan occasionally to bear in mind the fact that people were in the habit of dreaming before there was such a thing as psychoanalysis.
>
> —*Sigmund Freud*

Dreams and Dreaming in Greco-Roman Antiquity

In contrast to modern society and culture, in Greco-Roman antiquity dreaming and dream interpretation played a central role in a wide range of contexts.[1] In the Asclepian cult practice of incubation,[2] the dream was considered a sphere of communication shared by the god and the dreamer. The topic of the discourse was almost exclusively disease.[3] While sleeping in the temple, ill people were spontaneously restored to health by the god in their dreams, or received sometimes clear, sometimes encoded instructions for furthering the healing process. The dream was perceived in this particular function but was not the object of systematic research, although cases of healing that the priests recorded in praise of the god, always comprising the dream experience, might have allowed for this, too.

Physicians of secular medicine, such as Hippocrates, Rufus, and Galenus, also tried to evaluate the dream experiences of their patients—often in connection with the doctrine of the four humors or other criteria—as a supporting tool for the diagnosis of physical and mental illness. They could not do without a close scrutiny of the connection between dreams and state of health, yet research into the subject did not go beyond describing certain irregularities in the machine of the human body.[4]

Philosophers of all epochs tried to explain the source and significance of dreaming. Aristotle, the Stoics, the Epicureans—all came up with totally different explanations: dreams had their origin in exterior reality, or were caused by divine influence, or by the dreamer's psyche, or the functions of his or her body. Each of these explanations had an impact on the interpretability of dreams, that is, the question of whether they have a deeper meaning. Beyond this, dreams as an experience of virtual reality had epistemological implications, calling into question the validity of sensory perception and the human sense of reality. But even if in philosophy the experience of dreaming served apparently as a starting point for exploring some fundamental human problems, the results were not then reapplied to the phenomenon of the dream.

In magic, dreams and dream interpretation were the object of sympathetic praxis: magicians tried to provoke a certain dream image (and with it a certain materialization), or to control the behavior of other people through dreaming, or to use dreams to gain suprarational knowledge, for example, from the god or about the nether worlds.[5]

Within the Greek understanding of dreams, the key role belonged to mantic dream interpretation (or divination by dreams). To give a prognosis about future events, professional dream interpreters deciphered "ordinary" nocturnal dreams, when these could be classified as meaningful by specific criteria.[6] Although philosophers of all schools argued about the sense or non-sense of mantic dream interpretation, and the telling and interpreting of dreams are very popular themes in nearly every literary genre, we clearly still know very little about this widespread practice of interpretation—because the only (and subjective) testimony by a real dream professional offering us some more substantial information is the *Oneirocritica* (OC) of the Greek author Artemidorus (second century A.D.).[7]

The dream, or the observation that everyone dreams every night, was apparently a subject that could be approached from many different angles. We can explain this by the fact that the different approaches are based on the supposition of various dream types, or that they are focusing only on one or several phases of the dream phenomenon, that is, the formation of the dream; dreaming itself, along with the experiences the dreamer seems to have while dreaming; the dream narrative; reactions to the dream; and, of course, a dream interpretation (the last depending on the dream's assumed origin). These complementary approaches offer a complete picture of the dream in antiquity only when taken together. In fact, advocates of the different concepts of interpretation rarely disputed each other's legitimacy. For the real gap, rather than being located between the complementary models of explanation, lies between the assumption of interpretability and non-interpretability. Formulated more generally: it is between, on one hand, the presumption of a seamless continuum between the waking world and the dreamworld, so that the activities and perceptions of the waking state are simply carried forward to another level of consciousness; and, on the other, the presumption that dreams can be connected with another or higher truth hidden to those awake (hence the discontinuity of dreaming and waking).

The Epicureans advocated the most radical form of continuity and thus were the enemy incarnate for all those promoting interpretability.[8] This is because the Epicurean denial of divine influence on human life led directly to the denial of divination, including dream interpretation. For the Epicureans, dreams either originated in the continuous bombardment of the sense organs by atoms—a process that continued during sleep—or were simply a reflex to physical or sensory stimulation, or else the continuation and processing of daily activities upon another level of consciousness. Though the Epicureans had a deep insight into the connection between dream and dreamer, they did not go any further in their investigation of the body-mind phenomenon of the dream, toward what could have resulted in an understanding of what Freud would later call the "psychic apparatus."[9]

The Epicureans, in any case, represented a minority position. Even Aristotle, who thought dreams were primarily a result of external impressions made on the sense organs during sleep, conceded that dreams could be used for medical diagnosis. He also could not deny that some dreams announced the future, though, rationalizing, he preferred to explain this as mere coincidence.[10] For Aristotle also, despite all his doubts regarding divination through dreaming, the dream retains the quality of a space of significance, at once an alternative to the waking state and potentially useful to that state.

Particularly in his short treatise concerning *Diagnosis from Dreams*,[11] the physician Galenus, who lived approximately in the same time as Artemidorus, asserts that dream interpretation alone cannot serve as a reliable diagnostic tool, since a clear-cut distinction between the different dream types (meaningless, useful for medical purposes, prognostic) is not simple. His belief in distinct dream types was, it seems, solid enough to derive something like a division of labor in dream interpretation; when he believed he was faced with dreams belonging to another specialist's competence, he did not hesitate to refer the dreamer elsewhere. But he also accepted a less rational usage of dreams, believing, for instance, that in very serious cases of illness only divine intervention—dream healing—could help. In addition, he reports dreams of his father prophesying his son's medical career. But he himself was inspired by dreams to practice a spectacular method of operating, still presently in use.[12] According to his personal experience he could not, and would not, irresponsibly reduce the meaning of apparently polysemantic dreams to bodily stimulations or to signs showing the future. Therefore his motto could have been: "What can be observed is also correct" or perhaps even "*Anything goes.*"

The diviner Artemidorus carefully defines his own field of research as "allegorical" dreams that can be used for divination.[13] He nonetheless considers almost all other kinds of work with dreams as legitimate, if unequally useful (OC 4, 22). He approves of the way both the Asclepian cult and secular medicine use dreams, as long as the priests and doctors do not simply offer their interpretations in order to impress or take advantage of their naive clients. He even grants a role to the philosophers in this domain, although he does not expect any practical use of their reflections (OC 1, 6); but he strictly rejects dream manipulation through magical practices.

We thus see that in antiquity various ideas for both explaining and using the dream phenomenon coexisted, not readily reducible to a single, coherent conception. Even Aristotle's monistic approach is only one voice in this discourse. Because of this typological variety, the ancient Greeks were able to look at the dream phenomenon with less prejudice[14]—which made it possible to register the significance dreams could have for the awakened dreamer. Based on this typology of dreams, Artemidorus's *Oneirocritica* succeeded in describing—both encyclopedically and (with regard to his practical interest) systematically—the accumulated knowledge about dreams of his time.

Artemidorus

Artemidorus was born at the beginning of the second century in the culturally vibrant city of Ephesus in Asia Minor. He was a contemporary of the Emperors Hadrianus, Antoninus Pius, and Marcus Aurelius, as well as of the rhetor Aelius Aristides and the physician Galenus. Most of the evidence we have about the ancient understanding of dreams was handed down from this period, which saw the Roman Empire at its widest expanse, as well as the transition from pagan polytheistic religion to Christian monotheism.[15]

We know nothing about Artemidorus's education or social status, but can simply infer from his *Oneirocritica* that he was a very erudite man, and probably quite wealthy. He could already look back on at least 1,500 years of dream interpretation. The comprehensiveness and high standard of the *Oneirocritica* endow him with a double role: not only did he bring the pagan tradition to its culmination, but he also served as the mediator of classical dream research for both the Middle Ages and modern times.

The work's five extant books[16] display a unique linkage of theory and practice, and, as one would hope from a good textbook, Artemidorus presents, *en passant*, a profile of the perfect dream interpreter. Books 1 and 2 focus on the theoretical implications of dream interpretation, followed by a catalogue of dream elements and their possible contextualization. Artemidorus's enumeration follows the order of human life: he begins with the dream image "birth" and ends with the image of "death." Books 3 and 4 are an answer to those who found fault with the first two books but also contain supplements to and comments on the list of dream elements. In Book 4 Artemidorus attempts a synthesis of the preceding books; independently of special dream elements, he describes, on a theoretical level, the logical connection between dream elements and waking life. Book 5 is of a different nature, containing nearly 100 dreams and their "fulfillment" as exercises in analogy for the dream apprentice.

The *Oneirocritica*—the only extant work of ancient dream interpretation[17]—

has had an astonishing reception. Preserved after the pagan period in numerous Byzantine manuscripts and Arabic translations,[18] it was considered, from its widespread Latin translation in the Renaissance down to the eighteenth century, as the most exemplary scientific study of dreams. It was one of the first books to see print along with the Bible; a German edition (1597) actually goes back to Philipp Melanchthon.

One can distinguish roughly two lines of reception:[19] On one hand, in Roman Europe Artemidorus's *Oneirocritica* was transmitted in the form of epitomes, as excerpts for household use; many of the dream books still circulating in Italy can be traced back to these texts.[20] They reduce the Greek author's highly complicated interpretative system to standard symbolic meanings and leave out his general observations concerning dream formation. But the *Oneirocritica* also continued to be consulted by dream theorists and serious investigators well into the eighteenth century; we must not judge Artemidorus's work only in terms of popular reception. Despite the new approach of experimental dream research and its accomplishments, even Freud in his *Interpretation of Dreams* (1900) spoke of his ancient predecessor as an important, if unscientific, ally of his own method.[21]

Following this rather ambivalent evaluation, the approach to Artemidorus in the secondary literature has frequently, and fatally, been linked to psychoanalytical dream interpretation.[22] It seems to me, in general, that in evaluating Artemidorus, much depends on the observer's intention or ideological stance. Both the experience of resentful discussions and the reactions to various lectures I have delivered on ancient dream theory have convinced me that more is at stake here than either Freud or Artemidorus—namely, the question whether the interpretation of dreams, particulary Freud's, is really a serious field of research. In this context the ancient approach of divination is not considered for its own sake but is rather misused for the sake of assessing or disqualifying modern dream interpretation, the statements ranging from "all said before, nothing new" to "pure superstition" (the latter being either continued or overcome by Freud).

In fact, Artemidorus would be as out of place in our century as Freud would be in classical antiquity. From our vantage point, their respective concepts of the world are completed models, which we can neither add to nor subtract from. A high degree of sensitivity to differences between periods and cultures is consequently required here: we need to make allowances, *sine ira et studio*, for the discrediting of mantic praxis in later times, while always keeping in mind that our sense of this praxis has been distorted by the modest number of ancient testimonies at our disposal. Frequently, our understanding of what actually took place is only superficial, since a hasty identification with present-day esoteric practices interferes with a balanced estimation. But in classical antiquity divination had an entirely different significance than at present. It would be too easy to dismiss it—under the influence of Christianity or the natural sciences—simply as a form of superstition, particularly in an effort to formulate a history of mentalities pertaining to dreams and dreaming.

To evaluate Artemidorus's achievement, we need first to accept divination as a nonnegotiable basis for his pursuit of knowledge and then to take into account the intended goals of the *Oneirocritica*. In any event it serves no purpose to simply point, condescendingly, to the mantic context of Artemidorus's insights into the essence of dreams, in order to demonstrate their unscientific or nonserious nature.

The more complex aspects of divination—which is the attempt to investigate the connections underlying fate and the cosmos through natural and artificial means—constituted both an ancient mode for mastering life and a way of gaining knowledge or insight that, in the context of its time, can in no way be dismissed as irrational; at most, it might be considered extrarational. All disciplines of divination—whether reading intestines, augury (observing bird flights), or palmocritics (reading the lines in the hands)—are founded on an extreme determinism. The diviners believed that the course of fate, which a divine power has planned in minute detail, is manifest in recognizable fashion in a cosmic sympatheia running through all parts of the world, and that through observation and investigation, fate can be made predictable to a certain degree. These disciplines lay claim to solving the riddle of the future by reading the world's phenomena as a text—one either conveying direct statements about the future or making indirect suggestions of events to come. Artemidorus's interpretation of dreams is thus not simply a means of prognosis (explaining future, past, and present events) but also an imposing reservoir of knowledge about things of the world and their interdependence; thus his hermeneutic explanation of the world has its rightful place alongside the natural sciences.[23]

Of course not all amateur or professional dream interpreters had the far-reaching ambitions of Artemidorus or the Stoics, who even integrated divination into their philosophical system. But Artemidorus should not be measured against the standards of the *harioli impudentes*,[24] who made a fortune by deceiving credulous clients. Nor is a rehabilitation of Artemidorus as a "scientist" necessary, at least in the present essay; that would involve the question of what "science" is, a problem alien to the ancients in such a form. All we can do is to listen to Artemidorus himself and to what he has to say about his obsessive investigation into dreaming (OC 1, pref.):

> I . . . have not only taken special pains to procure every book on the interpretation of dreams, but have consorted for many years with the much-despised diviners of the marketplace. People who assume a holier-than-thou countenance and who arch their eyebrows in a superior way dismiss them as beggars, charlatans, and buffoons, but I have ignored their disparagement. Rather, in the different cities of Greece and at great religious gatherings in that country, in Asia, in Italy and in the largest and most populous of the islands, I have patiently listened to old dreams and their consequences. For there was no other possible way in which to get practice in these matters.

At the end of Book 3 Artemidorus adds the following: "I have thus in every respect passed through the school of experience, since I undertook nothing other than dedicating myself to dream interpretation, day and night." This lifelong theoretical and practical occupation with dreams enabled Artemidorus to write the *Oneirocritica*, a systematic textbook of dream interpretation. The work shows a highly secularized approach to the topic, and a claim to enlightenment that should not be underestimated. Like all diviners, Artemidorus wants to alleviate the fears of men and women, who cannot foresee the course of their lives. In addition he wants to purge dream interpretation of its occult or mystic tinge and lift it up to the standard of an applied science. But it seems to me that in striving for knowledge and for a rational penetration of his subject, Artemidorus goes far beyond mantic dream interpretation. He has higher goals, namely, the explanation of dreams, dream types, dream formation, and the possibilities for using dreams; moreover, he is engaged, as well, in a struggle to adequately describe his findings.

When the *Oneirocritica* is compared with later dream books such as the *Somnium Danielis*,[25] the independence of its descriptive and linguistic taxonomy becomes evident. Artemidorus had to find a language appropriate to his subject, that is, the connection between dreams and the waking world. This involved evaluating and presenting both the dream images and their potential realizations (empirically collected material) according to specific criteria. Neither the language of poetry nor philosophical terminology was suited for this purpose. Using philosophical terms, for instance, would have evoked highly specific concepts of thought and made necessary a definition of the particular meanings conveyed by specific terms. Since constantly evoking such a theoretical framework was impracticable, Artemidorus established his own terminology of different dream types (OC 1). Beyond this, he declared that he was not concerned with a philosophical approach, which in any event was incapable of solving the "problem" of dreams. Implicit in his choice of language is both a rejection and a reformulation of methodological and theoretical procedures.

By evaluating dream narratives and following up his client's life history, Artemidorus tried to find a logical connection between the dream world and the waking world, in order to explain the images of the night and render them useful for various ends. We can by no means reduce his method to setting up simple analogies between dream elements and future events; rather, Artemidorus works with numerous methodological extensions of context, such as the experiences and emotions of his clients, and facts and concepts of the natural sciences, linguistics, and literature. His dream interpretation is not only based on cosmic determinism, but also postulates the uniqueness of every single dream, since it is influenced by the life, character, education, and so on, of the dreamer.

Since Artemidorus opts for a tradition of dream interpretation differentiated according to the type and origin of the dream, he has to define his domain of research through the evaluation and classification of all sorts of dreams—including those which cannot be used for prognosis. Artemidorus tried to find a methodological approach to dreams, which, while adapting itself to each individual case, was by its nature repeatable and verifiable. He thus took account of the exigencies of a field of research that we might term "the dream and its place in human life"; this meant reconciling hypotheses about dream formation with others about the effects and contextualization of dreams in the waking state. The dream, understood as both a collective and an individual, intrapsychic and physiological phenomenon, together with its interpretation, takes its place (to use present-day terminology) somewhere between the natural and the cultural sciences. The dream cannot be seen independently of the dreaming subject; neither a specific dream image nor the capacity to remember dreams can be stimulated in an experimental situation. Therefore, the dream researcher has to have recourse to his own dream experiences as well as to those of others, with the proviso that translating the dream images into language only produces secondhand information concerning the actual, unobservable process. The neutral, professional service of dream interpretation, based on a demystified divination, provides the standardized conditions that scientific distance requires; simultaneously, it furnishes the necessary number of research objects. For this reason, the fact that Artemidorus does not perform any experiments does not imply a lack of scientific standards. It rather suggests that his approach is not only linked with the natural sciences but is at the same time a hermeneutic one. Comparisons with the natural sciences or medicine ought, then, not to be turned a priori to Artemidorus's disfavor:[26] in regard to the juncture of theory with practical application, the praxis of dream interpretation takes the place of empirical studies and experiments. We can observe a similiar procedure in the empirical school of medicine of Artemidorus's time.

Medicine and dream interpretation are circumstantial sciences that cannot gain direct access to the phenomena they are concerned with. They must rely on symptoms, clues, small signs, and inferences, juxtaposed and connected according to a specific hypothesis concerning their meaning.[27] To be sure, this observation applies equally to Freud's psychoanalytic interpretation of dreams. From this vantage, granted the very different contexts, the interpretative methods of Freud and Artemidorus gain a certain proximity. A detailed description of this proximity, particularly manifest in the praxis of interpretation, is the focus of the following discussion—doubtless an abrupt change of scene, impossible without a foreshortening of perspective.

Artemidorus and Freud

Today dream research is no longer based on a typology of dreams. Instead, we observe a preference for monistic explanatory models.[28] The study of dreams is still concerned with the same fundamental topics as in classical antiquity: the origin and interpretability of dreams, or put more neutrally, the significance of dreaming. Experimental dream research and psychoanalytical dream interpretation, understood not as contrary but as complementary approaches, treat the subject in different ways.

Experimental dream research seeks to track down the origins of dream formation in the brain and to map out the physiology of dreaming. Such physiological research is not interested in the impression a dream can make on an individual, inducing its interpretation or narration. Once the conclusion was reached that dreaming is primarily a physiological phenomenon, the question of its sense and meaning for humans in the waking state seemed pointless.[29]

In his *Interpretation of Dreams*, published in 1900, Sigmund Freud took a position completely opposed to that of strict natural science, predominant in the late nineteenth century; he also rejected the appraisal—prevalent in intellectual circles at least since Romanticism—of dreams as a means for reaching insight beyond Enlightenment rationalism. Aware of his own achievements and his status as an outsider, he took a step back from the contemporary scientific stance, thus drawing close to the impartiality and speculative curiosity of the pagan dream interpreters (based in folk belief, from his perspective), who considered dreams to be fundamentally interpretable structures. But in a brilliant reapplication of the discoveries of his age, Freud connected this insight with the explanatory model of the natural sciences, thus going beyond divination, Christian morals, and natural science. He overcame the determinism of both divination and Christian eschatology, replacing them with the determinism of the human psyche. This concept marks the greatest difference between Freud and ancient theory: on one side, messages from the gods; on the other, the "message" from the Unconscious. It is Freud's contribution to the Enlightenment that the Unconscious is not conceived as an exterior power, like the pagan gods or fate (or the Christian God), but is rather located within the human being. It is, however, not so readily perceptible as to have outgrown the numinous, but in fact operates as an éminence grise that even determines the existence of the proud Ego, so very sure of its rationality, in its waking state. In this respect the Unconscious certainly has, once again, a divine or demonic character, because in Freud's schema the Ego is still very much decentered. In place of a generally valid course of fate, there is the fate of the individual psyche, not so entirely unalterable, but at least as pitiless as the gods.

In the setting of a psychoanalytic cure, dream interpretation can be understood as an entrée to the patient's unconscious processes, but it is clearly distinguishable as an individual element in psychoanalytic technique—in fact as the core or seed of analysis itself. The interpretation takes place in conversation and interaction between analyst and client. But on a metatheoretical level, Freud also included hypotheses from natural science concerning the origin of dreams and the mechanisms of their formation. By this methodological marriage of scientific and hermeneutic approaches, Freud hoped to prove that "a dream turns out to be a meaningful psychic structure, with its appropriate place in the mind's waking activity,"[30] but also that, on a more abstract plane, its interpretation allowed conclusions concerning the operation of the entire psychic apparatus. For Freud the latent content of a dream is always wish fulfillment (or its opposite), which is encoded by the dream work, even if the manifest dream image points to other, less important meanings. He saw scientific progress precisely in this rigorous reduction to one explanation of the latent dream content.

In every respect, worlds separate Freud, the founder of modern nonexperimental dream interpretation, from Artemidorus, the theorist of dream divination. They do not share the same cultural background, and their relationship certainly cannot be defined in terms of "classical antiquity as the forerunner of modernity." This is particularly so since Freud's direct contact with Artemidorus appears to have been modest, and numerous transformations in intellectual history took place in the centuries between them. Still, we should not judge a comparison between these dream interpreters as pointless[31] just because of their different intellectual contexts, since this would deprive us of precious insight into the dream phenomenon itself. In fact, stated provocatively, Freud and Artemidorus both discovered a comparable approach to dreams, which takes into account the nature of the phenomenon as well as the possibility of its investigation. This tells us something about the dream as an object of research, which, from the perspective of the researcher, has remained relatively stable. A consequence of this continuity is that a typology of dream interpreters (or dream researchers) could be established. And, indeed, there are remarkable parallels not only between the prefaces to Freud's and Artemidorus's books on dreams, but also in the general tenor of their arguments. The vagueness of what is being investigated drives both of them to a sober meticulousness, systematization, and rationalization as counterweights to the dreams' fantastic and enigmatic qualities. Neither Artemidorus nor Freud show any interest in the manifest dream images (those pictures and sensations that arise while dreaming); both take them simply as starting points for interpretation, or as bearers of a message not identical with the visual images.[32] Both of them fashion themselves as dream interpreters par excellence; their argumentation thus sometimes reveals an almost unbearable dogmatism. Perhaps their truth claims can be explained in this way: since the dream as an individual product nonetheless remains strange and mysterious even to the dreamer, and since many empirically unconfirmed explanations have already been suggested, they believed that the mystery required a solution, once and for all.

The difference in perspective between Freud and Artemidorus is a result not of the object of their research, but of their differing sociocultural contexts—that is, of the significance dreams had in their respective societies. Freud removed the dream from the experimental laboratories of the natural scientists and put it back into a doubtless narrow context of interpretation—the setting of the psychoanalytic cure. He stakes no claims to a special social function for his interpretation of dreams (I am not referring to psychoanalysis in general and its possible wider applications). This context also determined the choice of clients for dream interpretation—individuals who had to cope with short- or long-term psychic or psychosomatic problems, were members of the Viennese middle and upper classes, and had hopes for an improvement in or explanation of their problems. Freud, however, claimed a general human relevance for his ideas, because, on the one hand, certain phenomena were simply more manifest in the neurotics he examined than in the average neurotic human being; on the other hand, he thought he had an objective foil to the clinically derived material in his own self-analysis, which actually was the nucleus of *The Interpretation of Dreams.*[33]

If we take Artemidorus's word for it, his clientele were not members of any particular social group, nor did he focus primarily on people who were physically ill or those with manifest psychopathological symptoms. The chief aim for those using his services was certainly not self-knowledge or self-realization. We actually discover among them the entire spectrum of his contemporary society, since for many people the various disciplines of divination had the status of a psychohygienic "technique for existence" (Foucault). Because there are no extant authentic records from clients, we can only speculate as to why dream interpretation possessed such long-lasting popularity. Probably the interpreter's success rate was of least importance. Along with an interpretation of the dream, those who consulted dream interpreters or other masters of prognosis perhaps needed help in making a decision or wanted to gain control of contingent events, or relief from hopes and fears, which makes sense in a time of poor medical care and risks connected with travel. Many of the interpretations do, indeed, concern the state of health or life expectancy of a client or someone else.[34] In Artemidorus's time, any decision was apparently preferable to none. Possibly, an unusual dream was a catalyst, or at least offered an opportunity for those not accustomed to self-reflection to talk about themselves with someone else. Perhaps it was, then, not very important if a prognosis actually came true. Significantly, Artemidorus himself did not see the dream interpreter's primary function in the act of interpretation itself. Thus in his description of the dream image "diviner, dream interpreter" (OC 3, 21; cf. 2, 20), we learn that

> if a man dreams that he has become a prophet and has been celebrated for his predictions, he will have experience in many areas and will take upon himself, in addition to his own anxieties, those of others. For the prophet is concerned not only with his own troubles, but also with those that are of no concern to him, the troubles brought to him by the people who seek his advice.

Artemidorus apparently kept in contact with his clients beyond the actual consultation;[35] many of them also seem to have consulted him more than once on their own initiative.

In spite of their different presuppositions, the object of research is fundamentally similar for both Freud and Artemidorus—another person's dream narrations. They not only interpret these in a particular setting for the sake of the client, but also evaluate them to promote their own research. Some methodological difficulties result from this situation. For one thing, as in any science based on evidence, the two researchers have to do with a reflected image of the phenomenon they are examining. The narration of a dream does not reproduce the dream's incoherent thought processes in pure form. When dream images, usually consisting of pictures, are transformed into language, the interpreter is already working with a mediated and rationalized construct. Its conciseness depends, of course, on the competence and credibility of the narrator. To this we should add that dream interpretation is a special case of interpreting texts or literature, which means that all problems inherent in the latter are problems of dream interpretation as well—above all the variety of meanings individual texts can have, or the dependence of interpretations on the perspective of the interpreter. Actually both researchers describe the relationship between dream text and the meaning behind it with concepts borrowed from rhetoric or poetics, and both interpret dreams through the language of narration. Artemidorus defines the significant dream as *allegorikos*, thereby evoking, from the start, the discrepancy between surface and deeper meanings; in Freud's vocabulary, mechanisms of dream work such as "condensation," "displacement," and so on, can be linked to metaphor, metonymy, and other tropes.

For both researchers, the research situation, which is not completely predictable and is subject to disturbances, requires backing up interpretations that necessarily vary from client to client by exploring the dreams of many people; it also requires balancing an apparent arbitrariness with consistently available hypotheses concerning the meaning of the dream. Since both see dreams as something concerning the entire human being, a simple dream narration, for example in written form, is sufficient for neither: their methods call for a situational, individual evaluation of the dreamer as well as for a supraindividual hypothesis of interpretation. For Freud, a constant revision of research results and the steady perfection of the consultant's art are defined in the juncture of research and treatment; in Artemidorus's case there is a similar linkage between research and consulting.

Both researchers introduce the communicative situation into their deliberations as at once the source of insight and the medium of its application. Whereas Artemidorus simply advises dream interpreters to take heed of their own spontaneous evaluation of the client and his situation (as a form of implicit professional knowledge), Freud, in the studies following his *Interpretation of Dreams*, enlarges the principle of directly observing the researcher (that is, usually, himself), resulting in the concept of transference—a concept that, however, no longer represents a specific feature of dream interpretation per se.[36]

Freud saw neither the transference nor the *fundamentum inconcussum* of psychoanalysis, the Unconscious, as the major difference between his method of interpretation and that of Artemidorus; the distinction lay rather in the setting of communication, which in psychoanalysis is dominated by the patient's associations. In the survey of dream literature, which was added to the fourth edition of the *Interpretation* (1914),[37] Freud stated that Artemidorus explained his clients' dreams without any input on their part (something which can be said about Freud's own alternative method of interpretation by symbols, developed under Jung's influence). But a careful reading of the *Oneirocritica*, apparently known to Freud only from secondary sources such as Büchsenschütz's *Traum und Traumdeutung im Alterthume*,[38] reveals a different story: Artemidorus's interpretations took place in a partly structured conversation, within which the client had to contribute to the evaluation of the dream by not holding back certain necessary information. The interpreter took both the motifs and elements of the dream in question and the real life of the dreamer as coordinates of the conversation. Although he might seem to lose contact with the manifest dream image by the sequence of associations or the interpretation of individual elements, he always had to reapply his results to the dual system of dreamer and dream image.[39]

For the sake of better defining this relationship, Artemidorus proposes, in the theoretical portion of the *Oneirocritica*, some questions meant to serve as the basis for exploring every dream image. In part, these concern the classification of dreams and their concrete significance in the life and future of the dreamer. But they also concern the nature and number of events to which the dream can be related. It is clear from the following example (OC 4, 30) that the interpreter has collected information about the client and sorted it out by using his professional expertise, in order to arrive at an interpretation:

> Many dreams come true for those whose characters are similar to the dreamer's and for his blood relatives and namesakes. For example, a woman who had a husband dreamt that she was married to another man. Since her husband was not sick, the dream did not signify that she would bury him and be free to marry another man. Since the woman did not have anything for sale, the dream did not signify that she, like a bride, would sign a contract. Since her daughter was not yet ready for marriage, it did not mean that she would give her in marriage and, in this way, see not herself but her daughter married to another man. Since she was not sick, the dream did not portend her death. For marriage and death signify one another because the circumstances surrounding both a marriage and a funeral are similar. She had a sister, however, with the same name, who was sick at the time and who died. And so what would have happened to her, had she been sick, happened to her sister whose name was the same.

Artemidorus did not deny that in many cases it was nothing but the dream interpreter's intuition that connected the dream with its fulfillment, possibly only after it had actually occurred (cf. OC 3, 64). Yet he could not arrive at even the simplest conclusions, including even the primary distinction between a significant and an insignificant dream, without the help of his clients, who had to give away very intimate details of their lives. Sometimes, however, the interpreter became a voyeur in his own interest (OC 4, 59):

> You must examine closely, moreover, the habits of men before the dream, that is, you must carefully inquire into them. And if you are unable to find out anything definite from their own mouths, you should put them aside for the present and find out about them from other people, so that you will not make a mistake.
>
> For example, someone dreamt that he practiced fellatio with his own wife. Another man, moreover, dreamt that his wife practiced fellatio with him. Even after a long time, none of the things that are signified by a fellatio dream, and which ordinarily happen to other men, actually happened to either of them. . . . Some time later, I discovered that both of the men were in the habit of practicing fellatio and of having mouths that were not clean. And so it was natural that nothing happened to them. For they were simply seeing the objects that ordinarily aroused their passions.

The dream, in Freud's view, is totally determined. As a consequence he has to rely on the patient's cooperation to define the contexts evoked by the dream or individual dream elements. This is particularly manifest in the interpretation of the Irma dream, which was part of his self-analysis.[40] Only after he has given a very detailed report about the circumstances of the dream and the parallels between waking life and dream experience, as far as he can recall them, does he offer an explanation of the dream's latent content. The other case studies from his psychoanalytic practice also show that the analyst, following specific guidelines, interrogated the dreamer about the differences and similarities between the waking world and the dream experience. Structurally, this procedure corresponds to Artemidorus's distinction between allegorical and meaningless dreams, but also to setting the dream in different contexts of the waking world in order to define its latent content. Particularly after his introduction of the symbol as a second pillar of the interpretative process, in the fourth edition of the *Interpretation*, Freud also confronts his clients with definite interpretations. One might well ask if Freud's statement that he made dream interpretation the client's task should be accepted only in qualified form—or even if it is mainly an ideal hardly realizable in practice. But here the answer rests with the psychoanalysts.

For both Freud and Artemidorus, the structure underlying the formalized conversation is constructed of implicitly or explicitly expressed hypotheses about the formation and composition of dreams: in practice, however, these are degraded to a metatheory (or metapsychology), which cannot be constantly referred to. Resting partly on personal empirical observation or on complicated hypotheses derived empirically, as well as from the tradition of research, this structure embodies the basic assumption of any dream interpretation: that beneath the surface of often bizarre, senseless, or even apparently unequivocal dream images, other significations may be hidden. Such an approach, however, rests necessarily on a complex sequence of presuppositions. In regard to these we can distinguish three different categories: (1) the stimuli from which dreams originate; (2) the material that is being processed; and (3) the mechanisms processing the material into the manifest dream image.

In the *Oneirocritica* Artemidorus describes in detail only the "allegorical" dream image. He does not contend that a god (or another power of destiny) delivers the message in the way the dreamer receives it. Rather, he states that the work of formation is achieved exclusively by the soul (OC 1, 2), which serves as the recipient of an external code or stimulus (whatever its nature my be). Nevertheless, each individual soul transmutes the message in a different fashion according to life circumstances, the surrounding culture, and the dreamer's level of learning. For Artemidorus, in converting the message into special images the soul plays the role of a censor. In contrast to Freud, this censorship has a positive connotation: dream messages are coded in order to prompt reflection in the dreamers about themselves and their place in the world. Here, as with Freud, the dream is simultaneously an object of interpretation (as a text) and an interpretation of the interpreter-dreamer (but this, in fact, holds true for almost every sort of dream interpretation).

Despite the external source of the stimulus, for Artemidorus the dream is still fundamentally an intrapsychic phenomenon. For this reason the encoding process can be reconstructed to a certain extent, with the client's help, and by comparison with things and events in the waking world. Artemidorus readily concedes that he does not know the final origin of these interconnections and that there are some factors of uncertainty, such as the precise time or number of the anticipated events. The interpreter's insufficient talent or lack of knowledge can be additional factors. Contrary to what many modern critics have asserted, such a confession of limitations is a sign not of Artemidorus's incompetence, but of the integrity of a researcher honestly interested in his subject.

In the history of dream interpretation, Artemidorus's approach occupies an intermediate position between antiquity and modern times. Taking recourse to the tradition of dream interpretation, he presents a typology of dreams according to their stimuli, in which he defines precisely the central subject of the *Oneirocritica*—allegorical dreams, which can be used to predict the future. According to his own account, he wrote other treatises—regrettably not extant—on all dream types evoked by various stimuli. Despite his vast and differentiated knowledge of dreams, he offers only rudiments of a comprehensive theory of dream formation; nor does he explore what Freud would later call the "psychic apparatus" more deeply than is necessary for his typology. But even if a typology of dreams has only a moderate scientific status, in his description of individual dream types Artemidorus reaches the level of general principles. For example, he explains that the meaningless dreams of people interested in dreams and their meaning are subject to similar, or even identical, principles of formation as the allegorical dreams of other people, operating just as much through encoding, condensation, and displacements (OC 4, preface). He might, of course, have transferred this hypothesis as well to dreams caused by physical or emotive stimulation. Artemidorus also observes that, in dreaming, only material that the dreamer has received previously can be used for encoding—something, he explains, that can be observed in the dreams of learned people (OC 4, 59).

We might thus formulate matters as follows: Artemidorus developed a verifiable, rational, and systematic research apparatus, taking into consideration probability, empiricism, the results of previous dream researchers, and a general determinism. This also includes the intuitions of the interpreter, who plays a significant role in the research situation, along with the willingness of the client to furnish personal information. This constellation of subjective and objective factors precludes the total petrification of research—an eventuality in any case inappropriate to the dream phenomenon, with its shifting phases and obvious multivalence.

As suggested earlier, in its details the picture Artemidorus draws of the transformation of the received message into a dream image shows certain similarities with Freud's "overseers" (*Werkmeistern*) of the "dream-work," that is, "condensation," "displacement," and "secondary elaboration."[41] But Artemidorus does not develop any general laws of psychic process, such as Freud's dream work, since on the one hand he is presenting a typology of dreams, formed according to different laws, and on the other, he does not understand dreaming as a purely intrapsychic event. Inasmuch as Freud's reading of Artemidorus clearly did not reach down to such details, we can assume that what is at work here is a structural parallel generated by the nature of the research object and by shared basic assumptions, for example, the distinction between latent content and the manifest dream image.

In his *Interpretation of Dreams*, Freud laid down general principles of the act of dreaming, which he understood as a model for the process of the entire psychic apparatus. In doing so, he gets rid of a typology of dreams and postulates instead the equal status of all dreams, all formed by the same mechanisms. Juxtaposed with Artemidorus's typological model, Freud's vision naturally appears to involve a more refined and differentiated understanding of dreams. While in his survey of dream stimuli and dream material Freud hardly goes beyond Artemidorus, his concept of dream work (that is, the interplay of mechanisms transforming the material into the structure of the manifest dream) constitutes an original discovery. Once deciphered, the dream, as a product of the Unconscious, no longer appears to be a rebus, but rather an organization of thoughts or a story, its essential function being to express a repressed wish or a number of such wishes. The dream's manifest content now simply presents a version, distorted by the censor, of what is actually being expressed: for Freud, the dream content is a translation of dream thoughts into another mode of expression, whose semiotic system and syntax can be learned through a comparison with the original.

Although Freud's research hypothesis addresses the psychic apparatus in its entirety, similarities with Artemidorus emerge when he applies his theories to the practice of psychoanalytic technique: to characterize the dream stimuli, Freud reverts to a typology of dream materials, which are responsible for the dream's individual quality. For, according to his concept of dream work, infantile experiences, recent events, and physical and sensory stimulation, as well as timeless symbolic representations, are placed in a new context in the manifest dream image. The latent content of a dream can only be discovered by explaining the origin of its materials.

But Artemidorus's method of dream interpretation is not simply based on a typology of dreams, their stimuli, and the material processed; it also sets the dream images and their meanings in relation to different contexts of the waking world. An allegorical dream need not exclusively concern the dreamer: Artemidorus knows other contextual categories such as political and cosmic dreams, pointing respectively to changes in political affairs or to cosmic anomalies such as earthquakes or total eclipses of the sun.

Already in the 1950s, Michel Foucault argued in his introductory essay to Binswanger's *Traum und Existenz* that Freud's explanation of dream activity was too narrow; it is not enough to explain the latent dream content exclusively in terms of masked wish fulfillment (something corresponding roughly to Artemidorus's category of emotional dreams). In a much later work, *Le souci de soi*, Foucault confirms this judgment of psychoanalytical dream interpretation, though without explicitly mentioning Freud. He shows that Artemidorus postulates a reciprocal representation of things; for example, sexual intercourse in a dream does not merely denote sexuality, but can also be related to different contexts not necessarily related directly to the dreamer. Freud, on the other hand, suspects sexual fantasies to be hidden behind superficially innocent activities performed in dreams, such as eating or flying; and this relation of signification is not reversible. As Foucault's German promoter Seitter put it aphoristically, playing on a famous phrase of Hölderlin's, Foucault seems to consider Freud's dream interpretation to be "*die richtige in dürftiger Zeit*" ("the right one for scant/scarce times").[42] This bon mot hardly does justice to Freud's importance, but neither does it speak to Artemidorus's accomplishment.[43]

The Greek dream researcher recognized the dream as a biological, cultural, political, and individual phenomenon. His interpretations are distinctly bound up with his clients' language, Greek; the meaning of the dream is determined by the surrounding culture. Negatively this means that neither the *Oneirocritica* nor Artemidorus's method of interpretation can claim universal validity. At most, someone living in a non–Greek-speaking country, but who knows Greek, could have used Artemidorus's theoretical remarks; he could *not* have translated the enumeration of dream elements schematically. Artemidorus was well aware of the ethnocentric quality of his interpretation (I use the term 'ethnocentric' positively). He even proposes a way to overcome it, advising the apprentice in dream interpretation to acquaint himself thoroughly with the manners and mores, flora and fauna, and so forth, of the country where he wishes to practice (OC 4, 4). Only in this way could he learn to define the connection between dream image and future event, always keeping in mind that the individual dreamer is a determining factor, as well. And since all such contexts have an influence on the dream's formation, the dream, inversely, can furnish information about contexts, in reciprocal interrelationship: in the dream, the dreamer mirrors the various contexts—cosmos, state, family, circle of friends—to which he is bound.

Freud does not consider social and cultural factors when he says there is nothing more egoistic, anarchic, and asocial than the dream.[44] Since, for the most part, he defines the effect of the dream within the framework of the entire psychic apparatus, he believes that his hypotheses can be applied to the dreams of all human beings, whatever their culture, period, and language. That in fact dream language depends on the language and culture of the corresponding waking world was something first recognized by those psychoanalysts forced to emigrate to non–German-speaking countries during the Third Reich.[45] Although Freud was fully aware of the variety of material from which the manifest dream image is formed (the day's residues, memories stored up but inaccessible in the waking state, physical stimuli, and so forth), he invariably sees the dream's deeper sense, its latent content, as a hidden wish fulfillment or its contrary. Given these limits, he no longer takes notice of the dream's role as an important mode of processing real life, influenced, among other factors, precisely by the social and cultural life of the dreamer.

In Artemidorus's open system of interpretation, dream narratives draw close to the mode of sociological evidence that—like literature or jokes—can be examined as mirroring or assimilating social processes. Although this was certainly not Artemidorus's aim, his work at least allows for this option. But investigations of this kind are rare even in our time. I know of two examples: in *Das Dritte Reich des Traumes*,[46] Charlotte Beradt portrays the process by which, before its eventual triumph, National Socialism's totalitarian system gradually made its way into the citizenry's dream world. And Ullrich Ahrens has recently completed a "secondary analysis of literature,"[47] meant to examine the dream and its sozialization from an intercultural perspective. This study evaluates all the ethnographic data available on dreams; "socialization" means the way the dream is treated by a specific ethnic group or culture.

Epilogue

Set against the experimental dream research now being conducted in Zürich under the guidance of Inge Strauch,[48] the methods of dream interpretation proposed by both Freud and Artemidorus seem to be of only historical interest. This, however, allows us in turn to reevaluate both Freud and Artemidorus in a manner that is free of bias. It is in any case striking that the latest methodological approach combines experimental research with interviewing the dreamers. This procedure, combining psychology and physiology, tries to verify hypotheses about the formation of dreams experimentally. Measurements of brain waves are juxtaposed with a precise evaluation of dream images and of the materials that seem to constitute them. The criteria of classification correspond to a remarkably high degree with those in Artemidorus—the social status of the dreamer, a comparison of dream and waking worlds, and so on.

As the starting point for further work on the meaning of dreams, we again have recourse to a dream typology, in which specific effects shaping dreams are studied along with clearly observable functions of the dream for the waking state: problem solving, inspirational dreaming, anxiety dreams, wish dreams, and so on. Being more rigorously oriented toward the dream phenomenon itself and its phases, this mode of dream research comes very close to Artemidorian dream interpretation in its potential openness, though there is, of course, no question of direct influence.

Still, for the time being, so-called psychophysiological dream research has consciously avoided offering definitive explanations for the dream phenomenon. Researchers are content to describe the dream as something depending to a high degree on waking life and, in particular, as a reflection of social processes and social status conveyed through the interaction of the dream ego and other dream elements.

It thus seems that there is yet no clear-cut answer to the question of the origin, meaning, and significance of dreaming. Or, as Theodor W. Adorno put it in his *Minima Moralia*:

> *Zwischen "es träumte mir" und "ich träumte" liegen die Weltalter. Aber was ist wahrer? So wenig die Götter den Traum senden, so wenig ist es das Ich, das träumt.*

> Epochs separate "a dream appeared to me" from "I dreamed." But which is more true? It is not the gods who send the dream, but it is not the Ego that dreams either.

Notes

My work on dream research began with a project at the Sigmund Freud Institute (Frankfurt/Main) on "The Heritage of Antiquity in Freud's Psychoanalytic Dream Research" (May 1990–September 1992 and December 1992–March 1993), funded by the Volkswagen Foundation in the Forschungsschwerpunkt "Antike in der Moderne."

1. For an excellent introduction to this subject, see Latacz 1984. On Artemidorus's epoch see Cox Miller 1994. (Cf. my short review, with certain reservations concerning method [Walde 1995]).

2. For instance in Epidauros (see Herzog 1931). On the background to incubation—the common practice of sleeping within a temple in order to receive a dream vision from the healing god—see Graf 1990 (with additional references). This use of dreams has a remarkable present-day sequel in Christian places of pilgrimage. On this tradition, see Deubner 1900.

3. Including tapeworm and abnormal pregnancies. Asclepius occasionally did offer help in cases lying outside his medical competence, such as the location of lost objects.

4. For an overview see Oberhelman 1983.

5. See Eitrem 1991.

6. In contrast to incubation or certain magic practices (e.g., placing laurel leaves under a pillow produces a specific dream experience) the dreams involved here were not supposed to be induced or anticipated in a fixed manner. On Artemidorus's attitude toward magic, see below.

7. Cited in text as (OC). I have made use of Pack's edition (1963). Throughout this chapter translated citations are taken from White (1975), with the reservation that sometimes his translation is superficial and not close enough to the Greek original.

8. See chapter 9 in this volume.

9. With the constant bombardment of the sense organs by atoms, the Epicureans were postulating an external stimulus that, in its haphazard and aimless nature, was meant as an antithesis to the divine and purposeful evocation of a specific image. From this perspective, the only usable criterion would thus be the connection between dream and dreamer.

10. The text *De somnis* discusses the origin of dreams from sensory impressions received in sleep. *De divinatione ex insomniis* treats the various forms of dream interpretation, which Aristotle—rather than refuting with concrete and provable arguments—views with healthy skepticism (see esp. 462b and 463b).

11. *De dignotione ex insomniis libellus*, in Kühn 1965, pp. 832–835.

12. Kühn 1965, 10: 609 (dreams of the father); 11: 315 (method of operation); 19: 18–19 (healing by divine interventions). Cf. Oberhelman 1983: 37–39.

13. OC 1, 2: "Allegorical dreams . . . are those which signify one thing by means of another: that is, through them, the soul is conveying something obscurely by physical means . . . . *Oneiros* is a movement or condition of the mind that takes many shapes and signifies good or bad things that will occur in the future. Since this is the case, the mind predicts everything that will happen in the future, whether the lapse of time in between is great or small, by means of images of its own, called elements, that are natural products." In addition, the allegorical dream is characterized by the dreamer's distinct memory of it upon waking, by its marked discrepancy to the waking world and by an absence of prompt fulfillment. Cf. as well OC 4, 1.

14. Christianity marginalized dream research by forbidding divination. See chapter 10 in this volume.

15. Cf. Cox Miller 1994.

16. Aside from minor lacunae it is probably the complete text.

17. I deliberately avoid the term "dream book" since it evokes medieval and modern books for popular use.

18. The manuscript tradition is described in various essays by Pack in several numbers of *Transactions and Proceedings of the American Philological Association* 1941–1967 (e.g., Pack 1965) as well as by Blum 1936.

19. I leave aside those writers who have discussed Artemidorus's work in relation to topics other than the dream, e.g., Foucault 1984; Hahn 1992; Näf 1995.

20. See chapter 8 in this volume.

21. In uncritical reliance on Büchsenschütz or Theodor Gomperz, Freud ascribed the role of magician rather than diviner to Artemidorus (cf. Freud [1900], 98–99). This imprecise use of the term "magic"—typical of Freud's time—led to an essentially inaccurate understanding of Artemidorus's accomplishment. (To be sure, a more accurate reading would have changed nothing in Freud's own theories.) It is certainly true that points of contact exist between divination and magic, since they are based on the same premise of the world's interconnectedness (cosmic sympathy); the purpose of serious mantic praxis, however, was knowledge, not a manipulation of the cosmos.

22. See, for example, Price 1986 and Jürss 1991.

23. See Hogrebe 1992.

24. "Shameless charlatans": Ennius in Cicero *de Divinatione*. I 58, 132.

25. German translation in Brackertz 1993.

26. Here I take issue with Price 1986. Cf. n. 36 on Freud.

27. On methodological premises of research based on such evidence, see Ginzburg 1989.

28. Good survey in Strauch and Meier 1992.

29. In this context, the research goal is not only dreaming, which often serves as the basis for exploring other, more complex events occuring in the brain, such as epilepsy or migraine.

30. Freud [1900]: 1.

31. Contra Price 1986, whose approach completely neglects the research object.

32. Freud states that dreaming, per se, is not a creative act (445); Artemidorus postulates that any use of dreams except dream interpretation lacks seriousness (OC 1, Preface).

33. In the preanalytic studies of hysteria, the social position of the patients Freud chose had been more balanced. Already in the preface to the first edition of the *Interpretation* ([1900], xxxiii–xxiv), Freud indicated that he could only analyze the dreams of neurotic patients and his own dreams; toward the end of his life, he took a criticial perspective regarding this partiality.

34. One question not treated in the *Oneirocritica* is how dream interpreters brought home bad news to their clients.

35. Albeit primarily for reasons of professional egoism; otherwise he could say nothing concerning a dream's realization and hence the validity of his prognoses.

36. Freud's introduction of this subjective factor has laid him open to the charge of being unscientific (cf. Whitebook 1995).

37. Freud [1914] 98ff.

38. Büchsenschütz 1868.

39. Both Freud and Artemidorus have to focus on single elements of the dream narrative. But while in Freud's dream analysis a single element can be the basis for discovering a variety of associations and meanings, Artemidorus tries to uncover a dream image's full significance from an element that seems to be the determining one. The precise recall of a dream—one of Artemidorus's characteristics of an important dream—can of course be of no importance to Freud.

40. Freud [1900], 106ff.

41. This is a result of the theory of decoding, as text 1 (dream) and text 2 (life) have to be related somehow.

42. Seitter 1992: 144.

43. Seitter 1992: 143 calls the *Oneirocritica* a "spätantike(es), eingestandenermassen epigonale(s) Traumbuch"—an opinion far less insightful than Foucault's.

44. Freud's most precise formulation of this statement is the ninth of his *Introductory Lectures on Psychoanalysis* [1916/1917], "The Censorship on Dreams," 136–148.

45. Cf. Kurzweil 1989.

46. Beradt 1994 [1966].

47. Ahrens 1996.

48. Strauch and Meier 1992.

References

Ahrens, Ullrich. 1996. *Fremde Träume. Eine ethnopsychologische Studie*. Berlin.

Beradt, Charlotte. 1994. *Das Dritte Reich des Traumes*. Frankfurt (first published 1966).

Blum, Claes. 1936. *Studies in the Dream-Book of Artemidorus*. Uppsala.

Brackertz, Karl (tr. & ed.) 1993. *Die Volkstraumbücher des byzantinischen Mittelalters*. Munich.

Büchsenschütz, B. 1868. *Traum und Traumdeutung im Alterthume*. Berlin.

Cox Miller, Patricia. 1994. *Dreams in Late Antiquity: Studies in the Imagination of a Culture*. Princeton, NJ.

Deubner, Ludwig. 1900. *De incubatione capita quattuor*. Leipzig.

Eitrem, Samson. 1991. "Dreams and Divination in Magical Ritual." In Christopher A. Faraone and Dirk Obbink (eds.), *Magica Hiera: Ancient Greek Magic and Religion*. New York and Oxford, 175–187.

Foucault, Michel. 1984. *Histoire de la sexualité*, 3: *Le souci de soi*. Paris.

Freud, Sigmund. *The Interpretation of Dreams*. [1900] *Standard Edition of the Complete Psychological Works of Sigmund Freud*. Vol. 4. London.

———. *Introductory Lectures on Psychoanalysis*. [1916/1917]. *Standard Edition of the Complete Psychological Works of Sigmund Freud*. Vol. London.

Ginzburg, Carlo. 1989. "Clues: Roots of an Evidential Paradigm." In *Clues, Myths, and the Historical Method* (Baltimore), pp. 96–125. (Orig. Ital.: "Spie. Radici di un paradigma indiziaro." In Aldo Gargani (ed.), *Crisi della ragione: Nuovi modelli nel rapporto tra sapere e attività umane*. Turin, 1979, 57–109.)

Graf, Fritz. 1990. "Heiligtum und Ritual. Das Beispiel der griechisch-römischen Asklepieia." In Olivier Reverdin and Bernard Grange (eds.), *Le sanctuaire grec*. Vandoeuvre and Geneva, 158–199.

Hahn, Istvan. 1992. *Traumdeutung und gesellschaftliche Wirklichkeit. Artemidorus Daldianus als sozialgeschichtliche Quelle*. Konstanz, (Xenia 27).

Herzog, Rudolf. 1931. *Die Wunderheilungen von Epidauros. Ein Beitrag zur Geschichte und zur Religion*, Leipzig [Philologus Suppl. 22, 3]).

Hogrebe, Wolfram. 1992. *Metaphysik und Mantik. Die Deutungsnatur des Menschen*. Frankfurt.

Jürss, Fritz. 1991. "Zum Problem des Traums," in the German translation of *Oneirocritica*: Artemidor, *Traumkunst*, Leipzig, 5–17.

Kühn, C. G. (ed.) 1965. *Claudii Galeni opera omnia*. 22 vol. [1821–1833]; Hildesheim, Vol. 6.

Kurzweil, Edith. 1989. *The Freudians: A Comparative Perspective*. New Haven and London.

Latacz, Joachim. 1984. "Funktionen des Traums in der antiken Literatur," in Therese Wagner-Simon and Gaetano Benedetti (eds.), *Traum und Träumen*, Göttingen, 10–31. (Reprinted in Joachim Latacz, *Kleine Schriften zur Literatur der Griechen und Römer*, Stuttgart and Leipzig, 1994, 447–467.)

Näf, Beat. 1995. "Der Körper in der Traumdeutung des Imperium Romanum," in *Symbolik des menschlichen Lebens*, Bern and Frankfurt, 1995 (Schriften zur Symbolforschung 10), 101–119.

Oberhelman, St. M. 1983."Galen on Diagnosis from Dreams," *Journal of the History of Medicine* 38, 36–47.

Pack, Roger A. (ed.) 1963. *Artemidori Daldiani Onirocriticon Libri V*, Leipzig (=OC).

———. 1965. "On Artemidorus and His Arabic Translator," *TAPA* 96, 313–326.

Price, S. R. F. 1986. "The Future of Dreams. From Freud to Artemidoros." *Past and Present* 113, 3–37.

Seitter, Walter. 1992. "Afterword" in *Traum und Existenz* by Ludwig Binswanger. Bern.

Strauch, Inge and Barbara Meier. 1992. *Den Träumen auf der Spur. Ergebnisse der experimentellen Traumforschung*. Bern.

Walde, Christine. 1995. Review of Cox Miller, Patricia. *Dreams in Late Antiquity: Studies in the Imagination of a Culture. Museum Helveticum* 52, 259.

White, Robert J. (ed. & tr.) 1975. *Artemidorus Daldianus. The Interpretation of Dreams*. Park Ridge, NJ.

Whitebook, Joel. 1995. "Athen und Mykene. Zur Integration klassischer und neuerer psychoanalytischer Theorie." *Psyche* 49, 207–226.

8

On the Mantic Meaning of Incestuous Dreams

Cristiano Grottanelli

Among the many aspects of ancient dream divination, the most problematic is surely the paradoxical quality of the mantic use of incestuous dreams. I have identified three main problems, one of which is common to dream divination in general, while the other two are specific to the interpretation of incestuous dreams. The first and more general problem was described by Angelo Brelich in his essay "The Place of Dreams in the Religious World Concept of the Greeks," published in Roger Caillois's and G. E. von Grunebaum's *The Dream and Human Societies*.[1] Though Brelich described the contents of ancient and modern dream books as a "chaos of absurdities" and spoke of "unrestrained folly" as inspiring such lore, I define this problem less dramatically as the existence of different, even of contrasting interpretations for similar dreams in the same corpus.

A second problem has been very briefly mentioned by Michel Foucault in his book *Le souci de soi*,[2] whose first two chapters are dedicated to the dream book of Artemidorus of Ephesus, better known as Artemidorus of Daldis, who wrote in the second century C.E. Artemidorus often presents dreams containing incest with the mother as good omens, and this is paradoxical, Foucault writes, because in principle that author establishes a correlation between the moral and the mantic evaluation of dreams. "May one deduce from this paradox," Foucault asks, "that incest between a son and his mother is not considered condemnable? Or should we consider this just an exception to Artemidorus' rule, accepted by that writer?"

To these two problems one should add a third and more serious one, consisting of the contrast between some ancient classifications of incestuous dreams as unworthy of interpretation and useless for divination, and the actual use of such dreams by diviners, and especially by Artemidorus of Ephesus.

1

Let me start with the first problem. One source seems to show that the *same* ancient text may contain apparently contrasting interpretations of similar incestuous dreams, and that the contrast may depend upon the different situations or the different personalities of the dreamers, and also upon the details of the dreams.

In the first book of his *Oneirocritica* (OC), Artemidorus dedicated a long and complex discussion to the meanings of men's incestuous dreams in divination. His chapter 78 dealt with dreams in which the dreamer had intercourse with his own son, with his own daughter, and with his own brother or sister, while chapter 79 was dedicated to the various meanings of a man's dreams of having intercourse with his own mother. Artemidorus's general observations about the meaning of such dreams are found at the beginning of chapter 79. "The discussion about dreams of a man's incest with his mother," he states, "which is very complex and may be divided into many parts, has escaped the attention of many dream critics. The simple fact that such an intercourse is dreamt of is not in itself sufficient to reveal the dream's meaning, because the types of intercourse and the various positions of the bodies imply different outcomes." A long typology of forms of intercourse between a man and his mother follows,[3] and the possible meanings of each type are presented; further variations in meaning are determined by different circumstances, such as the relationship existing in reality between the dreamer and his mother, or the composition of the dreamer's household. Depending on such circumstances, incestuous dreams are presented by Artemidorus as announcing a positive or a negative outcome.

Though other types of incest are discussed (OC 1, 78), copulation with the mother (OC 1, 79) is treated much more thoroughly, and the range of the symbolic values attributed to motherhood by Artemidorus may be compared to the complexity of that author's treatment of kinship relationships or of types of sexual encounter (see table 8.1). Here I shall quote only those symbolic meanings of the mother that correspond to the homology between her and the Earth. Four different aspects of the mother : Earth homology appear in the *Oneirocritica*, referring respectively to the fatherland or mother country (*patris*), to the earth as primal matter, to landed property, and to agriculture.

The mother country, *patris*, is mentioned three times. To dream of having sexual intercourse with one's own mother according to the laws of Aphrodite (frontal penetration) and while one's own mother is alive in the waking world, Artemidorus says, "is a good omen for all demagogues and political leaders, because the mother is the symbol of the mother land [*sēmainei gar tēn patrida hē mēter*]. So, just as one who has intercourse according to the laws of Aphrodite has power over his partner's whole body while she follows him willingly, thus the man who has such a dream shall rule over all his country's affairs." If one dreams of having the same type of intercourse after his mother's death in the waking world, he adds, and if the dreamer is traveling outside his own country, he shall return to it; but if he dreams the same dream while he is in his own country, he shall have to leave

Table 8.1.
Artemidori *Oneirocritica* 1, 79: Incest and Mother : Earth Homology

Mother (in Waking Life)	Type of Intercourse	Dreamer (in Waking Life)	Meaning
living	frontal penetration	demagogue politician	control of *polis*
		traveling outside the mother country	return to mother country
?	from behind	residing in the mother country	expulsion from mother country
dead	frontal penetration	residing in the mother country	expulsion from mother country
		traveling outside the mother country	return to mother country
		ill	death
		disputing over land, property	obtaining land, property
		practicing agriculture	fertility
?	mother riding above	ill	death
		healthy	good omen

it, "because after having committed such an outrage he is not allowed to remain by his mother's fireplace." If a dreamer dreams of having sex with his own mother from behind, he shall be rejected by his mother or by his mother country.

The homology between the mother and earth as matter (*hulē*) appears in the following passage: if the dreamer is ill while he dreams of having intercourse with his own mother, and if his real mother is dead in the waking world, "he shall die immediately: for the body of a dead person dissolves into the matter it is composed of, and as the human body is mostly made up of earth, it is transformed into its original matter; and we call the earth 'mother' [*kai tēn gēn* (*oude hautēn*) *ouden hētton mētera kaloumen*]. And for a man who is ill, what may it mean to copulate with his own dead mother, if not to mingle with the earth?" The same symbolic homology lies behind Artemidorus's statement that if a man dreams of having sex with his own mother while he is lying on his back and she is riding above him, he shall surely die soon if he is ill in the waking world, "because the earth is the nurse and the mother of all, and the earth is above the dead, and not above the living [*gē(i) gar eoiken hē mēter, epeidē trophos pantōn kai geneteira hē gē: hautē de tōn nekrōn anōthen kai oukhi tōn zōntōn ginetai*]." (Artemidorus adds that according to some interpreters this type of sexual intercourse means that the dreamer will soon die, but according to him this interpretation is correct only if the dreamer's health is bad, and otherwise the omen is favorable, because this position is the most enjoyable for a man, as it requires no effort on his part.)

As for landed property, here I am interested only in the statement that "to dream of having sex [according to the laws of Aphrodite] with one's mother after she has died [in the waking world] is a good omen for dreamers who are fighting in court over landed property, for those who wish to buy land, or for those who intend to practice agriculture." The connection between this type of incestuous dream and agriculture is debated, however, for, as Artemidorus states, "some say that this dream is unfavorable if the dreamer is an agriculturer, because he is sowing seed into dead soil, and so he shall reap no fruits [*hōs epi nekran gar tēn gēn katabalei ta spermata, tout'estin akarpēsei*]"; but Artemidorus thinks this interpretation is not correct, unless the dreamer dreams of feeling repentance or pain because of this union.

These few selected examples of just one symbolic homology show how complex and consistent the interpretation of symbolic dreams was in the only ancient dream book we possess in nonfragmentary form. In his essay, Angelo Brelich argued that, although Artemidorus's description of the functioning of dream interpretation presented itself as an explanation of its symbolic logic, it was in reality simply a secondary rationalization of a matter that was intrinsically diverse and even chaotic. Should we agree with Brelich, or should we envisage Artemidorus's systematic treatment as an expression of the inner, or the implicit, logic of traditional Greek dream divination? The fact that we know so little of the actual contents of all other Greek and Latin dream books makes it impossible to answer this question with any assurance. In Dario Del Corno's book, *Graecorum de Re Onirocritica Scriptorum Reliquiae*[4] all the extant data are collected, and these amount to little more than thirty-three names of supposed authors of such books—including some mythical names such as that of the Egyptian god Horus or that of the first *Puthia*, Phemonoe.

Other facts point to contrasting answers. For instance, it is discouraging to discover that other ancient dream books, such as the fragmentary Egyptian ones, or the Babylonian,[5] are made up of simple homologies that do not seem to be consistent from one text to another. More specifically, incestuous dreams are interpreted in contrasting ways in two of the extant Egyptian dream books.[6] The oldest of these is the dream book included in the *Chester Beatty Papyrus* 3, a hieratic text written at the time of Ramses II but possibly containing material that goes back to the Twelfth Dynasty. In section 3.5 we read: "(If a man sees himself in a dream) while he has intercourse with his own mother: (THIS IS A) GOOD (OMEN): his family will stick to him," and on the following line: "(If a man sees himself in a dream) while he has intercourse with his own sister: (THIS IS A) GOOD (OMEN): he shall inherit." The *Copenhagen Dream Book* (*Carlsberg Papyrus* 13) is one of the five main fragmentary dream books in Demotic: it should be dated to the second or third century C.E. In section b. 2 we find a list of "the types of sexual intercourse people may see [in a dream]" with the respective mantic meanings, and the extant forty lines contain a woman's possible dreams, the last of which is incestuous: "If her son copulates with her, the son she has shall come to a bad end." When I asked my colleague Edda Bresciani to comment upon such dream omens, she interpreted the different mantic evaluations of incestuous dreams attested by the two texts as resulting from historical change in Egyptian attitudes to incest, and she showed no interest in my suggestion that the different perspectives adopted by the texts (a man's dreams in the hieratic dream book, a woman's in the demotic papyrus) could have something to do with the different evaluations. In any case the inconsistencies of the Egyptian tradition may indicate that dream divination had no intrinsic coherence and that Artemidorus's logic was idiosyncratic. On the other hand, Artemidorus was a professional practicing dream diviner, who may have differed from the others simply because he catered, or wished to cater, to the sophisticated elite of the oriental provinces of the Roman Empire.[7] Moreover, his frequent quotations from many books by other dream diviners may indicate that he felt himself somehow integrated into that category, even though G. W. Bowersock is probably right in describing him as a snob.[8]

So my first problem remains unsolved. Of course, it would be easy to argue that seeming incongruities in one corpus of dream omens may be explained as internal variations *within* one and the same system ruled, on one hand, by the inner logic of symbolic discourse, and, on the other, by a set of culture-specific values expressed by symbolic homologies. This would be a good counterattack on Brelich's skepticism. But in the case in point, such a statement may be transformed into something more than a *petitio principii* only if we accept Artemidorus's mantic logic as a credible representative of ancient Greek dream divination.

2

The functioning of Artemidorus's dream divination would have been exemplified just as clearly if I had chosen other aspects of that author's symbolic system to illustrate its structure. To quote but one example: the symbolic connections between the mother and the dreamer's profession or trade also shape various interpretations offered by the *Oneirocritica* and function in very similar ways. If I have chosen the homology between mother and Earth to exemplify the symbolic discourse of Artemidorus, it is because that correspondence allows me to continue my discussion of the interpretation of incestuous dreams in divination by examining other sources in which that symbolic homology plays a similar role. By discussing such sources, I intend to show that one aspect of the use of incestuous dreams for divination is characterized by a high degree of consistency, which should be interpreted as the result of historical continuity. In the case of the mother : Earth homology, such continuity is a particularly lasting one, because the sources attesting its use extend over a period of at least 700 years. The sources in question, the most ancient of which dates to the fifth century B.C.E., are the writings of Greek and Latin historians; the central theme is, in all cases, the acquiring or the maintaining of political power (table 8.2), which corresponds well to Artemidorus's use of the mother : Earth homology in connection with the future of demagogues and politicians.

In the two cases relating to the Greek world, the story is about a dream

Table 8.2.
Incestuous Dreams and Political Power

Text	Protagonist	Dream	Interpretation
1. Herodotus 6, 106–108	Hippias son of Peisistratus		
2. Pausanias 4, 26	Comon the Messenian		
3. Dio Cassius 37, 52.2	C. Julius Caesar		
4. Dio Cassius 41, 24.2	C. Julius Caesar		
5. Suetonius *Divus Iulius* 7, 2	C. Julius Caesar	*visus erat per quietem stuprum matri intulisse*	*coniectores ad amplissimam spem incitaverum arbitrium terrarum orbis portendi interpretantes, quando mater, quam subiectam sibividisset, non alia esset quam terra, quae omnium parens haberetur*
Plutarch *Life of Caesar* 32, 9	C. Julius Caesar		

interpretation that turns out to be only partially correct. Herodotus (Histories 6, 107) tells us that Hippias, the son of the Athenian *turannos* Peisistratus, betrayed his city in the hope of regaining his power and guided the Persian enemies to Marathon. "In the past night he had seen a vision in his sleep, in which he thought that he lay with his own mother [*opsin idōn toiēnde: edokee ho Hippiēs tē(i) mētri tē(i) heōutou suneunēthēnai*]. He interpreted this dream [*sunebaleto ōn ek tou oneirou*] to signify that he should return to Athens and recover his power, and so die as an old man in his own mother country [*katelthōn es tas Athēnas kai anasōsamenos tēn arkhēn teleutēsein en tē(i) heōutou gēraios*]; and, being the Persians' guide, he made the ships anchor when they had put in at Marathon, and set the barbarians in array when they were landed. Now, while he dealt with such matters, he started to sneeze and to cough more violently than he normally did; and, since he was rather old and most of his teeth were loose, the violence of his cough caused one of his teeth to fall out. It fell into the sand, and Hippias did all he could to find it; but the tooth was nowhere to be seen, and he said lamentably to those who stood by: 'This land is not ours, nor shall we be able to subdue it; my tooth has all the share of it that was meant for me.'" Hippias's interpretation of his dream, involving his return and his death in his mother country as well as the recovery of his power (*arkhē*), corresponds well to the interpretations we find in Artemidorus's dream book in connection with politicians; but the omen comes true when his tooth, and not his whole body, takes possession of a portion of his native soil and is buried in it. This is a typical case of the irony of omens that come true while also escaping the wishful interpretations of ambitious men, so frequent in Herodotean historiography.

A reversal of the same *topos* is found in Pausanias's account (*Messenia* 26) of the Messenian recovery of their native land after the Spartans were defeated by the Thebans at Leuktra (371 B.C.E.). In this case the initial interpretation of an incestuous dream is less positive than the final outcome. "A year before that victory," Pausanias writes, "the *daimōn* foretold to the Messenians their return to Peloponnese. It is said that in Messene on the Strait the priest of Heracles saw a vision in a dream: it seemed that Heracles Manticlus was sent by Zeus as a guest to Ithome [in the Messenian territory]. Also among the [Messenian refugees living in the Lybian territory of the] Euesperitae, [the Messenian leader] Comon dreamt that he lay with his dead mother [*Komōn suggenesthai nekra(i) tē(i) mētri*], but that afterwards she came to life again [*anabiōnai*]. He hoped that as the Athenians had recovered their sea power, the Messenians would be restored to Naupactus [the harbor town that had been offered to the Messenians by the Athenians as a base against the Spartans in the Peloponnesian War]. But the dream really indicated the recovery of Messene [*to de ara edēlou to oneiron anasōsesthai Messēnēn*]."

The most famous case of a dream announcing power over land by showing the dreamer's intercourse with his own mother differs greatly from these two narratives presenting dream interpretations as an unsatisfactory type of guesswork. It is the famous dream Gaius Julius Caesar is said to have dreamt in the accounts of three ancient historians; in all those narratives the dream announces precisely what is later achieved by the dreamer: absolute power and control over the whole earth. Dio Cassius (Roman History, 37, 52.2; 41, 24.2) and the later Suetonius (*Divus Iulius*, 7, 2) both place the dream in the year 62 B.C.E., when Caesar was twenty-eight. The young man was beginning his *cursus honorum* as a *quaestor* in Spain when he dreamt of having intercourse with his own mother (Dio: *tē(i) mētri suggignesthai onar edoxe*; Suetonius: *visus erat per quietem stuprum matri intulisse*). This happened in the city of Gades by the shore of the Atlantic Ocean, where Caesar had just visited the sanctuary of Hercules Gaditanus. The exact relationship between Caesar's visit to that shrine and his dream is not clear in our two sources; but certainly Caesar availed himself of professional dream interpreters. Their response was clear: Dio states that they announced great power (*kai para tōn manteōn emathen hoti en megalē(i) dunamei estai*: 37, 52.2) and that from their interpretation of his dream Caesar derived a hope of conquering monarchic rulership (*kai ap'autou tēn elpida tēs monarkhias . . . elaben*: 41, 24.2). According to Suetonius, the interpreters announced that Caesar would conquer the whole world (*coniectores ad amplissimam spem incitaverunt arbitrium terrarum orbis portendi interpretantes*). *Ad amplissimam spem* in Suetonius's account corresponds well to the *elpis* mentioned by Dio Cassius, but the Greek text is centered upon the quality of Caesar's future power, while the Latin is concerned with its extension in space. The idea that the whole earth will be conquered is immediately connected by Suetonius to the symbolic homology that ruled the mantic interpretation offered by the *coniectores*: Caesar is destined to rule the *orbis terrarum*, the interpreters say, "because the mother whom he had seen in his power was none other than the earth, which is regarded as the common parent of all mankind" (*quando mater, quam subiectam sibi vidisset, non alia esset quam terra, quae omnium parens haberetur*). Clearly, the symbolic homology referred to here is not the correspondence between the mother and the mother country, as in the stories about Hippias and Comon, but the homology between the mother and the Earth, justified by the circumstance expressed by Artemidorus with the sentence *trophos pantōn kai geneteira hē gē*.

Both Dio and Suetonius connect the dream omen to the *topos* of the *imitatio Alexandri* that ties the two great conquerors and statesmen together. According to both accounts, Caesar wept in the sanctuary of Hercules Gaditanus when he saw a statue of Alexander the Great, because at his age the Macedonian king had conquered the world, while he, Caesar, had performed no great deed. In his narrative, Suetonius uses the same terminology for Alexander's accomplishment (*quia iam Alexander orbem terrarum subegisset*) and for the interpretation of Caesar's dream by the *coniectores* (*arbitrium terrarum orbis*). Though he also mentions this episode involving the *imitatio Alexandri*, Plutarch, our third source for Caesar's incestuous dream, does not connect it to the dream in his *Life of Caesar* (the dream is found in 32, 6). In his account, Plutarch places the dream in the night preceding the famous crossing of the Rubicon (January 10, 49 B.C.E.), thirteen years after Caesar's *quaestura* in Spain, which was the turning point in that statesman's career as well as in the institutional history of ancient Rome. During that night, we are told, "Caesar had an unlawful dream: He thought that he was having an unmentionable intercourse with his own mother" (*onar idein ekthesmon: edokei gar autos tē(i) heautou mētri mignusthai tēn arrēton mixin*). No interpretation of the dream is given here, but the terminology used for the dream (*ekthesmon, arrēton*) points to its horrible contents and surely connects it to the terrible, unlawful decision taken upon the following day, which prepared Caesar's conquest of absolute power while breaking the rules of the Roman Republic.[9]

3

As I have already stated, these narratives presenting the incestuous dreams of political leaders show the continuity of dream divination that lies behind one of Artemidorus's symbolic homologies. I must add that the treatment of Caesar's incestuous dream by Suetonius and Plutarch points to the second problem presented at the beginning of my paper, namely, the contrast between the unlawful and shameful contents of such dreams and their possible interpretation as omens of future power. I shall discuss this second problem now, and I shall begin by explaining why I do not think it is possible to do away with that problem by denying that the dreams under discussion were really envisaged as incestuous by those who interpreted them as good omens.

In his introduction to the volume *Il sogno in Grecia*,[10] my friend Giulio Guidorizzi quotes some of the texts I have analyzed so far to prove that incestuous dreams corresponding to the Oedipus myth were rather frequent in the dream experience of ancient (Greek and Roman) societies. This statement is accompanied by a critical evaluation of Georges Devereux's book *Dreams in Greek Tragedy*,[11] where one reads that incestuous dreams, as the experience of Freudian psychoanalysts has proved, are not present in an explicit form in the dream experience of modern patients, and that the same must be true of antiquity, when dreams expressed incest not directly but symbolically. In the present occasion, it is neither possible nor necessary to discuss the problem of the validity of Freudian theories for the study of dream experiences other than the Western and modern; a good treatment of that problem may be found in an important article by Simon Price.[12]

As to the existence of explicit accounts of incestuous dreams in the ancient world, I tend to agree with Guidorizzi against Devereux. Though we will never know what dreams were actually dreamt in antiquity, I think the texts I have discussed do not allow any doubt about the existence of accounts of incestuous dreams; to them one should add Guidorizzi's main proof, that is, the passage in Sophocles' *Oedipus Rex* (vv. 975–983) in which Iocaste says to Oedipus that many men have dreamt of having sex with their own mothers (*polloi gar ēdē kan oneirasin brotōn / mētri xunēunasthēsan*).

Though I tend to agree with him on this point, I have problems with Guidorizzi's further argument, which raises a most important question, the same question raised four years earlier by Foucault. "To Devereux's denial of explicit incestuous dreams," Guidorizzi adds, "we may respond by observing that the incest taboo had a different meaning in Greek culture, or more precisely that on a deeper level this type of dream was not really incestuous: indeed in the mythical and symbolic system constructed by Greek culture, the theme of 'the wedding with the mother' may be inserted in the context of the symbolic homology between the earth and the fecund mother, that appears both in mythical narrative and in the language of divination" (p. XXVI).

It would be easy to criticize Guidorizzi's position by repeating that the homology between the Mother and the Earth he presents as central is only one of the symbolic equations applied in the interpretation of incestuous dreams in Greek and Roman antiquity. But the central question raised by Guidorizzi's response to Devereux concerns the quality of such dreams: "On a deeper level," my Italian friend writes, "this type of dream is not really incestuous." Here my perplexity is still stronger.

In my opinion, Artemidorus dissolves the horror of incest in his detailed discussion of different types of the dreamer's intercourse with his mother, involving different evaluations and omens (and culminating in the worst type, oral sex with the mother but also with other partners). Yet in one case at least, even frontal penetration, the type he defines as being in accordance with the laws of Aphrodite, is presented as guilty (*amartema*), obviously because it is incestuous, and portends the dreamer's expulsion from his mother country. The use of terms such as *ekthesmon* and *arrēton* in Plutarch's description of Caesar's dream, or *stuprum* in Suetonius's text on that same dream, proves that the intercourse in question was looked upon as unlawful and horrid by those authors, even though they presented the dream as announcing a glorious destiny. Finally, while Oedipus's tragic adventure is not a dream, and should be used only with great care, the Sophoclean passage I have just quoted, containing Iocaste's statement about incestuous dreams, is a further indication not only that such dreams were said to be dreamt, but also that the incest obsession was presented as causing horror (*phobos*, v. 980; cf. 976). Iocaste says such an obsession is meaningless, and explains that one lives more lightly if one ignores it (vv. 982–983).

By suggesting the removal of the incest obsession, Iocaste is adopting a strategy that makes a good deal of sense, and not only to a Freudian. But most of the texts we have examined ignore such a sensible strategy. In such texts—in spite of what I would call the symmetrical removal strategies of Devereux and Guidorizzi—incestuous dreams are really said to be dreamt, the dreams are really perceived as incestuous, and their contents are interpreted symbolically as announcing future positive events. In spite of the seeming contradictions, all these different attitudes to incestuous dreams seem to coexist. This raises questions, touched upon by Michel Foucault—and, in my opinion, the same questions Devereux and his opponent were striving to deal with in their treatments of Greek incestuous dreams. First of all, did ancient dream lore perceive the contradiction between the awful contents of such dreams and the successful future they could be announcing? Second, is there evidence in our ancient sources that enables us to reconstruct the inner logic—and thus the possible solutions—of that contradiction?

4

To deal with such questions, one should consider that in the sources I have quoted the interpretation of incestuous dreams often involves terms and concepts of authority and hierarchical superiority (and of course such superiority is attributed to the partner in the sexual union who was considered the "active" one) and also of violent force. In Artemidorus's text, just as in his treatment of the guilty quality of incestuous intercourse in dreams, there is much reassuring rationalization. In his interpretation of incestuous dreams for demagogues and politicians, the dreamer's power, expressed by the verbal form *arkhei*, implies persuasion, and willingness on the part of his partner; the control of the city's matters given to the dreamer in the portended future is probably freely offered to him by his fellow citizens. But the *arkhē* Hippias hoped to regain after dreaming his dream is clearly presented by Herodotus as the power of a *turannos* who is also a traitor. Caesar's dream was interpreted by the specialists as announcing *arbitrium terrarum orbis* in Suetonius's text (*Div. Iul.* 7, 2); while according to Dio it portended *megalē dunamis* (37, 52.2) or even (41, 24) *monarkhia*. All these terms expressed absolute power, while the last (*monarkhia*) refers explicitly to the institution that was most hated in the value system of the Roman Republican tradition.

In my opinion, these homologies between incestuous dreams and absolute power point to a connection between the guilty quality of unlawful sexual intercourse and the violent and unruly (even unlawful) aspects of the power portended by some dreams containing such encounters. The proper symbolic context in which such a connection should be placed has been presented convincingly by such scholars as Jean-Pierre Vernant,[13] and Nicole Loraux[14] in their writings on the incestuous *turannos* in Greek political thought. I need not remind readers that the Greek title of the *Oedipus Rex* refers to Oedipus as a *turannos*. It is more important in the present context to quote what Diogenes Laertius (third century C.E.) tells us of another *turannos*, Periander of Corinth, who ruled approximately between 625 and 585 B.C.E. (see table 8.3).

In his work on the lives of the most famous philosophers (1, 96), Diogenes Laertius says Periander's mother Krateia, who was enamoured of her son the *turannos*, would meet him secretly to have sex with him. Periander was pleased with this, but when the secret was discovered, he was so distressed that he became extremely strict with all his subjects. This tradition may go back at least to the fourth century B.C.E.[15] The mother's name surely refers to her son's power, but Nicole Loraux[16] was mistaken when she translated it as Authority, because *kratos* means "strength, energy," and the adjective *krataios* means "strong." In Hesiod's *Theogony* Kratos and Bia, "strength" and "violence," were respectively the son and daughter of Styx ("hate"), who never abandoned powerful Zeus. If we keep all this in mind, the story of Periander and Krateia will appear to be a symbolic construction in which the incestuous union between a son and his own mother expressed not the homology between the mother and the fertile earth, but the homology between the mother and the son's power based upon strength. This is the guilty secret of the *turannos*; when the secret is revealed, the power of the incestuous *turannos* becomes even heavier for his subjects (see table 8.3).

In this tradition about Periander and his mother, the incest theme is central, but there is no dream. The connection between incestuous dreams and the figure of a *turannos*, which we have already found in Sophocles' *Oedipus Rex*, is presented in the context of a totally different genre by Plato in the ninth book of his *Republic*. Plato uses dreams to illustrate the various parts and functions of the human soul (*psukhē*); these various aspects of the human soul he uses to describe various types of human beings; and finally the human typology he has thus constructed is the tool he employs to illustrate the main kinds of political order. Plato's discussion of dreams is found (*Republic* 9, I = 571 A–572 B) at the beginning of his description of the *anēr turannikos*: some dreams, we are told, express the lawless (*paranomoi*, 571 B; cf. *anomon*, 572 B) desires of men, "those that are awakened in sleep [*peri ton hupnon*] when the rest of the soul, the rational, gentle and dominant one, slumbers, but the beastly and savage part, replete with food and wine, gambols and, repelling sleep, makes an effort in order to satisfy its own instincts. . . . In such case . . . [the beastly part of the soul] does not shrink from attempting to lie with a mother in fancy [*mētri gar epikheirein mignusthai, hōs oietai*], or with anyone, human, god or animal. It is ready for any foul deed of blood; it abstains from no

Table 8.3.
Incestuous Dream, Real Incest, Power

Protagonist	Incestuous Dream	Real Incest	Type of Power
Hippias	Intercourse with the dreamer's mother		Hippias is a *turannos* (and a traitor)
Caesar	Intercourse with the dreamer's mother: *stuprum* (Suetonius); *arreton mixin* (Plutarch)		*arbitrium orbis terrarum* (Suetonius); *megale dunamis, monarkhia* (Plutarch)
Oedipus		Intercourse with the mother	Oedipus *turannos*
Periander		Intercourse with the mother	Periander is a *turannos*

food, and, in short, avoids no extreme of folly or shamelessness." The *anēr turannikos* is the type of man whose soul is dedicated to the satisfaction of such unlawful desires and dominated by the beastly part. Incest is thus typical of that kind of man, and incestuous dreams express the part of the soul that dominates the soul of the *turannos*.

So, at the specific level of Plato's philosophical discourse, this theory contains the connection between incestuous dreams and tyrannical power. In other words, Plato's theory helps us to deal with an aspect of the second problem related to the ancient interpretation of incestuous dreams. But if we go back to our historical sources, it will appear clearly that those narratives are too complex and diverse to be explained by a simple correspondence between incest and absolute power. Let us consider Hippias first. In Herodotus's account, the interpretation based upon the homology between incest with the mother and *arkhē* is presented as the wrong interpretation, dictated by the hubris of the *turannos* and traitor. Note that it is Hippias's interpretation of his own dream. As for Caesar, the great conqueror and political innovator is judged by authors writing between the first and the third century C.E., and thus in the context of a political system based upon the constitutional revolution initiated by Caesar himself. It is thus obvious that the story of Caesar's incestuous dream must be interpreted as the product of anti-Caesarian propaganda, repeated and reshaped by the senatorial elite that remained faithful to the ideal values of the Republic and more or less explicitly opposed the imperial autocracy. But the different authors did not choose identical strategies in presenting Caesar as comparable to Hippias and even to Oedipus. Only Plutarch, our oldest source, connects his dream directly with the Rubicon; Suetonius and Dio Cassius retain the unlawful quality of his dream while being less explicit about the ambiguous nature of his power. Yet their outlook is also different from that of Artemidorus, who goes so far as to connect the incestuous dreams of politicians to a power probably offered to the dreamer by the will of his fellow citizens.

Before I conclude the discussion of my second problem, a note of warning is necessary. I must state most clearly that the evidence examined so far is only helpful in solving one specific aspect of the favorable meaning of incestuous dreams in ancient divination: the connection between such dreams and future political power. I am still unable to justify the fact that in many dream books, and already in the Egyptian texts I have dealt with, some dreams of incest with the mother portended a positive future in contexts different from that of political sovereignty. I must repeat that my choice of the homology between the mother and the mother country (or the Earth) leaves out other aspects that are just as frequent, at least in Artemidorus's text and in Egyptian dream books, and that it was chosen precisely because it allowed me to exploit evidence that could suggest a possible, *partial* solution of the problem posed by Foucault.

5

Plato's discussion of incestuous dreams differs from the other texts I have examined not only because it ties the incestuous dreams to the *turannos*. In Platonic dream theory, incestuous dreams, like other dreams of unlawful behavior and desires, are presented as devoid of any precognitive potentiality. The relationship between this theory and the mantic use of incestuous dreams constitutes the last of the three problems I deal with in the present paper (see table 8.4).

Plato's denial of the precognitive value of unlawful and beastly dream visions was expressed indirectly by the philosopher, and directly by those who followed his theory. In the passage I have just quoted (*Republic* 9, I = 571 A–D) Plato described the type of dreams that arose from the beastly part of the *psukhē*; in the lines that follow, he dealt with the opposite type of dreams, dictated by the rational part of the soul, and dreamt by dreamers who fell asleep after having tamed the appetitive and passionate parts.

In such dreams, Plato says, the best part of the soul "may in isolated purity examine and reach out toward and apprehend some of the things unknown to it, past, present or future" (*auto kath'auto monon katharon skopein kai oregesthai tou kai aisthanesthai ho mē oiden, ē ti tōn gegonotōn ē ontōn ē kai mellontōn*) (572 A). In Greek linguistic tradition, and already in the Homeric poems, the triadic knowledge of present, past, and future is typical of divination: by these words Plato is thus explicitly defending the mantic value of the best kind of dreams and clearly, if implicitly, denying that the worst type has such a value. The basic principle here is the connection between truthfulness and lawfulness, as shown by the philosopher's subsequent statement that in the case of pure and rational dreams the dreamer "is most likely to apprehend truth, and visions are least likely to be lawless" (572 A–B).

In the first book of Cicero's *De divinatione* (1, 29), in which the author's brother Quintus argues in favor of divination, a translation of the Platonic passage I have

Table 8.4.
Useless Dreams

Author	Dream Type	Description	Causes	Use for Divination
Plato, fourth century B.C.E.	One of two types	Unlawful, irrational, involving the lowest parts of the soul. Incestuous dreams included.	Caused by too much food or drink.	None
Cicero, first century B.C.E.	One of two types (*falsum somnium*)	Plato's description quoted. Incestuous dreams included.	Caused by too much food or drink.	None
Artemidorus, second century C.E.	One in a complex typology (*enupnion*)	Expresses the dreamer's present, leaves no trace after waking.	Caused by too much or too little food and by various passions (fear, desire).	None (it does not express the dreamer's future)
Macrobius, fourth/fifth century C.E.	One of five types (*enupnion* or *insomnium*)	Contains fears and desires (ambition, food, sex). Leaves no trace after waking.	Caused by too much or too little food and by various passions (fear, desire).	None

discussed so far is presented. After having described a precognitive dream he qualifies as *divinum*, Quintus tries to answer the possible objection that, while some dreams are precognitive, many others are untrustworthy. Possibly, he says, such dreams are not false, but their meaning is hidden from us. "But even if one grants that some dreams are false, why should we declaim against those that are true? Indeed, true dreams would be much more frequent if we went to our rest in a proper condition. But when we are burdened with food and drink our dreams are troubled and confused" (*Sed sint falsa quaedam; contra vera quid dicimus? Quae quidem multo plura evenirent, si ad quietem integri iremus. Nunc onusti cibo et vino perturbata et confusa cernimus*). At this point, what "Socrates says in Plato's *Republic*" (*quid Socrates in Platonis Politia loquatur*) is presented at length, and Quintus declares that he has reproduced Plato's very words (*Haec verba ipsa Platonis expressi*). Obviously, Quintus states explicitly that incestuous dreams (dreams in which the dreamer *cum matre corpus miscere videatur*) are false (*falsa*) in order to defend Plato's general theory that some dreams are precognitive (*vera*).

In his *Commentaria in somnium Scipionis* (a learned commentary on a famous passage of Cicero's *De republica*), Ambrosius Macrobius Theodosius, whose *floruit* should be placed around the year 400 C.E., classified dreams in five main types: the *oneiros* or *somnium*, the *horama* or *visio*, the *khremathismos* or *oraculum*, the *enupnion* or *insomnium*, and the *phantasma*, called *visum* by Cicero (*Comment. in somn. Scip.* 1, 3. 2). The *insomnium* and the *visum* are presented by Macrobius as not worthy of discussion because they are useless for divination (*cura interpretationis indigna . . . quia nihil divinationis adportant*). The *enupnion* or *insomnium* is said to result from the preoccupations of waking life. Its contents are ruled by the desire to obtain, or by the fear of losing, honors and positions, as well as by sexual desires or various terrors. Such dreams may be determined by excess or lack of food, and this peculiarity of the *insomnium* is clearly an echo of Quintus's quotation of Plato in *De divinatione*.

Though incest is not mentioned in Macrobius's description of the *insomnium*, this late reappearance of the Platonic model of false dreams is important because it takes us back to Artemidorus,[17] while presenting a theoretical position that is totally incompatible with Artemidorus's mantic discourse. For, on one hand, Macrobius's typology of dreams is surely connected to, if not actually derived from, the typology we find at the beginning of Artemidorus's *Oneirocritica* (1, 1). On the other hand, Artemidorus dedicates a part of his treatise to the mantic interpretation of dreams that should be considered useless for divination if classified according to the criteria Macrobius inherited from (Plato and from) Cicero—and among such dreams the incestuous ones mentioned by Plato and by Cicero, but not by Macrobius, nor by Artemidorus, are especially prominent.[18]

If we look at Artemidorus's description of the type of dream he calls *enupnion* and contrasts with the trustworthy dream or *oneiros*, we find that such a type is caused by sexual desire, by hunger, or by indigestion (and in such cases it derives directly from the body), or by passions such as joy or distress (and in those cases it comes from the soul). In all cases it expresses the dreamer's present and not his or her future. In a passage precisely echoed by Macrobius, Artemidorus adds that "this type of dream is called *enupnion* not because it is seen in sleep [*hupnos*], for the *oneiros* is also enacted during sleep, but because it is an activity that takes place during sleep and then disappears entirely," while the activity of the *oneiros* lives on after the dreamer has awakened from his or her sleep. It is clear that Artemidorus's *enupnion* corresponds well to Macrobius's description of *insomnium* or *enupnion*; given the Platonic derivation of Macrobius's description of that type, it is virtually impossible to believe that incestuous dreams were not classified in this category by the late Latin author. Did Artemidorus reason in a different way? It is impossible to answer this question with certainty. Surely incestuous dreams correspond well to Artemidorus's *enupnion*, but just as surely a long tradition presented them as an important object of mantic interpretations. The contradiction remains and is very difficult to resolve.

6

I shall conclude by looking once more at the problems I have dealt with, and by summarizing the tentative solutions I have submitted. My first problem was the variety of interpretations offered by ancient texts for incestuous dreams. When they are found in different chronological contexts, such different interpretations may plausibly be explained by historical change (as has been suggested in the case of the Egyptian dream books or in the comparable one of the Andean dream interpretations studied by Bruce Mannheim[19]). But in the case of Artemidorus's *Oneirocritica*, the different outcomes portended by such dreams in the same text can possibly be envisaged as the inner variations of a complex system ruled by the logic of symbolic discourse and by culture-specific values presented as symbolic homologies, though such an explanation must remain hypothetical.

My second problem, the contrast between the shameful and the impure quality of incestuous dreams and the positive outcome they are often said to portend, should not be explained away by denying the real existence, or the negative aspects, of such dreams. In particular, the Greek theme of the incestuous *turannos*, and the long-lasting success of that theme from the fourth century B.C.E. to the third century C.E., help us understand why in some cases unlawful behavior in dreams is interpreted as predicting the dreamer's conquest of a power that may also be qualified as unlawful. But other cases are more difficult to solve.

Finally, Plato's discussion of the *anēr turannikos* and of his unlawful desires, expressed also by incestuous dreams, leads to my third problem, represented by the paradoxical classification of such dreams by some authors (and among them possibly Artemidorus) as mere reflections of the dreamer's present, and thus as devoid of any precognitive value. This problem is the hardest to solve. I shall only add that when the modern European translators of the *Oneirocritica*, such as the sixteenth-century Pietro Lauro Modonese[20] or the nineteenth-century F. N. Krauss (whose German version was read by Sigmund Freud),[21] omitted the whole section on incestuous dreams, they did so for obvious "moral" reasons. But, though they were not aware of it, their intervention was also a rationalization that eliminated a possible inconsistency in their author's great achievement.

Appendix: Incest in Modern Dream Books

Even if I had not shared Angelo Brelich's interest in modern dream books, I would not have been able to avoid a sensational encounter with contemporary dream divination, and more specifically with the mantic interpretation of incestuous dreams toward the end of the second millennium C.E. For during the academic year 1992–1993, I taught the history of religions at the Instituto Universitario Orientale di Napoli, and so I spent about two days a week in that exotic city where the *Lotto* is the most popular game in town after soccer, and piles of dream books are sold in the streets, containing instructions on how to deduce lottery numbers from dreams. I bought many such books—they were very cheap, the average price being about ten dollars—and I still possess five different volumes, two of which are anonymous and bear the following titles: *L'antica cabala del Lotto—La vera smorfia*[22] and *Il grande libro dei sogni—La smorfia.*[23] *La vera smorfia—*

Il mezzo più sicuro di vincere al Lotto[24] is the title of a book of which I possess two copies, one with a red and the other with a yellow cover, identical reprints of a small volume published in Loreto, 1776, presented as the work of two authors, Fortunato Indovino and Albumazar da Carpenteri (figure 8.1). My fifth book is attributed to a certain Gustav Anders and called *Dizionario dei sogni—10.000 sogni interpretati e relativi numeri cabalistici.*[25] The contents of all these books are practically identical, consisting of lists of numbers, from 1 to 90, followed by dream items, alphabetical lists of dream items followed by numbers, and tables depicting dream items accompanied by the corresponding names and numbers (figures 8.2 and 8.3). Four of them also contain lists of dream items followed by the mantic interpretations of such items, with or without the corresponding number. In *L'antica cabala del Lotto, Incesto* corresponds to number 37, *Incestuare* to 76, and *Incestuoso* to 88. In *Il grande libro dei sogni, Giacere con la madre* ("to lie with one's own mother"), number 50, is followed by the caption *denota sicurezza* ("denotes security"), while the apparently more secure *giacere con donna* ("to lie with a woman"), 60, is captioned *denota malanno* ("denotes misfortune"); *incesto*, 61, is said to denote ruin (*denota gravi accidenti, ruina*). According to Gustav Anders's *Dizionario dei sogni, Incesto* is also a negative dream omen: *Sognare rapporti incestuosi significa che state per perdere una posizione rispettabile e che subirete una perdita negli affari.* I will not translate the words attributed to Anders, because Philippa Waring's *Omens from Your Dreams: An A–Z to the Mysteries of Sleep,*[26] states under *Incest*: "For instance, a British book of dream lore, published in the 1920s, told its readers: 'To dream of incestuous practices denotes you will fall from honourable places and will also suffer loss in business'"—and this statement amounts to a word-by-word translation of the sentence in the *Dizionario dei sogni.* Here important questions arise for modern philologists: there is no reason to think that the author or redactor of the British dream book published in the 1920s quoted from an Italian prototype of Anders's book, or that the influence traveled in the opposite direction, that is, from the British book to the *Dizionario dei sogni.* I will not even try to tackle the problem, though I think the two passages derive from an unknown common source. I prefer to point to two important aspects of this popular tradition of dream books.

First: the conservative quality of the tradition in question. The formula *Giacere con la madre. Denota sicurezza* I found in *L'antica cabala del Lotto* is already present in my two copies of the booklet by Fortunato Indovino and Albumazar da Carpenteri published in 1776. But this persistence through two centuries seems insignificant if one compares it to the persistence of the same formula attested by a medieval text that was pointed out to me by Jean-Claude Schmitt.[27] The text in question is a dream book, preserved in Latin and in Old English, belonging to the well-known type of *Somnialia Danielis* and listing a series of dream items with the mantic interpretation of each item. In this list we find the following items: "[LXVII] *Cum sorore concumbere, dampnum significat*; [LXVIII] *Cum matre, securitatem significat*; [LXIX] *Cum virgine concumbere, anxietatem significat*, [LXX] *Cum coniuge sua concumbere, anxietatem significat.*" The correspondence between item LXVIII of this text and the formula *Giacere con la madre. Denota sicurezza* is perfect, while items LXIX

Figure 8.1. *Il mezzo più sicuro di vincere al Lotto* (1776), Frontispiece.

IL MEZZO PIU' SICURO

PER VINCERE AL LOTTO

O SIA NUOVA

LISTA GENERALE

De' Sogni, col Nome di tutte le coſe, e numeri corriſpondenti all' Eſtrazioni

DI ROMA, E NAPOLI

OPERA

DI FORTUNATO INDOVINO

E DI

A L B U M A Z A R

DA CARPENTERI

Deſcritta, ed accreſciuta di due Smorfie, e di 90. figure del Giuoco Romano

DALL'ANONIMO CABALISTA

Con l'aggiunta delle 19. Tavole del 1500. di Rutilio Benincaſa, e il modo di adoprarle, ed altre diverſe Cabale; di più l'interpretazione, o ſia ſpiegazione de' Sogni; con la Tariffa de' prezzi, ed in fine l'Eſtrazioni uſcite dal 1750. fino al preſente.

LORETO MDCCLXXVI.

Per Federico Sartorj Impreſſore di S. CASA
Con Licenza de' Superiori.

Figure 8.1. *(continued)*

Figure 8.2. *Il mezzo più sicuro di vincere al Lotto* (1776), pp. 104–105.

Figure 8.2. *(continued)*

Figure 8.3. *Il grande libro dei sogni* (1990), pp. 8–9.

73. Uno Spedale con Letti. 74. Una Grotta. 75. Un Bramante e un Pellegrino.

76. Una Fontana. 77. Bufala. 78. Acquacedrataio.

79. Ferraro ossia Magnano. 80. Corriere con Postiglione. 81. Giuocatori di carte.

Figure 8.3. *(continued)*

and LXX can well be compared to *Giacere con donna. Denota malanno.* This is not the right place—and I am not the right person—to speculate further on this continuity, but surely the matter deserves attention, and a careful research on the historical links between the different dream books across a whole millennium would be rewarding.

The second aspect I wish to mention is the process of adding new and often incongruous statements to the traditional ones. This may be exemplified by reading from Philippa Waring's *Omens from Your Dreams*, where the statement quoted above is followed by the mention of "a recent dream study, published in America," that "underlined the importance of resisting the pressure being placed upon the subject" by incestuous dreams, because "the consequences of giving in could be disastrous." The principle underlying this process is the idea that the new may be added to the old in total disregard of the respective theoretical assumptions. Surely the same general principle accounts for a curious aspect of another dream book of the same Italian series I have discussed, which I purchased in Rome in 1995: *La nuovissima Smorfia vincente. Segni. Numeri. Lotto.* In this volume, the section devoted to divination is replaced by a similar alphabetic list of dream items, each of which is followed by what the editor calls *una decifrazione psicologica.* In the short introduction (pp. 5–8) the ancient tradition of dream divination and the theories of Freud are compared.

Would it be possible to suggest that the same principle of mixing different materials without worrying about contradictions explains the coexistence in some contemporary European dream books of two contrasting mantic evaluations of incestuous dreams, represented respectively by the series "to lie with one's own mother denotes security" and by the series "incest denotes ruin"? Surely such a suggestion is the exact opposite of my tentative interpretation of Artemidorus's seeming incongruities as aspects of a complex but coherent system. And surely there is some logic in the juxtaposition of the apparently diverging interpretations we find in modern dream books, because incest in general is consistently qualified by those texts as negative, while the specific type of incest consisting of intercourse with one's mother is always presented as a positive omen: the former is associated with insecurity, while the meaning of the latter is said to be the exact opposite. Angelo Brelich may well have been too pessimistic in his judgment of modern dream divination, as well as of the corresponding ancient practice.

Notes

1. Brelich 1966: 294–295.

2. Foucault 1984. I have used Pack's edition (1963) of Artemidorus.

3. The literary evidence for the existence of a rich conventional taxonomy of sexual intercourse in the Greek and Roman tradition is ample, and the same may be said of the evidence from the visual arts. For the Roman world, a good bibliography and some plausible suggestions are found in Richlin 1992. Foucault's contribution to the study of ancient sexuality is important, but a healthy reaction to Foucault's too rapid generalizations, as well

as to the Foucaultian views of Winkler 1990, is to be found in Bowersock 1994: 77–98 (the chapter is called "The Reality of Dreams").

4. Del Corno 1969.

5. Oppenheim 1956; Oppenheim 1966.

6. Bresciani 1994: 484–486; 719–724. I have also consulted Sauneron 1959: 33–38, with slightly different translations.

7. Bowersock 1994: 79–87.

8. Bowersock 1994: 81.

9. On the literary and semantic aspects of this episode, see Poli 1993.

10. Guidorizzi 1988: XXVI.

11. Devereux 1976: XXV–XXVI.

12. Price 1986.

13. Vernant 1986.

14. Loraux 1993.

15. On the attribution and dating of this narrative, see Loraux 1993: 22–23.

16. Loraux 1993: 22.

17. For the classification of dreams in antiquity and later, see Kilborne 1987, Le Goff 1985.

18. For the social implications of Artemidorus's classification of dreams, see Bowersock 1994: 79–87.

19. Mannheim 1987.

20. Artemidoro di Daldi 1976.

21. See Bowersock, 1994: 84.

22. Anonymous 1992.

23. Anonymous 1990.

24. Indovino and Carpenteri 1988 [1776].

25. Anders 1991.

26. Waring 1993.

27. Förster 1910.

References

Anders, Gustav. 1991. *Dizionario dei sogni—10.000 sogni interpretati e relativi numeri cabalistici.* Padova, La Fenice Libri.

Anonymous. 1990. *Il grande libro dei sogni—La smorfia.* La Spezia, Fratelli Mellita.

Anonymous. 1992. *L'antica cabala del Lotto—La vera smorfia.* Milano, Mariotti.

Artemidoro di Daldi. 1976. *Dell'interpretazione dei sogni, nella traduzione di Pietro Lauro Modonese.* Milan.

Bowersock, G. W. 1994. *Fiction as History: Nero to Julian.* Berkeley, Los Angeles, London.

Brelich, Angelo. 1966. "The Place of Dreams in the Religious World Concept of the Greeks." In G. E. von Grunebaum and Roger Caillois (eds.), *The Dream and Human Societies.* Berkeley and Los Angeles, 293–302.

Bresciani, Edda. 1994. *Letteratura e poesia dell'antico Egitto.* 2nd ed. Turin.

Del Corno, Dario. 1969. *Graecorum de Re Onirocritica Scriptorum Reliquiae.* Milan.

Devereux, Georges. 1976. *Dreams in Greek Tragedy.* Oxford.

Förster, Max. 1910. "Beiträge zur mittelalterlichen Volkskunde IV. 5. Das lateinische-altenglische Pseudo-Danielsche Traumbuch in Tiberius A III." In *Archiv für das Studium der neueren Sprachen und Literaturen* 44, N.S. 25, 39–69.

Foucault, Michel. 1984. *Histoire de la sexualité, 3: Le souci de soi*. Paris.

Guidorizzi, Giulio (ed.). 1988. *Il sogno in Grecia*. Rome-Bari.

Indovino, Fortunato and Albumazar da Carpenteri. 1988 [1776]. *La vera smorfia—Il mezzo più sicuro di vincere al Lotto*. Napoli, Stabilimento "Arte Tipografica" s.a.s.

Kilborne, Benjamin. 1987. "On Classifying Dreams." In Barbara Tedlock (ed.), *Dreaming: Anthropological and Psychological Interpretations*. Cambridge, 171–193.

Le Goff, Jacques. 1985. *L'imaginaire médiéval*. Paris.

Loraux, Nicole. 1993. "Melissa, moglie e figlia di tiranni." In Nicole Loraux (ed.), *Grecia al femminile*. Rome-Bari, 6–37.

Mannheim, Bruce. 1987. "A Semiotic of Andean Dreams." In Barbara Tedlock (ed.), *Dreaming: Anthropological and Psychological Interpretations*. Cambridge, 132–153.

Oppenheim, A. Leo. 1956. "The Interpretation of Dreams in the Ancient Near East with a Translation of an Assyrian Dream Book." In *Transactions of the American Philosophical Society*, n.s. 45 Part 3, 179–373.

Oppenheim, A. Leo. 1966. "Mantic Dreams in the Ancient Near East." In G. E. von Grunenbaum and Roger Caillois (eds.), *The Dream and Human Societies*. Berkeley and Los Angeles, 341–350.

Pack, Roger A. 1963. *Artemidori Daldiani Onirocriticon Libri V*. Teubner, Leipzig.

Poli, Diego. 1993. "Il rischio del transito." In Diego Poli (ed.), *La cultura in Cesare (Quaderni linguistici e filologici dell'Università di Macerata, V)*, Vol. 2. Rome, 473–486.

Price, Simon R. F. 1986. "The Future of Dreams: From Freud to Artemidorus." *Past and Present* 113, 3–37.

Richlin, Amy. 1992. *The Garden of Priapus: Sexuality and Aggression in Roman Humour*. New York and Oxford.

Sauneron, Serge. 1959. "Les songes et leur interprétation dans l'Egypte ancienne." In *Sources Orientales II. Les songes et leur interprétation*. Paris, 18–61.

Vernant, Jean-Pierre. 1986. "Le tyran boiteux: d'Oedipe à Périandre," in Jean Pierre Vernant et Pierre Vidal-Naquet, *Mythe et tragédie*, Vol. 2. Paris, 45–77.

Waring, Philippa. 1993. *Omens from Your Dreams: An A–Z to the Mysteries of Sleep*. London, Chancellor Press.

Winkler, Jack. 1990. *The Constraints of Desire*. New York and London.

9

Idolum and Imago

Roman Dreams and Dream Theories

Hubert Cancik

1. The Dream in Roman Religion

1.1. Practiced Religion

1.1.1. (a) Dreams and dream interpretation do not have a specific place in Roman public religion. However, the Romans did much to develop divination. There was a college that specialized in augury; it interpreted species, numbers, and direction of flight as well as the cries of birds. The *haruspices* analyzed the entrails of sacrificial animals, read the signs on the livers, and interpreted lightning flashes and monstrosities of all kinds. In addition, the Romans cultivated ecstatic inspirational prophesying: the Sibylline sayings, preserved in oracular books, which were elucidated by the quindecemvirs. None of these, however, specialized in dreams. Dreams were not an element of Roman state religion in their own right.

In the rare event that the gods indicated their will through a dream, the dream was dealt with through the official channels generally prescribed for omens affecting the state.[1] An example:[2] the great games of Jupiter were once interrupted by an evil sign without it being noticed. Therefore, Jupiter appeared three times in the dreams of a disbelieving peasant, demanding the "renewal" (*instauratio*) of the games. Finally, afflicted with a terrible disease, the peasant reported his dream to the senate, that is, the consuls. The peasant immediately recovered from his illness, and the senate "examined" the dream and ordered the games to be repeated. In this manner the dream was integrated into the Roman system of prodigies (*prodigia*).

(b) When the cult of Asclepius was taken from Epidauros to Rome in 291

B.C., the practice of incubation was adopted as well: the patient found his remedy in a dream vision. However, only a few inscriptions are known from the shrine on the Tiber island that testify to cures induced by incubation. To my knowledge, no traces of this dream oracle are evident in the poetry and prose of Rome.[3] Cicero recommended seeing a doctor rather than dreaming in the temple of Asclepius; Cicero also intended for "all authority of dreams to be lifted."[4]

The contrast with Greek religion is considerable. Early in the third century A.D., Tertullian draws up a list of dream oracles:[5] Amphiaraos near Oropus, Amphilochos near Mallus, Sarpedon in the Troad, Trophonius in Boeotia, Mopsus in Cilicia, Hermione in Macedonia, and Pasiphae in Laconia. Although the list, which Tertullian adopted from his older contemporary Hermippus of Berytos, is not complete, it is notable that no mention of an Italian dream oracle is made, not even of the Asclepius shrine on the Tiber island in Rome.

1.1.2. (a) Thus, dreaming was only of minor significance in Roman public religion, namely within the framework of the prodigia and the cult of Asclepius. In their private religion, however, the Romans made great use of dream interpretations, to the great annoyance of the official cult functionaries. Privately, the Romans turned to independent specialists, who interpreted dreams for payment. For Cicero, these *coniectores somniorum* were on the same level as the street *haruspices* and the circus astrologers, as the Marsic augurs and the interpreters of lots, as necromancers and the (dream?) interpreters of the Isis religion.[6] Contrary to augury, interpretation of oracles, analysis of entrails, and the *procuratio* of prodigies by the state's specialists, the hustling of the private specialists was generally an unwelcomed 'parallel religion,' viewed as pure superstition, trickery, and avarice. If divination was to be tolerated, the state needed to monopolize the privilege of interpretation.

(b) The "Lots of St. Gall" provide an example par excellence of the interpretation of private dreams. The *Sortes Sangallenses* are a subancient collection of oracle replies that have come down to us in the Codex 908 of St. Gall (sixth century A.D.).[7] Parts of the collection date back to the third or fourth century A.D. As demonstrated by parallels to other collections of oracles[8] and the Italian bronze lots,[9] the method and numerous interpretations date back to the Republican era. Roman lot oracles existed in Praeneste, Antium, Ostia, Caere, Clitumnus, and Patavium.

The casting of lots was used to decide various problems of daily life, as we can see from the following examples from the *Sortes Sangallenses*:[10] Should I take a trip? Should I make my will? Is my business partner deceiving me? Will I succeed in my attempt to flee from slavery? Will I win the court case? Will I receive the inheritance, the treasure, the office? The relevant answers regarding the significance of dreams are as follows:

II/no. V	*Visum utilem (!) non est; sed cave ne incurras inimicorum insidias.*
III/no. VI	*Visa fantasmatae sunt.*
IV/no. VII	*Observa istum visum, ne forte in laqueo incidas.*

V/no. VIII	*Vera sunt visa; observa, ne aliquo damno incurras.*
VI/no. IX	*Visa vera sunt et lucrabis.*
VII/no. X	*Magnum visum vidisti, ut scias; honorem cum hereditatem* (!) *tibi significat.*
VIII/no. XI	*Non utilem visum vidisti; observa hora mala.*
IX/no. XII	*Visum bonum vidisti; unde non speras, lucravis.*

Thus, the meaning of the dream was indicated through the casting of lots. Should the cleromancy have been performed in an urban temple—such as a shrine of Fortuna—and not by a private entrepreneur or a traveling soothsayer with an interpretation manual, the private dream was bound to public religion. For example, the lots were cast or drawn from a special cup (phimós) in front of the god's image with either dice or engraved sticks.[11]

1.2. The Dream in the Scheme of Divination Types

1.2.1. Even in antiquity, both religious scholars and philosophers tried to integrate divination into their systems, such as the doctrine of the soul, epistemology, theology, cosmology, or the four-elements theory (Varro). The following divination scheme has come down to us through a Roman augur and student of the skeptical academy:[12]

genera divinationis (Cicero, *De divinatione* 1, 6)

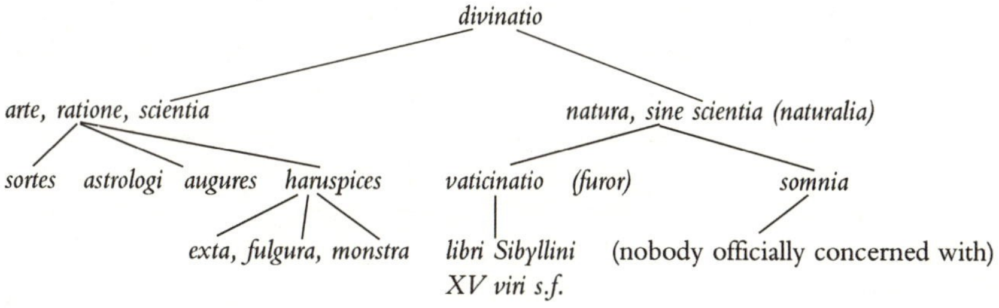

Probably the scheme stems from the Stoic tradition, in which clear models were particularly popular. The Stoics were also known for their division according to *ars* and *natura*, and they devoted significant treatment to themes of "divination" and "dream."[13] Cicero, our source of this scheme, generally relied on Zeno and Kleanthes for his account of divination.[14] He cites—probably only indirectly—the following definition from Chrysippos's book *On Dreams* (*Peri enupniōn*):[15] *Somniorum coniectionem esse vim cernentem et explanantem, quae a diis hominibus significentur in somniis.* "The interpretation of dreams is a faculty which is critical and exegetical of those things which are indicated to men by the gods in their dreams."

Aside from these three earlier Stoics, Cicero cites a number of younger Stoics as sources for his treatise: Diogenes of Babylon, Antipater of Tarsos, and the five books on divination by Poseidonios of Apamea. Poseidonios was the most recent of these treatises and probably Cicero's immediate source. All these works on divination certainly also treated dreams.

Cicero drew his theories and many examples of Greek dreams from the Stoic tradition.[16] It is striking that Cicero made no mention of what is, to my knowledge, the only Latin work "On Dreams." His friend, P. Nigidius Figulus (ca. 100–45 B.C.), a polyhistor and Pythagorean like M. Terentius Varro, wrote of private augury, entrails, and astrology, as well as of dreams.[17] Aside from Nigidius, at the end of the Republic clearly no Roman monographs existed that treated either divination or dreams.

About 210 A.D., Tertullian compiled a catalogue of authors who had written on dreams:[18] Artemon, Antiphon, Strato, Philochorus, Epicharmus, Serapion, Cratippus, Dionysius Rhodius, Hermippos. Among these nine names there is not one Latin author. Tertullian uses the last of these as his source—Hermippos of Berytos, who left us the list of dream oracles. No works of these authors have come down to us. On the other hand, Tertullian did not use the only book on dreams that has come down to us, written by his older contemporary, Artemidorus of Daldis.

1.2.1. The longest dream in Roman literature fills the sixth book of Cicero's treatise *On the State*. Cicero replaces the philosophically offensive journey into the underworld of the Pamphylian Er as described in his model, Plato's *Republic*, with a dream of the young Scipio, in which his father teaches him about the nature and fate of the soul. However, even the dream—like eschatological myth—had to be justified as a form of philosophical communication.[19] Early in his commentary on Cicero's *Somnium Scipionis*, which encompasses two volumes (ca. 400 A.D.), Macrobius developed the following dream theory.[20] There are five types of dreams: *somnium, visio, oraculum; insomnium, visum*. Only the first three forms are suitable for divination. *Insomnium* only mirrors the troubles of the body (gluttony, hunger), the soul (love, the threat of an ambush), or profession (to win or lose an office). The *visum* appears in the transitional state between sleeping and waking and causes anxiety and nightmares.

Macrobius explains that the dream of Scipio, on the contrary, combines the characteristics of vision, oracle, and dream in a narrower sense. It is a vision because he sees the sites at which the soul will tarry after death; it is an oracle because honorable persons teach him; it is a dream "because the profundity of the things he is told is concealed by a cryptic wisdom and can only be revealed through the science of interpretation."[21] In the narrower sense, however, the dream itself has five aspects:

(a) It concerns the dreamer personally, who learns what lies ahead for him (individual eschatology): *somnium proprium*.
(b) It also concerns the future of other humans: *somnium alienum*.
(c) It concerns the dreamer and other persons together: *somnium commune*.
(d) It predicts the victory of Rome, the downfall of Carthage, and Rome's future history: *somnium publicum*.

(e) The dreamer sees the heavens, the paths of the stars and the earth from above: *somnium generale.*

The dream that Cicero composed for the finale of his analysis of the state is thus a perfect divination dream. Clearly, this dream theory was neither thought up by Macrobius nor created specially for the introduction to his commentary on the *Somnium Scipionis.* The parallels to Cicero and Artemidorus demonstrate that here we are dealing with dream theory just as the much scorned *coniectores somniorum* had developed it.[22]

1.3. Summary

This analysis of dreams in Roman public and private religion demonstrates that in Rome dreams were relatively insignificant when compared to other types of Roman divination or to Greek religion. This explains Cicero's radical rejection of dream interpretations in his treatise *On Divination,* which he wrote after having been a member of the high college of augurs for ten years—a rejection even of "clear," "theorematic" dreams. Each dream interpretation is a result of superstition; superstition needs to be eradicated in the interest of true religion. This is the tone struck in the conclusion of his work on prophesying—a notable contribution to religious enlightenment in ancient Rome.[23]

Perhaps one could compare the dream's relative insignificance and its clearly subordinate role in Roman religion to additional peculiarities within this religion. Three analogies could be mentioned in this context:

(a) The limitation of inspirational divination to the interpretation of the "canonized" and secret Sibylline books through a *collegium* of specialists;
(b) The repression of the Dionysian cults in Italy since 186 B.C.;
(c) The regulation of the Mater Magna religion at the time of its adoption in Rome (201–196 B.C.).

This conclusion appears to confirm the old stereotype of the sober Roman: without fantasy, pedantic, not possessing either original myths or original mysteries. We will see, however, that Roman religion did not represent all of Roman culture.

2. *Idolum—Imago*: Lucretius on Dreams

2.1. "The Confused Dreams" (Cic. div. 2,59,122)

2.1.1. Somnia divina putanda non sunt. "Dreams are not to be considered as divine."[24] According to Cicero, this is also valid for clear dreams; he has already dismissed the "bewildering and confused" ones.[25] Complete wildness can rage freely in dreams while reason sleeps. Following Plato, Cicero's first example of this type of dream is one of intercourse with the mother or with anyone else, whether man or god, often even with a wild animal; then "slaughtering somebody, or heinously staining oneself with the blood of murder and making many things impure and revolting arbitrarily and shamelessly." These dreams can be taken into account neither within religious divination nor within the philosophical reflection about this practice.

2.1.2. Cicero claims that dreams cannot be "observed." Thus they are not objects suitable for empirical study:[26] "There are innumerable variations. Nothing can be thought so absurd, so disjointed, or so monstrous that we cannot dream it: How can we, then, grasp these infinite, original [dreams] in our memories, or describe them as a result of our observations?"

Stars are subject to natural laws; astrology is a science. Dreams are not subject to natural laws; a science of dreams is thus not possible. In this manner, muddled, fantastic, disorderly dreams are excluded by both Stoic and Academic philosophy. They are useless for divination and do not attest to the existence of sympathetic coherence in the universe or of providence. Accordingly, Epicurean theology, which relieves its gods of all worries about humans and the world, provides a different, more open access to the world of dreams. We begin with Lucretius's atomistic theory of perception.

2.2. "Everything Is Full of Images" (Cic. div. 2,67,137)

2.2.1. Idolum—Imago—Simulacrum (a) Atomistic philosophy interprets dreams both physically and sensually. Dreams are not sent by the gods, as the "atomic" gods do not trouble themselves with the world or humans. Therefore, dreams are no prodigies. Neither are they proof of the immortality of the soul, though we often dream of dead persons. But dreams are proof of the existence of gods, their human form, and their fortune, which humans cannot disturb either through pleading or praise.[27]

(b) Dreams do not stem from memory;[28] rather, they penetrate the sleeper from without.[29] All things and persons—even the gods—continuously release vague images (*idola, imagines, simulacra*) which fly through space in all directions:[30]

principio hoc dico, rerum simulacra vagari
multa modis multis in cunctas undique partis
tenuia . . .

These images are exact doubles in substance, but they are infinitely more delicate than their originals; they are not symbols of the objects themselves, but reproductions that are identical in color, form, quality, and size. They stimulate the senses, which in turn release their own images; these then enter the mind:[31] "Everything is full of images."[32] Dream images are so delicate that they can penetrate the body directly without mediation of the senses.

(c) The dream images do exist; they are physically determinable, as is everything else in this world. Thus, according to the enlightened and religio-critical philosophy of Lucretius, even the mythical crossbreeds have an existence. They are not lies of the poets; rather, they are hybrids of images of various origin such as man and horse, or dog and woman: Centaurs, Scylles, Cerberus. These images have their own movement: They can appear in thin air *sponte sua* (4,746).[33]

Lucretius, as a poet, was extremely fascinated by this world of images. An overview of his theory of perception in the fourth book of his didactic poem serves to illustrate his emphases.

2.2.2. The Structure of Lucretius's De rerum natura, book 4 The psychology of perception and thought is the topic of the fourth book. The first and larger section of the book reiterates the *eidola* teachings of the Greek atomists (vv. 1–822). Lucretius proves the existence of *eidola* and describes their particular nature: they are particularly small, delicate, and invisible, and their genesis and movement are rapid. Lucretius applies this theory to perception and thought (vv. 216–822), sight, hearing (vv. 524–614), taste and smell (vv. 615–721). He inserts an abrupt caesura at this point, at which he clarifies yet again in theoretical formulations the relationship between perception and thought; there is no significant difference between the two, according to his conception. He begins the book's second large section at this point (vv. 823–1287). He does not, as one might expect, outline an epistemological theory; rather, he applies the theoretical teachings to psychologically interesting anomalies such as "sleep/dream" and "love."

In this text, Lucretius demonstrates a specific interest in the imaginative activities of consciousness. The imaginary figments are to be assigned directly to these imaginative activities of consciousness. Therefore, Lucretius has already described in great detail the phenomena of mirror and echo effects, of shadow, perspective, and refraction in the first section of his book; he describes the anomalies and exceptions in greater detail than the activities of perception and thought which are, in his view, "normal." True to Lucretius's particular psychological interest, the conclusion of his fourth book—*De rebus Veneriis*—does not constitute some exterior facet, perhaps springing from some biographical experience that can no longer be verified; instead, it is the logical consequence of the structure that underlies the whole of the fourth book. Both the imaginative activities of consciousness and the imaginary objects fill the fourth book from the outset. It is not surprising that Lucretius closes the book with the dangerous effectiveness of these figments. He therefore deals with the Seven Dreams and the pathology of love at the close of his fourth book. The structure of this fourth book is probably Lucretius's original work; it cannot be derived from his Greek sources.

2.3. The Seven Dreams (4,1011–1036)

2.3.1 At the penultimate point of the fourth book, prior to the pathology of love, the treatise *De somno et somniis* constitutes the climax of the theory of perception. The 133 verses (4,907–961 and 4,961–1036) are marked by their own internal proem. The part on dreams is nearly twice as long as that on the physiology of sleep (4,916–961).

The passage can be divided into three subsections:

(a) The repetition of the activities of humans, while awake, in dreams (962–986)
(b) The repetition of the activities of animals, while awake, in dreams (987–1010)
(c) The seven dreams

The first examination of human dreams (962–986) shows friendly images:[34] on one hand, the practice of professionals—solicitors, generals, seamen, and, as the highlight, "us poets." The latter continue to compose on the nature of things even in their dreams; then, on the other hand, there is a long theatre dream. The second examination of human dreams is oppressive. It is difficult to see why Lucretius brings in seven frightful dreams just at the end—is it only to prepare us for the horrors of the pathology of love?[35]

The following dreams are described:

1. War: the dreamer screams as though (*quasi si*) he was about to be strangled.
2. Animal fight: the dreamer screams as though (*quasi*) he was about to be devoured.
3. Many talk in their dreams and "very often" in the process divulge their secrets.
4. Falling dream: the dreamer falls headfirst as though (*quasi*) from a high mountain, he wakes with a start, and is beside himself (*quasi mente captus*).
5. Thirst dream: the dreamer drinks the whole river and yet remains thirsty.
6. Urine dream: the dreamer "often" believes he is sitting on the latrine and "wets" the precious Babylonian sheets.
7. Pollution dream: in puberty, images of some beautiful body "often" penetrate the sleeper, he spills "enormous floods" of sperm, "as if [*quasi si*] everything was carried through" and soils his gown.

The seven dreams are arranged according to the principles of increasing length and intensity.[36] The real traces of the dreamed experience become ever stronger: shouts, *corporis aestus*, urine, semen. Lucretius stresses that "many" people "often" dream of such things.[37] The illusionary nature of the dreamed events is emphasized by the phrase *quasi* ("as if"), which is repeated five times. On the other hand, the idols are real; they really do penetrate the body of the sleeper and arouse him. The poet was obviously very interested in the blending of imaginary experiences with reality.

2.3.3. Thanks to atomistic philosophy, the abandonment of divine providence, and the human art of divination, a Roman poet was able to create a text called "On Sleep and Dreams," as we find it at the end of Lucretius's fourth book on the philosophy of nature. The continuation of the text confirms this interpretation.

The last of the Seven Dreams serves as a transition to the pathology of love. Dreams can rob humans of their reason.[38] The idola of a removed beloved can drive the lover into a frenzy:[39]

ulcus enim vivescit et inveterascit alendo
inque dies gliscit furor atque aerumna gravescit.

Lust cannot be satisfied by sexual pleasure. Rather, the lover, confronted with the images of his beloved, finds himself in a situation similar to dreaming he had an overabundance of water yet was unable to quench his thirst with the dream's images (vv. 1097 ff.). The pathology of love demonstrates human susceptibility to the imaginary figments, whose physics, mechanics, and perception are described in the fourth book.[40]

3. Dreams in Latin Literature

3.1. Imaginary Motives and Imaginative Activities of Consciousness

3.1.1. In agreement with classical dream interpretation, classical literature describes primarily "clear" dreams and those depicting the future, which corresponds to its respective dream interpretation. The dream is used as a prospective connective, that is, compositionally, and thus sets the stage for an action. A quote from a seer or an oracle could often stand in its stead. Memory dreams, which mirror moods, feelings, and desires of the dreamer rather than an action, appear only rarely. Those dreams consisting mainly of action are generally less psychologically interesting. However, an increase of psychological elements in the history of classical literature is certainly evident here. A compilation of the dream elements and their logical connections from all the dreams of antiquity, however, results in a surprising dearth of scope. A comparison between the dream texts of antiquity and those of modern psychology demonstrates a much greater diversity and breadth in the latter. The range of themes and motifs in these dreams seems to be much greater than in those of classical antiquity. The following genuine dream elements can be found in the literature of antiquity: attempting to grasp the dream image; sudden changes of scenery, which cross the natural spatial boundaries; dreams in which the dreamer has the urge to stretch, to urinate, or in which the dreamer falls or is hindered in some way; a few dreams of memory and anxiety; nightmares; some erotic dreams; and very rarely dreams in which lifeless objects are transformed into living beings. In addition, these imaginary motifs in antiquity are limited to several typical situations. Thus, the blending of reality and the dream world in the literature of antiquity only occurs during drowsiness; that is, the interspersion of reality with dream elements rarely exists. In modern literature, on the other hand, one can readily observe the reversal of dream world and reality—a modern expansion of a motif already laid out in antiquity.

The same development is apparent in the literary history of dream motifs as of other imaginary or unreal motifs: they are abundant in the pre- and postclassical literature, but are repressed during the classical and classicistic epochs; they are more extensive in all periods of Roman literature, including its classical era, than in Greek literature. They are quite widespread in modern mannerist literature.

3.1.2. Roman literati linked the dream motif to other imaginary motifs and imaginative acts of consciousness. They placed the dream in twilight, the ambivalent hours between day and night, or in the phases of parting, of waiting, of fluctuation, before a battle.

The texts of Ovid and Lucan, two postclassical poets of the early Empire, serve to illustrate this set of motifs and the embedding of the dream motif. Understandably, dreams could develop easily in the metamorphic, mythical world Ovid had created; myth is the subject matter Ovid used for psychological experiments. Ovid very often applied the possibilities that are contained in motifs such as dream, twilight, mirror, and echo to depict imaginary and unreal scenes. Lucan or Statius may have surpassed Ovid in individual instances, such as in the poetry of horror. Nonetheless, Ovid's work is the most mannerist of the literature in antiquity, insofar as it is rich with mannerist motifs.

3.2. Ovid's Dreams

3.2.1. Dream and Metamorphosis (Ovid, Metamorphoses 7,634–643: The Dream of Aiacus[41]) While watching swarming ants in a high oak tree one day, Aiacus, King of Aigina, requests Zeus to provide him with as many subjects as there are ants in the tree. He falls asleep, and his troubles continue. In his dream, he continues to see the oak tree and the army of ants. Then the ants

> A nobler Form, and larger Bulk receiv'd,
> And on the Earth walk'd an unusual Pace,
> With manly Strides, and an erected Face;
> Their num'rous Legs, and former Colour lost,
> The Insects cou'd a Human Figure boast.

The dream continues the experience of consciousness and is a typical wish dream. It appears to continue in reality:

> I wake, and waking find my cares again,
> And to the unperforming Gods complain.
> And call their Promise, and Pretences vain.
> Yet in my Court I heard the murm'ring Voice
> Of Strangers, and a mixt uncommon Noise:

But I suspected all was still a Dream,
'Till Telamon to my Apartment came,
Op'ning the Door with an impetuous Haste,
O come, said he, and see your Faith and Hopes surpast:
I follow, and, confus'd with wonder, view
Those Shapes which my presaging Slumbers drew:
I saw, and own'd, and call'd them Subjects . . .

It is the Myrmidons, the ant people.

Ovid clearly depicts the blending of the dream experience and reality for the awakening dreamer; thus, this passage can be termed a description of irreality: the imaginary figments gain reality. The fact that the animal of metamorphosis is an ant accounts for another mannerist motif. Ovid appears to have inserted the dream motif into the Aiacus story. With Ovid, a realization of dream experiences is quite possible, as the "real world" of the metamorphoses possesses many characteristics of a dream world.

3.2.2. Nightmare (Ovid, Metamorphoses 8,816–829: The Dream of Erysichthon) Similarly, Ovid embroiders reality with dream elements in another of his dream narratives; however, Erysichthon's dream is a nightmare, not a wish dream. Generally on bad terms with the goddess Ceres, Fames (hunger) nonetheless obeys her order and enters Erysichthon's house (816 ff.):

'Twas Night, when entring Erisichthon's Room,
Dissolv'd in Sleep, and thoutless of his Doom,
She clasp'd his Limbs; by impious Labour tir'd,
With battish Wings, but her whole self inspir'd;
Breath'd on his Throat and Chest a tainting Blast,
And in his Veins infus'd an endless Fast.
The Task dispatch'd away the Fury flies
From plenteous Regions, and from rip'ning Skies;
To her old barren North the wings her Speed,
And Cottages distress'd with pinching Need.

To this event, which is formulated in mythological language, Ovid then links the account of the dream experience and the sleeper's reaction to what he experienced in the dream (823 ff.):

Still slumbers Erisichthon's Senses drown,
And sooth his Fancy with their softed Down.
He dreams of Viands delicate to eat,
And revels on imaginary Meat;
Chaws with his working Mouth, but chaws in vain,
And tires his grinding Teeth with fruitless Pain;
Deludes his Throat with visionary Fare,
Feasts on the Wind, and banquets on the Air.

This dream experience continues in reality. Erysichthon devours all that the earth, the oceans, and the air provide, yet constantly demands more. The meal's original purpose suddenly changes completely, the hunger increases, until finally (877 f.):

> His Muscles with a furious Bite he tore,
> Gorg'd his own tatter'd Flesh, and gulp'd his Gore.

The narrative closes with this paradox, and thus describes perfectly the perverse character of the event. This perversion, however, is a blending of dream world and reality, which could be described schematically as follows:

The normal:		
	in the dream:	Eating—not being satiated
	in reality:	Eating—being satiated
Perversion:		
	in reality:	Eating—as in the dream, not being satiated

Ovid contrasts his description of Erysichthon, who could devour the whole world yet starves, to hunger (*Fames*). Like a living corpse, he nourishes himself with a few meager herbs (vv. 799 ff.). His description contains elements of morbid nightmare poetry.

3.2.3. The Erotic Wish Dream (Ovid, Metamorphoses 9,468–517: The Dream of Byblis) Here Ovid also links the dream motif with the theme of perversion. What interests us in this context, however, is the fact that Ovid describes not only how reality continues to exist within the dream, but also how the dreamt experience influences the conduct of the dreamer in reality. Thus, "irreality" is also the theme of this passage.

Byblis loves her brother Caunus. While conscious, she forbids herself to dwell on this; in her dreams, however, she feels it permissible to live her desires (vv. 468 ff.):

> Yet waking still she watch'd her struggling Breast,
> And Love's Approaches were in vain address'd,
> 'Til gentle Sleep an easy Conquest made,
> And in her soft Embrace the Conqueror was laid.
> But oh too soon the pleasing Vision fled,
> And left her blushing on the conscious Bed[.]

Naturally, she awakens doubtful and uncertain (vv. 479 f.):

> How bless'd, how pleas'd, how happy shou'd I be!
> But unregarded now must bear my Pain,
> And, but in Dreams, my Wishes can obtain.

She then experiences the complete desire of the dream once again in her memory: *ut meminisse iuvat.* In this manner, Ovid reconciles the following imaginative activities of consciousness: dream, vacillation, and memory. But by realizing Byblis' dreams, memory goes one step beyond the dreamed experience. The perverse character of her wishes is indicated by a play on words (vv. 483 f.):

quam bene, Caune, tuo poteram nurus esse parenti!
quam bene, Caune, meo poteras gener esse parenti!

Ovid continues the realization of the dreamed experience with a fourth imaginative activity of consciousness. Byblis interprets her dream and seeks to discover hints pointing to possibilities of realizing her desires (she lists numerous mythological examples of siblings married to one another). By doing so, she anticipates such fulfillment, and is only hindered by renewed vacillation. Finally, after much hesitation—Ovid indicates this through a series of consecutively briefer questions and answers—she resolves to write a letter to her brother confessing her love for him. While she is writing the letter, however, new doubts overcome her, and only after much hesitation does she send it. This narrative barely touches on the dream itself and contains few imaginary elements. However, the story demonstrates the connection between various imaginative activities of consciousness.

3.2.4. Morpheus and Metamorphosis (Ovid, Metamorphoses 11,633 ff.: The Dream of Alcyone) The dream of Alcyone, in which her drowned husband appears with a wet beard and dripping hair, contains few genuine dream elements. On the contrary, Ovid often emphasizes that Morpheus, who appears instead of Alcyone's husband, resembles Ceyx completely in his gestures, voice, and appearance. Upon learning of the death of her husband, Alcyone cries in her sleep and tries to hold on to the dream's escaping image; she wakes herself with her own cries. After awakening—the reaction typically begins during the dream—she has no doubts of the dream's significance, because of Morpheus's close resemblance to her husband. But more important than this dream narrative itself in the context of our study is the description of the dream godheads Ovid gives in the preceding passage. Using genealogical mythology, he outlines a theory of dream images whose most important facet—to be expected of a work titled *Metamorphoses*—is their ability to transform. Juno sends Iris to the House of Sleep. She proceeds through a wonderful mannerist landscape with a specific lighting effect: a rainbow shines through the dimming twilight. Similarly, in Statius's *Thebaid* (10,112 ff.), Iris arrives in the cave of Somnus:[42]

Vague dreams of countless shapes stand round about him, true mixed with false, flattering with sad, the dark brood of Night, and cling to beams and doorposts, or lie on the ground.

The latter two verses call to mind portrayals of bats. Statius's lighting effect is similar: in the cloud-wrapt chambers of Night (v. 84) the rainbow shines (vv. 118 ff.).

In Ovid's description, Iris enters the House of Sleep, forces back the dreams that bar her way, and delivers Juno's order to the god of sleep (vv. 633 ff.):

> The God, uneasy till he slept again,
> Resolv'd at once to rid himself of Pain;
> And, tho' against his Custom, call'd aloud,
> Exciting Morpheus from the sleepy Crowd:
> Morpheus, of all his numerous Train, express'd
> The Shape of Man, and imitated best;
> The Walk, the Words, the Gesture could supply,
> The Habit mimick, and the Mein bely;
> Plays well, but all his Action is confin'd,
> Extending not beyond our human Kind.
> Another, Birds, and Beasts, and Dragons apes,
> And dreadful Images, and Monster Shapes:
> This Demon Icelos, in Heav'n's high Hall
> The Gods have nam'd; but Men Phobetor call.
> A third is Phantasus, whose Actions roul
> On meaner Thoughts, and Things devoid of Soul;
> Earth, Fruits, and Flow'rs he represents in Dreams,
> And solid Rocks unmov'd, and running Streams.
> These three to Kings, and Chiefs their Scenes display,
> The rest before th'ignoble Commons play.

3.2.5. (Ovid, Epistulae ex Ponto 1,2,41–50: Ovid's Self-Portrait) Leaving the remaining dreams in the *Metamorphoses* aside,[43] we now turn to a dream portrayal from Ovid's own life; the dreams depicted in his other works indicate that his dream life was probably quite vivid. Early in a letter written during his banishment (*Epist. ex Ponto* 1,2), Ovid describes all of his agony, which refuses to leave him even at night when all creatures are at peace. All the fears worrying him during the day reappear at night and suppressed wishes make themselves felt (vv. 41 ff.).

3.3. Lucan on the Dreams of Pompeius

3.3.1. The first dream of Pompeius (3,8–35) which Lucan tells in his epic on the civil war between Pompeius and Caesar is an anxiety dream: *plena diri horroris*. It contains few imaginary elements, as the main body of the text consists of a speech. The awakening is topical: Pompeius grasps for the dream image in vain.[44]

More important than the dream itself are the circumstances in which it is dreamed as well as the connection this dream has to Pompeius's second one, told at the beginning of the seventh book. It is significant that the first dream is placed in a state of suspense—the departure of the fleet—just as the second one is placed before the start of the great battle. Lucan links the fleet's departure to the twilight motif, which he has long been preparing (since 2,86). The dream is set at the end of a long scene of hesitation and vacillation. The sun sets after the dream (vv. 40 f.). All the narrated events take place at the beginning and end of a day; the day itself remains empty.

3.3.2. Pompeius's second dream is a theatre dream: Pompeius sees himself entering the Roman theatre which he had built.[45] Lucan depicts the dream (7,7–24) after the great magical scene of the sixth book and before the great battle of Pharsalus (48 B.C.). However, the necromancy ends at dawn (6,828 ff.). Thus, Lucan reiterates through the twilight motif one of the most important themes of the magical scene: the perversion of all nature through the arts of Erichtho. The beginning of the seventh book takes up the theme of perversion (7,1 ff.): the sun rises later than the eternal law of Nature had called.

Pompeius's dream, however, takes place at this time, as the end of the dream informs us. It is a typical dream occuring in twilight. But the dream itself does not contain imaginary or fantastic elements of any kind, although the introduction to the depiction of the dream is as follows (7 f.): "the night deceived restless sleep with a vain image" (*nox . . . sollicitos VANA DECEPIT IMAGINE somnos . . .*). The dream becomes psychologically significant through Lucan's interpretations as well as through the particular circumstances of the dreamer.

The first of Lucan's various attempts at interpretation—none of them excludes the other—refers to the wishful character of this memory dream. As such it is somewhat unusual in classical literature, as these dreams are typically prospective. But Lucan writes: "the anxious mind fled back to happy times." *Refugit*, however, points to Lucan's second category of interpretation, which in modern terms is called repression: The dreamer replaces the threatening present situation with a joyful experience of the past (*contraria*). Lucan sees this process as containing the usual ambiguities (*solitas ambages*) of the dream. Both interpretations—as wishful dream and as memory dream—complement each other: both cause repression. Lucan offers another possible interpretation—Fortuna showed him his home—and to this he links thoughts (vv. 24b ff.) which illuminate the contrast between dream and reality. The dream serves to "mirror together" present and past so as to emphasize the contrasts. Lucan returns to the content of the dream with the words, "They applauded in the same way in the theatre." The dream is a theatre dream, and thus a characteristic example of Roman dreaming:[46] Pompeius sees himself at the height of his power, entering the theatre which he had built, while the masses cheer him on. This final scene of the dream marks an additional connection between dream life and reality. At the end of the dream the sun, Lucan writes, had overcome the stars, and in the camp the soldiers shouted (vv. 45 ff.). The time confirms that it is a dream occurring in twilight. The content of the dream, which we now know to be both a wish and an anxiety dream quite similar to the one described early in the third book, certainly corresponds to antiquity's other twilight dreams.

Through his depiction, Lucan accomplishes an implicit further connection between dream and reality based on subtle psychological experience. Simply by placing the "noisy soldiers in front of Pompeius's tent" and the "cheering masses in the theatre" in close proximity to each other, Lucan clarifies the following: that the dream has transformed the noise of the soldiers who are eager to go into battle to the cries of the masses in the theatre. The delay at the beginning (v. 1) is compensated by a sudden acceleration and precipitation of the events—they plunge headlong into ruin. The dream covers up the stimulus to awaken; in doing so, it serves to prolong sleep. Thus, this dream not only actualizes past events by utilizing memory, it also actively focuses on mastering a present misfortune. Although a memory dream, the connection between wish fulfillment and the reinterpretation of the stimulus to wake up makes it clear that it is also one of those dreams that attempt to solve future problems.

The dream says, as it were, "Just keep sleeping, Pompeius"—even Lucan applied such an apostrophe to the sleeper—"keep sleeping. You have already won this difficult battle at Pharsalus, just as you won all your earlier battles; you are entering your theatre while the throng is cheering you on."

I know of no other description of a dream in classical literature that describes the activities of consciousness developed in a dream as concretely, precisely, and in such detailed fashion. The dream Lucan narrates transcends the boundaries of time: it overcomes past and present with the help of images that memory snatches away from the past; wishes and hopes, fears and happy memories are unified within it.

4. Summary and Conclusion

4.1.

In contrast to Greek religion, the dream was not an element of the public religion of the Romans in its own right. Divination was well developed; however, there were no specialists in the interpretation of dreams. There were no dream oracles. Cicero's explicit aim in his treatise *On Divination* (44 B.C.) was to "do away with all authority of dreams," even to drive out all dream prophecy.

How are these findings to be viewed in relation to Roman religion more generally? Can we derive any conclusions for Roman culture in general from these specific religio-historical findings? Do they substantiate the stereotype of the sober Roman, of the particular Roman rationality founded on law and militarism?

4.2.

Roman literature and philosophy supplement the picture suggested by religio-historical findings. Poets from Ennius to Ausonius portrayed dreams, particularly the "confused" ones, which were so disruptive to religious divination. A memory dream of Pompeius is particularly noteworthy, which Lucan (7,1–47) poeticized in close connection with contemporary historical literature. Ovid, however, is the most important source. Dreams as literary elements are particularly suitable for metamorphoses. Lucretius examined the imaginary activities of consciousness within the framework of atomistic philosophy: *plena sunt imaginum omnia*—"everything is full of images" (Democritus). These images have their specific reality: they penetrate men through the pores and produce dreams. Optic and acoustic phenomena and illusions (refraction, reflection, echo, shadow, perspective, monsters, sleep, dream, love) create an imaginary world of atomic idola (*simulacra, imagines*). Mythical crossbreeds (centaurs) are not merely poetic lies, but hybrids of atomic images.

4.3.

The texts of the poets and philosophers on dreams and dream interpretation show that some circles of classical Roman society had a clearly worked-out consciousness of the semiotic nature and the artificiality of their culture: their culture contains a "second nature" (*secunda natura*), created by human *ratio* and *ars.*[47] "Art," however, imitates nature, insofar as it is creative. "Creation and generation are the specific traits of art," says Stoic teaching:[48] *artis maxume proprium esse creare et gignere.* Philosophers and poets apparently were able to comprehend these facets of Roman culture more clearly than religion or theology. Therefore Roman religion does not "represent" Roman culture. As to dreams: one cannot draw conclusions from religion alone.

Notes

Translation from the German by Christine Baatz.

1. *Cicero, De divinatione* 1,2,4: *nec vero somnia graviora, si quae ad rem publicam pertinere visa sunt, a summo consilio neglecta sunt.* Cicero's example is the temple of Iuno Sospita which had been restored because of a dream of Caecilia, daughter of Baliaricus.

2. Cic. *div.* 1,55, with reference to his source, the history of L. Coelius Antipater; cf. Livius 2,36; Macrobius, *Saturnalia* 1,11,3–5.

3. (a) *CIL* VI 8; *IG* XIV 966 (2nd cent. A.D.). (b) Cf. Vergil, *Aeneid* 7,81 ff. and Ovid, *Fasti* 4,649 ff. (dream oracle of Faunus). (c) In the sanctuary of Asklepios at Sikyon there were two images of Hypnos and one of Oneiros: Pausanias 2,10,2.

4. Cic. *div.* 2,123: . . . *tollitur omnis somniorum auctoritas.*

5. Tertullian, *De anima* 46,11; source: Hermippus of Berytos (2nd cent. A.D.). Dream oracles in Italy: of Faunus in Tibur, of Podaleirios and of Kalchas in Apulia.

6. Cic. *div.* 1,132; cf. 2,127. Cicero calls them *coniectores somniorum, haruspices vicani, de circo astrologi, Marsus augur, sortilegium, psychomantia, Isiaci coniectores.*

7. Dold 1948; Demandt 1991.

8. Cf. the *Sortes Astrampsychi*, Browne 1983; Champeaux 1990.

9. (a) *CLE* 331 = *CIL* I 1438–1454 = I 2^2 2173–2189; the origin of these brass sticks is not exactly known; epoch: second half of first century B.C.; there is no dream among them. (b) Cf. *CIL* XI 1129: preimperial *sortes* (Parma).

10. A survey of the subjects in Dold 1948: 11 f.

11. Cf. Heinevetter 1912, esp. p. 40.

12. Cic. *div.* 1,6,11–12; cf. 1,3,5 et al.—cf. Pease a.l.

13. Cf. Pease 1963, Cic. *div.* 3,71 and *SVF* II nr.1187 ff. Varro has a division following the four elements: *geomantia, hydromantia, aëromantia, pyromantia* (Isidor, *Etymologiae* 8,9,13; cf. Servius, *Comm. Aen.* 3,359); he therefore cannot be Cicero's source here; Cicero does not indicate a special source for his scheme.

14. Cic. *div.* 1,3,6: *uno* (libro) *de somniis.*

15. Cic. *div.* 2,63,130 = *SVF* II nr.1189; he might have taken the quotation also from Chrysippos's books on divination, cf. *SVF* II nr.1183 (Chrysippos, *On Divination.* 2 books), and from the dream book *SVF* II nr.1199. 1201. 1202. 1204. 1205. 1206.

16. Cicero takes evidence for Roman dreams out of Roman historiographers, cf. Pease 1963, Cic. *div.*, pp. 24, 27.

17. The work is referred to in Lydus, *De ostentis* 45: *oneiron epi skepsis.*

18. Tertullian, *De anima* 46,10. Cf. Waszink 1947: 285 f.

19. Macrobius, *Comm.* 1,2,5.

20. Macrob. *Comm.* 1,3,1–20.

21. Macrob. *Comm.* 1,3,12: *est somnium quia rerum quae illi narratae sunt altitudo tecta profunditate prudentiae non potest nobis nisi scientia interpretationis aperiri.* Cf. 1,3,10: *Somnium proprie vocatur quod tegit figuris et velut ambagibus non nisi interpretatione intellegendam significationem rei quae demonstratur. . . .*

22. Macrob. *Comm.* 1,3,2: *phantasma quod Cicero . . . visum vocavit*; cf. Artemidorus I 2; IV (Prooem.).

23. Cic. *div.* 2,148 f.

24. Cic. *div.* 2,61,126.

25. Cic. *div.* 1,29,60, from Plato, *Republic* 9 pp. 571b–572c.

26. Cic. *div.* 2,71,146.

27. Lucretius 5,1169–1182; cf. Cic. *De natura deorum* 1,18,45–49.

28. Lucr. 4,765.

29. Cf. Cic. *div.* 2,120: . . . *animos dormientium . . . externa et adventicia visione pulsari.*

30. Lucr. 4,724 ff.

31. Lucr. 4,750 f.

32. Cic. *div.* 2,67,137 on the doctrine of Democritus.

33. The atomists' *idola—spectra* as a world of ghosts: Cic. *Epistulae ad familiares* 15,16,1.

34. Structure: I. theme; II. examples: 1. professions, 2. theatre dream; III. end and transition to the dreams of animals.

35. Also the pollution dream has negative connotations, as shown by the last words: *vestemque cruentant.*

36. Two (four), three, two, four, two (lacuna?), four, seven verses. We may assume that there is a lacuna in the fifth dream: see s. 4,1100; vv. 1020 f. possibly include two dreams.

37. The words *saepe* and *multi* occur seven times in this passage.

38. Lucr. 4,1022: *mentibus capti.*

39. Lucr. 4,1068 ff.

40. Seneca uses a similar wording when dealing with this danger (*Epistulae morales* 13); according to him, too, the desire of men cannot find limits in those "idle and vain" figments—neither in pleasure, nor in fear, nor in hope.

41. P. Ovidius Naso, *Metamorphoses.* Translation: Garth et al. 1732 (Reprint London 1976).

42. Statius, *Thebaid.* Translation: Mozley 1969.

43. Ovid, *Metamorphoses* 9,685–701 (dream of a pregnant woman; desire dream); *Met.* 15,21–33: Hercules appears to Myscelos in dream (characteristics of a nightmare); *Met.* 15,653–664: incubation dream without imginary elements, but connected to the description of dawn.

44. Further dreams in Lucan: 1,185 ff. (an *imago ingens patriae* appears to Caesar during the night); 5,505. 808; 6,283; 9,674.

45. Rose 1970: 477–485 compares Pliny *Epistulae* 1,18 to *contraria* (nothing analogous in Artemidorus) and Homer, *Iliad* 10,199–201 and suggests an imitation of Homer by Lucan. Cf. Rutz 1970: 509–524; Cancik 1970.

46. As to "theatre dream" cf. Fronto, *De feriis Alsiensibus* 3: *donat et multa somnia amoena, ut quo quisque studio devinctus esset, ut histrionem in somniis fautor spectaret.* It is significant that Fronto gives just this example.

47. Cic., *De natura deorum* 2,60,152. Cf. Cancik 1979.

48. Cic. *De nat. deor.* 2,22,57.

Bibliography

Bailey, Cyril (ed.). 1966 [1947]. *Lucretii de rerum natura*, 3 vols., Oxford.

Beard, Mary. 1986. "Cicero and Divination: the Formation of a Latin Discourse." *JRS* 76, 33–46.

Bloch, R. 1963. *Les prodiges dans l'antiquité classique.* Paris.

Bouché-Leclerq, A. 1879. *Histoire de la divination dans l'antiquité.* Paris.

Browne, G. M. (ed.). 1983. *Sortes Astrampsychi.* Leipzig.

Cancik, H. 1970. "Ein Traum des Pompeius (Lucan, Pharsalia VII 1–47)." In W. Rutz (ed.) *Lucan*, Darmstadt 546–552 (Wege der Forschung 235).

———. 1979. "Römische Rationalität. Religions- und kulturgeschichtliche Bemerkungen zu einer Frühform des technischen Bewusstseins." In P. Eicher (ed.), *Gottesvorstellung und Gesellschaftsentwicklung* (Forum Religionswissenschaft 1). Munich, pp. 67–92.

———. 1991. "La religione romana (I)." In: *Princeps urbium. Cultura e vita sociale dell'Italia romana.* Milan, 339–416.

———. 1994. "La religione romana (II)." In: *Storia delle religioni, a cura di Giovanni Filoramo. 1. Le religioni antiche.* Bari, 349–408.

———. 1995. "Cicero als Kommentator. Zur Formgeschichte von Ciceros Schriften 'Über den Bescheid der haruspices' (56 v.Chr.) und 'Über die Gesetze II' (ca. 52 v.Chr.)." In J. Assmann and B. Gladigow (eds.), *Text und Kommentar. Archäologie der literarischen Kommunikation* 4, Munich, 293–310.

Champeaux, Jacqueline. 1990. "Sors oraculi: des oracles en Italie sous la République et l'Empire." *MEFRA* (*Mélanges d'Archéologie et d'Histoire de l'Ecole Française de Rome, Antiquité*) 102, 271–302.

Del Corno, D. 1978. "I sogni e la loro interpretazione nell'età dell'impero." *ANRW* 2, 16.2. Berlin and New York, 1605–1618.

Demandt, Alexander. 1991. "Die *sortes Sangallenses.* Eine Studie zur spätantiken Sozialgeschichte." In *Atti dell'Accademia romanistica constantiniana. 8. Convegno internazionale*, 635–650.

Deubner, L. 1900. *De incubatione capita quattuor.* Lipsiae.

Dold, Alban. 1948. *Die Orakelsprüche im St. Galler Palimpsestcodex 908 (die sogenannten 'Sortes Sangallenses').* Vienna.

Fürbringer, F. 1912. *De somniis in Romanorum poetarum carminibus narratis.* Jena.

Heinevetter, F. 1912. *Würfel- und Buchstabenorakel in Griechenland und Kleinasien.* Breslau.

Hüttig, A. 1990. *Macrobius im Mittelalter. Ein Beitrag zur Rezeptionsgeschichte der Commentarii in Somnium Scipionis.* Frankfurt am Main.

Kany-Turpin, José and P. Pellegrin. 1989. "Cicero and the Aristotelian Theory of Divination by Dreams." In W. W. Fortenbaugh and P. Steinmetz (eds.), *Cicero's Knowledge of the Peripatos.* New Brunswick, London (Rutgers University Studies in Classical Humanities 4).

Kessels, A. M. 1969. "Ancient Systems of Dream-Classification." *Mnemosyne* ser. 4, 22, 389–424.

———. 1973. *Studies on the Dream in Greek Literature,* Diss. Utrecht.

Luterbacher, F. 1967 [1904]. *Der Prodigienglaube und -stil der Römer,* Darmstadt.

P. Ovidius Naso. 1732. *Metamorphoses.* Translated by Sir Samual Garth, Dryden, et al. Reprint London 1976.

Pease, A. St. (ed.). 1963 [1920–1923]. *M. Tulli Ciceronis de divinatione.* Darmstadt.

Rose, H. 1970. "Der Traum des Pompeius." In Werner Rutz, (ed.), *Lucan.* Darmstadt, 477–485 (Wege der Forschung 235).

Rutz, Werner (ed.). 1970. *Lucan.* Darmstadt, (Wege der Forschung 235).

———. 1970. "Die Träume des Pompeius in Lucans Pharsalia." In Werner Rutz (ed.), *Lucan.* Darmstadt, 509–524 (Wege der Forschung 235).

Schetter, W. 1961. "Das Gedicht des Ausonius über die Träume (Ephem. 8)." *RhM* 104, 366–378.

Schmitt, A. 1994. "Das Bewusste und das Unbewusste in der Deutung durch die griechische Philosophie." *Antike und Abendland* 40, 59–85.

Schofield, M. 1986. "Cicero for and against divination." *JRS* 76, 47–65.

Siniscalco, P. 1984. "Pagani e Cristiani antichi di fronte all'esperienza di sogni e di visioni." In V. Branca et al. (eds.), *I linguaggi del sogno,* Firenze, 143–162.

Statius. 1969. *Thebaid with an English Translation by J. H. Mozley,* vol. 2. Loeb Classical Library, London, Cambridge, Mass.

Stearns, J. B. 1927. *Studies of the Dream as a Technical Device in Latin Epic and Drama.* Princeton.

Ussani, V. Jr. 1955. *Insomnia. Saggio di critica semantica.* Rome.

Waszink, J. H. 1947. *Tertullian, De anima.* Amsterdam.

10

Dreams and Visions in Early Christian Discourse

Guy G. Stroumsa

> Who is such a stranger to human experience as not sometimes to have perceived some truth in dreams?
>
> —Tertullian, *De anima* 46

Introduction

In the absence of a Christian Artemidorus, we possess no early Christian "key to dreams." Gershom Scholem once remarked that no Buddhist monk ever dreamt of the Blessed Virgin Mary. Could we imagine a Christian monk in fifth-century Egypt, for instance, dreaming of Dionysos? The answer is, most probably, negative. A more serious question is whether the Christians saw their God in dreams and visions in the same way as the pagans saw theirs. What kind of impact did Christianity have upon the perception of dreams and visions? Through the specific case of the dramatic mutation of Western culture with the advent of Christianity, it is the problem of the cultural and religious determination of dreams and visions which will be raised here.

In early Christian discourse, there is no way of distinguishing clearly between dreams and visions. "I had the following vision . . . " (*uideo in horomate hoc*) writes Perpetua, for example, making it clear only later ("I awoke"), that it was a dream.[1] In all probability, most dreams of the early Christians were of a rather mundane nature, and did not involve visions of divine or of demonic figures. Such dreams, however, did not seem to count, and hence were not reported. On the other hand, waking visions, obtained in a state of ecstasy, were reported in the same terms as visions obtained during sleep, that is, dreams. Hence any study that focuses on dreams while ignoring visions is bound to remain deeply flawed.[2]

The early Christian writers, who perceived dreams and visions as referring to basically the same phenomenon, were adopting an attitude already found in the Hebrew Bible. A good example is Joel 2:28, which was paraphrased in Acts 2:17, and thus became a *locus classicus* for describing and justifying dreams and visions among Christians:

> And it shall come to pass afterward, that I will pour out my spirit upon all flesh; and your sons and your daughters shall prophesy [*we-nib'u*], your old men shall dream dreams [*halomot yahalomun*; 70 *enupniois enupniasthèsontai*], your young men shall see visions [*hezionot yr'u*; 70 *horaseis opsontai*].[3]

In her recent *Dreams in Late Antiquity: Studies in the Imagination of a Culture*, Patricia Cox Miller treats the subject as if both pagan and Christian dreams equally reflected late antique culture, in which both pagans and Christians would have partaken to the same extent.[4] My approach here will be precisely the opposite: in my view, religious beliefs and allegiances do make a difference, sometimes a radical one, in the perception of dreams as in other aspects of anthropology. From the second to the fifth century, Christian thinkers developed an approach to dreams that reflected a new interaction between Greek and Hebrew traditions. They also expressed serious reservations about most dreams and visions.

The striking difference between pagan and Christian dreams is a fact that has been recognized, but which remains to be explained.[5] In the following pages, I shall examine to what extent the religious beliefs of Christians in the Roman empire informed their understanding of dreams and visions. I shall also attempt to show that we can identify an early Christian discourse on dreams and visions, distinct from other similar discourses in late antiquity, and that this discourse reflects the new anthropology, the new perception of the person, developed by Christian thinkers.[6]

It should be noted that we do not have a record of the dreams of most Christians from the first centuries, but only the highly reflective testimonies of a few adult men, most of them intellectuals, and of a single young woman, the African martyr Perpetua. These few precious documents reflect the way or ways some Christians perceived their dreams and spoke about them—what they decided to emphasize and where they chose to keep silent. It is from these documents alone that we can attempt to retrieve early Christian discourse about dreams. In the words of Gilbert Dagron: "*Seront donc significatifs d'une époque ou d'une culture non ses rêves, mais ce qu'on en dit et ce qu'on en fait.*"[7]

We cannot retrieve the dreams of the early Christians themselves. As a rule, we can assume that most of their dreams were quite similar to those of contemporary pagans and Jews, and that the Christian attitude toward these dreams was *usually* not different from that of non-Christians to their own dreams. We can, moreover, isolate the discourse on those dreams and visions that are described as being specific to the Christians and are the exception to the rule, and identify their nature.

This discourse in its turn informed the Christian perception of the world, the relationships in the Christian mind between reality and illusion, body and spirit, sleep and awakening—what the French call the *imaginaire.*[8] The representation and the role of dreams reflect anthropological attitudes, as well as perceptions of the divine. The mapping of dreams and their role is directly related to cultural or theological presuppositions. In a sense, then, dreams and visions should be studied in the larger context of historical anthropology.[9]

Christianity began as an enclave culture, or even as a radical counter-culture that defined itself through the rejection of most prevalent attitudes in the Greco-Roman world. In the fourth century, however, due to the conversion of the Empire, we can witness a major mutation of the supernatural world, which involves a radical simplification or impoverishment of the pantheon. The gods have disappeared, or have become transformed into minor demons. The victory of monotheism entailed the ordering of the demonic world under the single power of Satan, forever rebelling against the good creator God, the God of Israel.[10] Christianity thus played a crucial role in the formation of the medieval *imaginaire,* both in Byzantium and in the West. The analysis of the shape of dreams and visions in early Christian discourse can thus help us to better understand this dramatic process.

In a sense, however, the place of dreams in the medieval *imaginaire* seems paradoxically closer to their place in pagan antiquity than to the place they occupied in the Christian psyche. This stems from the fact that in the Middle Ages, Christian culture was well established and defined with clear boundaries, whereas in late antiquity we cannot yet really speak of such a culture.[11]

Hellenic Divination and the Second Religiosity

Like everyone else, the early Christians were well aware that dreams were a universal phenomenon. In Tertullian's *De anima,* written before the end of the second century, we have the first sustained discussion of dreams by a Christian writer. Tertullian states that the majority of mankind learn to know God through dreams: "*et maior paene uis hominum ex visionibus deum discunt.*"[12] In this statement, he recognizes clearly the universality of dreams, and yet he does not refer to the divine in general, or to the gods, but to God, *deum,* that is, the one and true God of the Christians. But most men and women around him were, of course, pagans.

Christian intellectuals, as newcomers to a long tradition of reflection on dreams, were unable to offer a systematic alternative to the cultural premises they were rejecting. It is probably no mere chance that the classification of dreams by a pagan, Macrobius, informs all the medieval perception of dreams.[13] As Jacques Le Goff pointed out, it is only with Isidore of Seville, in the seventh century, that we can detect the birth of a specifically Christian oneirology.[14]

Chesterton's apothegm—"Dreams are like life, only more so"—would not have been easily understood in the Hellenistic world, where sleep was perceived as being dangerously close to death. Tertullian calls sleep "the very mirror" of death, or its "mirror and image."[15] In sleep, as in death, the soul was separated from the body, a conception reflected, for instance, in late antiquity by the Gnostics or by a Iamblichus.[16] For Tertullian, who basically accepts Stoic ideas, sleep represents "a temporary suspension of the activity of the senses, procuring rest for the body only, not for the soul."[17] If sleep is close to death, for a Christian, awakening resembles resurrection of the dead.[18] Dreams were thus believed at once to permit communication of the soul with the dead, and to be a most fitting vehicle for divine revelations. The ambiguous status of dreams permitted a vision, blurred as it might be, of the netherworld, and offered a link to a domain not otherwise accessible to humans. Dreams also offered, together with knowledge of the suprahuman world, solutions to various daily problems. The status of dreams was also related to their power. Plutarch's attitude here is typical of traditionally minded intellectuals in the second century C.E.:

> The dreams, children of Night and messengers of the Moon. . . . This oracle has no fixed location. It moves in all places among men, in dreams and in visions. It is from there that dreams, mixing error and confusion with simplicity and truth, are being dispersed in the whole universe.[19]

For Plutarch, then, dreams and visions can be compared to oracular phenomena. Since one observed a disconnection of soul and body in sleep, dreaming can be perceived as a shamanistic trance of sorts. The shamanistic character of vision and dreaming is reflected in various religious traditions of antiquity, from the Pythagoreans and Orphics to Sasanian Zoroastrianism.[20]

It was easy to see the gods in the ancient world. One could see everywhere the statues of the gods, in the temples, and in the streets of the cities. Seeing the god was desirable, and very common.[21] The vision could happen in different conditions; it could happen while awake, in a state of ecstasy, as in the *Poimandres*; it could also consist of a conversation with the god, in waking and without ecstasy, as is the case with Thessalos the doctor. It could happen during sleep; it could also be induced, through a process known as incubation, usually at the temple of the god.[22] Aelius Aristides is of course the most famous instance of such a cultivation of incubation, but he is certainly not an isolated case. Aelius Aristides was a hypochondriac intellectual living under the Antonines, a contemporary of Artemidorus who spent years in the temple of Asclepius in Pergamon, taking careful notes of his dreams.[23] It should however be pointed out that the Greek interest in dreams was not shared by the Romans, who had little interest in this kind of symbolism.

The common presence of visions of the gods in the Hellenistic world reflects at least two traits of ancient thought. The first is the important role images played in it. Here the Christians, like the Jews, are the exception. The second is the relative lack of interest the ancients had for the continuity of affective life. One has even been able to consider this lack of interest as responsible for the perception of dreams as mainly divinatory, and of their visions as essentially similar to waking vision.[24]

In the early Roman empire, religiosity underwent deep changes. A new accent was put on subjectivity and on personal choice in religious matters. In this context, one can even speak of a "second religiosity."[25] Plutarch's dramatic description of the death of Pan underlines the perceived failure of oracles in the early empire.[26] This failure was ipso facto perceived as that of the professional seers who had been traveling through the places of heaven and Hades, telling what they had seen to simple mortals. Under such circumstances, the dream-vision report assumed a new status and dreams became the locus par excellence of religious revelation.

Early Christian attitudes reflected an ethos vastly different from the traditional ethos of the Hellenistic world. Up to the fourth century, Christianity remained essentially an aniconic religion, which did not favor visions of the Deity.[27] The success of Christianity, moreover, both reflected and encouraged the transformations of pagan religiosity. In a sense, it epitomized them. The failure of the pagan oracles was paralleled, among Jews and Christians, by the final closing of prophecy, with the contemporary closure of the canons, of both New Testament and Mishna.[28] But the widespread refusal to recognize the validity of guilds of professional seers, together with the presence of dream books, also reflects the "demotization" of both dream interpretation and of religious visions. Anyone dreamed and could cultivate visions, provided he or she reached a certain state of mind attainable through ascetic practices, in particular fasting and prayer. Methods known throughout antiquity to encourage the appearance of visions and dreams were now popularized by the Christians; on the one hand, anyone could become an ascetic (what Max Weber called a "religious virtuoso"); on the other hand, dream interpreters had been officially forbidden.

Divination and Incubation

Dreams belong to the general field of mantics, divination of the future. As such, they were to be encouraged and induced by various ascetic practices, such as fasting.[29] Dreams were also connected to conversion among pagans, as shown by the dream of Isis in Apuleius's *Metamorphoses*.[30]

The Christians attributed the methods of divination in use in the first centuries C.E. to evil genii and polemicized in very harsh terms against them.[31] They remained, however, unable to develop theoretical arguments against divination itself.

Among the various methods of divination known in the Greco-Roman world, oneiromancy was not only widespread, it was also a science that could be learned, in principle, by everybody—although dream interpretation usually remained the privilege of specialists.[32] It was also the only method the Christians did not reject in categorical terms, a fact noted by Franz Cumont.[33] Already the Hebrew Bible, while rejecting divination, had recognized its existence and power. Even about oneiromancy, moreover, the Christians expressed serious doubts. Tertullian not only suggests that Christians must intepret dreams in a new way; he also rejects dream interpreters.[34] Indeed, dream interpreters, the specialist intermediaries, were banned from baptism in the early Church. Any adult was considered capable of interpreting his or her own dreams. In the words of Synesius of Cyrene, a Neoplatonist turned Christian in the fourth century, "At twenty-four years of age, it is inexcusable for a man still to need an interpreter for his own dreams."[35]

Oneiromancy in its most commonly established form, incubation, lived on in late antique Christianity, where the martyr's tomb replaced the god's temple. Christian incubations in churches, where the titular saints appear, and at the tombs of martyrs, continued for a long time after the fall of paganism. In our sources, the finding of the *reliquiae* of martyrs often happens following dreams. Dreams thus played a crucial role in the *inventio* of martyrs' relics,[36] as well as in hagiographies,[37] a fact emphasized by Gilbert Dagron. It should be pointed out in this context that Augustine, among others, fought the proliferation of such practices and that thanks to his influence, the council of Carthage put an end to a real contagion of dreams and revelations. Canon 83 of that council objects to *martyria* where incubation is sought for the apparition of the martyr or saint.[38]

Prophecy

The Hebrew Bible refers, of course, to many dreams and visions, from the dreams of Joseph to those of Daniel and the visions of the prophets (or the dreams of the false prophets). The early Christian writers, who knew the relevant Biblical passages by heart, built their hermeneutical rules on them. For Origen, the phenomena of prophecy and of dreaming are closely related to one another:

> All who accept the doctrine of providence are obviously agreed in believing that in dreams many people form images in their minds, some of divine things, others being announcements of future events in life, whether clear or mysterious. Why then is it strange to suppose that the force which forms an impression on the mind in a dream can also do so in the day time for the benefit of the man on whom the impression is made, or for those who will hear about it from him? Just as we receive an impression in a dream that we hear and that our sense of hearing has been physically affected, and that we see with our eyes . . . so also there is nothing extraordinary in such things having happened to the prophets when, as the Bible says, they saw certain marvellous visions, or heard utterances of the Lord, or saw the heavens opened.[39]

This important text reflects Origen's attempt at interpreting the phenomenon of prophecy, and especially prophetic vision, by comparing it with dreaming. It is also worth noting that he does not object to the predictive dimension of dreams.

Beyond the Bible, the early Christians also had at their disposal the large and varied corpus of Apocalyptic and pseudepigraphic literature, with its emphasis on visions of the divinity or of its angels. This whole literature, Bible and Pseudepigrapha of the Old Testament, constituted the foundation of the Christian attitude to dreams and visions.[40] Biblical dreams and visions were not only legitimate; they were also canonical. But it is precisely their canonical status that also highlighted the difference between them and other, more mundane and common dreams. Such common dreams could not usually boast of a similar direct divine origin. Most often, then, it was to be feared that they came from the devil. Augustine summarized the *opinio communis* of Christian thinkers when he said that any revelation which does not have its origin in God comes from the demons.[41]

For the Jews as well as for the Christians, prophecy had ended with the closure of the canon. This does not mean that there are no significant differences between Jewish and Christian approaches to dreaming and vision in late antiquity. Jews, like Christians, believed that some dreams could point to future realities, as did prophecy. But unlike the Christians, they could not make use of Hellenic literary traditions, which they ignored. Hence, perceptions of dreaming in Rabbinic texts, and in particular in Midrash, are strikingly different, in their approach as well as in their tone, from those in Patristic literature.[42] Midrash is a literary genre that is much more popular than most writings of the Church Fathers. And the Christians' constant preoccupation with Satan has no parallel in Jewish texts, where there is no obsessive fear of demons comparable to that found in many early Christian texts. Finally, in some of the Patristic texts we can identify the blossoming of a new depth of psychological insight that has no parallel in Rabbinic literature. Altogether, the perception of a radical fight between the two opposite powers carried out within the individual is much less present in Jewish than in Christian contexts.

Early Christian discourse on dreams and visions was shaped by two closely connected phenomena—on the one hand, the encouragement given to larger numbers of people to seek visions, and, on the other hand, the attempt to discourage, repress, and limit the world of dreams. These are the two sides of a consistent effort to domesticate dreams and visions, to transform them into the instrument of a direct link with God after the closure of the Biblical canon: revelations after the age of Revelation, as it were.

In a theology that proclaimed the era of revelation to be closed, that God had already said in both Testaments whatever he wanted and needed to tell mankind, the revelatory nature of dreams was problematic. The gates of revelation cannot be hermetically closed, even in a monotheistic religion with canonical writings. In early Christianity, as well as in Rabbinic Judaism and later in Islam, dreams and visions were endowed with a new status, liminal and ambiguous, which kept open the possibility of a continued revelation of God.[43] The opening, however, remains narrow. For a Christian dream to be religiously significant, it must come from God. But since God usually reveals himself in the canon of Scripture, now closed, a true Christian dream must remain something of an exception.

Christian suspicions about dreams were enhanced by the very nature of Christianity as a monotheistic religion. As Erik Peterson showed a long time ago, monotheism entails a single legitimate religious authority.[44] The idea of a single

God as well as that of a single bishop imply a single legitimate source of truth and thus militate against the plurality of valid dreams. The drastic limitation of valid dreams was also a result of the notion of divine transcendance (and of the world as God's creation), a notion that impedes easy passage between the world of humans and the divine realm.

Classifications of Dreams

For the early Christians, Homer remained to a large extent *terra incognita*.[45] Ignorance of Homer meant the absence of the *loci classici* of dreams and their interpretation in Hellenic culture throughout the ages.[46] Instead of the Homeric writings, which were the closest that Greek culture had to a holy writ, the Christians had the Bible. Although the New Testament includes some highly interesting visions, which became topical in Christian literature, it is not particularly rich in dreams.[47] The Septuagint, on the other hand, provided the Christians with a large body of dreams, such as those of Joseph or Daniel. For the Christians, the only true dreams were those that had been sent by God through angels, and which possessed a symbolism grounded in Scripture. But although the Christians were unable to make a simple and direct use of the long and rich Hellenic tradition of dream interpretation, they could not invent a fresh approach to dreams. They accepted Greek ideas, seeking to adapt them to their specific needs. In particular, they made good use of the various taxonomies of dreams that they found in widely circulating dream books. The best instance of this procedure, perhaps, is found in Tertullian's reference to "the entire literature of dreams," where he singles out Hermippus of Berytus from among a long list of authors.[48]

Different methods of dream interpretation competed for attention in Hellenistic times, and there was no single authoritative theory.[49] Aristotle's tractate on dreams, for instance, had little influence. Similarly, Artemidorus's useful distinction between a mere dream (*enupion*), and a significant, prophetic dream (*oneiros*), which is of Homeric origin, did not leave a clear mark, and this distinction is not generally observed in Hellenistic literature.[50]

In the late fourth century, the pagan Macrobius proposed in his *Commentary to the Dream of Scipio* a taxonomy of dreams that was to become the most important single source for the perception of dreams in the Latin Middle Ages.[51] According to him, dreams, of which there are five main types, often tell the future. Most dreams are true, and all are interesting. This approach clearly remains in line with the Greek classifications of dreams.

Stoic approaches have a particular importance in our context. According to the Stoics, dreams could come from the gods, from the demons, or from the soul. This tripartition of dreams lies at the basis of the first Christian tractate on dreams, in chapters 45 through 49 of Tertullian's *De anima*. For Tertullian also, dreams come from one of three sources: from God, from the devil, or from the soul (*a deo, a daemonio, ab anima*):

> But the Stoics are very fond of saying that God, in his most watchful providence over every institution, gave us dreams amongst other preservatives of the arts and sciences of divination, as the especial support of the natural oracle. So much for the dreams to which credit has to be ascribed even by ourselves, although we must interpret them in another sense. As for all other oracles, at which no one ever dreams, what else must we declare concerning them, than that they are the diabolical contrivance of those spirits who even at that time dwelt in the eminent persons themselves . . . [52]
>
> The third class of dreams will consist of those which the soul itself appparently creates for itself from an intense application to special circumstances . . .
>
> Those [dreams], moreover, which evidently proceed neither from God, nor from diabolical inspiration, nor from the soul . . . will have to be ascribed in a separate category to what is purely and simply the ecstatic state and its peculiar conditions.[53]

Although this text is at times difficult to understand, the last passage makes clear that there are three kinds of dreams, classified according to their source, the ecstatic state (*proprie ecstasi*) excluded. The most important point, perhaps, is that Christians can rely, *grosso modo*, on Greek classifications, but that they should interpret dreams differently from pagans. Let us comment briefly on Tertullian's classification.

God

The *Vision of Perpetua*, in the *Acts of the Martyrs*, mentions a conversation of the future martyr with God. Perpetua is said to be "talking to God," *fabulari cum domino*. Voice and vision are mentioned together: *profecta est mihi vox*, "a voice was adressed to me" and also *ostensum est mihi hoc*, "this was shown to me." Note the passive voice: the dreamer is the recipient of a vision, rather than its active proponent. This significant fact refutes the suggestion that Christians sang and listened to texts but did not gaze on idealized forms of their God, and that their dreams emphasize singing angels rather than visions of the Divinity.[54] Indeed, many Christian texts describe dream visions of the deity, or of angels, that often do not differ significantly from various pagan visions. The difference between pagan and Christian discourse on dream and vision must be sought elsewhere.[55]

A striking example of such a dream vision is the so-called *Vision of Dorotheos*, an anonymous text found on a single papyrus, which has not elicited the attention it deserves.[56] The vision takes place at midday, in the king's palace, and during sleep. The vision is that of God in his own palace, similar to that of the *basileos*. I quote here the beginning of this text:

> Surely, it is not for me, this sinner, that from heaven the pure God has sent Christ, his own image, to the world as a bright light, while putting in my heart a desire for a graceful song. When I was sitting alone in the palace in the midst of the day, sweet sleep fell upon my eyelids. You do not know and cannot believe all the splendour that appeared to me then. I sit well awake and singing in the

> daytime all that has appeared, but it baffles me to describe in words all the splendid supremacy of the Immaculate that appeared to me.
>
> I deemed to be standing in the porch and to behold the Lord in His palace, who is immortal and unborn, and grown from himself. This no man on earth has ever set eyes upon, nor the moon, nor the sun, nor the stars. Neither night nor cloud comes near to where the All-seeing lives, the eternal Lord who looks to every side. This is how my heart pictures it . . .

The great interest of the text lies in its imagery of the divine palace, which is reminiscent of the late antique Hebrew texts describing the "Divine palaces," the so-called *Hekhalot* literature.[57]

One of the most famous dreams in Christian literature is that of Jerome. In a letter to his female disciple Eustochium, Jerome tells of the dream he had "many years ago," while he was "on [his] way to Jerusalem, to wage [his] warfare."[58] Jerome's dream, or rather nightmare, was sent by God, while Satan assaulted Jerome with other methods. The theme of the dream is well known: Jerome, "caught up by the Spirit," is brought before the shining "judgment seat of the Judge."[59] Asked about his identity, he says: "I am a Christian," but the Judge anwers: "Thou liest, thou art a follower of Cicero, not of Christ" (*Mentiris, ait, Ciceronianus es, non christianus: "ubi thesaurus tuus, ibi et cor tuum"* [Matt. 6:21]). Upon this, the dumbfounded Jerome receives the lashes of the whip, and suffers even more from "the fire of [his] conscience." Most interesting in our context, however, is the ending of Jerome's report. The proof that his dream is true, that it is of divine origin, that "this was no sleep or idle dream," lies in the fact that "long after [he] woke up from [his] sleep," he could see and feel on his shoulders the painful traces of the lashes he had received in the dream. In other words, the true dream becomes reality, ceasing ipso facto to be a dream.

Jerome's attitude to dreams is typical of the strong suspicion about dreams among Patristic writers, and in particular in monastic literature.[60] An example of this literature can be seen in Diadochus of Photike, a Greek spiritual writer close to the Messalian movement, who had a deep influence on the Byzantine tradition. Diadochus discusses the possibility of seeing God in dreams and visions. Can the religious virtuoso (the "athlete") see the glory of God in a vision of the physical senses, or in a dream?[61] Diadochus denies the possibility of a vision of God in this world. Such visions, of a figure of light, for instance, should be rejected as coming from the enemy (that is, Satan). As to dreams, he recognizes the possibility of good dreams side by side with evil ones. Since by far most dreams, however, are evil, misleading images and diabolical mystifications, it is a sign of virtue never to trust a dream. If it so happens that God sends us a vision that we reject, Jesus Christ, in his goodness, will forgive us, since he knows well that this attitude is dictated to us by the ruse of the demons.[62] Diadochus here stays in line with Tatian, who in the second century had compared the demons responsible for sending us dreams with bandits who kidnap for a ransom.[63]

The Devil

Tertullian had already pointed out that while some dreams might come from God, most must be attributed to the devil. Indeed, the devil is the predominant presence in most Christian dreams.[64] He usually sends dreams to men, but can also appear in dreams sent by God. This is the case, for instance, in the third dream of Perpetua, who describes how she sees the devil, as an Egyptian of horrible appearance (*foedus specie*).

Perhaps the most sustained and incisive discussion of the demonic or diabolical origin of most dreams is that of Evagrius Ponticus, whom one of his best students has called "a philosopher in the desert." Indeed, Evagrius, toward the end of the fourth century, offers a theory of monastic praxis. In his *Praktikos*, written as a basic regulation for the life led by the monks of Egypt, Evagrius mentions eight categories of demonic dreams, which he parallels to the eight *logismoi*, or evil thoughts (cf. Cassian).[65] "The demons wage a veritable war against our concupiscible appetite," he tells us; for this combat they employ phantasms.[66] The attacks of the devil upon man do not end with spiritual progress. On the contrary, Satan makes special efforts to wound purified souls: "The greater the progress the soul makes, the more fearful the adversaries that take over the war against it."[67] The constant war the monks must wage against Satan and his temptations is a well-known theme in monastic and hagiographic sources, and has left a deep imprint on literature, as anyone familiar with Flaubert's *La tentation de Saint Antoine* knows.

It should not come as a surprise to us if dreams retain a central place in those trends in early Christianity that sought to revive mythological patterns of thought. Dreams and visions played a significant role in the thought of Gnostics, Montanists, and other heretics and schismatics of the first centuries. Indeed, dreams can play a double role; they can serve to establish a truth as well as to upset an authority. Hence the important role of dreams and visions in the foundation of sects.[68]

From Valentinus and Montanus in the second century to the sixteenth-century miller described by Carlo Ginzburg in *The Cheese and the Worms*, the *imaginaire* (or "cosmology") of marginal and radical groups thrives on dreams and visions—on personal, highly subjective perceptions of religious truth, which do not pass through the channels of institutionalized and hierarchical religion.[69] The Montanists, for instance, linked dream, ecstasy, and prophecy. The origin of the Montanist view of prophecy must be found in their propensity for ecstatic phenomena.[70]

The *Pseudo-Clementine Homilies* is an apocryphal popular novel of the fourth century that contains much material going back to early Jewish-Christian literature. In the form of a dialogue betwen Simon Magus and Peter, the seventeenth homily, chapters 14 through 18, preserves the most interesting and detailed discussion of dream, vision, and prophecy in early Christian literature.[71] The confrontation between the two radically different conceptions starts with Peter pointing out that while the prophet can be inherently trustworthy, "he who trusts to apparition or vision and dream is insecure." The main reason for this insecurity lies, of course, in the possibly demonic origin of the dream or vision: the sleeper is unable to check the dream and to ascertain its source. Simon, on the other hand, claims that the dreams and visions of just men can be trusted: "If he who has had the vision is just, he has seen a true vision." For him, "it seems impossible that impious men should receive dreams from God in any way whatever." Peter answers that on the authority of the Bible, even the impious, such as Abimelech and the pagan Nebuchadnezzar ("who worshipped images"), can see true dreams and visions. This important text has not received the attention it deserves. The argument concerning the legitimacy of dreams and visions is linked in the *Homilies* to Jewish-Christian traditions about the mystical vision of God. It seems to have stood at the very heart of the struggle of nascent Christianity to define itself as a religion rather than as a radical sect.

At this juncture it should be recalled that Simon is called Magus. The early Christian tradition associates the arch-heretic directly with magical powers. The magician has the power to evoke dreams, and receives power from dreams. This association of magic and dreams is already well established in Greek literature.[72] Its reflection in early Christianity, where Satan has inherited most magical powers, is an interesting and complex problem, which deserves separate treatment.

The Soul

Following his Stoic sources, Tertullian refers to sleep as a natural function:

> Since, then, sleep is indispensible to our life, and health, and succour, there can be nothing pertaining to it which is not reasonable, and which is not natural.[73]

In sleep, he goes on, we observe a temporary separation of the body from the senses: "Our only resource, indeed, is to agree with the Stoics, by determining the soul to be a temporary suspension of the activity of the senses, procuring rest for the body only, not for the soul also." Consequently, the Christians must take dreams seriously, as "incidents of sleep, and as no slight or trifling excitements of the soul."[74] According to this conception, the soul continues to be active during sleep, while the body rests, dreams being the fruit of this activity. Tertullian states specifically that dreams which do not originate in God or the devil come from the soul.[75]

The psychosomatic understanding of dreams is further developed in the fourth century by Gregory of Nyssa, in his *Treatise on the Creation of Man*, one of the most interesting examples of fourth-century Patristic anthropology.[76] For Gregory, the dream reflects a sickness of the soul. The only legitimate activity of the spirit, according to him, is that of intelligence, of rational thought, while the representations formed by imagination during sleep are only appearances. This is so because only the senses permit the union of soul and body. Since, during sleep, most faculties of the soul are resting, we cannot speak of sensorial or intellectual activity. In sleep, only the nutritive part of the soul remains active, retaining images of waking vision and echoes of sensory activities, printed in memory. All this is shaped into a new form by chance. In other words, human imagination is at work in dreams, and the mind gets lost in muddled and inordinate confusions. The mind during sleep can be compared to smoke: at once active and powerless. Through this detailed theory, Gregory can explain the ambiguity of dreams. They do sometimes offer a certain predictive vision of things to come, but this vision must remain blurred. This is what is called *ainigma* by dream interpreters.

Gregory, who seeks to offer a scientific explanation of dreams, relates them to the past activities of the subject. In this context, his acceptance of the possibility of predictive dreams is somewhat intriguing. But this reflects the status of Biblical dreams. Such are, for instance the dreams of Joseph in Pharaoh's prison (Gen. 40) and those of Daniel. But Gregory immediately limits the relevance of such examples. The prophets were granted future knowledge by divine power, and thus have nothing to do with our topic. The predictive character of dreams in the Bible, including those of the Egyptian and Assyrian kings,[77] reflects God's desire to reveal the hitherto hidden wisdom of the saints. Such needs, says Gregory, do not exist at the present.

Except for prophetic dreams, therefore, human dreams may vary in their expression, but all are influenced by the physical disposition of the subject. As a proof of the psychosomatic nexus revealed in sleep, Gregory mentions the case of an acquaintance of his whom he himself had treated, and whose serious case of indigestion had caused him delirium. Gregory notes that the very same symptoms (sweat, for instance) could have been caused by a dream. In both cases, illness and sleep, the intelligent part of the soul had been deactivated. Indeed, says Gregory, many doctors agree that illnesses are linked to what the sick see in their dreams. Moreover, he adds that the moral state of the person is also significant in the formation of dreams. He sums up his discussion of dreams by saying:

> It is not reason, but the irrational part of the soul which informs these products of imagination; it is from things which kept one busy during the day that dreams fashion images.[78]

Gregory's discussion of dreams strikes one as strongly positivistic. There may have been religious significance to dreams in the Bible, but as a natural phenomenon, dreaming must be treated with the analytical tools of medical doctors, who should seek to identify the relationships between psychic and somatic phenomena. One should note that not only God but also Satan is strikingly absent from this sharp analysis. This absence emphasizes the differences between Gregory and discussions of dreams and dreaming in monastic literature.

As mentioned above, Evagrius insists on Satan as the origin of human dreams. But it is in the strongly psychological tone of his approach that Evagrius's real originality lies. The phantasms used by the demons to attack the soul are a spiritual cancer, as it were. Dreams are one of the direct consequences of such unhealthy growth of the soul:

> Natural processes which occur in sleep without accompanying images of a stimulating nature are, to a certain measure, indications of a healthy soul. But images that are distinctly formed are a clear indication of sickness. You may be certain that the faces one sees in dreams are, when they occur as ill-defined images, symbols of former affective experiences. Those which are seen clearly, on the other hand, indicate wounds that are still fresh.[79]

More than any Christian or pagan writer before him, it would seem, Evagrius seeks to define psychic health, and to analyze the content and tonus of dreams in order to measure this health. Health is peace, quiet, lack of movement—what Evagrius calls, after Clement of Alexandria and in the wake of the Stoic thinkers, *apatheia*.[80] Active or violent dreams, on the other hand, reflect the fight of the demons against the soul.[81] Such a fight entails what one can perhaps call a neurosis, diagnosed by the growth of passions and the terror the dreams imprint on the soul.[82] It is not possible to completely avoid the display of images during sleep, but it is possible, at least for the ascetic, to avoid being disturbed or moved by these images. Hence,

> The proof of *apatheia* is had when the spirit begins to see its own light, when it remains in a state of tranquility in the presence of the images it has during sleep and when it maintains its calm as it beholds the affairs of life.[83]

Evagrius's radical psychologization of dreams, his insistence that they reflect the state of health of the soul, set a new tone in Western discourse on dreams. What counts most for him is not so much the fight of the devil against the individual as the concrete reaction of the soul to his attack, and the ways in which it can attain peace by identifying the source of its dreams, thus mastering them. There is no need, I think, to emphasize the modernity of this tone.

Evagrius's understanding of dreams is based on a mythological element, namely, the power of Satan and his fight against God, a fight waged on the battlefield of humanity, soul and body. But the strong psychological interest in dreams developed by Evagrius neutralizes this mythological element. In a sense, we may thus speak of the real *Entmythologisierung* of dreams accomplished by Evagrius.

Having recognized the psychosomatic character of dreams and the fact that they reflect a neurotic state of the soul, the monastic authors propose, as treatment, to discuss all dreams with a therapist, that is, a wise man, an elderly monk, or *gerôn*, who functions also as a spiritual leader and counselor. This counselor is asked to interpret the dream (or to interpret it away), and to counsel on sexual dreams.[84]

Evagrius's deep interest in the psychological side of dreams is paralleled in the West by Augustine. Augustine's remarkable psychological sensitivity left a deep mark on his multifaceted reflection on dreams. His writings on dreams, both autobiographical and theoretical, have been analyzed carefully in the beautiful study of of Martine Dulaey, and it is unnecessary to repeat her findings.[85] I shall therefore only refer to a few passages of Augustine's discussion of dream and *ekstasis* in his *De genesi ad litteram*.

Augustine notes the paradoxical status of the soul during dreams, when it is at once vigilant and the prey of corporal images which it imagines to be real bodies.[86] When asleep, he points out, one may be aware that the images which appear in the dream are not real, while at the same time retaining the illusion that they reflect reality. Altogether, Augustine's main contribution to the discourse on dreams is his emphasis on their being essentially a psychological phenomenon, and not a privileged access to truth.[87] Here, as elsewhere, Augustine stands on the dividing line between antiquity and the modern mind. He is thus able, more clearly than anyone before him, to see prophecy and dream as two phenomena opposed to one another.[88]

Ekstasis

Augustine's discussion of *ekstasis*, and of the difference between prophecy and dream, focuses upon the case of Paul's ascension to the third heaven (2 Cor. 12: 1–4).[89] To what kind of vision did the Scripture refer—to a physical vision of the senses, or to a spiritual one? And was the Apostle asleep or awake when taken to the third heaven? In other words, should we speak of a dream or of a case of ecstatic vision?[90] To sort out these possibilities, Augustine is forced to distinguish between different kinds of visions. There are, he says, three types:[91] The first is in the proper sense, through the eyes, by which we read the letters. The second is vision of the human mind (*spiritus hominis*), thanks to which we can develop mental representations; the third is the intuition of the intellectual soul (*mens*), thanks to which we contemplate through intelligence (*dilectio*) itself. This third type is intellectual (*intellectuale*) vision, and it permits what is often described as mystical vision.

In Christian vocabulary, *ekstasis* refers, first of all, to Adam falling asleep in Genesis 2:21, where Hebrew *tardema* is translated as *ekstasis* in the Septuagint. Tertullian had already offered a definition of ecstasy: "This power we call ecstasy, in which the sensuous soul stands out of itself, in a way which even resembles madness" (*excessus sensus et amentiae instar*).[92] For him, as we have seen, "the ecstatic state and its peculiar conditions" was to be considered a separate kind of dream, side by side with divine, satanic, or psychic dreams.[93] In such a taxonomy, therefore, ecstasy is not clearly differentiated from dreams; rather, it is a special kind of dream. In this sense, Jacques Le Goff has been able to speak about "*cette forme suprême du rêve qu'est pour les chrétiens l'exstase*," pointing out that only in the Middle Ages would a clear distinction between dream and vision be worked out.[94]

Ekstasis, which involved having visions while remaining awake, was well known to the early Christians, as the above reference to Paul already suggests. Again, one should note that the vocabulary often does not distinguish between *ekstasis* and dream. Hence, in *The Pastor* of Hermas 1.3 "I fell asleep" may either refer to *ekstasis* or to a trance.[95] The same difficulty in differentiating clearly between dreams and visions arises in monastic literature. Among anchorites, various phenomena such as visions, dreams, hallucinations, and ecstasy cannot easily be distinguished.[96]

The psychosomatic understanding of dreams in Patristic sources raises the question whether one can influence the content of dreams, or evoke a vision. In principle, says Tertullian, dreams remain under control of a man's will. Tertullian however points out that just as different diets will produce different sleeping conditions, so will they have a direct influence on dreams, and on ecstatic visions, which belong to the broader category of dreams. Hence Tertullian's suggestion that fasting might contribute to visions. The catch here is that ascetic practices are not the privilege of Christians alone, but are also well known to pagans: "For even demons require such discipline from their dreamers as a gratification to their divinity. . . . " Therefore, Tertullian points out, Daniel's fast was not meant to bring ecstasy, but rather to please God through humiliation of the body.[97] Ecstasy, indeed, should remain, as Philo had said, a *sobria ebrietas*. The dreams of Perpetua, similarly, are preceded and prepared by fasting. This careful and even diffident attitude of Tertullian toward fasting is characteristic of the general tone of Christian authors, and stands at the root of the use of fast and prayer in monastic literature. Their aim is not to induce dream and ecstasy, but, on the contrary, to prevent dreaming.

Conclusion

In a sense, we may perhaps speak of a "demotization" of dreams in late antiquity, due mainly to the Christian suppression of dream interpreters. This trend, however, does not mean that everyone had religiously important, or significant, or legitimate dreams to the same extent. With the emergence of a new perception of dreams in the early Christian centuries, the number of valid, significant dreams sent by God becomes drastically limited. But, since most dreams are sent by the demons, and in particular by their leader, Satan, significant and legitimate dreams and visions usually remain those of religious virtuosi, that is, monks, nuns, and saints, who know best how to avoid the devil's traps.

The ambiguous developments delineated above suggest the later transformation of dreams in two directions:

1. Dreams into utopias: when the collective side of dreams is emphasized, we witness what can be called a *continuatio apocalyptica*. Dreams and visions are recruited to the cosmic war against Satan and his hosts. In the ancient world, dreams often had a political significance, particularly the king's dreams. This political significance of dreams had disappeared in early Christian discourse. This disappearance was linked to the early Christian process of *Entpolitisierung*.[98] But as we have seen, even within an "enclave culture" dreams could reflect, in various schisms or heresies, a power struggle, the claim for an alternative source of revelation and religious

authority, and a direct contact with the divine, which would not be mediated through the Church hierarchy.

A new, collective approach to dreams developed. Accordingly, these dreams no longer predicted the future, but were transformed into utopias describing the ideal society. Christian utopias represent the immersion of the individual dream-vision within the apocalyptic messianic tradition.[99]

As a consequence of this apocalyptic way of thought, dreams and visions are often related to conscience, guilt, and penance. In a sense, dreams and visions will represent for Christian conscience the window into a different, new, redeemed reality. Such a dualist pattern between present reality and messianic expectations reflected in utopian dreams will become a major factor in the discourse on dreams, and even in the implicit perception of dreams, in Western thought throughout the centuries. In that sense, one may also argue that it lies at the root of Freudian psychoanalysis.

2. Dreams and visions as they had been known in early Christianity provided one of the major building blocks for Christian mysticism. Visions soon became reinterpreted as mystical experiences or as tours of heaven, as in Dante's *Divine Comedy*. The birth of Christian mysticism also reflects the transformation of the psychology of dreams and visions. Christian psychology reflects a turning inward and the equivalence of the inward/upward metaphors. Hence the visions of the upper world are also an enlightenment of the soul, and dreams come to be understood as a reflection of the state of the dreamer's soul.

If the Christian bearers of true visions are profoundly different from shamans and other specialists of religious ecstasy in ancient or archaic religions, this is at least partly due to the fact that the fundamental structure of Christianity prevents the easy dissociation between soul and body. Indeed, Christianity emphasizes, both explicitly and implicitly, the essential unity of the human composite, made in the image of God, and to be reunified after death at the time of resurrection.

As we have seen, in the new discourse dreams reflect the state of the soul rather than predicting the future. Simon Price has noted that while Artemidorus was interested in dreams as a key to the future, the Freudian revolution transformed them into mirrors of the self, as keys to the unconscious. In other words, Artemidorus's position is predictive, while Freud's is introspective.[100] As I have tried to show in the preceding pages, the basic attitude of many early Christian thinkers toward dreams and their significance reflects a major departure from that of Artemidorus.[101] One may argue, therefore, that early Christian discourse on dreams and visions represents the passage from ancient to modern attitudes. This passage is a direct consequence of the radical transformation of the supernatural world effected by fourth-century Christianity.[102] In a sense, the Freudian revolution began with the early Christian *Entzauberung der Welt*. If von Grunebaum's suggestion that we no longer need *Wahrtraum* is true, we owe this, in great part, to the anthropological revolution achieved by the early Christian thinkers.[103]

At the beginning of his *Menschliches, Allzumenschliches*, Nietzsche devotes a few pages to dreams. According to him, dreams entail the belief, common to ancient, simpler civilizations, in another world, parallel to this one. Dreaming is thus the source of all metaphysics. Nietzsche sees a direct link between this dichotomy of worlds and the dichotomy between body and soul. Hence, for him, the belief in spirits, and eventually in gods, is also a consequence of the seriousness granted to dreams. Dreaming, according to this perception, would be, to use the Marxist metaphor, an opium that lures men into abstaining from action and from revolt. It is at least an implicit conclusion of the preceding pages that the early Christian discourse on dreams and visions does not fit Nietzsche's approach. In its impoverishment and its strictures, it announces the birth of the modern, *entzaubert*, person.

Notes

1. This appears in the third dream; cf. the second and the fifth dreams. I quote according to Musurillo 1972. The dreams of Perpetua have been the subject of much research. See, for instance Amat 1985: 66–86, Robert 1982, and the feminist approach of Miller 1994: 148–183. See further Shaw 1993: 28, n. 63; and Bowersock 1995: 32–34. These studies refer to previous literature. On the broader context of martyrs' dreams, see Mertens 1986: 5–46.

2. For studies treating together late antique dreams and visions, see for instance Del Corno 1978: 1605–1618; Hanson 1980: 1395–1427; Consolino 1989: 237–256.

3. Prophetic literature also reflects violent arguments about dreams, since dreams can be perceived as the instrument of false prophecy, as in Jeremiah 23:25–28: "I have heard what the prophets said, that prophecy lies in my name saying, 'I have dreamed, I have dreamed.'" My thanks to R. J. Z. Werblowsky for calling this passage to my attention. In the Hebrew Bible, dreams can come "stealthily" (Job 4:12), but they can also be a major means of divine revelation (Gen. 28, 37, 41, 1 Kings 3); in Num. 12:6–8 it is through dreams that Yahwe makes Himself known to the prophets. See further Ottoson. On the question of dreams and visions in the New Testament, see Oepke. Oepke notes that the New Testament is relatively poor in dreams. See further Berger 1991: 125–129.

4. See my review of her book in *Journal of Religion*, 76 (1996), 469–470.

5. Fox 1987: 410, notes that approved dreams in Christianity had an obedient tone, unlike anything in Artemidorus's book.

6. On early Christian discourse, see Cameron 1991.

7. Dagron 1985: 37. See also E. R. Dodds's chapter on dream pattern and culture pattern in Dodds 1951. His main concern is not so much the dream experience of the Greeks as the Greek attitude to the dream experience.

8. There is no real English equivalent to *imaginaire*. "Cosmology" as used by sociologists has a less broad frame of reference than *imaginaire*. On the *imaginaire*, see Patlagean 1985; Kaufman 1985.

9. See n. 3 above. For a study of dreams from the perspective of social history, see the pioneering study of Burke 1973: 329–342.

10. Le Goff 1985: 293. Le Goff rightly emphasizes the significance of the passage from the demons to Satan.

11. On the Western medieval reflection on dreams, see Kruger 1992.

12. Tertullian, *De anima* 47.2 (65 Waszink). We are lucky to possess an admirable edition of and commentary upon this text: Waszink 1945. I quote the translation in the

Ante Nicene and Nicene Fathers, Vol. 3. The treatise on dreams extends from ch. 45 to 49.

13. On this text, see for instance Stahl 1952.

14. Le Goff 1985: 290.

15. Tert. *De an.* 42, end; 50, beginning.

16. See Iamblichus, *Mysteries of Egypt*, 3.7. On Gnostic perceptions, see MacRae 1976.

17. Tert. *De an.* 53. See further Tert. *De an.* 45: in sleep, the body rests, and is disconnected from the soul. Cf. Cyprian, *Ep.* 9 (*PL* 4, 253).

18. Tert. *De an.* 53, *in finem*.

19. Plutarch, *De sera numinis vindicta* 22.

20. For Sasanian Zoroastrianism, see Shaked 1995: 49. For the Greek tradition, see Kingsley 1995.

21. See for instance the enlightening remarks of Versnel 1987: 42–55. See further Festugière 1944: 310 and Festugière 1960: 95–98. He analyzes the heavenly visions of Asclepius in Aelius Aristides' *Sacred Tales*. Hermann Usener had insisted long ago on the importance of seeing the gods through their images in the ancient world.

22. On Christian incubation, see for instance Leclerq. The most careful study of the passage from pagan to Christian incubation is still Deubner 1900.

23. On him, see Behr 1968, and in particular, ch. 8: "The Interpretation of Dreams in Antiquity." See further Michenaud and Dierkens 1972, [*non vidi*], and A. J. Festugière's translation of the *Sacred Tales*, with a preface by J. Le Goff and notes by H. D. Saffrey: Aelius Aristide 1986. In his history of autobiography in antiquity, G. Misch refers to the *Sacred Tales* as an "oniric autobiography." On Artemidorus, see A. J. Festugière's translation of Artemidorus (1975).

24. See Refoulé 1961: 470–516, esp. 498.

25. See for instance Dulaey 1973.

26. Plutarch, *De defectu oraculorum* 419 c.

27. Although some esoteric traditions, inherited from Judaism, seem to have sought the vision of God. On these traditions, see Stroumsa, *Hidden Wisdom*, 1996.

28. On canonization processes in early Christianity, see Stroumsa 1994.

29. See for instance Philostratus, *Life of Apollonius of Tyana*, 2.37; cf. Cicero, *De divinatione*, 2.58.119; these and other texts are quoted and discussed in MacDermot 1971: 1, 41–45. On the practice of fasting in order to elicit dreams, see Fox 1987: 396.

30. This is in contradistinction to the thought of the rabbis, for whom the dream of a gentile does not count as a legitimate motive for conversion.

31. See Bouché-Leclercq 1879–1880: I, 93–94.

32. On dream interpretation in the ancient world, see Hopfner.

33. F. Cumont, 1949, 92: "*L'oniromancie est le seul mode paien de divination que l'Eglise n'ait pas répudié.*" On oneiromancy, see for instance Ps. Chrysostom, *PG* 64, 740–744, = Suda, s.v. *prophèteia*. This text is quoted by Dagron (1985: 40, n. 15) as a very influential text arguing that predictive dreams also exist for Christians, but that among the pagans, such dreams come from a pernicious art, while among the Christians, they come from virtue.

34. See Fox 1987: 392. On the Christian condemnation of divinatory dreams, see Devoti 1987: 119 and n. 46.

35. Synesius of Cyrene, *De somniis*. This work had been translated into Latin by Marcilio Ficino.

36. See Deubner 1900: 56 ff., and Delehaye 1912.

37. See for instance B. Flusin's comment on visions in the hagiography of Saint Anastasius the Persian, from sixth-century Palestine (Flusin 1992: 2, 142: "*La vision de Jean* [John of the Heptastomos] *est à la fois trop transparente et trop générale pour prêter à un long*

commentaire. . . . Il n'est pas un thaumaturge, capable par sa prière d'infléchir le cours des événements et de protéger la ville. Il devient un simple visionnaire, en un sens le successeur des prophètes, capable, parce qu'il est dioratique, de voir et de faire connaître aux autres le vrai sens de l'Histoire . . . "

38. See Dagron 1985: 40.

39. Origen, *Contra Celsum*, 1.48.

40. The New Testament apocrypha, in particular the *Apocryphal Acts of the Apostles*, are relatively rich in dreams and visions, but the status of this literature soon became problematic in mainstream Christianity, due to its popularity among various Gnostic groups and the Manichaeans.

41. Augustine, *De divinatione daemonorum*.

42. See for instance Stemberger 1976; Niehoff 1992. And see chapter 11 in this volume.

43. See Brague 1995, esp. 72, where Brague points out that in medieval Islamic thought some dreams are identified to the Koranic *mubashshirāt*, the continuation of prophecy after its official end, as it were.

44. Peterson 1951; cf. Schindler 1978.

45. Fox 1987: 377.

46. The bibliography is immense. See for instance Byl 1979.

47. Cf. n. 3 above.

48. Tert. *De an.* 46; see the important remarks of Waszink 1947 in his commentary, *ad loc.*

49. On these, see for instance Kessels 1969.

50. In *Odyssey* 14.495, for instance, *enupion* is put in opposition to *oneiros*. Elsewhere in Greek literature, *enupion* is usually the equivalent of *oneiros*, or *opsis enupiou*, the vision of a dream. See for instance Herodotus, *Historiae* 8.54. Cf. the distinction betwen *rêve* and *songe* in French. Philo, among others, does not distinguish between *enupion* and *oneiros*.

51. Le Goff (1985: 279) reminds us that this text will be fundamental in the twelfth-century renewal of reflection on dreams.

52. Tert. *De an.* 46.

53. Ibid. 47.

54. Fox 1987: 394.

55. See Hanson 1980.

56. See Kessels and Van der Horst 1987.

57. On this literature, see Schäfer 1992.

58. Letter 22.30, written in 383–384; text in Labourt 1949; 144–146. On this text, see Antin 1963.

59. " . . . *cum subito raptus in spiritu ad tribunal iudicis pertrahor, ubi tantum erat ex circumstantium claritate fulgoris ut proiectus in terram sursum aspicere non auderem.*" It is significant that at the end of the vision, when Jerome returns to earth, the text has "*reuertor ad superos*," which makes it clear that the throne of the judge is situated in the underworld, and not in the heavens.

60. See Guillaumont 1979. Benz (1961: 22) notes that the Christian distrust toward dreams came earlier than that toward visions. See further Benz's fundamental study, Benz 1962.

61. Diadoque de Photicé 1966: ch. 36–40, pp. 105–108.

62. Ch. 38, p. 107: *kalôn te kai phaulôn oneirôn.*

63. Tatian 1982: 36–37. For other second-century warnings from dreams sent by demons, see for instance Irenaeus, *Adversus haereses*, 1.16.3, Justin Martyr, *Apology*, 18.3, and Tertullian, *Apology*, 23.1.

64. On the devil in the early Christian tradition, see Forsyth 1987. Forsyth, however, does not study dreams.

65. I quote according to the translation of J. E. Bamberger, OCSO, Evagrius Ponticus, *The Praktikos: Chapters on Prayer* (1978).

66. Evagrius Ponticus, *Praktikos* 54.

67. Ibid. 59.

68. On the function of dreams in sect foundation, see Benz 1962: 253–266; Fox 1987: 399. Le Goff (1985: 284) refers to the importance of dreams among Ebionites, Valentinians, Carpocratians and Montanists; see further Dulaey 1973: 37–41.

69. On Gnostic literature, see in particular the rich study of Filoramo 1990. See esp. 51, where Filoramo rightly insists on the implications of a radical dualist anthropology for the perception of dreams. For some of the most important sources, see Eusebius, *Historia ecclesiastica* 4.7.9, Irenaeus, *Adversus haereses* 1.25.3 (about the Carpocratians honoring demons which send them dreams, "*oniropomps*"), Hippolytus, *Philosophoumena* 6.26, and the *Cologne Mani Codex* 4 and 23. See also Pagels 1978: 426 ff. Doresse 1958: 170, had already pointed out that in the vocabulary of the Gnostics, "I fell asleep" was a *terminus technicus* alluding to ecstasy. On one of the most interesting examples of vision among the Gnostics, see Casadio 1989.

70. This is one of the main points of Labriolle 1913. On visions among the Montanists, see Fox 1987: 404–410.

71. Text in Rehm 1953. Cf. Pseudo-Clementine *Recognitiones*, 2.62. I quote the translation in the *Ante Nicene and Nicene Fathers*. A. Le Boulluec is preparing a new annotated translation of this important text for the Sources Chrétiennes series.

72. See Eitrem 1991. See further Stroumsa, "Dreams" (1999).

73. Tert. *De an.* 43.

74. Ibid. 45, beginning.

75. Ibid. 47, end.

76. *De opificio homini* was written in 379. The discussion of dreams is in ch. 13.

77. Gen. 39:20–41:57 and Dan. 2.

78. Gregory of Nyssa, *De opficio homini*, 13.

79. Evagrius Pntikos, *Praktikos* 55.

80. Ibid. 56.

81. Ibid. 59.

82. Ibid. 54.

83. Ibid. 64.

84. See Dagron (1985: 43) on Evagrius, Barsanuphius, and John of Gaza's *Questions and Answers*, where the devil is the source of even visions of Jesus Christ. Dagron (1985: 46–47) points out that the monastic authors ask one to doubt such revelations. For Barnasuphius and John, no vision whatsoever is legitimate and true. Cf. the concept of *directeur spirituel* in post-Tridentine French Catholicism.

85. Dulaey 1973. See also Amat 1985; Crevatin 1988. In the Confessions, Augustine refers to various dreams of his mother Monica; see *Conf.* 3.11; 5.9; 6.1; 6.3; 6.13.

86. Augustine, *De gen ad lit.* 12.2.3. I quote according to the edition in the *Bibliothèque Augustinienne*, 332 ff.

87. Cf. Le Goff 1985: 300.

88. See esp. Augustine *De gen ad lit.* 12.30.

89. Augustine *De gen ad lit.* 12.3.6–8.19.

90. Ibid., 12.5.14.

91. Ibid., 12.6.15. On visions in Christian literature, see Adnès. See also "Epiphanie," *Reallexikon für Antike und Christentum* 5, 832–905.

92. Tert. *De an.* 45.

93. Ibid., 47 end.

94. Cf. Cyprian, *Ep.* 9, *PL* 4, 253.

95. Fox 1987: 383.

96. Refoulé 1961: 480; Dulaey, 1973: ch. 3.1; MacDermot 1971. See further Benz 1961, Benz 1962.

97. Tert. *De an.* 48 *in finem.*

98. For an analysis of this concept in Weberian terms, see Kippenberg 1991.

99. For medieval utopias, see Gardiner 1993.

100. Price 1986.

101. Hanson (1980: 1421) argues to the contrary that early Christian dream visions are not significantly different from those in the Hellenistic and Roman world.

102. Le Goff 1985: 293.

103. See von Grunebaum 1966: 20.

References

Adnès, P. "Visions." *Dictionnaire de Spiritualité* 16, 949–1002.

Aélius Aristide. 1986. *Discours sacrés.* Translated by A. J. Festugière. Paris.

Amat, J. 1985. *Songes et visions: L'au-delà dans la littérature latine tardive.* Paris.

Antin, Dom P. 1983. "Autour du rêve de Saint Jérôme." *Revue des Etudes Latines* 41, 350–377.

Bamberger, J. E. 1978. *The Praktikos: Chapters on Prayer.* Evagrius Ponticus. Cistercian Studies Series 4. Kalamazoo, MI: Cistercian Publications.

Behr, C. A. 1968. *Aelius Aristides and the Sacred Tales.* Amsterdam.

Benz, E. 1961. *Dreams, Hallucinations, Visions.* New York.

———. 1962. *Die Vision: Erfahrungsformen und Bilderwelt.* Stuttgart.

Berger, K. 1991. *Historische Psychologie des Neuen Testaments.* Stuttgarter Bibelstudien 146/147; Stuttgart.

Bouché-Leclercq, A. 1879–1880. *Histoire de la divination dans l'antiquité.* Paris, reprint New York, 1980.

Bowersock, G. W. 1995. *Martyrdom and Rome.* Cambridge.

Brague, R. 1995. "L'impuissance du Verbe qui a *tout* dit." *Diogène* 170, 49–74.

Burke, P. 1973. "L'histoire sociale des rêves." *Annales ESC* 28.

Byl, S. 1979. "Quelques idées grecques sur le rêve, d'Homère à Artémidore." *Les Etudes Classiques* 47, 107–129.

Cameron, A. 1991. *Christianity and the Rhetoric of Empire: The Development of Christian Discourse.* Berkeley, Los Angeles, London.

Casadio, G. 1989. "La visione in Marco il Mago." *Augustinianum,* 123–146.

Consolino, F. E. 1989. "Sogni e visioni nell' agiografia tardoantica: modelli e variazioni sul tema." *Augustinianum* 29.

Crevatin, G. 1988. "Agostino e il linguaggio dei sogni." *Versus: Quaderni di studi semiotici* 50/51, 199–215.

Cumont, F. 1949. *Lux Perpetua,* Paris.

Dagron, G. 1985. "Rêver de Dieu et parler de soi: le rêve de son interprétation d'après les sources byzantines." In T. Gregory (ed.), *I sogni nel medioevo.* Lessico intellettuale europeo 35. Rome.

Del Corno, D. 1978. "I sogni e la loro interpretazione nell'età dell'impero." *Aufstieg und Niedergang der Römischen Welt* (*ANRW*), 2.16.2.

Delehaye, H. 1912. *Les origines du culte des martyrs.* Bruxelles.

Deubner, L. 1900. *De incubatione.* Leipzig.
Devoti, D. 1987. "Sogno e conversione nei Padri: Considerazioni preliminari." *Augustinianum* 27.
Diadoque de Photicé. 1966. *Oeuvres Spirituelles.* E. des Places, S. J. (ed.). Sources Chrétiennes 5ter, Paris, Cerf.
Dodds, E. R. 1951. *The Greeks and the Irrational.* Berkeley, Los Angeles, London.
Doresse, J. 1958. *Les gnostiques d'Egypte.* Paris.
Dulaey, M. 1973. *Les rêves dans la vie et la pensée de saint Augustin.* Paris: Etudes Augustiniennes.
Eitrem, S. 1991. "Dreams and Divination in Magical Ritual." In C. A. Faraone and D. Obbink (eds.), *Magika Hiera: Ancient Greek Magic and Religion.* New York, Oxford, 175–187.
Festugière, A. J. 1944. *La révélation d'Hermès Trismégiste.* 1. Paris.
———. 1960. *Personal Religion among the Greeks.* Berkeley, Los Angeles.
———. (trans.) 1975. Artémidore, *La clef des songes: Onirocriticon.* Paris: Vrin.
Filoramo, G. 1990. "Diventare Dio: la palingenesi gnostica." In *Il risveglio della gnosi ovvero diventare dio*, Bari, 45–83.
Flusin, B. 1992. *La vie D'Anastase le Perse.* Paris.
Forsyth, N. 1987. *The Old Enemy: Satan and the Combat Myth.* Princeton.
Fox, R. Lane. 1987. *Pagans and Christians.* Hammondsworth.
Gardiner, E. 1993. *Medieval Visions of Heaven and Hell: A Source Book.* New York, London.
von Grünebaum, G. E. 1966. "The Cultural Function of the Dream as Illustrated by Classical Islam." In von Grünebaum and R. Caillois (eds.), *The Dream and Human Societies.* Berkeley, CA.
Guillaumont, A. 1979. "Les visions mystiques dans le monachisme oriental chrétien." In *Aux origines du monachisme chrétien.* Spiritualité orientale 30; Bégrolles en Mauge, 136–149.
Hanson, J. S. 1980. "Dreams and Visions in the Graeco-Roman World and Early Christianity." *ANRW*, 2.23.2.
Hopfner, Th. "Traumdeutung." *Pauly Wissowa Realencyklopädie*, 7.A.2, 2233–2245.
Kaufman, P. 1985. "Imaginaire et imagination." *Encyclopedia Universalis* 9, 776–783.
Kessels, A. H. M. 1969. "Ancient Systems of Dream Classification." *Mnemosyne* 22, 389–424.
Kessels, A. H. M. and Van der Horst, P. W. 1987. "The Vision of Dorotheus (Pap. Bodmer 29), Edited with Introduction and Notes." *Vigiliae Christianae* 41, 313–359.
Kingsley, P. 1995. *Ancient Philosophy, Mystery and Magic: Empedocles and Pythagorean Tradition.* Oxford.
Kippenberg, H. G. 1991. *Die vorderasiatische Erlösungsreligionen in ihren Zusammenhang mit der antiken Stadtherrschaft.* Frankfurt.
Kruger, S. F. 1992. *Dreaming in the Middle Ages.* Cambridge Studies in Medieval Literature 14; Cambridge.
Labriolle, P. 1913. *La crise montaniste.* Paris.
Labourt, J. (ed., trans.). 1949. *Lettres de Saint Jérôme*, vol. 1. Paris, Belles Lettres.
Leclerq, H. "Incubation." *Dictionnaire d'Archéologie Chrétienne et de Liturgie*, 7, 51–517.
Le Goff, J. 1985. *L'imaginaire médiéval.* Paris.
MacDermot, V. 1971. *The Cult of the Seer in the Ancient Middle East.* London.
MacRae, G. W., S. J. 1976. "Sleep and Awakening in Gnostic Texts." In U. Bianchi (ed.), *Le origine dello gnosticismo.* Supplements to Numen 12; Leiden, 496–507.
Mertens, C. 1986. "Les premiers martyrs et leurs rêves." *Revue d'Histoire Ecclésiastique* 81,
Michenaud, G. and Dierkens, T. 1972. *Les rêves dans les discours sacrés d'Aélius Aristide.* Bruxelles.

Miller, P. Cox. 1994. *Dreams in Late Antiquity: Studies in the Imagination of a Culture.* Princeton.

Musurillo, H. (ed., trans.). 1972. *Acts of the Christian Martyrs.* Oxford Early Christian Texts; Oxford.

Niehoff, M. 1992. "A Dream Which Is Not Interpreted Is Like a Letter Which Is Not Read." *Journal of Jewish Studies* 43, 58–84.

Oepke, "*onar.*" In G. Kittel (ed.). *Theological Dictionary of the New Testament,* 5, 220–238.

Ottoson, "*Chalôm.*" In G. J. Botterweck and H. Ringgren (eds.), *Theological Dictionary of The Old Testament,* 4, 421–432.

Pagels, E. 1978. "Visions, Appearances and Apostolic Authority: Gnostic and Orthodox Traditions." In B. Aland (ed.), *Gnosis: Festschrift für Hans Jonas.* Göttingen.

Patlagean, E. 1985. "L'histoire de l'imaginaire." *Encyclopedia Universalis* 9, 249–269.

Peterson, E. 1951. "*Monotheismus als politisches Problem.*" In *Theologische Traktate.* Munich.

Price, S. 1986. "The Future of Dreams: From Freud to Artemidorus." *Past and Present* 113, 3–37.

Refoulé, F. 1961. "Rêves et vie spirituelle d'après Evagre le Pontique." *La Vie Spirituelle, Supplément* 14, 470–516.

Rehm, B. (ed.). 1953. *Die Pseudo-Klementinen.* GCS 42; Berlin.

Robert, L. 1982. "Une vision de Perpétue martyre à Carthage en 203." *Comptes Rendus de l'Académie des Inscriptions et Belles Lettres,* 228–276.

Schäfer, P. 1992. *The Hidden and the Manifest God.* Albany, N.Y.

Schindler, A. (ed.). 1978. *Monotheismus als politisches Problem? Erik Peterson und die Kritik der politischen Theologie.* Gütersloh.

Shaked, Sh. 1995. *Dualism in Transformation.* London.

Shaw, B. D. 1993. "The Passion of Perpetua." *Past and Present* 139, 3–45.

Stahl, W. H. (intr., trans.). 1952. *Macrobius, Commentary on the Dream of Scipio.* New York.

Stemberger, B. 1976. "Der Traum in der rabbinischen Literatur." *Kairos* 18, 1–42.

Stroumsa, G. G. 1994. "The Body of Truth and Its Measures: New Testament Canonization in Context." In H. Preissler and H. Seiwert (eds.), *Gnosisforschung und Religionsgeschichte: Festschrift Kurt Rudolph.* Marburg, 307–316.

———. 1996. *Hidden Wisdom: Esoteric Traditions and the Roots of Christian Mysticism.* Studies in the History of Religions 70; Leiden.

———. 1999. "Dreams and Magic among Pagans and Christians." In Stroumsa, *Barbarian Philosophy: The Religious Revolution of Early Christianity,* Tübingen, 191–203.

Tatian. 1982. *Oratio ad Graecos.* M. Whittaker (ed., trans.). Oxford Patristic Texts. Oxford, Clarendon.

Versnel, H. S. 1987. "What Did Ancient Man See When He Saw a God?: Some Reflections on Greco-Roman Epiphany." In D. avn der Plas (ed.), *Effigies Dei: Essays on the History of Religion.* Studies in the History of Religion 51; Leiden.

Waszink, J. H. 1947. *Tertullian, De anima.* Amsterdam.

11

Communication with the Dead in Jewish Dream Culture

Galit Hasan-Rokem

for Raanan Kulka

Mortals are immortals and immortals are mortals,
the one living the others' death and dying the others' life.

—*Heraclitus of Ephesus*

The frequency with which dead people appear in dreams and act and associate with us as though they were alive has caused unnecessary surprise and has produced some remarkable explanations which throw our lack of understanding of dreams into strong relief.

—*Sigmund Freud*

1

Dreams are visual experiences that are necessarily transformed into words in order to turn them into meaningful communication, not just among individuals, but also between the dreaming individual and her/himself. Their presence in culture is thus characterized by a semiotic complexity of levels in which the seen and the heard, the spoken and the shown, are intensely interrelated, but also marked in their difference. Defying Lessing's taxonomy of media and Kantian categories of perception, they seem to elude both time and space, while turning the elements of both into categories that are radically transformed by the cognitive and expressive uniqueness of the phenomenon of dreaming. Thus they resemble other states in which numinous and supernatural experiences occur.

As visual vehicles of meditation, memory, and interpretation, they present themselves doubly: snapshots from an internally generated *terra incognita* but also stylized maps of the same; metonyms as well as metaphors of inner journeys. They thus invite interpretation both as fragments of a whole never to be completely perceived and as synecdochic keys to a comprehensive symbolical code. It is this mental, communicative, and semiotic indefiniteness of dreams that has turned them into an enigmatic epicenter of interpretative praxis in many cultures.

This essay is about the nexus of dreams and death in Jewish textual tradition. Although it is not possible to characterize "the Jewish way" of dreaming or interpreting dreams, some themes are persistent enough to be regarded as central, or as keys. Death, one such key theme, powerfully focuses the existential and epistemological potential of dreams. Its manifestations in Jewish dream culture problematize other central concepts and practices of the culture, among them monotheism, visual representations of the sacred, divination, and the afterlife.

Dreams have been given a privileged position in Jewish culture since biblical times. The tension and oscillation between totality and utter fragmentation that are implicit in dreaming correlate them strongly to human experience vis-à-vis the divine as articulated in Hebrew religious literature since its emergence.

Leo Oppenheim's comprehensive study of dream interpretation in the ancient Near East bears ample witness to the fact that dream interpretation carried an enormous weight in the birthground of Hebrew culture.[1] Dreams gained importance far beyond the domain of private life—for example, in major decisions of a political character; this pervasiveness is intricately interwoven with the expressive articulation of the presence of holiness in the world of humans. The centrality of dreams in early Sumerian and Semitic texts enabled Oppenheim to delineate one of the terminological constructs still governing much of the discussion of dreams in the Bible and in rabbinic literature, namely prophetic dreams and symbolic dreams, or the dream as prophetic vision, as riddle or enigmatic message.

It should thus not surprise us that dreams have a special, marked position in biblical texts, and are inserted into them in a way which reflects their central status in the construction of religious fantasies and norms.

While the text does not inform us if Abraham's initiation into the unity of the one God included a dream vision, Jacob—the patriarch who fathered the tribes of Israel—did have a major dream experience. Jacob's dream of the ladder and the angels portrays a formidable *axis mundi* through which the building blocks of Israelite identity—patriarchy, electedness, and the land of Canaan—traffic between heaven and earth.

The dream texts of the Hebrew Bible concern, in general, leaders and kings (Jacob, Joseph, Gideon, Solomon, and Nebuchadnezzar). Two lacunae call for attention: there is no dream dreamt by a woman, and there is no appearance of a dead person in a dream. The correlation between the two omissions may be understood by recalling the visit of Saul to the witch of Endor, who conjures up an apparition of the dead Samuel. The practice she specializes in is absolutely forbidden and practically extinguished by the monarch himself. To attain communication with the dead, Saul has to transgress a prohibition ordered by his own authority, and to conceal his own identity.

The story of Saul's visit to the necromancer is inserted in the sequence of narratives describing David's preparations for his future position as a king. "Now Samuel was dead and all Israel had lamented him and buried him in Ramah, his own city. And Saul had driven away the necromancers and magicians from the land" (1 Sam. 28:3). The information about Samuel's death is redundant, since it was already mentioned (1 Sam. 25: 1). Its reappearance in the verse about Saul's puritan measures against the mediators of the world of the dead is thus of special significance. It is precisely the death of Samuel—who anointed Saul but also kept chastising him, and who was Saul's main source of information about God's will—which seems to have motivated Saul's drastic reform. Saul tries to free himself from Samuel's patronizing presence even as a dead soul. Thus he drives away the necromancers very much like the father of Briar Rose (Sleeping Beauty), who orders the destruction of all the spindles in his kingdom. Saul's ambition to prove his personal autonomy is, however, doomed to fail in the crisis that has befallen him: the Philistines are preparing for war and David recruits popular support against the king. Moved by fear caused by the sight of the mass of Philistine soldiers, Saul tries to establish communication with God via all the legitimate mediators—through dreams, by *Urim* (a divinatory device managed by the high priest), and through prophets—but with no success. The technique of *Ovot*—necromancy—is his last hope. Tragically for Saul, the apparition of the dead prophet Samuel can only reinforce what already seems obvious: God has abandoned the king.

The precise mode of mediation between Saul and Samuel—and through Samuel with God—is presented in the story in a regrettably unclear way. It seems, however, that only the conjuror herself sees the dead person, whereas the client only hears him. The separation of sensory systems in communication with the dead echoes the strong sense of detachment and fragmentation that is the hallmark of the perception of the dead by the living in Jewish culture.

One particular verse in the Endor narrative has caused the interpreters severe trouble: "And the king said unto her, do not fear, what have you seen, and the woman said: I saw gods rising from the earth" (1 Sam. 28:13). Two pieces of linguistic information are essential. First, "Do not fear, what have you seen" is actually a paronomastic conundrum (*al tirei ki ma rait*) in which fear and seeing are equated. Saul, who only hears and does not see the vision, articulates the paradox, "Do not see what you have seen." Even though the primary meaning of Saul's words is clear, they also convey the awe of the numinous, visual experience embodied in the dead and the divine. Second, the word translated in English as "gods" has the exact form of the word usually translated as God—*Elohim*. It is from the plural form of the verb "rising" (*olim*) that the subject's identity as gods rather than God may be derived, and even then the *pluralis majestatis* is also a possibility. The Aramaic translation, Targum Jonathan, quotes the woman as follows: "I saw the angel of God rising." Rashi's medieval commentary elaborates as follows: "'I saw gods rising from the earth'—two angels (or messengers) Moses and Samuel, because Samuel feared [the same verb as in verse 13] that he was summoned for trial, so he brought up Moses along with him."[2] The commentator

Radaq (Rabbi David Qimchi) mentions the Talmud passages but actually prefers the metaphoric understanding, "Big as gods (or God?)," whereas a later interpreter (Metsudat David) glosses the above-mentioned plural form as *pluralis majestatis*, that is, the One.

This whole discussion points to the complexity and paradoxicality of the status of the visual numinous experience in Israelite, and later Jewish, culture. God's words to Moses, "There shall no man see me and live" (Exod. 33:20), and the ailing king Hezeqia's self-pitying words quoted by the prophet Isaiah, "I shall go to the gates of Sheol . . . I shall not see Yah, Yah in the land of the living" (Isa. 38:10–11), as well as the description of the revelation at Sinai, "And all the people saw the voices" (Exod. 20:18)—all this suggests an unresolved contradiction concerning visual communication with the divine. If a living man who sees God will not live, are the dead in the presence of God—and can they see him? Can Yah not be seen in the land of the living? Or perhaps He is only in the land of the living? The complexity of the relationship of being alive, being dead, seeing, and God is a knot in the depth of the textual web.

That there are no dead in dreams in the Bible stems from a general apprehension toward the dead, which permeates the cultural registers of ancient Israel represented in the biblical corpus. Communication with the dead is relegated to the domain of folk religion, stamped as pagan, or rather idolatrous. When a glimpse of such traffic is shown, it is practiced by a woman, to point out its dubious status.

The communication of women with death and the dead is not restricted to this one instance in the Hebrew Bible. Lamentation for the dead is a feminine practice in biblical culture, as it had been in ancient Greece and in the Mediterranean area for generations.[3] Moreover, it is the creation of woman in Genesis 2 that provides the narrative incentive for turning the Edenic immortal Adam into a mortal man. She becomes his woe-man, so to speak.

Hava, the name of the first woman, is associated with life, which is given to her by Adam. This resonates both with his own being, "a living soul" (*nefesh ḥaya*, Gen. 2:7) and the totality of living creatures (Gen. 1:24, 2:19) as well as with the description of the snake as one of "the living creatures of the field" (*ḥayat ha-sade*, Gen. 3:1). The verbal inscription of her name thus places her in the domain of life and foregrounds that part of her cultural meaning. In the narrative, however, she both embodies and contradicts the fantasy of eternal life invested in Edenic existence.

The term for Adam's "deep sleep" (*tardema*) is taken up by Elihu in his oration directed to the suffering Job. Elihu's use of the word suggests the intimate relationship between living and sleeping, or rather living and dreaming: "In a dream in a vision of the night, when deep sleep falleth upon men. . . . He keepeth back his soul from the pit and his life from perishing. . . . He will deliver his soul from going into the pit, and his life shall see light. . . . To bring back his soul from the pit, to be enlightened with the light of the living" (Job 33:15, 18, 28, 30). Significantly, Elihu extends the life-giving power God invests in humans from the preventive measure of "keeping back from the pit" (*yaḥsokh nafsho mini shaḥat*) to "delivery from going into the pit" (*padah nafshi me'avor ba-shaḥat*) to the explicitly redemptive "to bring back his soul from the pit" (*lehashiv nafsho mini shaḥat*). Elihu thus provides a powerful articulation of the idea that, although sleep resembles death, human beings need dreams for their well-being, perhaps even for their survival.

2

Whereas Elihu in his speech proposes that dreaming vitalizes the dreamer her/himself, in Jewish dream culture from late antiquity onward, in marked contrast to biblical texts on dreams, dreaming serves as a major vehicle to revitalize dead others as actual presences in the lives of dreamers.[4]

There are numerous and varied appearances of the dead in dreams in rabbinic literature. Such an appearance may be presented as having a perfectly practical function. One such instance is actually the textual hook on which the lengthy passage on dreams in the Palestinian Talmud (*Ma'aser Sheni* 4–5) hangs. The Mishna portion being discussed states:

> Whosoever tells his son that the second tithes [which he reserved] are in this nook and he finds them in another nook, they are [declared] ordinary; that he left a hundred [coins] and he finds two hundred, the difference [the other hundred] is ordinary; two hundred and he finds one hundred, all of it is tithes.

It seems quite evident that the reason why the father himself cannot be consulted is that he has departed for a distant place or, more likely, that he is dead.

The following Talmudic discussion elaborates on the issue:

> There was a man who was worried about his father's money. His father appeared in his dream and told him the sum and the location of the money. It was brought before the rabbis who said: What is said in dreams does not weigh in either direction. (Ibid.)

The initial reaction of the rabbis sounds completely acceptable from a rational point of view. On the other hand it is followed by a long passage with examples which, at least to some degree, prove the opposite. These texts clearly indicate the complexity of rabbinic views on dream interpretation.

This compexity reflects the formal aspect of the multivocal structure of rabbinic literature of late antiquity. Rabbi So-and-So says one thing, Rabbi Somebody Else says another thing: the very structuring of the text as dialogue and as a chain of tradition embodies a dialogical interaction that presents itself to us as a true celebration of disagreement. Significantly, the categorical rejection of the halakic significance of dreams, or even of their significance in general, is in this case attributed to a collective voice, "the rabbis." Its initial position in the sequence of dreams in *Ma'aser Sheni* perhaps overstates its normative, representative, and authoritative character, and presents the other views quoted (from individuals) as subversive. As our knowledge of the intricate procedure of turning the oral traditions of the Talmudists (*Amoraim*) into a written work is still very incomplete, it is difficult to judge whether this seeming opposition beween authority and subversion stems from the dynamics of the oral tradition itself or if it has been superimposed by the editorial organization of the materials.

The discussion initiated by the example of the man who dreamt the place where his father had deposited his tithes leads to the presentation of additional dreams:

> A man came to Rabbi Yossi ben-Halafta and told him: I saw in my dream that I was told: Go to Cappadocia and you will find your father's fortune. He [Rabbi Yossi] asked: Did that man's [the dreamer's] father ever go to Cappadocia in his lifetime? He answered: No. He [Rabbi Yossi] said to him: Go and count ten rafters in your house and you will find your father's fortune under rafter *kappa*. (Ibid.)

The interpretation of Rabbi Yossi seems to refer to the position of the Greek letter *kappa* in the alphabet as tenth, rather than to its numerical value, twenty, paralleling the numerical system practiced in the Hebrew alphabet. (In the Babylonian Talmud version, *Berakhot* 55b, "*kappa*" is interpreted as the term for the rafter and the number ten is derived from the end of the word "*docia*"—"*deka*").

I have elsewhere discussed the central motif of both the above dreams: a father who leaves a fortune to his son who is compelled to complete a task, often to solve the riddle, in order to inherit it.[5] The motif reflects the father-son relationship between God and Israel, which is widely represented in rabbinic narratives, especially in parables. The relationship is thus constantly tested in numerous narrative renderings. But in this case the issue is also the basically enigmatic character of the individual's identity, which seeks reaffirmation in a mode paralleling it in its elusiveness. Knowledge about the legitmacy of lineage is reached in a dream.

The second dream text presents in an extremely condensed form—characteristic of the poetics of rabbinic literature in late antiquity—the semiotic complexity of the audial and the visual, in line with our earlier remarks. Thus the dream is a hybrid of a message dream and a symbolic dream, the classical categorization of Artemidoros, which has become a standard division in European folk interpretation of dreams as well as in the scholarly discourse on the subject. The dreamer sees a dream, but its contents are verbal, almost like a realization of the sacred, synesthetic metaphor applied in the description of the revelation at Mount Sinai: "And the people saw the voices" (Exod. 20:18). This cognitive process seems to proceed in an implied, almost automatic manner. The hypostatization of the heard voice as a visible entity, which is simultaneously to replace the visible and to eradicate it, represents a level of theological epistemology that problematizes the whole perception of visual reality. The synesthetic construction questions sensory experience by distorting its usual framework. Likewise dreams very often employ the power of the senses but also belie this same power. The mixture of sensory systems, like the above-mentioned separation between them, is common to dream experiences and experiences of the numinous.[6]

The sequence of dreams in the Palestinian Talmud tractate *Ma'aser Sheni* continues with some examples in which dreams are interpreted to communicate incestuous wishes or wish-fulfillments (the two possibilities are within a fairly sensible interpretative range of the text). These texts have been especially central for understanding the rabbinic influence on Freud's theory of dream interpretation, based on dreams and interpretations such as, "I saw an olive tree watered by olive oil . . . he knew his mother; I saw one of my eyes kiss the other . . . he knew his sister."[7] However, the perspective of this essay leads us to halt at another dream: "A man came to Rabbi Yishmael ben Rabbi Yossi and told him: I saw in my dream a star being swallowed. He said to him: May his spirit leave him [an extremely powerful curse], he has killed a Jew, as it is written: 'There shall rise a star out of Jacob'" (Num. 24:17; the blessing of Bileam). This is the only dream from the sequence in the Palestinian Talmud passage that employs a biblical verse as an interpretative key for a dream. In the much more extensive passage on dreams in the Babylonian Talmud (*Berakhot* 55a–57b), this technique is presented as a standard procedure of conversions. The dream may also be understood to imply an ethnic opposition between Jew and non-Jew.

The interpretation of the symbol is quite simple and does not differ in principle from the earlier ones in the passage in which no verse was applied. The fact that a verse is employed here may be a mere coincidence, but it may also be there because this dream, unlike the others, has moved from the area of tabooed sex and social status (in dreams I have not quoted) to that of death. It is the revelation of this subject that, more than others, either needs corroboration from a biblical source or, by association, leads the discourse to a text from the sacred corpus.

The dreams that have been discussed until now all lack the part which for most people who submit their dreams to interpretation must seem the most important—the realization of the interpretation in reality. In systematic dream books there are, as a rule, no such moments. The question of realization arises in the context of dream narratives, that is, when people tell their dreams not for the purpose of interpretation, but in order to construct a past reality, or even a biography, in which a dream, its interpretation, and its realization all play an important role. In such narratives the direction of the discourse turns from the future—which dominates some, but not all, dream-interpretative discourses—to the past; and the mode shifts from prescription to description.[8]

In the context of the legal discourse of the Talmud, which leaves most cases unresolved in the strictly pragmatic sense, thus open to future interpretation and extrapolation, the lack of solutions to enigmatic dreams is not surprising. This seems to me to reveal the speculative character of the rabbis' intellectual activity, despite the prevailing view of their interests as mainly pragmatic. Whereas the referential aspect of the text predominantly addresses the past, interpreting and reinterpreting Scripture, the conative aspect—focusing on the recipient—actively turns toward future generations.[9] The dialogical character of the rabbinic corpus is not limited to internal textual relations, which abound in the varieties of dialogue, but also evolves in an openly self-reflexive manner into the process of future-oriented interpretation.

The dreams in the passage from the Palestinian Talmud discussed above, where the result in reality is accounted for, present powerful examples of what is best characterized, I believe, as word magic. The magical effect of the interpreter's words is further stressed by the next account, where a woman comes to Rabbi Eliezer (variants: Elazar) and tells a dream—in which a rafter of her house was broken. His interpretation predicts the birth of a son, which indeed occurs. The symbolic aspect of the interpretation resonates with a standard metaphor in rabbinic language: a man's wife is called his house. The interpretation of birth in terms of breaking a rafter reveals an intimate knowledge of the connection between giving birth and rupture, danger and death.

After a while, however, the woman dreams the same dream again. She returns to ask for an interpretation. When she arrives for the second time, Rabbi Yishmael happens to have left his students alone; they do their best to replace him as dream interpreter. This proves to have fatal consequences as their interpretation reveals a much more one-dimensional understanding of the symbol of the broken rafter—so that death alone is projected, and the subtle and vital connection with giving birth is overlooked. The students interpret the broken beam as predicting the death of the dreamer's husband, which soon occurs. Upon hearing the wailing of the widowed dreamer, Rabbi Yishmael teaches his disciples an important lesson in dream interpretation: "You have killed a man. The dream follows its interpretation, as has been said: 'And it came to pass as he interpreted to us'" (Gen. 41:13; the master of butlers to Pharaoh concerning Joseph).[10]

More than any theoretical formulation in rabbinical texts, the dreamer's return to Rabbi Yishmael clearly states a rejection of static interpretations of dreams based on lists of symbols and their meanings. The interpretation proves to be absolutely dependent on a specific context of interpretation, on the personality of the participants, their knowledge, wisdom, and maturity, and their choice of those fate-laden words in which they choose to formulate their interpretation. It thus strongly resembles the hermeneutical praxis of Midrash, in which numerous, contextually recreated interpretations may grow out of reading one and the same biblical text. Interpretation of dreams, like the interpretation of sacred texts, is thus seen as the specific dialogue of a given individual in a personalized context.

Rafters seem to carry special significance in ancient dream lore. In one of the best-known dreams of antiquity—Penelope's in *Odyssey* 19, line 544—the eagle (interpreted as Odysseus himself) perches on the rafter of the gabled roof. The dream itself is followed by the most articulate version of early Hellenic oneiric theory, built around the famous image of the gates of ivory and the gates of horn. The rafter, however, connects the dream with intimate experiences inside the house, within the family and the married couple. In both the Greek and the Jewish examples, the rafter is interpreted as a male element which, together with the female image of house, constructs the union of man and wife (in rabbinic language *beta*—house—is explicitly also a term for wife; the Homeric term *melathron* may also mean "house" in later usage). In all the rafter dreams mentioned here, the dynamics of fragmentation of the whole, and the construction of a whole from fragments, seem to be central. Birth, which complements the structure of the family, occurs through a break in the female body. The death of the husband obviously truncates the wholeness of the family. And Odysseus's interpretation of his wife's dream (*before* she has recognized him) signals the imminent end of the long separation between them.

3

The passage on dream interpretation in the Palestinian Talmud, which has supplied the examples discussed above, is "recycled" (in a reformulated version) in *Midrash Rabba* on the Book of Lamentations. Many cultures privilege the theme of death in the discourse of dream interpretation. I hope that the discussion above has introduced some of the specific issues that arise in the context of a culture wrestling with the complexity and paradoxes of monotheism, and also laboring to shape meaningful connections between the latter and the human experiences of separation, fragmentation, individuality, and insecurity. In the Palestinian Midrash on Lamentations, *Eikha Rabba*, the theme of death in the text of dream interpretations echoes the central historical subject of the book—death and suffering caused by the destruction of the second temple in Jerusalem and Roman oppression. The dream narratives foreground the metaphysical as well as the universal aspects of this historical narrative.

Eikha Rabba presents a succession of riddle tales and dream tales. This sequence naturally stresses the interconnectedness of both genres and, in the process of reading, projects one genre onto another. Thus both the oneiric flavor of riddle images and the enigmatic character of dreams are highlighted.

The dream of the swallowed star, cited above, is also interpreted as the murder of a Jew in *Eikha Rabba*, on the basis, however, of a different Biblical verse, the image of the innumerable stars in God's promise to Abraham (Gen. 15:5). Both verses set the murder of an individual Jew in the context of a collective prophecy of a bright future for the people. While, on one hand, the transcendence of the group over individual mortality may be understood as a source of consolation, it also sharpens the total loneliness of the individual, most clearly embodied in each individual death. Similarly to death, which is inevitably experienced individually, dreams are a cultural practice rooted in a radically isolated experience; this experience can, moreover, only be communicated secondarily—unlike death, which usually cannot be communicated at all.

The most extensive text on dream interpretation in rabbinic literature is the passage of almost three folio pages in the Babylonian Talmud, *Berakhot* 55a–57b ff. This passage displays striking variety in form, contents, and genres as well as in ideological and epistemological approaches.

The text moves from a total denial of the ontological value of dreams to the view that a dream is a diminutive prophecy; from examples of how interpretation is the one and only factor that determines how the dream is going to be fulfilled in reality, to lists of dream symbols and their standard interpretations. This wide range of ideas is again possible because of the chorus of voices—or rather, the host of expressive solos—representing informants of at least three centuries (first century C.E. to fourth century C.E.), two countries (Palestine and Babylonia), and several cultural environments (late Hellenistic, Roman, Persian, Byzantine).

This text understates the role of dreams as conveyors of messages from the dead in comparison with other texts, both in the Palestinian sources already discussed and in the Babylonian Talmud itself. On the other hand, it includes a horror tale about the death of the wife of Rava (a Babylonian Jewish sage) as the result of a dream interpreter's negative interpretation—given because Rava did not pay him. Here again the magical power of the interpretative formula is highlighted. Since Rava's dreams, like those of his colleague Abaye (who paid the interpreter and therefore received benign interpretations), are mostly scriptural verses, the exposition of the inherent polysemy of the biblical text emerges as a by-product of the story.

4

This section of *Berakhot* masterfully expresses the delicate balance between psychological motivations and magical powers in the story of two Jewish sages, Rabbi Yehoshua ben-Hanania (Palestinian) and Shmuel (Babylonian), who are approached by two kings, a Roman emperor and the Persian king Shapur. The two rulers provoke the sages to enact Jewish wisdom by demanding that they predict what the emperor and the king will dream the next night. The sages recite two striking pictures, paralleling and mirroring each other, in which the ruler is captured by adversaries (the Roman by the Persians and vice versa) and forced to perform a menial task using a golden tool. The picture reminds us of Harold Bloom's remark about Rieff's commentary on the relationship between the dream and its message according to Freud: " . . . what matters is some protruding element, some element that seems hardly to belong to the text."[11]

The consecutive appearance of the two scenes as dreams is doubly coded in this context. One possibility is that the Jews are indeed able to foresee dreams, and thus their wisdom is of a magical character. The other is that the wisdom of Rabbi Yehoshua and Shmuel is psychological: they apply the device of suggestion, thereby determining the contents of the dreams rather than predicting them.

The double perspective of psychological and magical motivations lies at the center of the multifaceted picture of dream interpretation in rabbinic sources. It would be false to try to trace that ambivalence back to a sociological dichotomy such as popular (magical) and elite (psychological)—a solution sometimes offered by scholars. In the context of the paradoxes of monotheism in its correlation to human experience, the need to contain epistemological ambivalence may be a major reason for the central position of dreams. Along these lines, dreaming and dream interpretation may be understood as one of the expressive arenas in which a human and a superhuman perspective meet, communicate, and clash. Other such arenas are sacred texts and rituals.

5

The rites of the dead are conducted by the living. Often, however, eulogies and lamentations use the desperate second-person form, to prolong the liminal phase of parting, to halt the final detachment. The image of dreaming is suggestive of that fluid stage. By introducing it the rabbis present a possible bridge over the clear division between the living and the dead:

> R. Shimon ben Laqish said: The difference between us and the [dead] righteous is only in speech. R. Ishian [said]: The dead person hears his praise as if in dream. R. Shimon ben Laqish said: Those who are alive know what those who are dead do, and those who are dead know nothing about what those who are alive do.[12]

In a long passage in the Palestinian Midrash compilation *Bereshit Rabba*, from which the above is quoted, Ben Laqish deals with hindrances in communication between the living and the dead (he is discussing the immortality of the righteous). One of these hindrances is the inability to speak. In the Babylonian Talmud (*Berakhot* 19a), the same is said in the context of the question of whether the dead can hear eulogies. The discussion introduces a detailed list of the different stages of the decomposition of the body and the varying degrees of ability of the dead to hear during those stages.

The power of the text lies in its intense ambiguity: the dead are dreaming those alive—who are in a dream—and the dead appear in the dreams of the living. R. Ishian proposes the dream as a possible bridge between the worlds. His intuition correlates the dead with dreams, since that is where mortals are able to encounter them. A dead person is portrayed as sleeping and dreaming of those alive who are praising him. Thus those who are alive are the dream of the dead. R. Ishian's image comes quite close to the widely known notion of life as a dream. Ben Laqish's second sentence—"Those who are alive know what those who are dead do, and those who are dead know nothing about what those who are alive do"—may be seen as a reaction to the idea expressed by R. Ishian: since the dead dream the living, the living constitute for them the unknown sphere of the dream. It remains unclear what Ben Laqish means with the beginning of this sentence—"Those who are alive know what those who are dead do"—unless he is referring to the physical condition of the corpse.

One of the most compelling dream narratives about the communication between the living and the dead appears in the Babylonian Talmud (*Mo'ed Qatan* 28a):

> Rav Seorim, the brother of Rava, was sitting [and studying] in front of Rava. He saw him [Rava] "fall asleep" [dying]. He [Rava] said: Tell [the angel of death] not to cause me pain. The other answered: Are you not a "best man" [an important man] yourself? He answered: Once man's fortune is in the hands [of the angel of death] he does not mind him. He said: Please appear to me [in a dream, after death]. He appeared to him and asked: Were you in pain? He said: Like the piercing for bloodletting.
>
> Rava was sitting [and studying] in front of Rav Nahman. He saw him [Rav Nahman] "fall asleep" [dying]. He [Rav Nahman] said: Tell [the angel of death] not to cause me pain. Answered the other: Are you not an important man yourself? He answered: Who is important, who is safe, who is strong [facing the angel of death]? He said: Please appear to me [in a dream, after death]. He appeared to him and he asked: Were you in pain? He said: Like pulling a thread out of milk. But if God would tell me "Go back to the world where you were," I would not want it, since the fear is great.

This dream narrative presents the distance between the living and the dead as unusually close. The dying teachers and their disciples are even able to arrange a dream rendezvous across the border between here and eternity. The narratives are, however, permeated with feelings of insecurity and fear in the face of the moment of death. Both teachers reveal their weakness, turning to their disciples in a desperate attempt to alleviate the pain of death. According to the rabbinic ethos, disciples learn from their teachers by close observation and imitation, even of most intimate and quotidian behaviour. The function of the doubling of the narratives seems to be at least partly to show that even the manner of dying is transmitted from teacher to disciple, from R. Nahman to Rava. Rava, who occupies a special position in Babylonian Jewish magical tradition (the making of the Golem, Bab. Talmud *Sanhedrin* 65b), serves as the connecting link of the tradition; he learns from his teacher and teaches his own disciple the tradition of bridging over the limit of death and life—by dreaming.

Unlike Ben Laqish, the narrator of the double tale seems to think that the only ones who know what dying is really about are those who have already experienced death. The concluding words of R. Nahman remain enigmatic, and even the lexical choice for the word "fear" is unusual (*b'twty*). One could interpret the concluding sentence according to Stoic philosophy: death is where calm is, and returning to this world and its anxieties is undesirable. On the other hand, the enigmatic formulation at the end of the story conveys a countermessage to the story itself. Whereas the story seems to tell us that dreams are a possible channel of communication between the dead and the living, the final sentence reinforces the emotional presence of the impenetrable, unknown domain of death.

As in many other dreams in ancient Jewish sources, here, too, there is a striking visual component, although the dreams are primarily staged as audial communication. The two metaphorical descriptions of the pain of death function at first "sight" to familiarize the utterly unknown and to reassure the listener about the unthreatening proportions of the awesome moment. On the other hand the symbolic significance of blood and milk connects these fluids with a mystery of no less power than the moment of death—namely, that of birth. The red and white of the vital fluids introduce the perspective of the beginning into dreams dealing with the anxiety of the end. Thus a heightened sense of transformation is created that leads in (at least) two directions. Birth and death are the harmonious frame of a meaningful unit—life. The meaning lies in its very framing as a linear process. On the other hand, the occurrence of blood and milk in the description of death also transposes the departure from one life into birth in another one. Strangely, the introduction of the perspective of a new life into the story does not create a tone of consolation, but rather disrupts the equilibrium achieved by the framed span.

In Jewish culture of late antiquity, as in many other periods and places, midwiving and lamenting are both womanly arts. Thus the appearance of blood and milk, representing labor and nursing, may be seen as representatives of the "exotic" world of women in the all-male reality of teachers and disciples (especially in Babylonia). On the other hand, the relations between the men in these two narratives represent an alternative mode of intimacy, that of studying together, from which women are excluded. The pictures of blood and milk in these two dreams are carefully detached from the archetypal context of birth and nursing: bloodletting occurs in rabbinic texts as a perfectly acceptable male occupation (Abba Umna in Bab. Talmud *Ta'anit* 21b–22a). The lifting of the thread or the net from the milk brings to mind the preparation of cheese, which in the Middle East until this day may be done by men, unlike the preparation of other kinds of food. White and red are also the dominant colors in the passage called "the tractate on the gestation of the child" (Bab. Talmud *Niddah* 31a). There the vital fluids are blood and semen, and there is an operative collaboration—rather than separation—of female and male in conjunction with God. In contrast to the image of wholesomeness in the relationship man-woman-God projected in "the tractate on the gestation of the child," the two short stories about Rav Seorim, Rava and Rav Nahman also introduce fragmentation into the sphere of the divine by associating the process of dying with the ambiguous agent called the angel of death, rather than with God himself.[13]

An earlier passage of the *Niddah* text elaborates another aspect of the transcendental potential of dreams:

> Rabbi Simlai presented the text: What does the child look like in his mother's womb? He rests like a folded writing board [*pinax*], his hands on both temples, both forearms on both knees, both heels on both buttocks, and his head rests between his knees, the mouth sealed and the navel open; he eats from what his mother eats, drinks from what his mother drinks and does not excrete so as not to kill his mother, and when he has seen daylight the sealed opens and the open is sealed, otherwise he cannot live even for an hour. And a candle is lit on his head and he looks from one end of the world to the other, as it is said "When

> his candle shined upon my head and when by his light I walked through darkness" [Job 29:3]. And you should not wonder, since man sleeps here and sees a dream in Ispamia [Spain] and there are no days in which man has such pleasure as those days, as it is said "Oh that I were as in months past, as in the days when God preserved me" [Job 29:2]. Which days consist of months only and no years? The days of pregnancy. And he is taught all of Learning [Torah] as it is said . . . and when he goes out to the world an angel comes and hits his mouth so that he forgets all of Learning . . . " (Bab. Talmud *Niddah* 30b)

The comparison between the child in the womb and a dreaming person reaches beyond the simple technicality of explaining the ability of the unborn to see all of the world—exactly like a person who can dream about distant lands. The unborn is to R. Simlai like one who dreams the entire world, much like the dead are to R. Ishian in the *Bereshit Rabba* text quoted above. The dream of the unborn expands to include the entire Torah, which is then forgotten, in a Platonist manner, with the help of the angel's finger.

The framing of human life as a dream in rabbinic culture may well reveal the influence of other cultures, such as Greece or India. The distribution of the idea among the rabbis should in any case not be overrated, since it has been synthesized here from two separate texts of separate origin. The following, later text presents a somewhat inconsistent variation on the same theme:

> Rabbi Zecharya says: sleep at night is like this world, and awakening in the morning is like the world to come. And as at night man lies down and sleeps and his soul roams around in the world and tells him in the dream everything that comes along, as it is said "In a dream, in a vision of the night, when deep sleep falls upon men, in slumberings upon the bed; then he opens the ears of men and seals their instruction" [Job 33:15–16], likewise the souls of the dead roam in the world and tell them everything that comes along. . . . There are six whose voice runs from one end of the world to the other and their voice is not heard: when a tree which bears fruit is felled . . . when the skin of the snake falls . . . when a woman is divorced from her husband . . . when a woman is with her husband for their first intercourse . . . when the child comes out of his mother's womb . . . and when the soul leaves the body—the voice runs from one end of the world to the other, and the voice is not heard. And the soul does not leave the body until it has seen the divine Presence [*Shekhina*] as it is said "For there shall no man see me and live" [Exod. 33:20].[14]

This text is somewhat later than the classical rabbinic period (approximately eighth century C.E.) and is characterized by a typically didactic tone. The ideological proposition which states that this world is sleep, and the world to come the awakening, is consistent with the view that life is a dream. But that view is soon followed here by the comparison of death with sleep. The motif "Sleep is one sixtieth of death" (and Bab. Talmud *Berakhot* 57b, and "a dream is one sixtieth of prophecy") is widened to include the world as the dream of the dead. It seems as if the author(s) conceptualize separately the experience of dying and death and the idea of the world to come, as if it were not the dead who are supposedly populating the world to come.

The passage on the worldwide sounds that are not heard constructs a group of phenomena united by their deep and truly tragic pathos. They are all irreversible transformative changes, involving loss and some violence. In this context it makes sense that first mating and birth, as well as the molting of the snake, which are all in principle positive changes, are grouped together with the falling fruit tree, divorce, and death. The cluster highlights on one hand the violent, hurtful side of apparently positive changes and, on the other, the liberating, generative aspects of the sadder ones. The inherent ambivalence of the total human process is made very concrete.

The tree felled while it carries fruit is to me the most enigmatic image of the six. Unlike the others, it arouses an empathy that is perfectly disinterested, as it describes an experience which we never have and will never be part of. It thus activates an almost purely poetic-aesthetic sense of compassion (even if environmentalists may see here an ancient prefiguration of some of their ideas).

The three first images echo the world of Eden: the tree, the serpent, and the expulsion (the Hebrew word for divorce is identical to the word for expulsion); the last three express the human condition after Eden—sex, birth, and death. The rabbinic configuration can no longer separate the two stages. Thus the beings of Eden are tainted by loss, whereas dreaming serves as a re-creation of possibilities which are experienced as lost, that is, as having existed in the ideal past.

What does the oxymoronic universal, unheard sound signify? Probably something similar to the sound of the atomic explosion as described by a deaf and mute survivor in the Swedish poet and Nobel Prize laureate Harry Martinson's dystopian epic poem "Aniara": "One mute as stone began to describe / the worst noise he ever heard, / soundless."[15]

The oxymoron is an intensification of synesthesis. Synesthesis, mixing the senses, puts the concept of sensory reality, and especially the possibility of representing it in words, into a state of insecurity and ambiguity. Oxymoron, made of impossible sensory connections and combinations, explodes the distinction of separate sensory systems. Both are part of the intricate mechanism by which dreams condense and distort reality. They also are means of uttering the ineffable, of giving form to the transcendent. Along these lines the passage in *Pirqe de-Rabbi Eliezer* ends: "And the soul does not leave the body until it has seen the divine Presence" (*Shekhina*).

6

Medieval and premodern Jewish culture transmitted rabbinical dream lore in various modes of expression. One such is the creation of handbooks, similar to the adaptations made of Artemidorus's *Oneirocritica* in almost every European language.[16] These Hebrew dream books, which are still reproduced in almost unchanged form, organize some of the rabbinic texts, mainly large portions of the passage from

Berakhot, in an alphabetic—or some other systematic—order. They are composed as dictionaries where the dream symbol is presented as a word in a foreign language, and its traditional interpretation as the definition in translation. The emergence of dream books that standardize the relationship between dream symbols and their meaning introduces a radical change into the communicative process and therefore to the cognitive status of dream interpretation. Whereas rabbinical literature, as we have seen, highlights the interpersonal context of interpretation, dream books seem to contract the contextual connotations into conventionalized denotations. The *Berakhot* passage is the nearest to a dream book that classical rabbinic culture produced. Although not exactly a standard list of interpretations, its frequent reference to biblical texts, which appear both in dreams and as interpretative devices, serves as a more stable textual framework for dream interpretation than most other rabbinic texts on the subject, which interpret dreams contextualized in narratives. But even in the *Berakhot* passage, the fact that the the rabbis see texts as eternally open to reinterpretation generates a potential for the recontextualization of the interpretations of dreams.[17]

There are, however, numerous other instances of oneiric creativity in Jewish culture after the end of the classical rabbinical period (after the eighth century C.E.). One that has been central for the construction of the tradition of dream interpretation both in the responsa literature and in folklore is the rich and varied corpus of dream narratives as well as discussions on dreams in the context of Ashkenazi Hassidism—German Jewish Pietism—of the twelfth century.[18] It is significant that the twelfth century constitutes a real peak in the articulation of the return of the dead in Western Christianity, as Jean-Claude Schmitt has recently shown.[19]

Much of the Ashkenazi Hasidic material, which has since been endlessly recycled by rabbis all over Europe and the Mediterranean countries, discusses or portrays the appearance of the dead on a level of quotidianity that seems quite rare in the rabbinical literature. Rabbis in the sixteenth century are asked what to do when a dead person comes in a dream and asks to be removed from his grave because he is buried next to a heavy sinner. One dead man is said to have asked in a dream that his clothes be buried with him. In this case the rabbi showed special resourcefulness by suggesting that the clothes be distributed to the poor, so that the dead man's soul be clothed with charity in its eternal abode. There is no doubt that dreams serve in this cultural sphere as the major mode in which the dead are believed to communicate with the living—more so than the living with the dead.

Modern Jewish dream culture in its Israeli manifestation draws upon a variety of traditions. The main features of rabbinic dream interpretation now cooexist with a variety of other components of dream culture acquired through centuries of cultural interactions.

Moroccan Jews, as well as other ethnic groups in Israel today, construct the cult of deceased holy men and saints upon oneiro-biographies of the worshipers and their objects of worship, creating networks of oneiro-communities.[20] Communication with the dead is accepted, matter-of-factly. Important collective and private events are communicated through dreaming. In a recently published folk book containing a Sephardi woman's repertoire of dream narratives, the dreamer herself writes in her introduction that dreams are, for her, signs of a world in which life and death exist in harmony without pain. They open up the possibility of meeting her dear ones, both the living and the dead. In her own words, "They have made me believe in a life after this one."[21]

7

> At that moment I was not selective. After having locked the door of the bathroom behind me, I took off my clothes and mounted my bed, that is I entered the bathtub and prostrated myself in it. Rabbi Nahman of Braslav used to say, The Holy Name Blessed be He conducts His world with mercy every day better and better. For me it is not so. Every new day which the Holy One Blessed be He gives me is harder.
>
> But still I fell asleep and slept. How do I know that I slept? From the dream that I had. What did I dream, I dreamt that a great war came upon the world and I was called out to war. I swore an oath to the Lord that if I return home in peace from the war, whatsoever comes forth from my house to meet me, when I return from the war, I shall bring as a burnt offering. I returned home in peace and lo, here I myself come forth to meet me.[22]

The story in which this dream is recounted opens with the narrator's landlady in Berlin dreaming that he—the narrator—will bring back her son who has disappeared at the front in World War I. The story was written by Agnon in 1949, after World War II and after the Holocaust. The narrator-protagonist, a Polish Jew who has left his home in Palestine, is moving from one place to another in Germany, mostly by trains. The story has been criticized for "not having a center which holds."[23] It is, however, a story about the destruction of the inner center and becoming a Wandering Jew, upon whom others project dreams of omnipotent, miraculous rescue, and who himself dreams about exorcising an immense guilt—that of survival—by becoming a burnt offering. The crossing point between life and death is, in this dream, moved into the self.

Agnon lived in an intellectual milieu in which psychoanalysis had an integral place. His stories are replete with psychoanalytic insights and motives. The German context of this specific story may have triggered a heightened articulation of psychoanalytic discourse (although some stories that occur in Poland are also like this, for example, "A Simple Story"). It is, however, the despair of the Holocaust that resonates through the reality of the First World War, a displacement of ineffable mass death transformed back into a "normal" war. The disappearance into total invisibility of an entire Jewish culture positions ideas of transcendence on an extremely sharp edge. Collective nightmares can truly melt the center of the self with sacrificial flames.

Even if Agnon had not mentioned Rabbi Nahman of Braslav in the paragraph leading to the dream, the dream itself might have reminded the reader of one of Rabbi Nahman's own dreams:

> And I saw in the dream that it was the Day of Atonement [*Yom Hakippurim*], and it was clear to me that every Day of Atonement one person is sacrified, and the high priest sacrifices him. They were looking for one for the sacrifice, and I agreed to be the sacrifice. And they asked me to make a written commitment, and I did so. Later, when they wanted to sacrifice me, I regretted it and wanted to hide. But then I saw that the crowd surrounded me, so how could I hide? I left the town and while I was leaving I turned back and entered into the town. And I looked around and saw that I was back in the town! So I wanted to hide among the non-Jews. I thought that if the community will come and ask them for me, they will certainly hand me over to them. Another one to be sacrificed in my place was found. And yet I fear the future.[24]

The religious imagery of sacrifice links ritual and dream as stages of the enactment of the battle between the identity of the individual and the need to destroy the uniqueness of individuality—and this in the face of the monotheistic conduct of a world that often presents itself as chaotic and senseless. Both Rabbi Nahman and Agnon seem to accept the despotism of the One, but their dreaming rebels against the violence of that despotism as it reaches into internal space.

The relationship in Jewish culture between the human and the divine is rooted in radical separation and division. It is thus not surprising that the act of creation itself is structured as a series of divisions, between high and low, wet and dry, man and woman, and, finally, mortal and immortal. Jewish dream culture echoes this basic structure: dreams become very complex means of bridging the division, even of transposing it in paradoxical ways, such as changing roles between dreams and dreamers, the living and the dead.

Notes

1. Oppenheim 1956.

2. Based on a passage in Palestinian Talmud *Hagiga* chapter 2, paragraph 2 and Babylonian Talmud *Hagiga* 2b.

3. Alexiou 1974; Nenola-Kallio 1982: 97–111; Hasan-Rokem 1996a: 121–140.

4. Kristianpoller 1923; Stemberger 1976; Niehoff 1992; Hasan-Rokem 1996a: 101–120. For comparative perspectives, see also Lewy 1978; Cox Miller 1994.

5. Hasan-Rokem 1987; 1996a: 50–77.

6. Chapter 5, this volume.

7. Bakan 1958; Bilu 1979; Miller 1981; Handelman 1982; Hasan-Rokem 1996a: 141–154.

8. Bowersock 1997 claims that whereas Artemidorus was mainly intrested in dreams as omens, his contemporaries who wrote fictional prose presented mainly "Freudian" dreams that express fears, anxiety, and other similar states of mind.

9. Jakobson 1960.

10. When I told one of the senior administrators at the Hebrew University about the

topic of our symposium at Hubertusstock, she reacted as follows: "You know, a neighbor on David Yellin Street where I lived when I was young had a dream about the roof falling down. She went to a rabbi (whose name I don't know) and he told her that her husband would die. She came frightened to Rabbi Arye Levin who lived nearby and told him in panic the dream and the rabbi's interpretation. He said: 'That rabbi killed your husband, because as the dream is interpreted you get it.' This is a true story that I can tell you. He really died within a year or so."

11. Bloom 1987: 5.

12. *Midrash Rabba* for Genesis, *Bereshit Rabba* Vatican MS version, Theodor-Albeck edition p. 1237; Variants: Pal. Talmud, *Avoda Zara* ch. 3 paragraph 1 *Midrash Zuta* Ecclesiastes, Qohelet Zuta, ed. S. Buber, ch. 9.

13. In the Palestinian version of the "gestation" theme, in the *Midrash Rabba* for Leviticus, *Vayiqra Rabba* 14, 2–3 (Margaliot-Margulies ed. esp. pp. 302–305), the interaction is exclusively between God and the woman.

14. *Pirqe de-Rabbi Eliezer* ch. 34 in the Warsaw edition with the Luria commentary, and in the Horowitz edition; ch. 33 in the Higer edition. I thank Dina Stein for the insight and the reference.

15. Martinson 1954: 45.

16. See chs. 7 and 8 in the present volume.

17. For the relationship between the rabbis' interpretation of texts and their dream interpretations, see Lieberman 1962; Kugel 1986; Niehoff 1992; Hasan-Rokem 1996b.

18. Harris 1963; Dan 1971; Trachtenberg 1974: 230–249.

19. Schmitt 1994.

20. Prof. Yoram Bilu, Hebrew University, Jerusalem; personal communication.

21. Raymond 1995: 54.

22. S. J. Agnon 1968, "Ad Henna," 7:76. (my translation)

23. Prof. Dan Laor, Tel-Aviv University; personal communication.

24. Sadeh 1983: 117.

References

Agnon, S. J. 1968. *Collected Works*. Tel Aviv.

Alexiou, Margaret. 1974. *The Ritual Lament in Greek Tradition*. Cambridge.

Bakan, David. 1958. *Sigmund Freud and the Jewish Mystical Tradition*. New York.

Bilu, Yoram. 1979. "Sigmund Freud and Rabbi Yehudah: On a Jewish Mystical Tradition of 'Psychoanalytic' Dream Interpretation." *The Journal of Psychological Anthropology* 2, 443–463.

Bloom, Harold. (ed.). 1987. *Sigmund Freud's The Interpretation of Dreams*. New York, New Haven, Philadelphia.

Bowersock, Glen Warren. 1997. *Fiction as History: Nero to Julian*. Berkeley, Los Angeles and London.

Cox Miller, Patricia. 1994. *Dreams in Late Antiquity: Studies in the Imagination of a Culture*. Princeton.

Dan, Joseph. 1971. "The Dream Theory of Hassidei Ashkenaz (German Pietists)." *Sinai* 68, 299–293 (Hebrew).

Handelman, Susan A. 1982. *The Slayers of Moses: The Emergence of Rabbinic Interpretation in Modern Literary Theory*. Albany, NY.

Harris, Monford. 1963. "Dreams in Sefer Hasidim." *Proceedings of the American Academy for Jewish Research* 31, 51–80.

Hasan-Rokem, Galit. 1987. "The Rhetoric of Intimacy—The Rhetoric of the Sacred." *Temenos* 23, 45–57.

———. 1996a. *Riqmat ha-ḥay im : ha-yetzira ha-ammamit be-sifrut ḥazal. Midrash ha-aggada ha-erets-yisraeli eikha rabba* (The Web of Life: Folklore in Rabbinic Literature. The Palestinian Aggadic Midrash Eikha Rabba). Tel-Aviv (Hebrew).

———. 1996b. "'A Dream Amounts to the Sixtieth Part of Prophecy': On Interaction Between Textual Establishment and Popular Context in Dream Interpretation by the Jewish Sages." In B. Z. Kedar (ed.), *Studies in the History of Popular Culture*. Jerusalem (Hebrew) 45–54.

Jakobson, Roman. 1960. "Closing Statement: Linguistics and Poetics." In Thomas A. Sebeok (ed.), *Style in Language*, Cambridge, MA, pp. 350–377.

Kristianpoller, Alexander. 1923. *Traum und Traumdeutung, Monumenta Talmudica* vol. 2, Vienna and Berlin.

Kugel, James. 1986. "Two Introductions to Midrash." In G. H. Hartman and S. Budick (eds.), *Midrash and Literature*. New Haven and London, 131–155.

Lewy, H. 1893. "Zu dem Traumbuche des Artemidoros," *Rheinische Museum für Philologie*, Neue Folge 48, 398–419.

Lieberman, Saul. 1962. *Greek and Hellenism in Early Jewish Palestine*. Jerusalem (Hebrew).

Martinson, Harry. 1956. *Aniara*, Stockholm.

Miller, Justin. 1981. "Interpretation of Freud's Jewishness, 1924–1974." *Journal of the History of Behavioral Sciences*, 357–374.

Nenola-Kallio, Aili. 1982. *Studies in Ingrian Laments*. Folklore Fellows Communications 234. Helsinki.

Niehoff, Maren. 1992. "A Dream Which Is Not Interpreted Is Like a Letter Which Is Not Read." *Journal of Jewish Studies* 43, 58–84.

Oppenheim, A. Leo. 1956. "The Interpretation of Dreams in the Ancient Near East with a Translation of an Assyrian Dream-Book." *Transactions of the American Philosophical Society* New Series 46/3, 179–373.

Raymond, Miryam. 1995. *Mifgashim ba-halom* (Dream Encounters). Introduction by T. Alexander. Hod Hasharon, Israel (Hebrew).

Sadeh, Pinhas. 1983. *Sefer ha-dimyonot shel ha-yehudim* (Fantasies of the Jews). Tel Aviv (Hebrew).

Schmitt, Jean-Claude. 1994. *Les revenants: Les vivants et les morts dans la société médiévale*. Paris.

Stemberger, Brigitte. 1976. "Der Traum in der rabbinischen Literatur." *Kairos* 18, 1–42.

Trachtenberg, Joshua. 1974. *Jewish Magic and Superstition—a Study in Folk Religion*, New York.

IV

Middle Ages and Modern West

12

Astral Dreams in Judaism

Twelfth to Fourteenth Centuries

Moshe Idel

Introduction

We live multidimensional lives. Among other things, we inhabit simultaneously a variety of times: a private one, consisting of birth, youth, maturity, and death; microchronic time, used below to refer to the rhythms of daily and yearly rituals; historical time, dealing with the events of groups and nations, described here as the mesochronos; and cosmic time, dealing with processes in nature and universe, which we call macrochronos.[1] Some mystics attempted to escape time altogether by reaching an ecstatic, atemporal experience. Everyone also experiences "oneiric time," which is a special form of private, conscious time. A person may inhabit some of these times at the same time; it is always interesting to explore the shifting balances between such times, balances that characterize different personalities or various cultures. Rather than attempting to distinguish between these religious cultures on the basis of their alleged definitive discrimination between times, and then describing a certain religion against the background of this choice, I suggest we examine ways different religions integrate various forms of time differently.

The concomitance of these times facilitates distinct interactions. The ritual microchronos may be related to a much larger natural or macrochronic rhythm. At the same time the microchronos may be related to historical time, the celebration of important past events or anticipation of future events. The existence of natural rhythms invites a relationship between private time, which may be regarded as random, and more comprehensive forms of order that encompass it. The attempt to correlate the two rhythms to exploit the potential of the former for the benefit of the latter is one of the main purposes of astrology and of some forms of magic.[2]

For a medieval Jew expected to perform the daily Jewish ritual, for example, multiple times included a *historia sacra* and also the impact of the astral order on private and public events, if he believed in astrology—as many Jews did in the Middle Ages. This average Jew would also expect the advent of the Messiah in historical, or what I propose to designate as mesochronic, time. The coexistence of these different forms was not simple, and dormant conflicts may be sensed. Thus, for example, it is not always easy to believe in the direct intervention of God in history while presupposing the efficiency of the astral order; or to believe in the efficacy of ritual while allowing astrology an important role. But, complex as these webs were, inner conflicts did not prevent an often fruitful coexistence. Answering different human needs, these forms of time were effective in different moments. Ordinary human behavior has much to do with the possibility of establishing a balance between them, so that the rhythm of life is not disturbed by an uncontrolled mixing. It is helpful to discriminate and to experience the plenitude of these forms of time in order to regulate what is commonly called the normal course of life.

I would like to address the relation between private time and the macrochronos, understood in this context as astral order. Astral order was considered active not only in external daytime reality but also at night, in sleep, in nocturnal time. Unlike many other kinds of time in Judaism, especially the *micro-* and *mesochronoi*, the period of sleep was not shaped by legal regulations; prayers were offered immediately prior to and after waking from sleep, but the realm of sleep was free from formal requirements. I shall present the astral dream as the intersection between the astral order and private life, a moment of insight, either a gift from above or a result of human initiative, enabling a person to peer into the future by means of a mantic relationship to the celestial forces that shape that future.

In many of the dimensions previously mentioned, time is not merely a succession of meaningless moments but rather instances following each other in accordance with a certain structure or order that provides the sequence with specific types of meaning. Structure is linked to meaning, and moments in time are charged with a specific import. One of the most influential ways of structuring the universe, shaping concepts of private and historical time, was (and is) the astrological order. Stars, spheres, and planets were conceived not only as celestial entities roaming in chaotic space, but also as powers ruling the lower world. While many Greek, Muslim, Jewish, and Christian philosophers and astrologers assumed a certain influence of the movements of the celestial bodies on the generation and decay of lower substances, in some circles the celestial bodies were thought to have an impact on lower processes by virtue of their spiritual, rather than their material, components. The spiritual elements of these bodies—*pneumata, ruḥaniyāt*, or *ruḥaniyyot*—were forces both immanent in them and present in processes below, and also endowed with the potential of being drawn down by capable magicians.[3] In a hierarchical vision of the world, everything higher was conceived of as naturally more powerful, governing lower events by forces emanated from above.

In medieval Aristotelian cosmogony, the motions of celestial bodies shaped all natural processes, such as the generation and corruption of bodies, the removal of one form and the impression of another. The lower entities were regarded as hylic, potential, fluid, corruptible by definition, compared to the supernal entities, which were more formative, active, and stable. Again, in this cosmogony, epistemology reflects the same order; human hylic intellect was seen as actualized by the separate, cosmic, or "agent"/"active" intellect. This downward emanation is one of the most comprehensive concepts of medieval thought in the West, shaped by most forms of Neoaristotelianism and Neoplatonism, by medieval astrology as well as by Kabbalah. Though sharing many elements, these hierarchies have, nevertheless, their own distinct structures. Neoaristotelianism and Neoplatonism were much more inclined toward a rigid order that presupposed a continuous stream of emanation downward, and human activity was mainly conceived, in this context, as preparation for the maximum reception of this emanation. Often this stream was a unified one, and its different effects were seen as dependent upon the recipients. In other words, differentiation is basically the effect of different receptions of one comprehensive and unified form of energy. Little, if anything, could be done to change the nature of the emanation or its strength or direction. Like broadcasting, it could have an infinite number of recipients, each according to specific capacities. Activities involved in establishing contact with the descending emanations are much more intellectual or spiritual, involving the purification of the soul or improvement of the activities of the intellect in order to better cleave to the emanations. These contacts are the culmination of moments of contemplation and, in more extreme forms, mystical experiences of union.

On the other hand, astrological and kabbalistic emanations were thought to be much more diversified. Presupposing a far more mythological supernal world, many kabbalistic theologies, and most astrological systems, play with the assumption that the different supernal powers, divine or astral, emanate different forms of effluxes, which can be captured in different ways through various rituals, objects, and moments. Moreover, according to some forms of Kabbalah, it is even possible to influence the nature of the descending effluxes by means of the commandments, performed with mystical intention, designed to control the relationship between divine powers and the forces emanated by the different constellations of divine manifestations.[4] In other words, astrological and kabbalistic rituals were felt to be much more influential because they entailed not only specific preparations but also the selection of powers one would like to capture, encounter, or even stimulate. The latter forms of ritual are much more concrete than those of the philosophers, and are similar to, and influenced by, some forms of theurgy found in the Hermetical traditions and some forms of Neoplatonism.[5] More than philosophical preparations, those proposed and embraced by astrologers and kabbalists can be called "techniques."

In what follows, I explore an issue that has been ignored by modern scholarship—the astral dream, a minor issue in the general economy of kabbalistic literature dealing with dreams. This marginality may be better understood against its salient background. Dreams in general, and those induced deliberately by certain practices, are important enough in Kabbalah; however, the main literary genre of this literature, called *she'elat ḥalom,*[6] has little to do with astral agents and deals more with a linguistic kind of magic directed at angels, conceived of in terms of more traditional Jewish views of late antiquity. The acceptance of the genre of *she'elat ḥalom* in kabbalistic literature marginalized the other brand of oneiric technique, based as it was upon astral concepts. Nevertheless, at least one recipe for receiving a dream connected explicitly to stars is available:

> *She'elat Ḥalom*: Fast and wash; afterward stand before the stars, where Ursa Major is,[7] and say in front of it: In the name of Stani, I conjure you, TzShNY BYH YH YH YH B'RY that you shall send me this night two sages who will reveal to me whatever I ask and demand from them in truth . . . until he will do my will, all the quests of my heart.[8]

Unfortunately, the Bodleian manuscript is the only one I know containing this recipe, and it has some illegible words. The content of this dream question is, however, devoid of a more comprehensive explanatory system, which would explain why and how stars are the source of dreams. Such systems existed, and I would like to point out the interactions between them and the phenomenology of dream and religion.

Rabbi Abraham ibn Ezra and the Anonymous *Sefer ha-Ḥayyim*

One of the most significant contributors to astral thinking in Judaism is the twelfth-century polymath Abraham ibn Ezra. An accomplished astronomer, a famous interpreter of the Bible, a distinguished linguist, and a great poet, ibn Ezra opened a new era in Jewish thought both by contributing to the development of astronomy in Judaism and by hinting at astrological implications of biblical episodes. The range of ibn Ezra's impact in these two domains still awaits comprehensive study, but it seems to me that no other author in the Middle Ages was given so much attention, judging by the number of supercommentaries dedicated to his biblical commentaries. In short, his assumption was that a certain ritual act or a building, if undertaken within a certain stellar configuration, would succeed to the extent of the affinity between the nature of the act or building and the nature of the stellar configuration at that time.[9] This is also the case insofar as dreams are concerned. In his commentary on Daniel 2:2–5:

> The *ḥartumim* know the essence of the dreams and how the soul sees visions during the night, and they called also to the *'ashafim* who know the pulse of the arm and what the changes in the body [depend] on. And the majority of dreams depend upon bodily changes. and he also called the *mekhashshefim*, who know the propitious hours to do certain deeds, so that they might have a look in order to know [the meaning of] the dream in accordance with the configuration of the

> stars in that hour.[10] He also called the *kasedim*, who know the future in accordance with their lore, when they know the moment of someone's birth.

Nebuchadnezzar's attempts to decode his dreams followed various paths, according to ibn Ezra, some of them reducing the dream to physical changes, others to the impact of celestial bodies. I am interested in the last two categories of occultists: the *kasedim* presupposed a deterministic attitude to events in life, which they viewed as dependent upon the stellar configuration at birth, and thus focused solely upon data in the past; the *mekhashshefim* interpreted dreams according to the hour of the dream, hence following the concomitant stellar configuration. The latter, however, implies a much more activist approach: if one knows the nexus between constellations and their effects below, one may not only decode the nexus retroactively but also stipulate a certain type of activity in advance. Thus "certain deeds" could be calculated in advance to ensure the best results. Elsewhere, ibn Ezra mentions the dream question explicitly, but without any astral implications.[11]

Ibn Ezra's view was adopted, anonymously, by *Sefer ha-Ḥayyim*, a theosophical treatise composed in the first third of the thirteenth century somewhere in Northern Europe, and attributed, according to some early evidence, to Abraham ibn Ezra.[12] There it is said that

> the *mekhashshefim* too know the propitious hour to do a deed, and in accordance with that hour they are able to know the dream of man, if he sleeps, by means of the configuration of the stars at that hour.[13]

The anonymous author elaborated upon ibn Ezra's statement, as this last sentence shows. *Sefer ha-Ḥayyim* was copied and preserved almost exclusively by kabbalists, as inspection of its earliest manuscripts shows. It is evident that the book was known to kabbalists in Italy at the end of the thirteenth century.[14] It seems that some syntheses between Jewish mystical concepts and Arabic magic are already evident in the Arabic writings of R. Yehudah ben Nissim ibn Malkah, who flourished in the middle of the thirteenth century, apparently in Northern Africa, long before the renewed intrusion of Arabic magic into the world of the Jewish elite of Spain.[15] However, astral rituals concerning dreams appear in Jewish literature, to my best knowledge, only at the end of the thirteenth century.

"Maimonides'" Kabbalistic Epistle

One of the first and most interesting discussions of oneiric techniques intended to induce an astral dream is found in a spurious epistle attributed to Maimonides. In some manuscripts it is entitled *Megillat Setarim*. It is quite evident that the forger was a kabbalist belonging to the ecstatic Kabbalah, but the precise date and place of the composition of this epistle is far from clear.[16] To Maimonides, who opposed astrology and was wary of uncontrolled activity of the imagination, was attributed the authorship of a kabbalistic letter, which discusses, positively, linguistic magic and astral dreaming.[17] This cannot be an example of ordinary pseudepigraphy, because views were attributed to Maimonides that were totally alien to his thought and even sharply criticized by him.[18] Thus we may assume that this attribution is a calculated effort to link the philosopher with those trends in Jewish thought that he either opposed or were quite alien to his worldview. Let me adduce the pertinent passage in the epistle:

> In the verse "And there I will meet with thee, and I will speak with thee from above the covering, from between the two *keruvim* which are upon the ark of the Testimony, of all things which I will give thee in commandment to the children of Israel":[19] You may find in it twenty-two words, hinted at in *Sefer Yetzirah*[20] when it was said: "Twenty-two letters, He engraved them and He extracted them and weighed them and permuted them and combined them, and He created by them 'the soul of all the formation,' and 'the soul of all the speech, which will be formed in the future' "[21] and these are twenty-two simple letters, and the intention was that all that was created, beginning with the spiritual forces of the angels to the human souls[22] has been engraved by the twenty-two words, and man will have knowledge of the hidden[23] and will remember what he has forgotten insofar as possible things. Know that Moses our master, blessed be his memory, all his comprehensions were the announcement of the divine nomos[24] as arranged out of all the names of the angels, when he was meeting with them always,[25] this being the reason of [the description of Moses][26] 'for he is the trusted one in My house.' And from this verse seven names emerge, which correspond to seven angels of the firmaments that are Saturn, Jupiter, Mars, Sun, Venus, Mercury, Moon, and they correspond to seven [types of] sacrifices of oxen, and corresponding to them the holidays are arranged according to sevens, and seven units of seven are the year of the Jubilee, and out of seven years is the Shemittah, and [at the end of the seven months], the New Year, and after seven weeks the reception of the Torah, and out of the seven days Sabbath, and corresponding to them the seven altars built by Balaam.[27] . . . And you already know, from what you have read with me concerning the science of astronomy,[28] that the Moon will turn into an opposite configuration in the seventh day; this is why her emanation onto the lower world will change. All this is a hint at and an observation[29] as to what will be emanated here from the movers of these seven planets.[30] Behold, this is the order of the seven names [emerging out of] the above-mentioned verse, and the first line consists of the first letters of the words, the second from the last letters and their vocalization is that of the Bible, forward and backward. These are the names:
>
> | | | | | | | |
> |---|---|---|---|---|---|---|
> | WLSh | W'M | HMSh | HMSh | H" | 'H' | "BY |
> | YKM | YKL | TNY | MRL | NTT | LRT | KLYL |
>
> And this is the way of [magical] use of this matter: Let him fast Wednesday, which is the day of Mercury, which is appointed for wisdom and the knowledge of the hidden things, and he should behave in an extremely pure manner and with a feeling of shame toward people. And when he goes to bed, he should wash all his flesh with water in the first hour of the night and clothe himself in a pure and clean robe and trousers, and he should sleep alone and pronounce

> those verses, one time with intense concentration[31] and a pure heart and humble spirit, and afterwards he should pronounce the above-mentioned names, and his heart is directed to heaven always. And you should do it so seven times, namely you should read the seven above-mentioned verses and the seven names of the angels,[32] and he should arrange in his mouth the doubt that he has, whatever it may be, after the perfect imagination and the evacuated thought.[33] And he should sleep afterwards on the left side[34] and you will find, in the midst of your sleep, that the spirit of the holy God will dwell upon you and the hair of your flesh will bristle,[35] when the sleep of *tremendum* comes upon you, and fear to your thoughts. During the dream at night you will see the visions of a man who will awake you from your sleep and will dispute with you and will tell you the secrets of wisdom, and twice as much understanding. Then he will appear as if he has a controversy with you showing to you the place that you were in doubt. The stronger your concentration[36] is and your compliance with the wondrous deed [greater], the doubt that you had will be explained in a truer and more correct manner and the firmament of your intellect will be purified from all great doubts by a strong catharsis, so that no room for doubt related to your question will remain.[37]

From many points of view, this astral vision in dream offers nothing new, insofar as astral elements are concerned. What I find more interesting and apparently characteristic of the kabbalistic version of the astral explanation, is the paramount importance of the linguistic aspect of the discussion. In magic in general, linguistic formulas recur. However, here is an explicit attempt to formulate a linguistic continuum that will enable the explanation of the efficacy of the linguistic device. Names do not only designate objects, nor do they only coexist with things, as in some natural visions of language; they are also entities permeating the spiritual realm and constituting a continuum between the angelic and the human worlds. Language, at least the special formulas mentioned above, is therefore seen as the very stuff of spiritual reality. The introduction of the quote from *Sefer Yetzirah* has precisely this role—to adduce a proof text for linguistic immanence.[38] The explanation of doubt, the substance of oneiric technique, is offered by Mercury, Hermes, the master of knowledge and hidden things. He appears in a dream vision and begins a dialogue with the dreamer. The way this dialogue is presented is reminiscent of talmudic discussion, when a person is taught how to understand a doubt about a text. This conversation is important from both historical and phenomenological points of view: in dreaming, as in wakefulness, revelation is more dialogical than apodictic. The dreamer is not asking for the gnosis of a hidden subject but would like to continue, on the nocturnal level, the reflection on and the elucidation of those matters that could not be elucidated upon wakening. Revelation is therefore put in the service of interpretation, and Hermes-Mercury comes in order to offer in a dream the clue to what could not be found in a lucid state of mind. The oneiric technique attempts to solve a hermeneutical quandary by resorting to Hermes.

Historically speaking, there can be no doubt that the spurious epistle was composed by a follower of ecstatic Kabbalah.[39] In this form of Kabbalah, revelation in a state of wakefulness is attained by means of divine names, and angels are thought to converse with mystics. What we see in this text is a nocturnal dream serving as the scene for the revelation that is usually said, in ecstatic Kabbalah, to take place in a state of lucidity. The main clue to the adjuration is the names that emerge from a verse dealing with divine revelation in the temple: God promised to speak from between the two *keruvim*. In the version of the medieval kabbalists, these two *keruvim* have been translated into the human inner faculties: imagination on one hand and intellect or thought on the other. These two capacities were described by Maimonides as necessary for prophetic experience, and I assume that the kabbalist must prepare them before going to sleep in order to have the divine message delivered from somewhere between them. This metaphorical reading of the *keruvim* is found elsewhere in the pseudo-Maimonidean literature, apparently in the same sense.[40] To a certain extent, the purifications of the dreamer mentioned in the epistle are reminiscent of that of the high priest who entered the holy of holies to obtain a revelation there. If this view is correct, we have a move from revelations once experienced in a state of wakefulness to those attained in dream. Indeed, the accomplished kabbalist is compared in this epistle to a prophet who knows whom to ask [and how to answer] by means of '*Urim ve-Tummim.*[41]

Let us explore further the restructuring aspects of this epistle. Language, intellect, and imagination, sleep and dream, are all described here as both the locus and the technique for ancient revelation. By restructuring the order of the letters of the verse dealing with divine revelation in the temple, a person could have a revelation in his own private temple. The new order of letters differs from the old in reflecting a more comprehensive cosmic order, which also informs the rhythm of the ritual. While in the temple the assumption was that God would reveal himself by his own initiative, in the case of the kabbalist it is the human initiative that triggers the experience. The strong God, who presided in the Israelite sanctuary and who revealed himself only in the sacrosanct locus between the *keruvim*, is now replaced by weaker entities, the angels, who can be induced to go everywhere. A more cosmic order created by the structure of sevenfold correspondences also makes it possible to plug into this order to initiate contact. It should be stressed that the temple, fixed in place, has been replaced by the extraordinary human experience during the dream. Unlike incubatory experiences well-known since ancient times (where the strength of the locus was crucial for eliciting the divinatory dream), in the kabbalistic epistle the place is basically irrelevant. This is why I prefer the term "oneiric technique" to "incubation," a term commonly connected to a sacred shrine or a sanctuary.[42] The hermeneutical moment should attract more of our attention; further on in the epistle, we read:

> My dear son, open your eye [and see] how the mysteries and the secrets of the divine lore will be revealed to you, and all that you have been in doubt regarding the interpretations of the Torah and its commentaries will be explained to you in the manner that I have revealed to you concerning its significance[43] and its

grandeur and its great power by the way of the true Kabbalah, and its experiment has been tested[44] by me.[45]

The strong emphasis is on the revelation of the interpretations of the Torah and of the secrets of Kabbalah (which can plausibly be viewed as secrets of the Torah). In other words, instead of relying on faithful and direct transmission of Kabbalah from master to student, the kabbalist is able to solicit kabbalistic secrets by mantic devices. The oneiric technique induces a dream, in which normal human spiritual powers are transcended by attracting supernal powers that are able to short-circuit problems left unsolved by regular consciousness. While this kabbalist would probably be reluctant to allow free creation of kabbalistic secrets by the lucid intellect, he was apparently ready to allow this for dreamed fantasies. The supremacy of the higher cosmic powers conferred special authority to the purported influx whose descent may be induced during the initiated dream. The special power of the names that emerge from anagrammatizing the biblical verse is also quite interesting: by changing the order of letters, one may obtain the power to reach the secrets of the Bible, a power that apparently does not exist in the regular sequence of letters in the canonic text. In other words, another order of letters, used to attain a special form of consciousness (the astral dream) helps one reach the inner sense of the Bible. The nexus between the names (allegedly found within the ordinary sequence of the biblical verses) and magical powers is already well-known in magical and mystical Jewish texts.[46] I am, however, not aware of a link between this nexus and dream visions prior to this kabbalist. "Maimonides" claims that he had great doubts, but Kabbalah helped him overcome them and open all the "doors of the perplexities and the clues of wisdom [which] have been delivered in my hands, and the interpretation of all that has been hidden from me."[47]

Why does this anagrammatization work? According to some Midrashic views, the Torah was not revealed in its primordial form, namely according to a different and much more powerful combination of letters.[48] Such an order, if retrieved, may transform the biblical text into a powerful book of magic. In our epistle, this theory is hinted at in the view that all of Moses' comprehensions "were the announcement of the divine nomos as arranged out of all the names of the angels." In other words, Moses arranged the Torah in accordance with the regular nomian order, namely the canonic one, while under its surface, or according to some techniques of decoding it such as the anagrammatic one used in the above example, it is possible to read in it the names of angels, instrumental in inducing astral dreams.

This explanation is corroborated by a passage written by a contemporary of the anonymous forger, the famous interpreter of the Pentateuch, R. Baḥia ben Asher. In his commentary on Deuteronomy 29:29: "The secret things belong to the Lord our God, but those things which were revealed belong to us," he writes:

You should understand also that from this verse emerges the name appointed[49] for the *she'elat ḥalom* by means of the combinations of letters, each and every name possessing three letters, altogether nine letters.[50]

The quote from the spurious letter may well be defined as a recipe for *she'elat ḥalom*. Thus, both in the pseudepigraphical epistle and in the tradition adduced by R. Baḥia, the technique for a dream question is based upon anagrammatizing a certain verse of the Bible where revelation or secrets are discussed, so that "names" emerge that are part of a technique for eliciting a revelatory dream. However, while Baḥia does not introduce the astral element that is crucial for the pseudepigraphic epistle, this element is crucial for the understanding of the "man" who appears in the dream. The nature of the "man" is significant for understanding the evolution of the oneiric practices in Kabbalah. He is definitively the imaginative representation of Mercury—but more as an embodiment of an astral power than an ancient Roman god. As such, he is an objective mentor, a celestial guide for the perplexed; the term "doubts" occurs in the epistle more than once.[51] This means that while we may assume a variety of astral mentors who may eventually be invoked to reveal themselves in a dream, none of them could be imagined, in the framework of the system espoused in this epistle, as a personal genius or an individual mentor. Private as a dream may be, the entity revealing itself within the dream is nevertheless conceived of in objective rather than subjective terms. Though a momentary creature of the imagination, the oneiric mentor is still the reflection of an objective, celestial entity selected because of specific attributes, as in the case discussed above where the power of disclosing the clues of wisdom and hidden secrets is mentioned.[52] Nothing in the above description suggests that the "man" is an alter ego, a double or a personal genius of the dreamer. This "objectivity" of angelic power is evident in the fact that a special time is mentioned as propitious for revelation in dream, namely Wednesday. The assumption, not an explicit theory, elaborated in this epistle is that every day, or night, presided over by another celestial power, is appropriate for dreams that inspire people for different purposes.

The anonymous kabbalist resorts to the phrase *ha-mal'akh ha-melitz* to designate the revealing angel[53] and assumes that revelations will take the form of allegory and parable,[54] allowing an enigmatic revelation in dreams that require intellectual effort to decode them.[55] But our description of the achievements of the astral dreamer would be incomplete without pointing out the importance of the nonscholastic attainments attributed to dream revelations. According to the epistle, the dreamer is able to receive not only details dealing with secrets of the Torah, but also a series of magical powers that have nothing to do with the Torah. It is this more magical aspect that seems to reflect the nature of the talismanic sources (plausibly of Arabic extraction) that influenced the epistle. The attainment of secrets seems to be an ideal grafted onto astral magic stemming from other forms of magic, like those related to the Prince of the Torah, namely the angel summoned down by the *Heikhalot* mystic in order to reveal the secrets of the Torah.[56] In other words, the anonymous kabbalist who attempted to portray Maimonides as a talismanic magician, while nevertheless resorting to Maimonidean epistemology, offered what can be described as the first synthesis between two systems that were initially quite different: the Aristotelian and the astro-magical. This synthesis has an echo in the writings of the late fifteenth-century thinker R. Yohanan Alemanno, the companion and teacher of Pico della Mirandola.[57]

Pseudo-Ibn 'Ezra's *Sefer ha-'Atzamim*

In several manuscripts, and also in print, there is a treatise titled *Sefer ha-'Atzamim*, attributed to ibn Ezra. This attribution has been duly rejected by most modern scholars, though there are still some who apparently regard it as the work of ibn Ezra.[58] An astro-magical treatise, it deals with talismanic theories in a manner much more explicit than the pseudo-Maimonides' epistle does. The approximate time of its composition is the latter thirteenth or the early fourteenth century, and I assume that the place is Spain. As Z. Edelmann (the editor of the pseudo-Maimonidean epistle) has pointed out, there are important convergences between the pseudo-Ibn Ezra treatise and the pseudo-Maimonidean epistle dealt with above.[59] A perusal of this magical book shows that a Neoplatonic attitude to reality informs its structure, though magical linguistics, plausibly stemming from Jewish sources, perhaps kabbalistic ones, are also influential. The main contribution of this treatise is not so much to the Spanish Kabbalah, which only rarely resorted to the concept of drawing down spiritual powers, but to the much later figure Yohanan Alemanno, mentioned above. The anonymous author draws heavily upon the Arabic view of drawing down spiritual forces from various astral bodies; this seems to be the first detailed treatment of this issue in a Hebrew source, which apparently incorporated paragraphs translated from Arabic. I would like to adduce just one passage which is pertinent for our topic:

> The spiritual force is the highest one among all the spiritual forces, and it is the agent intellect which was [also] called *Shekhinah*[60] and by [means of] him the drawer down of it[61] will know the Creator, blessed be He, and it will teach him during the time of mental concentration and while he is asleep, in hints, which are like answers to his questions that he asked it. And he[62] will interpret them and arrange them in the state of wakefulness, in an order and manner appropriate to the language of his generation, by means of parables and words and usages, in that language and custom . . . And there is a prophet upon whom emanation will descend in a state of wakefulness, without causing him to dream[63] or exhaust his power or cause him to fall asleep. But if he will not be an expert and know how to cause its descent and its worship and its sacrifices, it will kill him, and there was not one of them that was perfect in this matter but Moses, our master, blessed be his memory, and this is why it has been said[64] that he was prophesying by [means of] the shining mirror, whereas the other prophets did it only by means of the mirror that does not shine. And the explanation of it is that it was emanating upon him because of the scarcity of his dealing with sensible things, whereas the other [prophets] were not like him, because they were dealing with the matters of this world. This was coupled with the fact that they were not prepared and ready as he was, and this is the reason that this intellect was not descending upon them constantly, in the manner it was descending upon Moses our master, blessed be his memory, but only in a dream or terrifying visions.[65]

What the anonymous thinker has done here, in a manner reminiscent of the spurious letter, is to combine Maimonides' vision of prophecy (as the efflux stemming from the agent intellect, along with his distinction between Moses' sublime prophecy and that of the other prophets[66]) with the astral-magic vision of drawing down the emanation from above by ritual means. The astro-magical rituals described at length in this book are similar to those rituals described (and fiercely opposed) by Maimonides as characteristic of the Sabeans.[67] This work is also concerned with linguistic magic, attributed here explicitly to Aristotle,[68] though this issue is less central than in the epistle attributed to Maimonides. If the pseudo-Ibn Ezra treatise, or his sources, were composed before the epistle, the very attribution to Aristotle of linguistic magic dealing with divine names[69] could have inspired the attribution to Maimonides (an author deeply affected by Aristotelian thinking) of an alleged resort to linguistic magic. In one way or another, the two pseudepigraphic writings were designed to construe an interest in astro-magic either in Maimonides or in his main source, despite tension between Aristotle and Maimonides and the magical contents of astral theories.

Diurnal and Nocturnal Religious Tendencies

Remo Bodei has suggested recently that in wakefulness the personality is much more unified, while in the state of dreaming the various personalities tend to become more independent.[70] In other terms, while the normal state of consciousness is, theologically speaking, much more religiously centripetal, that of the dream (including astral dreams) is much more centrifugal. I would argue that processes that depend on macrochronicity are more prone to become centrifugal than those related to microchronicity. Centrifugal motion invites differentiation and plurality much more than centripetal motion. Or, to translate this more horizontal suggestion into vertical terms: the upward movement, namely philosophical and mystical attempts to ascend to the One, is much more centripetal, while attempts to draw down powers from above may be conceived of as much more centrifugal. Or, to attempt to offer another categorization: the upward unifying motion of the unitive mystics, striving toward one center of being, is characterized by unification and sometimes restriction of some human capacities, which also means a certain propensity to deprivation. The downward attraction of spiritualities of the planets means fulfillment, or plenitude understood as plurality; or, to use religious terminology (charged as it may be), polytheism and magic and, in one word, astro-magic. In temporal terms, astral dreams deal with plenitude as embodied by an open creation, and thus a future-oriented religious modality and the fulfillment of the personal needs of the individual.

Unitive mysticism is a much more past-oriented religiosity, attempting to regain a paradisiac state of consciousness, seen as disrupted by sin and embodied in "normal life." In terms of substance, the vertical movement of ascending is spiritualistic, attempting to simplify the complexity of the human aggregatus, elevating the material and transforming it into a more spiritual entity. The centrifugal motion attempts to transform the spiritual into something material and, consequently, the one into the multiple. Astral dreams are therefore concerned with solving a particular concrete problem not by reducing its importance or by transcending it in favor of a more sublime form of activity, but on the contrary, by breaking the spiritual into fragments in order to complete the particular. According to some texts, God dresses himself in a garment in order to reveal himself to man, while according to other texts, the mystico-philosophical ones, man divests himself of his materiality in order to become God. Theophany is the theological mode of the downward movement, whereas apotheosis is more concerned with anthropology, dealing as it does with the ascending movement.[71] However, different as those forms of religious experience may be, they not only coexist, as in the case of Alemanno's ladder of states of cognitions,[72] but sometimes may complement each other. The complexity discussed in my opening remarks is achieved not by the renunciation of one of these two forms in favor of the other, but by conjugating the two and thus also altering each of them as they become part of a more comprehensive scheme. The plenitude of the centripetal, with its concreteness of detail, may strive for meaning in the frame of the ascending mode, which transcends the existing order and unifies it. While astral dreams are related to the more immanentist approach, which is inclined to see *deus in rebus*, the ascending approach strives to see *omnia res in deo*. For our discussion, the salient fact is that two of the most important sources for the concept of astral dreams, the spurious letter of Maimonides and the spurious treatise of Abraham ibn Ezra, are forgeries attributed to the two most influential Jewish philosophers in the Middle Ages. I am inclined to assume that only by resorting to the pseudepigraphical genre could astral dream theory move from the margin toward a somewhat more influential position in Jewish thought. In other words, the anomian or sometimes even antinomian rites may be performed at night (according to some texts),[73] though they are forbidden in a state of wakefulness. The diurnal, conscious state of mind may be described as much more "monotheistically" inclined while the oneiric, nocturnal experiences may be described as much more "polytheistically" oriented.

Indeed, in one of the most interesting discussions of the danger of polytheism in kabbalistic literature, the early sixteenth-century R. Abraham ben Eliezer ha-Levi, though criticizing prayers addressed to angels, nevertheless defends the technique of *she'elat ḥalom* and *she'elah be-haqitz*, claiming that the kabbalist who resorts to this technique is explicitly mentioning the glory of God as the supreme entity.[74] This claim notwithstanding, it is striking that this kabbalist found it necessary to justify using the technique while attacking other forms of angel worship as idolatrous.

Notes

1. On the three types of time see Idel 1998c.
2. I shall be concerned here only with the astral aspects of magic and dream, as inspired

by views stemming from Greek and Arabic sources, as analyzed in the two studies of S. Pines (1980; 1988).

3. On these powers and the impact of the concept of spiritual forces, see the important studies by Pines 1980, 1988; also Idel 1995a.

4. On the relation between commandments and astral views, see Kiener 1987: 14–15, 20–22; Idel 1983b: 196, 203–208.

5. See Idel 1995a: 287–288, note 178.

6. On this literature see Lesses 1995; Werblowsky 1962: 47–48, 76, 142–144; Idel 1983a: 185–266; 1997.

7. *Ha-'agalah sham.*

8. Ms. Oxford Bodeliana 1965, fol. 183a.

9. On this theme see the important study of Langermann 1993.

10. Ibid.

11. Strangely enough, in his other commentaries on the biblical verses where the term *mekhashshef* appears, ibn Ezra does not offer this astrological interpretation. See, e.g., the two versions of his commentary on Exodus 7:12.

12. On this anonymous book see Dan 1968: 143–156 and Idel 1990a: 86–91.

13. Ms. Parma, de Rossi 1390, fols. 128b–129a.

14. At least the three earliest manuscripts of this book have been copied, anonymously, in Rome in the eighties of the thirteenth century. See Idel 1998a.

15. See Idel 1990b: 4–15 and Vajda's important study (1954).

16. See my suggestion that it might have been fabricated in Catalonia in the seventies or the eighties of the thirteenth century, Idel 1998b.

17. On this spurious letter see Scholem 1935a: 91–92; 1935b: 104–105; Idel 1998b.

18. Therefore, I assume that some views that the author mistakenly attributed to the great eagle show indeed that he was aware of attributing a view that was opposed by the philosopher.

19. Exodus 25:22.

20. This book was never mentioned by Maimonides. In my opinion, this was deliberate, because he opposed linguistic magic and mysticism that play such an important role in its cosmology.

21. *Sefer Yetzirah* 2:2.

22. *Nefashot 'Enoshiyot.* In print *nefashot ḥitzoniyot*, apparently, impure souls or demons.

23. *Ba-ne'elam.* So in ms. London, British Library Or. 19788, and *Liderosh 'Elohim* (Hamoi 1870). In *Ḥemdah Genuzah* (Edelmann 1856) the version is *Ba-'Olam*, which is a copyist's error.

24. *Ha-Nimus ha-'Elohi.*

25. *Tamid*, namely "in a constant manner."

26. Numbers 12:7.

27. Numbers 23:14.

28. *Ḥokhmat ha-tekhunah.* The anonymous forger is often insinuating a common study of Maimonides and his student, of Kabbalah and astronomy or astrology.

29. *He'arah.*

30. This view represents an Avicennian approach.

31. *Be-kavvanah 'atzumah.*

32. *Min ha-mal'akhim*, literally "from the angels."

33. *Maḥashavah penuyah.*

34. This is a recurrent recommendation for obtaining a divinatory dream, found in many recipes, already in ancient texts.

35. Cf. Job 4:15.

36. *Hitbodedutkha*. On this meaning of the term *hitbodedut* see Idel 1989a: 103–169.

37. Ms. London, British Library Or. 19788, fols. 4b–5a; *Liderosh 'Elohim*, fols. 19b–20a; *Hemdah Genuzah*, fols. 43b–44a.

38. On this concept see Idel 1995: 215–219.

39. This point has already been made by Scholem, see note 17 above.

40. See Idel 1989b: 43.

41. Ms. London, fol. 6a.

42. Incubation is often related not only to fixed places, such as temples, but also to strong gods that preside over these shrines, while the oneiric techniques as represented by the *she'elat ḥalom* literature are mobile and, while addressing the supreme deity, they involve the reception of the answers from weaker intermediary powers, such as angels.

43. *Ta'amah*.

44. *Nitztaddeq*, which means, literally, justified or verified.

45. Ms. London, fol. 5b.

46. See Scholem 1969: 28–29; Idel 1981: 28–29; Wolfson 1993: 45, 47.

47. *Ḥemdah Genuzah*, fol. 43a.

48. See Scholem 1969: 27.

49. *Shem mumḥeh*.

50. *Commentary on the Torah*, ed. Ch. D. Chavel, vol. III [Jerusalem, 1969] p. 436. The resort to this verse as part of an oneiric technique recurred later on in kabbalistic literature; see Idel 1983a: 206–209; Cordovero 1945: 4. Interestingly enough Cordovero too claims that the combinations of three letters are names of angels.

51. See the two quotes adduced above from the epistle.

52. The nexus between Hermes and interpretation, namely hermeneutics, is well known. See Plato, *Cratylus*, 408ab.

53. *Ḥemdah Genuzah*, fol. 44a, *Liderosh 'Elohim*, fol. 20b.

54. *Mashal u-melitzah*, ibid.

55. *Liderosh 'Elohim*, fol. 20b.

56. See Lesses 1995: 274–298.

57. Alemanno's views on astral dreams will be the subject of a separate study. See below, note 71.

58. Ed. M. Grossberg, [London, 1901]; Tishby 1989: 3, 904, note 142.

59. *Ḥemdah Genuzah*, fol. 43a note.

60. This designation of the agent intellect is implicit in several medieval texts, where the ten *sefirot*, of whom the *Shekhinah* is the last one, are identified with the ten separate intellects, of whom the agent intellect is the last one. See, e.g., Abulafia's text pointed out by Scholem 1961: 143.

61. *Ha-morido*.

62. Or it.

63. *Mi-beli she-yaḥlimehu*.

64. *Yevamot*, fol. 49b, *Sukkah*, fol. 45b. These texts have been widely exploited by medieval authors dealing with the issue of revelation.

65. *Sefer ha-'Atzamim*, p. 13.

66. *The Guide of the Perplexed*, 2:36.

67. See ibid., 3:29.

68. *Sefer ha-'Atzamim*, pp. 13–14.

69. See the passage from Picatrix to this effect; cf. Idel 1995a: 74. On Aristotle as a magician in the Middle Ages see the spurious *Secretum Secretorum*.

70. Bodei 1997.

71. On this issue see Idel 1996.

72. See for the time being the discussions found in Alemanno's passages extant in ms. Oxford 2234, fol. 106b; ms. Paris, Bibliotheque Nationale 849, fol. 28ab; *Sha'ar ha-Ḥesheq*, fol. 42a; ms. Oxford 1535, fol. 123a.

73. See Idel 1995b.

74. Cf. *Hora'ot be-'Inianei Mal'akhim*, ms. New York, Columbia 6H 13, fol. 37b.

References

Bodei, Remo. 1997. "Variationen des Ichs.", in *Die Wahrheit der Träume*, (eds.) G. Benedetti, E. Hornung, Munich, 227–248.

Cordovero, Moshe. 1945. "Derishot be-'Inianei Malakhim." Appendix in *Mal'akhei 'Eliyon*, Reuven Margaliot, Jerusalem.

Dan, Joseph. 1968. *The Esoteric Theology of the Ashkenazi Hasidism*. Jerusalem (Hebrew).

Edelmann, Z. (ed.). 1856. *Ḥemdah Genuzah*. Koenigsberg.

Hamoi, R. Abraham. 1870. *Liderosh Elohim*. Livorno.

Idel, Moshe. 1981. "The Concept of the Torah in Heikhalot Literature and its Metamorphoses." *Jerusalem Studies in Jewish Thought* 1, 23–84 (Hebrew).

———. 1983a. "Inquiries in the Doctrine of Sefer Ha-Meshiv." *Sefunot* 17 (ed.) J. Hacker, Jerusalem, 185–126 (Hebrew).

———. 1983b. "The Magical and Neoplatonic Interpretations of Kabbalah in the Renaissance." In *Jewish Thought in the Sixteenth Century*, (ed.) B. D. Cooperman, Cambridge, MA, 186–242.

———. 1989a. *Studies in Ecstatic Kabbalah*. Albany, NY.

———. 1989b. *Language, Torah and Hermeneutics in Abraham Abulafia*, (tr.) M. Kalus, Albany, NY.

———. 1990a. *Golem, Jewish Magical and Mystical Traditions on the Artificial Anthropoid*. Albany, NY.

———. 1990b. "The Beginning of Kabbala in North Africa?—A Forgotten Document by R. Yehuda ben Nissim ibn Malka." *Pe'amim* 43, 4–15 (Hebrew).

———. 1995. *Hasidism, Between Ecstasy and Magic*. Albany, NY.

———. 1996. "Metatron: Observations on the Development of Myth in Judaism." In *Myth in Judaism*, (ed.) Haviva Pedaya. Beer Sheva, 22–40 (Hebrew).

———. 1997. "Nachtliche Kabbalisten." In *Die wahrheit der Träume*, (eds.), G. Benedetti and E. Hornung, Munich, 85–117.

———. 1998a. "Abraham Abulafia and Menahem ben Benjamin in Rome: The Beginnings of Kabbalah in Italy." London, (ed.) Barbara Gavrin, forthcoming.

———. 1998b. "Abulafia's Secrets of the Guide: A Linguistic Turn." In *Perspectives on Jewish Thought and Mysticism*, (eds.) A. Ivry, E. Wolfson, and A. Ankush, Australia, 289–330.

———. 1998c. "Some Concepts of Time and History in Kabbalah." in *Jewish History and Jewish Memory, Essays in Honor of Yosef Hayim Yerushalmi*, (eds.) E. Carlebach, J. M. Efron, D. N. Myers, Hanover, London, 153–188.

Kiener, Ronald. 1987. "Astrology in Jewish Mysticism from the Sefer Yezirah to the Zohar." In *The Beginnings of Jewish Mysticism in Medieval Europe*, (ed.) J. Dan, Jerusalem, 1–42.

Langermann, Y. Tzvi. 1993. "Some Astrological Themes in the Thought of Abraham ibn Ezra." In *Rabbi Abraham ibn Ezra: Studies in the Writings of a Twelfth-Century Jewish Polymath*, (eds.) I. Twersky and J. M. Harris, Cambridge, 28–85.

Lesses, Rebecca. 1995. "Ritual Practises to Gain Power: Adjurations in Heikhalot Literature, Jewish Amulets, and Greek Revelatory Adjurations." (Ph.D. thesis, Harvard University, Cambridge, Mass.).
Pines, Shlomo. 1980. "Shi'ite Terms and Conceptions in Judah Halevi's Kuzari." *Jerusalem Studies in Arabic and Islam* 2, 165–251.
———. 1988. "On the Term *Ruhaniyyut* and Its Sources and On Judah Halevi's Doctrine." *Tarbiz* 57, 511–540 (Hebrew).
Scholem, Gershom. 1935a. "Me-Ḥoqer li-Mequbbal." *Tarbiz* 6, 90–98 (Hebrew).
———. 1935b. "Maimonides dans l'oeuvre des kabbalistes." *Cahiers juifs* 3, 103–112.
———. 1961. *Major Trends in Jewish Mysticism.* New York.
———. 1969. *On the Kabbalah and its Symbolism,* (tr.) R. Manheim, New York.
Tishby, Isaiah. 1989. *The Wisdom of the Zohar,* (tr.) D. Goldstein, Oxford.
Werblowsky, R. T. Z. 1962. *Joseph Karo, Lawyer and Mystic,* Oxford.
Wolfson, Elliot. 1993. "The Mystical Significance of Torah Study in German Pietism." *Jewish Quarterly Review* 84, 43–77.
Vajda, Georges. 1954. *Juda ben Nissim ibn Malka, philosophe juif marocain.* Paris.

13

Dreaming Analyzed and Recorded

Dreams in the World of Medieval Islam

Sara Sviri

for Professor M. J. Kister

"The veridical dream is one forty-sixth of prophecy," states an Islamic tradition attributed to the Prophet Muḥammad.[1] This statement implies that while prophecy has ceased, Muḥammad being the Seal of the Prophets, messages of divine origin can still be communicated through dreams, albeit on a smaller scale than prophecy. This possibility opened up important avenues for both mysticism and philosophy in medieval Islam. For Sufism it meant that divine inspiration (*ilhām*) could be granted to the friends of God (*awliyā' allāh*), the holy men of Islam. For philosophy it meant that in a state of suspension from the outer senses, a state which normally occurs during sleep or in deep contemplation, the human Intellect could become united with the Universal (or Active) Intellect and thus have access to transcendental truths. It was universally accepted that those who had cultivated their inner faculties and insights could decipher the encoded messages of their own dreams as well as those of others.

No wonder, therefore, that there exists a vast literature on dreams and dream interpretation in Islam. It is perhaps significant that in a conference on dreams held some thirty years ago a large proportion of the papers presented dealt with various aspects of dreams within an Islamic context.[2] In the comparative study of dreams in Islam, one can point to many contact points with other, older traditions. Some of the popular dicta concerning dreams—as, for example, the dictum opening this essay—came, directly or indirectly, from Jewish sources.[3] Practices of dream incubation, for which there is suggestive evidence in Islam,[4] had existed from time immemorial in the Near East[5] and in Greece.[6] Systematic attempts at analyzing the mechanism of dreaming and at defining the psychic components involved in it were part of epistemological and psychological disciplines inherited, via the Hellenistic schools of late antiquity, from ancient Greek philosophy. Dream interpretation, a genre that for centuries had produced encyclopedic volumes in Arabic,[7] could simulate the model supplied by Artemidorus's *Oneirocritica*, which had been translated into Arabic as early as the ninth century.[8] It could also make use of the (oral and written) cumulative Near Eastern vocabularies of dream symbols.[9] This, indeed, is a wide territory.

The areas covered by this essay, in contrast, are far from extensive. The presentation is divided into two parts. In the first part I have brought together samples from the writings of some medieval authors interested in the psychological components of dreaming, and in particular the role of imagination. In the second part I have reproduced an autobiographical document in which dreams dreamt by a ninth-century Muslim couple from Central Asia were recorded by the husband, al-Ḥakīm al-Tirmidhī, who, in his turn, was to go down in the Sufi tradition as one of the *awliyā'*. These dreams retain a personal as well as an archetypal aura. They were perceived by the author as teaching dreams; namely, as dreams guiding him on his spiritual journey and announcing his special rank on the hierarchical ladder of the "friends of God."

I

1

As is well known, ever since Artemidorus's *Oneirocritica* was translated into Arabic by Ḥunayn ibn Isḥāq in the ninth century,[10] Muslim writers on the subject of dreams and dreaming have studied and absorbed the literature and theories that were current in the Hellenistic philosophical schools of late antiquity.[11] Ya'qūb ibn Isḥāq al-Kindī (d. ca. 866), the earliest in a long line of Muslim philosophers,[12] in his *Epistle on the Nature of Sleep and Dream*,[13] maintains that the understanding of "sleep" and "dream" is based on the knowledge of the psyche (*nafs*) and its faculties, and in particular on identifying its two main, albeit polar, faculties: the sensible (*al-ḥissiyya*) and the mental (*al-'aqliyya*). Sleep, he says, is a state in which the psyche abandons the use of the physical senses. What the dreamer sees and hears in a dream comes, therefore, not from the senses but from a special psychic faculty which he names "the form-creating faculty" (*al-quwwa al-muṣawwira*)—"that which the ancient Greek sages called fantasy" (*fanṭāsiyā*).[14] Unlike the senses that bring forth the sensed objects in their physicality (*fīṭīnatihā*), fantasy, or imagination, produces them in their pure, noncorporeal forms. A similar process takes place when the mental faculty is at work in the waking state, when one is absorbed in thinking, and "sees" objects not via the senses, but via the form-creating faculty. Such purely formal perception, in sleep or in deep thinking, is considered by al-

Kindī much more refined and reliable than perception through the external senses, which are dependent upon sense organs, and which he, therefore, considers "secondary" (*ālāt thāniyya*). The physical senses can become damaged through illness and other external obstacles, and are restricted by the limited nature of natural phenomena; whereas imagination is much more expansive in its form-creating capacity. Thus, for example, in dreams a man can have wings and fly, or a beast can talk, which are improbable physical phenomena.[15] In producing such dream forms, the psyche, which is "knowledgeable, awake, and alive" (*'allāma yaqẓāna ḥayya*)[16] acts for the dreamer as a revealer of things to come, since in this way it points to, or prophesies, future events.

The precedence given to imagination over the physical sense organs, and the prophetic propensities of the psyche, were ideas developed also by al-Fārābī (d. 950)[17] and by Ibn Sīnā (d. 1037),[18] two Muslim philosophers who exerted an unprecedented influence on medieval discourse on dreams and on the understanding of the way in which imagination, as one of the functions of the psyche, operates in the twilight zone between sense perception and nonsensory visualization—between the world dominated by the senses and the world dominated by transcendent reality.

2

Medieval Arabic literature on dreams and visions—and in this term are included writings by non-Muslims—reiterates time and again the hierarchical polarization between knowledge acquired through the physical senses and knowledge of spiritual "meanings" (*ma'ānī*—referred to also as "ideas," "forms," "intelligibles," "universals") acquired through the inner, subtle senses that are activated in dreaming.[19] Jewish intellectuals, who were brought up on the same Hellenistic concepts in their Arabic garb as their Muslim compatriots, resorted in their writings to similar distinctions. Isaac Israeli, a North African Jewish philosopher of the tenth century, in his *Book on the Elements*, evaluates the transcendent nature of dream images, which do not conform with natural phenomena, in the following way:

> A man will behold himself during sleep as if endowed with wings for flying, and flying therewith between heaven and earth; and it will seem to him as if the heavens are open, and a voice is calling thence and speaking to him; and as if he is walking upon the waters of the sea and across great rivers; and as if the beasts are talking. The evidence lies in the fact that the character of these forms and images is spiritual, subtle, transcending the natural order, and contrary to what one experiences in waking condition. . . . We discover that they do teach us certain truths once some really intelligent person interprets them.[20]

He goes on to assert that there is a clear correspondence between these extraordinary images which are sometimes experienced by dreamers, and the spiritual images which are revealed to prophets:

> The prophets . . . armed themselves with those spiritual forms and revealed them to all and sundry in order that their fellow creatures might know their exalted qualities and their achievements having passed from the flesh to a spiritual state, since that which they made manifest transcends the natural order. From this point of view, there is agreement between all authors of books on religion and all who believe in prophecy that dreams are a part of prophecy.[21]

The mechanism of registering and retaining the dream images is explained by Israeli as the activity of the *sensus communis*, which, like imagination, with which it is sometimes identified, occupies a middle position between the inner and the outer senses:

> During sleep the *sensus communis*[22] (*al-ḥiss al-mushtarak*) sees forms intermediate between spirituality and corporeality . . . but knows them only in their corporeal aspects. . . . But once it knows their corporeal aspects, it transmits them to the imaginative faculty which resides in the anterior brain, and imagination receives them in a more subtle way since it is more subtle than the *sensus communis* and more remote from the corporeal sense, i.e., that of sight. Once the imaginative faculty has received them from the *sensus communis*, it transmits them to the memory and deposits them there. When the person awakes from his sleep, he claims these forms from the memory. . . . Remembering them, one seeks to understand their spiritual meaning through the cogitative faculty (*al-quwwa al-mufakkira*), because the latter possesses the power to scrutinise, discern, and combine. . . . When, therefore, the cogitative faculty of the person concerned is spiritual, pure, luminous, and hardly obscured by shells and darkness, intellect [i.e., the transcendent Universal Intellect—S. S.] will cause its light and brilliance to emanate upon it and make known to it its own properties, forms, and spiritual messages . . . and the difference between its spiritual forms and corporeal ones. Then . . . [cogitation] will interpret those dreams without fault.[23]

3

In a treatise on the art of poetry, written in Judaeo-Arabic by Moses ibn Ezra, an eleventh/twelfth-century Andalusian Jewish poet, we find yet another analysis of dreaming. Addressing the question whether a poem can be created during sleep,[24] and basing himself on Aristotle,[25] he too echoes the long-established understanding that dreams belong to a psychological realm which lies between the sensual and the spiritual. Dreaming, he explains, is an internal psychological happening that is activated during sleep, when the psychic energy flows inwardly, toward the internal senses, rather than outwardly, toward the external senses, as is the case in the waking state. Dreams are mental form constellations (*taṣwīrāt 'aqliyya*) perceived by the internal senses, which may emerge from two different sources: spiritual and sensual. Only dreams of the first kind, in which the forms emerge from a celestial origin, are veridical. The images constellated in these dreams represent subtle and spiritual ideas (*ma'ānī*). These ideas reveal to the dreamer's rational soul (*an-nafs an-nāṭiqa*) divine and hidden truths, and are perceived by the mental faculties (*al-quwā al-'aqliyya*), which, in their turn, are inspired by the Universal Intellect (*al-'aql al-kullī*). Interestingly, in this class of dreams no role seems to be assigned by Moses Ibn Ezra to the imaginative faculty. In the second class of dreams, however, those which derive from dense physical forms and which arise from the animal soul (*an-nafs ash-shahwāniyya*), the imaginative, form-creating faculty in conjunction with the *sensus communis* produce dreams that are false and inconsequential (*aḍghāth al-aḥlām*).[26] The imaginative faculty is seen here as participating with the inferior *sensus communis* but not—as in al-Kindī, al-Fārābī, Ibn Sīnā, and Israeli—with the higher mental faculties.

4

In the eighth chapter of the last book of the *Iḥyā' 'ulūm al-dīn* (The Revival of the Religious Sciences), an encyclopedic Sufi composition written at the end of the eleventh century, the author, Abū Ḥāmid al-Ghazālī (d. 1111),[27] offers a classic explanation for the phenomenon that allows nonprophets, through a vision which occurs in sleep, to have a glimpse into the realm of the unseen. Al-Ghazālī's exposition on dreams is contained in the final part of the *Iḥyā'*, which deals with eschatological matters.[28] After death, says al-Ghazālī, man is transported from the "world of possession and [sense] perception" (*'ālam al-mulk wash-shahāda*) to the "world of the angelic kingdom and the unseen" (*'ālam al-malākūt wal-ghayb*).[29] Dream visions too come from that realm, and therefore the perception of a dreamer to whom a veridical dream is conferred resembles the noncorporeal perception of the soul in the world to come. Both relate to a mode of inner seeing (*mushāhada*) that is independent of the outer senses. A veridical dream vision, which is by definition a weak version of prophecy, may be granted to the pious and righteous during their lifetimes. Al-Ghazālī explains that in a state of outer and inner purification the veil covering the heart is lifted and a vision of the future is revealed to the heart's eye. The heart, he explains, is like a mirror upon which forms (*ṣuwar*) and meanings (*ma'ānī*) are reflected. The source of these forms and meanings is the (Preserved) Tablet (*al-lauḥ al-maḥfūẓ*),[30] the heavenly book that records all created and preordained phenomena from the beginning of creation to its end. In the process of dreaming, it is suggested, a double act of mirroring is taking place: the Tablet mirrors the incorporeal forms that exist in the unseen, and the unveiled heart, in contemplating the Tablet, mirrors the images reflected there. When the heart is not obscured by the veils of desires and sense perception, visions from the world of the unseen may thus flash and become reflected upon its clear surface. This is best achieved in sleep, since in sleep the senses lie dormant and do not distract the heart.

Although the senses are dormant, sleep does not deter the imagination (*khayāl*) from being at work in the process of dreaming. Imagination, according to al-Ghazālī, is the faculty which, through imitation (*ḥikāya*), represents the noncorporeal meanings reflected upon the heart by means of producing analogous images (based on sense perception), which are then stored in memory (*ḥifẓ*).[31] When the dreamer wakes up, he remembers only the images. These images require interpretation, since they are no longer the original forms and truths (*ḥaqā'iq*), but only their symbolic representation. The interpreter of dreams, who has immersed himself in the science of dream interpretation (*'ilm al-ta'bīr*),[32] derives the meanings hidden behind the dream images by making relevant associations. Al-Ghazālī illustrates this in the following way:

> Someone told Ibn Sīrīn:[33] "I saw myself in a dream holding a seal by which I was sealing the mouths of men and the privies of women." Ibn Sīrīn said: You are a muezzin (*mu'adhdhin*) who calls for prayer on the mornings of Ramaḍān," to which the man responded, "You got it right!"

Ibn Sīrīn, suggests al-Ghazālī, interpreted the dream by associating the essential meaning of sealing, which is blocking or inhibiting, with the office of a *mu'adhdhin* calling upon the faithful to refrain from eating, drinking, and having sexual intercourse during the month of Ramaḍān. The dreamer's imagination, on its part, associated "inhibiting" with "sealing with a seal," and clothed the abstract, noncorporeal meaning in a graspable image. The function of the interpreter of dreams is thus to retrieve the original meaning that lurks behind the dream images.

In this short exposition al-Ghazālī loosely ties Orthodox Islamic tradition and Sufi images on the one hand with some concepts derived from the current philosophical theories referred to above on the other. But his prime interest is didactic rather than analytic, and his composition is aimed at an audience who might be interested in the *experience* of dreams and visions more than in a theoretical analysis of it. Hence, of all the internal senses discussed in the philosophical literature, that is, of all the cognitive and psychic components involved in dreaming, al-Ghazālī chooses to refer to imagination (and fleetingly to memory) alone. Neither the intellect nor the rational faculty figure in; instead, it is the unveiled heart, free from the control of desires, which receives the messages from the beyond by means of reflection.

5

Ibn al-'Arabī (d. 1240), the influential thirteenth-century Andalusian mystic, stands at the peak of the centuries-long development of theories and analyses of dream and imagination. Indeed, Ibn al-'Arabī employs earlier notions, but understands them in a way that is no less than a leap into epistemological arenas far beyond the limits of mental speculation. Well grounded in Aristotelian philosophy, he combines a philosophical understanding of the function of the imaginative faculty with insights inspired by his mystical tradition and experiences. From whichever angle imagination is viewed, says Ibn al-'Arabī, one is led to understand that it belongs to an intermediary realm; it is a *barzakh*. *Barzakh* is a term of Persian origin (?)[34] that appears in the Qur'ān (55:19) and is described as "something that separates two other things while never going to one side."[35] "When you perceive it," writes Ibn al-'Arabī,

> you will know that you have perceived an ontological thing (*shay' wujūdī*). . . . But you will know for certain . . . that there is nothing there in origin and root. So what is this thing for which you have affirmed an ontological thingness and from which you have negated that thingness . . . ? Imagination is neither existent nor nonexistent, neither known nor unknown, neither negated nor affirmed . . . [36]

An important ontological and epistemological insight emerges from Ibn al-'Arabī's investigation into the nature of imagination, whether in dreaming or in wakeful states: *all* existent things, he states, are at one and the same time existent and nonexistent. In Ibn al-'Arabī's words:

> The truth of affairs is that you should say concerning everything that you see or perceive, through whatever faculty perception takes place, "He/not He . . . " You do not doubt in the state of dreaming that the form you see is identical with what it is said to be; and you do not doubt . . . when you wake up that it was not it. You will not doubt in sound rational consideration that the situation is He/not He. . . . Every entity qualified by existence is it/not it. The whole cosmos is He/not He. He is the limited who is not limited, the seen who is not seen. . . . Know that the Manifest in the loci of manifestation—which are the entities—is the Real Being (*al-wujūd al-ḥaqq*), and that It is not It . . . [37]

Henri Corbin, in his extensive study of imagination and the world of the imaginal (*'ālam al-mithāl*)[38] in Islamic mystical philosophy, explains the doubling in the essence of the plane of imagination (*ḥaḍrat al-khayāl*) by using the analogy of the veil. "Imagination," he writes, "is subject to two possibilities, since it can reveal the Hidden only by continuing to veil it. It is a veil; this veil can become so opaque as to imprison us. . . . But it can also become increasingly transparent . . . "[39]

Dreams are phenomena in which imagination is displayed in all its complexity. Like images reflected in a mirror, dream images are both there and not-there. In their very essence dreams exemplify the ambivalent nature of existence, which is always both there and not-there. As an analogy Ibn al-'Arabī offers the example of a man looking in a mirror: what he sees is both there and not there. If he says, "I am there, in the mirror" he will be making a statement that is both true and untrue. This doubling is in the very nature of imagination. "The active imagination," explains Corbin, "is the mirror *par excellence*, the epiphanic place (*maẓhar*) of the images of the archetypal world."[40] The validity of visions and dreams as well as their true meaning depend on the access that the dreamer, or dream interpreter, has to the imaginal world (*'ālam al-khayāl wal-mithāl*).

In sleep, Ibn al-'Arabī says, as well as in mystical states such as "absence" (*ghaybūba, ghayba*), "annihilation" (*fanā'*), and "obliteration" (*maḥw*), the psychic attention is directed inward rather than toward the world of sense perception. In such states, the rational soul (*an-nafs an-nāṭiqa*), which is the highest component in the makeup of the human psyche, contemplates with its inner organs the images that have been stored in the treasury of the imagination (*khizānat al-khayāl*). These images have been accumulated and stored there via the continuous activity of the outer organs and the outer senses. For Ibn al-'Arabī too, as for the long line of his predecessors, imagination, in its capacity as mediator between the realm of the intelligibles, which is devoid of any corporeality, and the realm of the bodily senses, clothes an intelligible (*ma'qūl*), a noncorporeal idea, with formal images taken from the world of sensibles (*maḥsūsāt*).

> Imaginal things . . . are the meanings that assume shape (*tashakkul*) in sensory forms; they are given form by the form-giving faculty (*al-quwwa al-muṣawwira*) which serves the rational faculty.[41]

By transferring intelligibles into sensibles, imagination brings the two realms together; hence it facilitates a *coincidencia oppositorum*: "it brings together all opposites" (*al-jam' bayna al-aḍdād*).[42] It is through this function that human beings, especially during sleep, but also during extreme mystical states when the outer senses are completely at rest, can perceive something of the spiritual world, which is the world of reality (*ḥaqīqa*). Hence, imagination is instrumental in granting human beings the experience of the real, and in demonstrating the validity of the noncorporeal world of Truth.

In dreams, through the imaginative faculty (*al-quwwa al-mutakhayyila*), even divine attributes can be perceived in a corporeal form. The friends of God, says Ibn al-'Arabī, see images of highly spiritual beings such as angels, prophets, the Heavenly Throne (*al-'arsh*), and even God himself. He writes:

> The prophet said, "I saw my Lord in the form of a youth." This is like the meanings [i.e., spiritual entities—S. S.] that a sleeper sees in his dreams within sensory forms. The reason for this is that the reality of the imagination is to embody (*tajassud*) that which is not properly a body (*jasad*).[43]

Epiphanic visions of God are, as indicated above, both He and not-He (*huwa lā huwa*). They can be perceived only in the plane of imagination (*ḥaḍrat al-khayāl*) and in states such as sleep or mystical absence, when imagination takes over the plane of sense perception (*ḥaḍrat al-ḥiss*). For Ibn al-'Arabī, the plane of imagination is symbolized by Joseph, the archetypal dream interpreter in the biblical as well as in the Qur'ānic tradition. The ninth chapter of his *Bezels of Wisdom* (*Fuṣūṣ al-ḥikam*) is entitled "The Bezel of Luminous Wisdom in the Word of Joseph." In the opening lines of this chapter Ibn al-'Arabī writes:

> The light of this luminous wisdom expands to [embrace] the plane of imagination. This is the beginning of Divine inspiration granted to the people of Assistance (*ahl al-'ināya*). [This is supported by a *ḥadīth* transmitted in the name of] 'Ā'isha: "The first inspiration [granted to] the Prophet was a veridical dream. Every dream he had was [as clear as] the breaking of dawn. . . . "[44] . . . She did not know that the Prophet had said, "Men are asleep; when they die they wake up." . . . [Dreaming] is sleep within a sleep. Everything which comes about in this manner is named the plane of imagination. This is why it requires interpretation (*wa-*

> *lihādhā yu'abbaru*). In other words, something which in itself has one form appears in a different form, and [the interpreter] *crosses over* [*'ābir*] from the form seen by the dreamer to the form which is pertinent to the matter; for example, knowledge appears as milk. . . .[45] Later on when the Prophet was granted inspiration he was transported away from his ordinary senses . . . and became "absent" from those present with him. What took him over was the plane of imagination, though he was not in a state of sleep. In the same way, when the angel appeared to him in the form of a man, this too was from the plane of imagination. Although he was an angel and not a man he appeared to him as a human being. The observer who possesses knowledge transmutes this [form] until he arrives at the true form and says, "This is Gabriel . . . " Both perceptions are true: there is the truth of the sensual eye and the truth of this being Gabriel . . .
>
> Know that whatever is referred to as "that which is not God" (*siwā allāh*), in other words, the world, relates to God as shadow to man. It is God's shadow. This is the essence of the relation of [real] existence (*wujūd*) to the world. . . . The world is imagined, it does not possess a real existence, and this is the meaning of imagination, namely, you imagine that [the world] is a thing in itself outside God, but this is not so. . . . Know that you are imagination and whatever you perceive as not-you is also imagination. Existence is imagination within imagination, and real existence is nothing but Allāh from the point of view of His essence, not from the point of view of His names . . .[46]

Since dream images are sensual personifications of nonsensual realities, they need to be interpreted by someone who has access to knowledge of the intelligible world. The interpreter, like imagination itself, is mediating, crossing over, between the dreamer, the dream images, and the intelligible meanings that lie behind these images. He is also mediating between his own imaginative faculty and that of the dreamer. This mediation is borne out by the Arabic term assigned to interpretation: *ta'bīr* [from the root *'-b-r* : to traverse, to cross over]. . . . Says Ibn al-'Arabī,

> This is because the interpreter "crosses over" by means of what he says. In other words, . . . he transfers his words from imagination to imagination, since the listener imagines to the extent of his understanding. Imagination may or may not coincide with imagination. . . . If it coincides, this is called his "understanding" (*fahm*); if it does not coincide, he has not understood. . . . We only make this allusion to call attention to the tremendousness of imagination's level, for it is the Absolute Ruler (*al-ḥākim al-muṭlaq*) over known things.[47]

In the sixth chapter of the *Bezels of Wisdom*, which is concerned with Isaac, Ibn al-'Arabī gives an example for an outstanding case of a fateful misinterpretation of a dream: Abraham, he writes, saw in a dream that he was going to sacrifice Isaac. This, indeed, is based on a Qur'ānic verse according to which Abraham says to his son: "My son, I see in a dream that I shall sacrifice thee" (37:102). Further on in the same sūra (verse 105) God says: "Abraham, thou hast confirmed the vision."[48] But according to Ibn al-'Arabī, "[Abraham] did not interpret it [as he should have]." What had appeared in his dream was a ram in the form of his son, and Abraham accepted the dream at face value (*ṣaddaqa Ibrāhīm al-ru'yā*), instead of interpreting it according to its correct meaning. This, comments Ibn al-'Arabī, is why God had redeemed Isaac by means of "the great sacrifice" (*al-dhabḥ al-'aẓīm*). The idea behind this curious idiom is highlighted in the fourth chapter of *The Bezels of Wisdom*, dealing with Idrīs [=Enoch], where Ibn al-'Arabī explains that the form of Isaac, seen in Abraham's dream, was in fact a symbol for Abraham himself, since "the child is the essence of his father" (*al-walad 'ayn abīhi*). But Abraham fell short of making the right interpretation.[49]

A formal epiphany (*at-tajallī aṣ-ṣuwarī*) in the plane of imagination requires a special insightful knowledge by which God's intention, couched in a particular form, can be understood.[50] In Ibn al-'Arabī's own words:

> Through the science of [dream] interpretation a person comes to know what is meant by the forms of the images when they are displayed to him and when sense perception causes them to rise in his imagination during sleep, wakefulness, [mystical] absence, or annihilation.[51]

II

In the further reaches of the Islamic world, on the shores of the Oxus river (the Amu Daria), a ninth-century Muslim seeker went in search of inner knowledge. A personal account of his years of quest has been preserved.[52] Abū 'Abdallāh Muḥammad ibn 'Alī al-Ḥakīm al-Tirmidhī has left a document that is, to the best of my knowledge, the first autobiographical piece written, or at least preserved, in Sufi literature, and probably also in Muslim literature at large. In the Sufi tradition al-Tirmidhī's name has become associated with the doctrine, fundamental to his teaching, concerning the *awliyā'*, the friends of God, the holy men of Islam.[53] According to this doctrine, one of the routes by which God communicates with his elect is through dreams. This is based on the understanding of a Qur'ānic verse that reads: "Surely God's friends—no fear shall be on them, neither shall they sorrow. . . . For them good tidings (*bushrā*) in the present life and in the world to come (10: 62–64)."[54] "Good tidings," al-Tirmidhī writes in his *The Way of the Friends of God* (*Sīrat al-awliyā'*), "is a veridical dream . . . ; the dream of the faithful is God's word spoken to him in his sleep."[55]

In his autobiography, which is titled "The Beginning of the Matter" (*Bad' al-sha'n*), al-Tirmidhī has recorded a long series of personal dreams, as well as mystical experiences and key events in his life. Most of the dreams recorded were dreamed by his wife. Since al-Tirmidhī does not disclose her name, I shall refer to her simply as Umm 'Abdallāh, in the same way that he is called Abū 'Abdallāh. Although the dreams were given to her as divine messages for her husband, the document makes it clear that she is not just a mediumistic messenger. The dreams reflect also her own inner development. Significantly, al-Tirmidhī's record ends with Umm 'Abdallāh's own mystical experiences. This, then, is a document that describes the inner journey, through dreams and experiences, of a mystical couple, united in marriage as well as in the spiritual quest, whose inner and outer lives are closely knit together. In this respect, I think, it is not only a rare document, but also a rather rare and precious human experience.

In his autobiography al-Tirmidhī tells how for years, after his initial spiritual awakening which took place during a pilgrimage to the Ka'ba, he kept searching on his own, with no teacher, and without companions. He writes:

> The love of solitude came into my heart. I would go out into the wilderness and wander in the ruins and graveyards around my town. This was my practice, and I kept it tirelessly. I was looking for true companions who would support me in this, but I found none. So I took refuge in ruins and in solitary places. One day, while in this state, I saw, as if in a dream, the Messenger of God, peace be upon him. He entered the Friday mosque of our town and I followed him closely step by step. He walked until he entered the *maqṣūra* [the section reserved for the dignitaries] and I followed, almost cleaving to his back, stepping upon his very footsteps. . . . Then he climbed up the pulpit, and so did I. Each step that he climbed, I climbed behind him. When he reached the uppermost step he sat down and I sat down at his feet, on the step beneath him, my right side facing his face, my face facing the gates which lead to the market, and my left facing the people [in the mosque]. I woke up in this position.[56]

This is the first auspicious dream that al-Tirmidhī records. Traditionally, seeing the prophet in a dream is understood as a true event and must be taken at face value and not interpreted away.[57] Al-Tirmidhī does not find it necessary to interpret the dream. Its symbolic meaning is, to him, apparent.[58] The period that preceded this dream is described as intense, filled with ascetic and devotional practices. He talks of his determination and zeal, but also of his aloneness and confusion. In spite of his inner conviction he needs some external validation and guidance. The dream reflects an exceptionally close adherence to the Prophet, a "physical" closeness that heralds support, direction, and spiritual attainment.

The second dream al-Tirmidhī records again speaks for itself and does not require him to indulge in interpretation. He writes:

> A short time after this, while praying one night, I was overtaken by deep weariness, and as I put my head on the prayer rug, I saw a huge and empty space, a wilderness unfamiliar to me. I saw a huge assembly[59] with an embellished seat and a pitched canopy the clothing and covering of which I cannot describe. And as if it was conveyed to me: "You are taken to your lord." I entered through the veils and saw neither a person nor a form. But as I entered through the veils an [overwhelming] awe descended upon my heart. And in my dream I knew with certitude [*ayqantu*] that I was standing in front of Him (*bayna yadayhi*). After a while I found myself outside the veils. I stood by the opening of the [outer?] veil exclaiming: "He has forgiven me!"[60] And I saw that my breath relaxed of the fear.

This, no doubt, is more than a dream; it is a mystical experience. The dream is told in a laconic brevity that stands in contrast to the intensity conveyed. Alongside the depth of the personal experience the dream imagery links al-Tirmidhī with the ancient tradition of mystical encounters with the Lord who sits upon the Throne. The Throne image has clear biblical and prophetic connotations and is central for early Jewish mysticism of the Hekhalot and Merkabah literature.[61] "Certitude" (*yaqīn*)—inner mystical knowledge—and the description of the mystic's overwhelming proximity to God are themes that recur in many of al-Tirmidhī's works with reference to the *awliyā'*.[62]

From a certain point in al-Tirmidhī's spiritual journey his wife starts having dreams that contain a clear message for him. I know of no parallel to this phenomenon in Islamic literature. It is made clear that Umm 'Abdallāh herself becomes involved in the transformative process initiated through the dreams, and is told in one of them that she and her husband are on the same rung. Al-Tirmidhī writes that, while he was going through a period of great hardships, being harassed and persecuted by certain religious and political groups, his wife said to him:

> I saw in a dream, as if standing in midair, outside the house, on the path, an image of an old man, curly haired, wearing white clothes, sandals on his feet, and he was calling to me from the air (in the vision I was standing in front of him): Where is your husband? I said: He has gone out. He said: Tell him, the prince commands you to act justly, and he disappeared.

This is clearly a teaching dream. In spite of the persecution he encountered, al-Tirmidhī's position among his own companions had become that of a spiritual guide. He tells how people of his hometown started gathering in front of his door beseeching him "to sit in front of them" (*al-qu'ūd lahum*). He himself, however, does not have a spiritual teacher to turn to. His authorization, or license to teach (*ijāza*), comes by means of dream messages. Through the dreams of his wife he is being prepared for the role of master. The old man, white-haired, clad in white, is no other than Khiḍr, that teacher from the angelic plane of all those seekers who do not have a flesh-and-blood guide.[63]

A similar figure appears also in Umm 'Abdallāh's second dream. Al-Ḥakīm al-Tirmidhī writes:

> Now my wife kept dreaming about me, dream after dream, always at dawn.[64] It was as if she, or the dreams, were messengers for me. There was no need for interpretation, because their meaning was clear. This was one of her dreams:
>
> I saw a big pool in a place unknown to me. The water in the pool was as pure as spring water. On the surface of the pool there appeared bunches of grapes, clear white grapes. I and my two sisters were sitting by the pool, picking up grapes from these bunches and eating them, while our legs were dangling upon the surface of the water, not immersed in the water, only touching it. I said to my youngest sister: Here we are, as you see, eating from these grapes, but who has given them to us? And lo, a man came towards us, curly haired, on his head a white turban, his hair loose behind his turban, his clothes white. He said to me: Who is the owner of a pool such as this and of grapes such as these? Then

> he took me by the hand, raised me, and said to me at a distance from my sisters: Tell Muḥammad ibn ʿAlī to read this verse: "We shall set up just scales on the day of resurrection [so that no man shall in the least be wronged . . .]."[65] On these scales neither flour nor bread is weighed, but the speech of this will be weighed—and he pointed to his tongue—And it will be weighed with these and these—and he pointed to his hands and legs. You don't know that excess of speech is as intoxicating as the drinking of wine. I said: Would you, please, tell me who you are? He said: I am one of the angels; we roam the earth, and our abode is in Jerusalem. Then I saw in his right hand [a bunch] of young green myrtle [branches], and in his other hand two branches of fragrant herbs. While he was talking to me he was holding them in his hands. Then he said: We roam the earth and we call on the worshippers. We place these fragrant herbs on the hearts of the worshippers (*al-ṣādiqūn*), so that by them they could carry out acts of worship. And this myrtle we place upon the hearts of the just (*al-ṣiddīqūn*) and those who possess certitude (*yaqīn*), so that by them they could discern what is just. These herbs in summer look like this, but the myrtle is ever green, it never changes, neither in summer nor in winter. Tell Muḥammad ibn ʿAlī: Don't you wish that you could have these two? And he pointed to the myrtle and the herbs. Then he said: God can raise the piety of the pious to such a stage that they will need no piety. Yet he had commanded them to have piety, so that they should [come to] know it. Tell him: Purify your house! I said: I have small children, and I cannot keep my house completely pure. He said: I don't mean from urine. What I mean is this—and he pointed to his tongue. I said: And why don't you tell him so yourself? He said: . . . [What he does] is neither a grave sin nor a minor sin. In the eyes of people it is a minor sin, but for him this is a grave one. Why should he commit it? Then he moved the hand which was holding the myrtle and said: Because this is [as yet?] remote from him. Then he plucked out of the bunch which he was holding some of the myrtle and handed them to me. I said: Shall I keep it for myself or shall I give it to him? He laughed, and his teeth shone like pearls. He said: This is for you, and as for these which I am holding, I myself shall take them to him. This is between the two of you, because you are both at the same place together. Tell him: This is my last council to him. Peace be with you! Then he added: May God bestow on you, oh sisters, "green gardens" [happiness and fruitfulness], not because of your fasts and prayers, but because of the purity of your hearts. . . . I said to him: Why don't you say it in front of my sisters? He said: They are not like you and they are not your equal. Then he said: Peace be with you, and went away. I woke up.

As in the previous dreams, here too one is struck by the allusions to ancient traditions and teachings conveyed in the dream. The myrtle, for instance, is an ancient symbol for the righteous, the *ṣiddīq* (and in the Jewish tradition, the *zaddīq*). In the book of Zechariah (1:8–11), the prophet is shown a vision which is in many ways reminiscent of Umm ʿAbdallāh's dream images:

> I saw by night and behold a man riding upon a red horse, and he stood among the myrtle trees that were in the bottom. . . . Then I said: O, my lord, what are these? And the angel that talked with me said unto me, I will show you what these be. And the man that stood among the myrtle trees answered and said, These are they whom the Lord has sent to walk to and fro through the earth.

> And they answered the Angel of the Lord that stood among the myrtle trees, and said, We have walked to and fro through the earth, and behold, all the earth sitteth still, and is at rest . . .

The Arabic and the Aramaic words for myrtle (in Arabic *ās*; in Aramaic *āsā*) derive from a root that denotes "healing." The dream alludes to two levels of healing through spiritual teaching. The first is the level of ordinary worshippers (*al-ṣādiqūn*), which are symbolized by the fragrant herbs. Their healing is not altogether firm, but rather temporary, since "in summer they are like this," namely, withered, "and in winter they are green." This type of healing is inferior compared with the healing symbolized by the evergreen myrtle, conferred on the "just" (*al-ṣiddīqūn*) and on "those who have attained certitude."[66]

The hierarchical evaluation of *ṣādiqūn*, sincere worshippers compared with *ṣiddīqūn*, true mystics, is one of the main motifs of al-Tirmidhī's vast literary corpus. The relationship between his, or his wife's, experiences, and the development of his spiritual teaching is thus intriguing and worth noting. The dream brings good tidings also for Umm 'Abdallāh. She is distinguished from her sisters and is told in unambiguous terms that she and her husband "are together in the same place," and she too is given from the myrtle branches. Thus, through the dream, both wife and husband have become prepared for the next phase of their spiritual journey.

The next stage is inaugurated by a dream in which Umm 'Abdallāh is shown the spiritual transformation that is going to take place in her husband and in the world around him through his teaching. The dream points to her own deep involvement in this process: she becomes, or pledges to become, the custodian and protector of her husband's work. Without her his mission cannot be complete. Here is the dream:

> [In her dream] she was in the open hall of our house. . . . There were several couches there, upholstered with brocade. One of the couches stood next to the family mosque. She said: I saw a tree growing by the side of this couch, facing the mosque. It grew up to a man's height, and it looked very dry, like a withered piece of wood. It had branches, similar to a palm tree, but the branches were all dry, like wooden pegs or filings. Now from the bottom of the trunk new branches emerged, about five or six, and they were all green and moist. When these branches reached the middle of the dry tree it started stretching and extending upwards to about three times a man's height, and so did the branches too. Then from amidst the branches there appeared bunches of grapes. I heard myself saying: this tree is mine! No one from here to the other end of the world has a tree like this!
>
> I came closer to the tree and heard a voice coming from around it, although I could see no-one there. I looked at the trunk and saw that it had grown out of a rock, a big rock. By the side of this rock I saw another big rock which had a hollow, like a pool. From the trunk of the tree a brook emerged and its water, which was pure, flowed into the hollow of the rock and gathered there.
>
> Again I heard a voice calling me from the bottom of the tree: can you make

> a pledge to protect this tree so that no hand would touch it? Then this tree is yours. Its roots have stood in sand and soil; many hands have touched it, and its fruit became worthless, then rotted and dried up. But now we have placed the rock around it, and we have nominated a bird over it, to watch over the fruit of this tree. Look!
>
> I looked, and saw a green bird, the size of a pigeon. It perched on one of the branches, not on the green moist ones which grew from the bottom of the trunk, but on a dry one. . . . The bird hopped upwards, climbing from branch to branch; whenever it perched on a dry branch, which looked like dry pegs, it became green and moist, and bunches of grapes hung down from it. The voice said: if you protect this tree faithfully the bird will reach the top of the tree and the whole tree will become green; if not, the bird will stay here, in the middle. I said: I will; indeed, I will protect it! But there was no-one to be seen.
>
> The bird flew to the top of the tree, branch after branch, and the whole tree became green. When it reached the top of the tree I exclaimed with amazement: *lā ilāha illā 'llāh*! Where are all these people? Can't they see the tree and come nearer? And the bird answered from the top of the tree: *lā ilāha illā 'llāh*! I wanted to pick up a tender grape from the tree, but a voice said to me: No! Not until it has ripened! And I woke up.

In this dream too the images are ancient and archetypal; there is a magical numinosity in the transformation that takes place in front of Umm 'Abdallāh's eyes. For her, who has a complete and utter faith in her husband's mission and destiny, the dream speaks with prophetic truth.

"On another occasion," al-Tirmidhī writes, "she dreamed that she was sleeping with me on the roof. She said:

> I heard voices coming from the garden, and got worried, because I thought that there were guests whom we had neglected. I'll go down and feed them, I thought, and went to the edge of the roof in order to climb down, when the edge of the roof, where I was standing, descended until it reached the ground and stopped. I saw two dignified persons sitting. I approached and apologised. They smiled. One of them said: Tell your husband, "why do you bother with this green [grass, *ḥashīsh*]? Your task is to give strength to the weak and to be their support." And tell him [also this]: "You are one of the pegs of the earth, and to you is assigned a section of the earth." I said, "Who are you?" One of them said, "Muḥammad Aḥmad, and this is 'Īsā [i.e., Jesus]. Tell him," he added, "you are saying: Oh, King, oh, Holy One, have mercy on us! [It is you who should] become sanctified! Every piece of land which you bless will grow strong and mighty, and that which you do not bless will become weak and worthless." Tell him: "We have given you the Inhabited House": "[I swear] in the name of the Inhabited House."[67] May you have success!' Then I woke up.

In this prophetic dream al-Tirmidhī is assigned, by no less than Muḥammad and Jesus, the role of a "peg," one of the pegs [*awtād*] of the earth. In the theory of the *awliyā'*, the spiritual hierarchy consists of a fixed number of evolved human beings without whom the well-being of the world cannot be maintained. At the top of this hierarchy stands the "pole" (*quṭb*), which is sometimes referred to by al-Tirmidhī as "the Master of the Friends of God" (*sayyid al-awliyā'*). Under him come the "pegs," below which come the substitutes (*al-abdāl*). This hierarchy has become central to Sufi discourse and nomenclature.[68] The importance of this doctrine in the comparative study of the phenomenon of holy men in early Islam, and the evidence supplied by al-Tirmidhī's autobiography for such a study, must not be undervalued.

Information about Sufi women does not exist in abundance. We are fortunate to have access to this unique record that tells about a loyal, sincere, prophetic woman, whose dreams have been carefully and lovingly recorded by her husband. This unnamed woman from central Asia has become awakened, through her deep empathy with her husband's destiny, to her own inner quest. Alongside her dreams for him, al-Tirmidhī's autobiography records also Umm 'Abdallāh's own spiritual ripening through dreams. In one of these dreams she sees herself and her husband sleeping together in bed. The prophet comes and lies down with them.

In another dream, one of the last dreams in the document, and one which is meant for her alone, she sees the prophet enter their house. She wants to kiss his feet, but he does not allow it. "He gave me his hand," she told her husband, "and I kissed it."

> I did not know what to ask of him. One of my eyes had been badly inflamed, so I said: Messenger of God, one of my eyes has been infected with inflammation. He said: Cover it with your hand and say *lā ilāha illā 'llāh*, the One without partner, His is the kingdom and His is the praise, He revives and He kills, He holds the good in his hand, He is the omnipotent one. I woke up, and since then, whenever anything befalls me I repeat these words and the obstacle is removed.

The final passages of al-Tirmidhī's autobiography record Umm 'Abdallāh's own mystical experiences:

> After these dreams she felt an urge to search for truth herself. The first experience that she had, which confirmed the veracity of her dreams, was this: while she was sitting one day in the garden, five or six days after she had seen this last dream, the following phrases descended upon her heart: The light and guide of all things! You are He whose light pierces all darkness!
>
> She said: I felt as if something penetrated my chest, circled within my heart and enveloped it. It filled my chest up to the throat, I almost choked from its fullness. Heat spread through the cavity of my body, my heart was on fire, and all the sacred names appeared to me in their glory. Anything upon which my eyes fell, on the earth or in the sky; anyone whom I looked at, I saw as I have never seen before, because of the beauty and joy and sweetness [which filled me]. Then a verse in Persian descended upon my heart: We have given you one thing!
>
> Again I was filled with joy, elation and great energy. The next day [she said]

another verse descended on my heart: We have given you three things: Our glory, Our might and Our beauty!

Then, she said, I saw a glow behind me, and it stayed above my head as if in a dream, and in this glowing light these three things were revealed to me: the knowledge of the Divine Glory, the knowledge of the Divine Might, and the knowledge of the Divine Beauty.

Then I saw something shimmering and moving, and it was conveyed to me: These things are going to take place. All that moves is from Him; the might and the high rank are from Him, and so is the beauty and the merit. This fire that I first saw in the sky is from Him, and now I see it as sparks of emerald and silver, blown and kindled.

On the third day these words descended on her heart: We have given you the knowledge of past and future.

She remained in this state for some time, and then the knowledge of the names of God was revealed to her. Each day new names opened up to her, and the glowing light was upon her heart, and the inward meaning of the names was revealed to her. This lasted for ten days. On the tenth day she came to me and said that the [divine] name the Gracious was revealed to her.

With these experiences the autobiography ends, rather abruptly. Al-Tirmidhī seems to have left this personal and unique piece of writing unfinished.[69] Nevertheless, from the care with which these—as well as the rest of the dreams in the document—were recorded, one can gain insight into the importance assigned to teaching dreams in the doctrines concerning the holy men in early Islam. In this respect, al-Tirmidhī's autobiography stands out not only as a personal dream journal, but also, and most importantly, as a testimony of the *practical* and *experiential* way in which dreams were integrated into the transformative process of mystics in medieval Islam.

Notes

1. For an extensive list of sources and variants see Kister 1974: 71 n. 20; see also al-Ḥakīm al-Tirmidhī 1970: 117; 1965b: 151; al-Ghazālī n.d. 4, 459.

2. See chapters by G. E. von Grunebaum, H. Corbin, T. Fahd, F. Meier, F. Rahman, and J. Lecerf in von Grunebaum and Caillois 1966.

3. Cf. Babylonian Talmud, *Berakhot* 57b: "A dream is one sixtieth of prophecy"; see Alexander 1995: 245; see also ch. 11, this volume; note that ample comparative material is contained in pp. 55a–57b of *Berakhot* tractate, where dreams and dream symbolism are extensively discussed.

4. See Fahd 1978: 259f; see also idem 1987: 364; cf. also below n. 56.

5. See Oppenheim 1956: 187ff.

6. See e.g., Meier 1966; cf. Kingsley 1995: 284ff.

7. See e.g., al-Nābulusī 1884 (accompanied on the margin by two additional works on dream interpretation: [Pseudo-] Ibn Sīrīn, *Muntakhab al-kalām fī tafsīr al-aḥlām* and Ibn Shāhīn al-Ẓāhirī, *al-ishāra fī 'ilm al-'ibāra*).

8. See Fahd 1964.

9. Cf. the *Assyrian Dream-Book* in Oppenheim 1956: 256ff; see also Kister 1974: 99.
10. See above n. 8.
11. See Daiber 1995; Pines 1974; Walzer 1962.
12. See Jolivet and Rashed 1986.
13. See al-Kindī 1950.
14. Ibid.: 295.
15. Ibid.: 300; cf. the passage cited from Isaac Israeli below n. 20; cf. Pines 1974: 109.
16. Al-Kindī 1950: 303.
17. See Walzer 1962: 211ff; see also Walzer 1965, and Rosenthal 1992: 115.
18. See Goichon 1971; see also, and in particular, Corbin 1988: 308ff *et passim.*
19. On the "internal senses" see Wolfson 1935: 69–133.
20. See Altmann and Stern 1958: 136; cf. ibid.: 91.
21. Ibid.: 136.
22. On the *sensus communis* see Walzer 1962: 208ff; Altmann and Stern 1958: 140ff.
23. See Altmann and Stern 1958: 136–137; on al-Kindī's influence on Isaac Israeli see ibid.: 143–144.
24. See Halkin 1975: 120ff; Abumalham 1985: 132–147 (Arabic text) and 1986: 133–148 (Spanish text).
25. On the question of identifying the [pseudo-?] Aristotelian sources from which Ibn Ezra may have culled his ideas see Pines 1974: 132 n. 195 *et passim.*
26. On this term, which derives from Qur'ān 21:5, see Fahd 1995: 645.
27. See Watt 1965.
28. Cf. Wensinck vol. 4, 1962: 117.
29. On al-Ghazālī's distinction between *'ālam al-malākūt wal-ghayb* and *'ālam al-mulk wal-shahāda*, see Lazarus-Yafeh 1975: 503ff.
30. On the Qur'anic term *al-lauḥ al-maḥfūẓ* (The Preserved Tablet) see commentaries to sūra 85:22; see also Schimmel 1994: 155, 228.
31. On the "mimetic" aspect of imagination see Walzer 1962: 211ff; on the function of memory in storing dream images see, e.g., Altmann and Stern 1958: 137.
32. Cf. an-Nābulusī, a late authority on *oneirocritica*, who, with reference to Joseph's outstanding talent of interpreting dreams (Qur'ān 12:6), writes: "the science of dreams [is] the prime science since the beginning of the world; the prophets and messengers never ceased to study it and act upon it"—cited in von Grunebaum and Caillois (eds.) 1966: 7.
33. On Ibn Sīrīn (d. 728) as the paradigmatic dream interpreter in early Islam see Fahd 1966: 357; 1971: 947–948; 1987: 312ff, *et passim*; on the pseudo-Ibn Sīrīn, *Muntakhab al-kalām fī tafsīr al-aḥlām* see ibidem: 355f; see also Kister 1974: 67, 99 *et passim.*
34. On *barzakh* see Cara de Vaux in *Encyclopedia of Islam*[2] 1960: 1071–1072 and commentaries to the verses mentioned above.
35. Chittick 1989: 117; cf. Chodkiewicz 1993: 150.
36. Chittick 1989: 118; cf. Sviri 1997: 61–76.
37. Ibid.: 116–117.
38. Corbin has coined the term *mundus imaginalis* to render the Arabic *'ālam al-mithāl*—see Corbin 1976: 16 (based on Corbin 1971–1972); on *'ālam al-mithāl* see Corbin 1966: 406ff; see also Rahman 1966: 409ff.
39. See Corbin 1969: 187; cf. Wolfson E. R. 1994: 61ff.
40. See Corbin 1990: 88.
41. See Chittick 1989: 115.
42. This is related to a dictum attributed to the ninth-century mystic Abū Sa'īd al-Kharrāz who, when asked: "Through what have you known God?" answered: "Through

the fact that He brings opposites together"—see Chittick 1989: 115; cf. Corbin 1969: 188, 209; on the coincidence of opposites in Sufism see Sviri 1987.

43. Chittick 1989: 116.

44. Cf. Al-Bukhārī 1391/1971: vol. 9, 91.

45. Cf. Chittick 1989: 119; for canonical sources for this tradition see ibid.: 396, n. 6.

46. Ibn al-'Arabī 1946: 99ff.

47. Chittick 1989: 119.

48. English translation according to Arberry 1964: 460.

49. See Ibn al-'Arabī 1975: 78; cf. Ibn al-'Arabī 1975: 48, n. 8.

50. Ibn al-'Arabī 1946: 85ff.

51. Chittick 1989: 119.

52. See al-Ḥakīm al-Tirmidhī 1965a: 14–32; 1965b: 315–343; cf. Radtke 1994.

53. See e.g., al-Hujwīrī 1976: 210ff; cf. Chodkiewicz 1993: 27–32 *et passim.*

54. Arberry 1964: 204.

55. See Radtke 1992: 66–67 (Arabic text).

56. The fact that al-Tirmidhī wakes up sitting in the same position as in the dream may suggest that the dreaming took place in a mosque. If this be so, this may reflect a kind of *istikhāra*, a practice which echoes the ancient ritual of dream incubation—cf. Fahd 1978, and see above notes 4–6. For the Arabic editions of al-Tirmidhī's autobiography from which this and the following dreams are translated, see n. 52. For the English translation, cf. Radtke and O'Kane 1996: 17–18 and Sviri 1997: 61–76.

57. Cf. the *ḥadīth* "he who sees me in a dream sees [really] me, for Satan cannot embody me" (*man ra'ānī fī 'l-manām fa-qad ra'ānī fa-inna 'sh-shayṭān lā yastaṭī'u an yatamaththala bī*)—al-Ḥakīm al-Tirmidhī 1970: 116; see also Wensinck 1936–63: vol. 2, p. 200.

58. According to Ibn Khaldūn "dreams of plain import are from God," see Guillaume 1938: 213.

59. The Arabic *majlis 'aẓīm* is equivocal; Radtke translates here "eine gewaltige versammlung," see Radtke 1994: 248. Cf. Radtke and O'Kane 1996: 19.

60. The text reads: *'afā 'annī*, which may also be rendered "He has released me, He has set me free."

61. It is worth noting that a link with the Jewish tradition may be gleaned from later, legendary accounts of al-Ḥakīm al-Tirmidhī's experiences. Thus, for example, Farīd al-Dīn 'Aṭṭār (d. 1221), in his *Tadhkirat al-awliyā'*, relates the following anecdote as reported by Abū Bakr al-warrāq, allegedly al-Tirmidhī's disciple: "I set out with him," says Abū Bakr, "and within a little while I espied an arduous and harsh desert, in the midst of which a golden throne was set. . . . Someone apparelled in beautiful raiment was seated on the throne. The Shaikh [i.e., al-Tirmidhī] approached him, whereupon this person rose up and set Tirmidhī on the throne. . . . 'What was all that? [the disciple asked] What place was it, and who was that man?' 'It was the wilderness of the children of Israel,' Tirmidhī replied. 'That man was the pole.'"—see Arberry 1979: 244f.

62. See, e.g., Radtke 1992: 104, 122 *et passim*; cf. idem 1993: 490.

63. On al-Tirmidhī's link with Khiḍr in later accounts of his life see Arberry 1979: 244ff.

64. On the significance of dreams at dawn see Oppenheim 1956: 240f; cf. Alexander 1995: 233.

65. Qur'ān 21:47.

66. A more detailed analysis of the myrtle symbol see Sviri, S. "And the Myrtle Trees Are But the Righteous." Forthcoming.

67. *"al-bayt al-ma'mūr"*—Qur'ān 52:4.

68. See Radtke 1980: 91ff; cf. al-Hujwīrī 1976: 214.

69. For an interpretation which sees in these experiences an indication of al-Tirmidhī's final mystical attainment see Zimmermann 1984: 141.

References

Alexander, P. S. 1995. "Bavli Berakhot 55a–57b: The Talmudic Dreambook in Context." *Journal of Jewish Studies* 46, 230–248.

Altmann, A. and Stern, S. M. 1958. *Isaac Israeli: A Neoplatonic Philosopher of the Early Tenth Century*. Oxford.

Arberry, A. J. (trans.). 1964. *The Koran Interpreted*. Oxford.

——— (ed. & trans.). 1979. *Muslim Saints and Mystics* (*Excerpts from Farīd ud-Dīn 'Aṭṭār's Tadhkirat al-auliyā'*). London.

Chittick, William C. 1989. *The Sufi Path of Knowledge*. Albany, NY.

Chodkiewicz, Michel. 1993. *Seal of the Saints: Prophethood and Sainthood in the Doctrine of Ibn 'Arabī* (trans. L. Sherrard). Cambridge.

Corbin, Henri. 1966. "The Visionary Dream in Islamic Spirituality." In G. E. von Grunebaum and R. Caillois (eds.), *The Dream and Human Societies*. Berkeley and Los Angeles, 381–408.

———. 1969. *Creative Imagination in the Ṣūfism of Ibn 'Arabī* (trans. R. Manheim). Princeton.

———. 1971–1972 *En Islam iranien: aspects spirituels et philosophiques*. 4 vols. Paris.

———. 1976. *Mundus Imaginalis or the Imaginary and the Imaginal*. Ipswich.

———. 1988. *Avicenna and the Visionary Recital* (trans. W. R. Trask). Princeton.

———. 1990. *Spiritual Body and Celestial Earth* (trans. N. Pearson). London.

Daiber, Hans. 1995. "Ru'yā (2)." *Encyclopaedia of Islam*[2] 8, 647–649.

Fahd, Toufic (ed.). 1964. *Artémidore d'Éphèse: Le Livre des Songes traduit du Grec en Arabe par Ḥunayn b. Iṣḥāq*. Damascus.

———. 1966. "The Dream in Medieval Islamic Society." In G. E. von Grunebaum and R. Caillois (eds.), *The Dream and Human Societies*. Berkeley and Los Angeles, 351–363.

———. 1971 "Ibn Sīrīn." *Encyclopaedia of Islam*[2] 3, 947–948.

———. 1978. "Istīkhāra." *Encyclopaedia of Islam*[2] 4, 259–260.

———. 1987. *La Divination arabe: Études religieuses, sociologiques et folkloristiques sur le milieu natif de l'Islam*. Paris.

———. 1995. "Ru'yā (1)." *Encyclopaedia of Islam*[2] 8, 645–647.

Goichon, A. M. 1971. "Ibn Sīnā." *Encyclopaedia of Islam*[2] 3, 941–947.

Grunebaum, G. E. von and Caillois, R. (eds.). 1966. *The Dream and Human Societies*. Berkeley and Los Angeles.

Guillaume, Alfred. 1938. *Prophecy and Divination*. London.

Halkin, Abraham (ed. & trans.). 1975. *Kitāb al-mudhākara wal-muḥāḍara li-Moshe ibn Ezra*. Jerusalem.

Al-Hujwīrī, 'Alī ibn 'Uthmān al-Jullābī. 1976. *Kashf al-Mahjūb* (trans. R. A. Nicholson). London.

Ibn al-'Arabī, Muḥyi al-Dīn Muḥammad ibn 'Alī. 1975. *The Wisdom of the Prophets* (*Fusus al-Hikam*). (Trans. [from French to English] A. Culmer-Seymour) Aldsworth Gloucestershire.

Jolivet, J. and Rashed, R. 1986. "Al-Kindī." *Encyclopaedia of Islam*[2] 5, 122–123.

Kingsley, Peter. 1995. *Ancient Philosophy, Mystery, and Magic: Empedocles and Pythagorean Tradition*. Oxford.

Kister, M. J. 1974. "The Interpretation of Dreams, An Unknown Manuscript of Ibn Qutayba's *'Ibārat al-Ru'yā*." *Israel Oriental Studies* 4, 67–103.

Lazarus-Yafeh, Hava. 1975. *Studies in al-Ghazzālī.* Jerusalem.

Meier, C. A. 1966. "The Dream in Ancient Greece and Its Use in Temple Cures (Incubation)." In G. E. von Grunebaum and R. Caillois (eds.), *The Dream and Human Societies.* Berkeley and Los Angeles, 303–318.

Oppenheim, Leo, A. 1956. "The Interpretation of Dreams in the Ancient Near East, with a Translation of an Assyrian Dream-Book." *Transactions of the American Philosophical Society*, N.S., 46, 179–373.

Pines, Shlomo. 1974. "The Arabic Recension of *Parva Naturalia* and the Philosophical Doctrine Concerning Veridical Dreams According to *al-Risāla al-Manāmiyya* and Other Sources." *Israel Oriental Studies* 4, 104–153.

Radtke, Bernd. 1980. *Al-Ḥakīm at-Tirmiḏī: Ein islamischer Theosoph des 3./9. Jahrhunderts.* Freiburg.

——— (ed.). 1992. *Drei Schriften des Theosophen von Tirmiḏ.* Beirut and Stuttgart.

———. 1993. "The Concept of *Wilāya* in Early Sufism." In Leonard Lewisohn (ed.), *Classical Persian Sufism: From Its Origins to Rumi.* London and New York, 483–496.

———. 1994. "Tirmiḏiāna Minora: Die Autobiographie des Theosophen von Tirmiḏ." *Oriens* 34, 242–298.

Radtke, Bernd and O'Kane, John. 1996. *The Concept of Sainthood in Early Islamic Mysticism: Two Works by Al-Ḥakīm Al-Tirmidhī*, Richmond, Surrey.

Rahman, Fazlur. 1966. "Dream, Imagination, and *'Ālam al-mithāl.*" In G. E. von Grunebaum and R. Caillois (eds.), *The Dream and Human Societies.* Berkeley and Los Angeles, 409–419.

Rosenthal, Franz. 1992. *The Classical Heritage in Islam.* London.

Schimmel, Annemarie. 1994. *Deciphering The Signs of God: A Phenomenological Approach to Islam.* Albany, NY.

Sviri, Sara. 1987. "Between Fear and Hope: On the Coincidence of Opposites in Islamic Mysticism." *Jerusalem Studies in Arabic and Islam* 9, 316–349.

———. 1997. *The Taste of Hidden Things. Images on the Sufi Path.* Invarness, CA.

Walzer, R. 1962. "Al-Fārābī's Theory of Prophecy and Divination." In *Greek into Arabic.* Oxford, 206–219.

———. 1965. "Al-Fārābī." In *Encyclopaedia of Islam*^{2} 2, 778–781.

Watt, Montgomery, W. 1965. "Al-Ghazālī, Abū Ḥāmid." *Encyclopaedia of Islam*^{2} 2, 1038–1041.

Wensinck, A. J. 1936–1963. *Concordance et Indices de la Tradition Musulmane.* 8 vols. Leiden.

Wolfson, E. R. 1994. *Through a Speculum That Shines.* Princeton.

Wolfson, H. A. 1935. "The Internal Senses in Latin, Arabic, and Hebrew Philosophic Texts." *Harvard Theological Review*, complete vol., pp. 28, 69–133.

Zimmermann, Fritz, W. 1984. "Bernd Radtke, *Al-Ḥakīm al-Tirmidhī, ein islamischer Theosoph des 3./9. Jahrhunderts*—Review." *Journal of Arabic Literature* 15, 139–141.

Arabic Texts

Abumalham, Montserrat M. 1985. *Moshe ibn Ezra's Kitāb al-muḥāḍara wal-mudhākara.* (Arabic) Madrid, (1986, Spanish).

Al-Bukhārī, *Ṣaḥīḥ* (Arabic and English). 1971/1391. (Trans. Muhammad Muhsin Khān.) 9 vols. Beirut.

Al-Ghazālī, Abū Ḥāmid Muḥammad ibn Muḥammad. n.d. *Iḥyā' 'ulūm al-dīn.* 5 vols. Beirut.

Al-Ḥakīm al-Tirmidhī, Abū 'Abdallāh Muḥammad ibn 'Alī. 1965a "*Bad' sha'n Abī 'Abdallāh.*" In Yahya Othman (ed.), *Khatm al-awliyā'*, Beirut, 14–32.

———. 1965b. *"Buduww sha'n."* Ed. Masud Muhammad Khalid. *Islamic Studies* 4, 315–343.

———. 1965c. *Kitāb sharḥ al-ṣalāt wa-maqāṣidihā.* (Ed. Husni Nasr Zaydan.) Cairo.

———. 1970. *Nawādir al-'uṣūl fī ma'rifat aḥādīth al-rasūl.* Beirut, 1970 (reprint of Istanbul 1294/[1877]).

———. 1992. *Kitāb sīrat al-awliyā'.* In Bernd Radtke (ed.), *Drei Schriften des Theosophen von Tirmiḏ.* Beirut and Stuttgart, 1–134 (Arabic text).

Ibn al-'Arabī, Muḥyi al-Dīn Muḥammad ibn 'Alī. ca. 1946. *Fuṣūṣ al-ḥikam.* (Ed. Abū-l-'Alā' 'Afīfī.) Beirut.

Al-Kindī, Ya'qūb ibn Iṣḥāq. 1950. *Risāla fī māhiyyat al-nawm wal-ru'yā.* In Muḥammad Abū Rīda (ed.), *Rasā'il al-Kindī al-falsafiyya,* 1, Cairo, 283–311.

Al-Nābulusī, 'Abd al-Ghanī. 1302/1884. *Ta'ṭīr al-ānām fī ta'bīr al-manām.* Cairo.

14

The Liminality and Centrality of Dreams in the Medieval West

Jean-Claude Schmitt

Dreams—or more often their fleeting memory and reconstructed account (without which dreams could not exist in a social sense)—are universal. Also universal is the ambiguous status of dreams, fascinating and yet disturbing because they attest to an activity of the mind that takes place paradoxically at the very moment the person is submerged in a state of lethargy and inactivity often likened to death. Dreams are equivocal also because an individual perceives his or her own dreams as an entirely personal experience which nevertheless reflects a certain alienation, as if dreamed by another, and also somehow defamiliarizing faces of people who are otherwise familiar.[1]

Dreams are related to sensory experience (both "seeing" and "hearing") and produce "images" and "sounds" that appear real. Their plainly illusory nature, revealed gradually upon awakening, destines them to almost immediate oblivion if they are not recounted as soon as possible and thus transfixed. They manifest intense creativity but escape the control of individual reason or collective authority. As such, they arouse the mistrust and at times the reprobation of society, although they might also be seen as a privileged medium providing access to all that otherwise eludes objective consciousness: divine knowledge, the world of invisible beings (notably that of ancestors and the dead), foreknowledge, and signs of fate.

Dreams are also a historical phenomenon which, in different times and places, subscribes to different value systems and varies in content. The medieval West, like many other traditional cultures, can be said to have been a "religious culture," in its own, unique fashion. Dreams are, in effect, part of a general belief system, enriching the religious experience of individuals and society and extending the limits of knowledge concerning the mysteries of the above and beyond. Although by definition a personal experience, the dreams of an individual, from the moment they are recounted, put in writing, disseminated, and addressed to everyone, take on a collective value and a social significance; this explains the immense documentation on the subject. Generally speaking, in this society naturally connected to tradition, dreams, as an immediate recourse to a supernatural legitimating source, contribute to the justification of all innovations. The introduction of a new practice (e.g., the cult of images), a new doctrine (e.g., that of purgatory), the accession of a new dynasty, or the election of a new ecclesiastical dignitary must be announced, confirmed, and legitimized by dreams.

At the same time, as an individual experience they are seen to have personal value, as illustrated, for example, by the place of dreams in conversion narratives. This personal value is, however, quite different from that ascribed to dreams in our own culture. Far from referring to an autonomous ego—the value most frequently placed upon dreams in our time by psychoanalysis—it supposes a concept of the individual defined in reference to invisible divine might. For this reason, while the autobiographical narrative of a dream in this religious culture is, as we shall see, a way of affirming the individual, it also reveals the alienating structure of this relation of self to divine Other that compels the subject even in dreams.

The religious culture that gave meaning to dreams in medieval Christianity assumed a particular structure as a result of the dominant role of the Church which, through its clergy, claimed the role of mediator between hidden forces and humanity. Dreams, however, as a medium providing immediate access to hidden forces and knowledge, tend to bypass mediation or even to deny its value. Dreams thus reveal the basic limits of ecclesiastical power, showing it incapable of controlling all the arcana of individual religious experience, even if clerics assumed the essential role of saving the dream narratives from oblivion by recording, classifying, and judging them. In the medieval West, tension between the individual and the Church afforded the staging (and recording) of the oneiric experience a particularly dramatic character. This is confirmed by the theoretical and normative framework assigned to dreams by medieval scholars—the selective corpus of dream narratives, in connection with which I shall stress the role played by dreams in the historical development of that which I call Christian individuality.

Classification of Dreams

The original theoretical and normative framework within which medieval scholarship evaluated dreams developed from a dual heritage: pagan (Greco-Roman) and biblical (primarily Old Testament).[2] Rooted in this dual heritage is the view of dreams as interaction between the dreamer and invisible powers. Inter alia, this provided justification for pursuing the tradition of "dream keys" (*Somnialia Danielis*), which enabled the interpretation of each oneiric image as an auspicious or inauspicious portent. Oneirocriticism underwent great development in antiquity, at the hands of Artemidorus, for example, and Arab writers, who carried on the tradition. In the Latin West, from the tenth century on, the number of manuscripts of the dream keys attributed to the prophet Daniel increased. The keys are arranged in almost complete alphabetical order and are of a dual nature. They concern the gain (*lucrum*) or loss (*damnum*), happiness or unhappiness, health or sickness, longevity or shortness of life, hostility or peace, which can be expected based upon the oneiric appearance of one image or another.[3] The large number of these manuscripts must be the result of a keen interest in these lists during the Middle Ages. Dream narratives, however, as they appear in the narrative-chronicle sources, lives of saints, and so on, seem to have borrowed little from the dream keys. The logic of narrative and interpretation of dreams in these sources is, generally speaking, quite different from that of the keys. The narratives consider dreams both in their totality and in a unique personal or social situation, while the keys fragment the oneiric content into a myriad of discrete elements and isolated images, interpreting them according to an alternative logic, regardless of context. The contrast is so strong that it makes one wonder whether the "Dreams of Daniel" was ever used in a frequent or systematic fashion in medieval society, with the exception perhaps of the naturally limited literate church circles.

Rooted in this dual heritage—classical and biblical, and particularly in the latter—is a strong and basic mistrust of dreams. This does not rule out the possibility of recognizing the positive value of certain dreams. Critical exercise of such *discretio* would necessarily occur within the context of social attitudes that wanted saints, as well as kings, monks, and clerics, to enjoy a greater chance of experiencing truthful dreams, those of divine origin, than commoners, the illiterate, laymen, *rustici*, and, most of all, women. This pertains primarily to the High Middle Ages, during the first millenium, when the clerical ideology that dominated society exhibited a strong dualistic tendency: God versus the Devil, "true" dreams versus "false" ones, churchmen versus simple laymen—all according to a generalized and for the most part intangible distinction between "up above" and "down below." The Carolingian era, for example, showed a strong preference for royal dreams—something Paul Edward Dutton termed the "*via regia*" of dreams.[4] The emperor dreams and the dignitaries of the kingdom dream of him and for him, thereby forming an actual mode of government according to the body of information and divine "omens" concerning the fate of the empire in general and, more particularly, that of the sovereign, both in his existence down below and in his promised life up above. Thus dreams, notably those of monks who enjoy great visions from above, do not always spare the person and the decisions of the emperor, but their hard lessons must be tolerated since they unquestionably derive from true dreams and divine omens. Hence they provide the church hierarchy moderate powers of criticism (notably with regard to the sexual behavior of Charlemagne), warning, and pressure on the emperor. The monk Wetti of Reichenau, for example, a few days before his death, had a famous vision of Charlemagne being genitally tortured. The meaning of this image was easily read, and when Heito, the Bishop of Basel, and Walafrid Strabo, the abbot of Reichenau, took upon themselves to spread the story, though without explicitly naming the emperor, no one was fooled about the real target of this oneiric admonition. The following generation saw the "*Vision of a poor woman of Laon*" similarly enable a part of the secular and ecclesiastical aristocracy to reproach the emperor, Louis the Pious, for the brutal way in which he had blinded and disposed of his nephew, Bernard of Septimania.[5]

From the eleventh century onward, social and ideological evolution placed more importance upon modest and moderate solutions in all areas, opening unprecedented opportunities for breaking out of established ancient categories. The ambiguity of dreams was better taken into account, and the value of the dreams of the most humble was more readily recognized. Royal dreams and those of monks were far from forgotten but, in the words of Jacques Le Goff, the West witnessed a "democratization of dreams," as well as a "feminization," at least as far as their interpretation was concerned. (Women remained a minority among the recorded dreamers.) Female specialists in the interpretation of dreams begin to appear in the records, sometimes treated by the clergy as *vetulae*—old hags in collusion with the devil, but sometimes treated with admiration and respect when appearing to use their gifts as the Church hoped. *The Life of Saint Thierry*, written at the end of the eleventh century (soon after 1086) in the Ardennes, employs the well-known hagiographic *topos* of the pregnant woman's dream in aid of the saint's mother. In this case, the future mother of Thierry, disturbed by images seen in her dream, not doubting that her dream was true and untainted by diabolical illusions, was divinely inspired to consult a woman renowned for her gift of interpreting dreams:

> There was at that time in the area an old woman who lived in saintly continence, to whom, thanks to her merits, God had given, among her other virtues, the gift of telling the future—often, to many people. Because of her fame, the wife [of Gozon] came to her in the hope that she could interpret her dream. She confided in her after they had kissed and talked; trembling and weeping, she told her of her vision, first begging [the old woman] to pray for her, so that the vision would not forecast for her an unnatural event, and then begging her to tell her the meaning of the vision. After praying, invested with prophetic grace, [the old woman] said: "Have faith, woman, since what you have seen is a vision coming from God."[6]

This text wonderfully illuminates several important aspects of dreams and their interpretation: the ritual character of the entire sequence, the doubts with which the dreamer is plagued and, by way of contrast, the serenity of the old woman, confident in her ability.

At the beginning of the following century, the monk Guibert de Nogent never tired of praising his mother, who knew how to decipher his dreams, as well as those of her younger son and the men and women of her circle:

> Frequent visions, in which I figured together with other persons, made it possible for her to predict what was to happen, long in advance. I notice that some of these events undoubtedly occur or have occurred. Hence I expect the others to happen as well.[7]

In this period, the distinction between true dreams (of divine origin) and false dreams (those *fantasmata* that are nothing more than diabolical illusions) became less and less significant as more attention was devoted to dreams deriving solely from the human being, his or her mind and body. In these circumstances, the agonizing question of a dream's "truth" could not be answered with certainty, especially since the traditional social criterion—judging the trustworthiness of a witness based on that person's connections with the upper echelons of the social and religious hierarchy—played a lesser role.

Thus a medieval West not simply content with ancient classifications of dreams further developed them. One ancient classification of dreams, made famous by the commentary of Macrobius (c. 400) on the "Dream of Scipio," is recounted by Cicero in the sixth book of *The Republic.* Macrobius divides dreams into five categories, stressing their different natures but also, in Platonic tradition, the hierarchy to which they belong, from the most divine to the most closely related to human passions: prophetic vision (*visio*), nightmare (*insomnium*), ghostly apparition (*phantasma*), enigmatic dream (*somnium*), oracular dream (*oraculum*).[8] Christian authors departed from this classification early on, emphasizing other methods of classification better suited to the new ideology and to the Christian perception of relations between humanity and the divine. Augustine, in his twelve-book commentary on the book of Genesis, proposes the basic category of *visio spiritualis*, equally concerning both dreams and visions, as opposed to the *visio corporalis*, dealing with the physical sense of sight, and the *visio intellectualis*, the rational vision beyond every image—a rarity here on earth (Saint Paul, carried off to the "third heaven," perhaps experienced it), the almost face-to-face encounter of the elect with God. According to the three-part typology of dreams by their origin, first contrived by Tertullian (*De anima*)[9] and of no less importance in medieval Christianity, it is necessary to first ascertain the source of dreams, whether demonic (the most frequent), divine (if all ideological and social requirements have been met), or emanating from the person himself or herself, and influenced by the person's mind, daytime activities, and body. It was usually considered a bad sign when dreams were stimulated by overeating and drinking or by urges of the flesh (the usual explanation of nocturnal pollution). In his *Dialogues* (4, 50), written at the end of the sixth century, Pope Gregory the Great proposed six categories for the classification of dreams, which are basically a reiteration of the traditional three groups, doubled by combining the three simple types with each other, to form three mixed groups (e.g., reflection and revelation). The growing complexity of the typology expresses a heightened awareness of the difficulty in ascertaining the origin, and thus the value, of dreams.[10] The classification of Macrobius reemerged in the twelfth century in an anonymous work titled *Liber de spiritu et anima*, its lasting success assured by false attribution to Saint Augustine. It was in fact written by a Cistercian named Alcher de Clairvaux, and was as much an adaptation as a reiteration of his model, using the same words but not necessarily with the same meaning. *Fantasma*, for example, is charged with all the negative connotations ascribed to it by Christian culture, relating it to the deceitful influence of the devil.

At the same time, the growing diversity of categories of analysis reveals a desire to achieve a greater understanding of the psychophysiological components of dreams, as attested also by the fifteenth chapter of John of Salisbury's *Polycraticus*.

In the twelfth century, dreams could be said to have "come true." They were more accurately ascribed to the personality of the individual dreamer, and to concrete existence, emotions, and to sleep in its physical reality, at least as far as the influence of angels and demons was concerned. The course was set by monks such as Guibert de Nogent, and even a nun—the physician and visionary Hildegard of Bingen. The latter also spoke from personal experience, being credited with three autobiographical works documenting her visions (*Liber Scivias, Liber de operibus divinis, Liber vitae meritorum*), which she was careful to describe as neither dreams (*non in somnis*)—in which case they would have been suspect as possible diabolical phantasmata—nor the result of madness (*de phrenesi*) or sensory experience (*nec corporeis oculis aut auribus exterioris hominis*), but rather wakeful visions of the soul, of the "internal" eyes and ears of the intellect (*vigilans, circumspiciens in pura mente oculis et auribus interioris hominis*). This speaks of the enduring suspicion of dreams—gateway of the devil—and of the mistrust of the body and the senses. For this pioneer of "female mysticism," the wakeful *visio* is the highest form of revelation, even if—as Hildegard herself acknowledges—it is difficult to understand what constitutes a wakeful vision and what distinguishes it from a hallucination (*Quod quo modo sit, carnali homini perquirere difficile est*).[11] In another of her works, the medical treatise *Causae et curae*, the same Hildegarde presents a veritable psychophysiology of sleep.[12] Dreams also have their place, above all in connection with diabolical phantasmata and nocturnal pollution. The "treatment" is based on the combination and opposition of natural elements and bodily humors. Against diabolical phantasmata, for example, Hildegard recommends girding the patient crosswise with the skin of an elk and of a roe while reciting words of exorcism to repel demons and strengthen the patient's defenses. Observances and remedies continued to concern a world enchanted by the "*pensée sauvage*" of a symbolic and altogether religious approach to reality. However, the works of Hildegard and other twelfth-century authors demonstrated a growing concern with the mechanisms of the body and the mind, from which the rediscovery of Aristotelian scientific tradition in the following century would benefit, inter alia, in its copious treatises on sleep (*De somno*) and on dreams (*De somniis*).[13]

The Rhetoric of Dreams

The corpus of dream narratives confirms the liminal character of the status of dreams, but also the centrality of their functions in the medieval West. In the narratives (hagiography, chronicles, *exempla*, vernacular literature, etc.), dreams are referred to either as *somnia* (from the root *somnus*, sleep) or using a paraphrase in which the subject is portrayed as asleep at the time of the oneiric perception and awakening at the end of the dream. Dreams are thus well defined within the much greater province of the *visio*, or *visio spiritalis* in the words of Saint Augustine, as the perception of images, usually visual and auditory, but not corporeal (in contrast to sensory perception). As we have already seen in the case of Hildegard of Bingen, dreams were considered suspect by the clerical culture due to the elusive potential artifices of the devil.

Other types of "visions" a priori enjoyed a more favorable judgment at the hands of the clergy. This was the case regarding journeys of the soul to the above and beyond with the body asleep or in a cataleptic state. The tradition of these long "voyage" narratives was well established from the time of Bede (visions of Fursy and of Drythelm) and the great political visions of the Carolingian era (such as the visions mentioned above: *Vision of a poor woman of Laon*, and the vision of the monk Wetti), to the burgeoning of the genre in the twelfth century, with the visions of Tnugdall and the peasant Turckill actually depicting the imaginary geography of the above and beyond. The allegorical literature in the vernacular then seized upon the subject with Guillaume de Digulville's *Voyage de l'âme*, the *Roman de la Rose* by Guillaume de Lorris and Jean de Meung, and Dante's *Divine Comedy*.[14] These narratives explicitly refer to a temporary dissociation, during sleep, between the inert body, which lies as if dead, and the roving soul, which discovers invisible realms and beings before returning to the body. The *Roman de la Rose* cautions against the foolish beliefs of those who think the soul capable of traveling alone at night in the company of mythical figures demonized by the Church (Dame Abonde, the "*bonnes dames*") and fears that it will be unable to find the opening of the body upon its return:

> *C'est ainsi que maintes gens dans leur folie croient être des estries (du latin* strigae*: des sorcières) errant la nuit avec Dame Abonde; ils racontent que les troisièmes enfants ont cette faculté d'y aller trois fois dans la semaine; ils se jettent dans toutes les maisons, ne redoutant clefs ni barreaux, et entrant par fentes, chatières et crevasses; leurs âmes, quittant leur corps, vont avec les bonnes dames à travers maisons et lieux forains, et ils le prouvent en disant que les étrangetés auxquelles ils ont assisté ne leur sont pas venues dans leurs lits, mais que ce sont leurs âmes qui agissent et courent ainsi par le monde. Et ils font accroire aux gens que si, pendant ce voyage nocturne, on leur retournait le corps, l'âme n'y pourrait rentrer. Mais c'est là une horrible folie et une chose impossible, car le corps humain n'est qu'un cadavre, lorsqu'il ne porte plus en soi son âme . . .*[15]

This representation has been associated with the beliefs characteristic of shamanism in many traditional cultures.[16] This is consistent with the etymology of the French word "*rêve*," which evokes the concepts of bewilderment, madness, "taking leave of one's senses." The Old French *desver*, probably from the root **esver*, "to wander," signifies losing one's senses or being in a state of delirium: in dreams, the soul leaves the body and wanders. Medieval French did not yet possess the word "*rêve*," only the word "*songe*," deriving, as in other Romance languages (the Italian *sogno*, for example), from the Latin *somnium*. In medieval French, the common play on words "*songe/mensonge*" (dream/lie) demonstrates how greatly the suspicion of falsehood weighed upon the subject of dreams, in accord with the a priori mistrust characteristic of the scholarly interpretation of dreams. In the German "*Traum*" or English "dream," for example, the Germanic languages have preserved the ancient root *draugr*, which signifies one who is dead and returns to haunt the living. This etymology stresses the strong link between dreams and the world of the dead.[17] Only in French has the evolution of language produced a distinction between the terms "*songe*," which has become somewhat literary if not altogether rare, and "*rêve*," which came into common usage only in the seventeenth century. The distinction between these two words was contemporaneous with the transformation in scholarly representation of dreams due particularly to Descartes' *Treatise on Man* (1633), which for the first time described a physiology of dreams that reduced the process of dreams to the individual and the brain and nervous system, wresting it away from the old interpretative framework which laid stock in supernatural forces as well as in the collective and ritual dimension of the oneiric experience.

The new explanation proposed by Descartes was not isolated. It belonged to a series of discoveries, most notably affecting the field of optics. For Kepler, the explanation of sight as the reflection of light by the retina tended to stem from the ancient theories of extramission, whereby vision is the result of a force emanating from the eye that takes hold, externally, of the form of objects and draws this form into the eye so that it can be perceived. It is thus the aggregate of phenomena pertaining to sensory and oneiric vision that gave rise to a new explanatory, physiological, and individualistic paradigm. Paradoxically, the word "*rêve*," chosen to mark these changes, returns to some extent to the traditional representations it seemed to repudiate. It is the novelty of the word and not its etymological meaning that really seems to have marked this great heuristic change, which in due time paved the way for the Freudian "revolution" in *The Interpretation of Dreams*.[18]

One result of these transformations is that we no longer group dreams, which are considered both normal and essential to psychological equilibrium, with "wakeful visions," which we are more likely to place in the category of mental pathology, delirium brought on by intoxication, illness or emotional strain, or even fabrication. This was not the case in the Middle Ages. On the contrary, "wakeful visions" were reported in great numbers and were usually considered positively, a sign of the moral worth of those who enjoyed them, of their divine election and saintliness. We have already described how Hildegard of Bingen insisted that her visions be recognized as such and not as dreams possibly inspired by the devil or as the deliria of a "frantic person." In many cases, medieval narratives explicitly referring to a *somnium* specify that it was in fact a *visio* to certify its veracity. The Chronicle of the Abbey of Waltham, for example, written in the second half of the twelfth century by a canon of this abbey in southeast England, begins with an account of a wondrous dream dreamt by a blacksmith at the beginning of the previous century. For three successive nights, the venerable figure of Christ appeared to him in his sleep and ordered him, in an increasingly pressing fashion, to go find the parish priest and guide him to the summit of a mountain where they would discover, buried in the earth, a marvelous cross. The abbey itself was founded as a result of this holy "invention." It was therefore incumbent upon the chronicler to stress the divine nature of the foundational dream of the blacksmith. He describes in detail how the blacksmith sank into sleep after a hard day's work, and although he calls the experience a "dream," he quickly allays any doubts the reader might have by stating more precisely that the blacksmith's dream was in fact a "vision":

> One night this smith I have mentioned, this officer of the church, laid his limbs down to sleep, exhausted as usual by the work of his trade; of course, the more relentless toil shook his bones and relaxed all his muscles, the more surely did it induce a deep, restful sleep. So it was that when he was fast asleep he saw in a dream (in truth it was really a vision) a figure of divine beauty . . . [19]

This example, like many others, shows how heedful we must be of the constraints of the period, the rhetoric of dreams and visions, and through them the structures of belief and the prevailing criteria of verisimilitude and truth. The wakeful daytime vision, certified by witnesses judged trustworthy, most often members of the clergy, seemed to enjoy a level of authenticity not accorded to dreams. A visionary narrative one wished to be irrefutable would thus assume the traditional rhetorical form of a wakeful vision. It generally took the form of a story told to a third party, in the account of which the author—inevitably a cleric because only they could write—carefully unfolded the stages of the story's transmission, the names of its witnesses and those through whom it passed, thus certifying the truth of the story. On the other hand, when an author tells of a vision he himself experienced and which he himself can certify, he does not hesitate to refer to it as a dream, just as we might do, without fear of being suspected of fabrication. The distinction made in the written documentation, based upon which we distinguish between wakeful and oneiric visions, does not depend on the eventual objective reality of these experiences (at least not exclusively), but rather on the narrative rules of the genre and the belief system of the period. Autobiographical dreams are thus the opposite of reported visions.

This distinction is clear-cut, at least in the large corpus of medieval accounts of ghostly apparitions that I have studied.[20] Authentication by the Church was essential for the transmission of these accounts, and provided a format that served as a sort of imprimatur. The *Liber exemplorum*, an English Franciscan miscellany from the early thirteenth century, tells, for example, of a ghost that appeared in a dream to a layman of Ulster. A Franciscan monk by the name of Dunekan heard the story and recited it to Friar Robert of Dodington, who used it in a sermon, whence it reached the ears of the unnamed author.[21] The path of transmission is described in detail because it serves as confirmation of the content of the dream, and there is no reason to doubt that the story was believed by those who transmitted it—the monks in this case—and by the laymen who heard this *exemplum* supported by the aura of monastic authority in the context of a sermon. Remember that dreams had no social existence except as narratives, relevant not only to the individual but also to the social group that recounted, transmitted, and adapted them to its values and the framework of its beliefs.

The Self and the Dream

In certain cases, admittedly less numerous, it is the dreamer who put his or her own dream in writing and certified its veracity with personal *auctoritas*. Autobiographical dream narratives began to increase in number in the eleventh and twelfth centuries, when the tradition of oneiric narratives encountered another basic cultural trend of the period, one more aptly described as the deepening of Christian subjectivity than as the discovery of the individual. The monastic and clerical culture took up the thread, almost completely lost since Saint Augustine's *Confessions*, of Christian autobiography, or more specifically, autobiographies of conversion. The thread was not entirely broken during this period. The Carolingian *Liber revelationum*, for example, compiled (c. 840) and revised (854) by Archbishop Audrade de Sens, is an exception to the rule. The originality of this work might be explained by the polemic circumstances in which the author found himself. Asked to justify his own orthodoxy before Pope Leo IV, he submitted to the pontiff his written work, including a collection of revelations he had experienced. The first of these, entitled *oraculum divinum*, concerns the appearance of the ghost of Saint Peter, a suitable figure to make peace between the archbishop and the successor to Peter's own See! In chapter 8, the vision of the celestial tribunal clearly defines the limits of the Christian "ego" still existing during this period. Audrade also saw the emperor, Louis the Pious, led before God, to whom he explained that he had chosen his son Charles the Bald as his successor, and not Lothair, who had shown himself to be unworthy. God then brought Lothair before him and informed him that he had been deposed because of his presumption in saying "*Ego sum*," "I am."[22]

In the twelfth century, such assertions were no longer sanctioned by God or by humans, whereas dreams, the medium of immediate perception of divine will, had become the privileged instrument of personal conversion, whether "external" or "internal" (like that of Guibert de Nogent, whose path as a young oblate to finally assuming the monastic habit was marked by numerous autobiographical dreams, as he recounted toward the end of his life [c. 1115], in his *De vita sua*).[23] Even earlier, the monk Otloh de Saint Emmeran (died c. 1070) wrote a *Liber visionum*, comprising twenty-three visions. With the exception of the first four, all the visions are wakeful, and reported in the third person. The first four visions, on the other hand, are personal dreams recounted by Otloh from memory, although they date back many years. Each, however, marked an important turning point in the life of the young monk: his conversion in early youth, a conflict with Church authorities who forced him into exile at one point, and finally a nightmare, at a time when he was ill and in a dispute with his abbot. The dreams, at least those he recalled toward the end of his life in the then-novel pursuit of autobiography, are those that most powerfully touched his existence, his self-image, and his destiny. They were plainly interpreted a posteriori as signs of things to come, in accordance with divine plan.

This is no less true of dreams pertaining to "external" conversion, such as that experienced at the age of twenty by the Jew, Hermann of Cologne, the written account of which—the *Opusculum de conversione sua*—appeared, perhaps posthumously, in autobiographical form.[24] This pamphlet begins with an account of a dream the young Jew had in his thirteenth year. He dreamt that he was showered with gifts by the emperor and invited to dine at his table. The child did not understand the meaning of his dream and was not satisfied with the interpretation offered by an old sage of the local Jewish community. On business—collecting a loan—seven years later, he was given the opportunity to approach the Bishop of Munster and other clergymen, through whom he discovered the Christian faith and its cult, including the worship of images, which shocked him greatly at first. Following two further visions he was finally baptized, entered the Premonstratensian order, and became a priest. The final chapter of the pamphlet offers, a posteriori, an obviously Christan interpretation of the initial childhood dream, of which Hermann, by that time a Christian and a priest, was himself capable. The dream was said to have symbolically announced his conversion to Christianity as well as his calling to the priesthood, with the figure of the emperor representing that of God and the repast in the imperial palace symbolizing the altar of the Eucharist. It matters little here that this text, addressed to canons and nuns of the Premonstratensian order in Westphalia,[25] is written entirely from a Christian, ecclesiastical, and more precisely canonical perspective. Had Hermann never existed, it would be no less important to note the autobiographical form, still quite new at the time, of this narrative, and the very specific role played by the dream and its autointerpretation, embodying the history of conversion.

This same period, the twelfth to thirteenth centuries, also saw the development of allegorical literature in Latin (Alain de Lille) and in the vernacular (*Roman de la Rose*), going back to works of late antiquity (Macrobius, Martianus Capella) proposing original thinking on feelings, emotions, passions, and the province of the human soul, as well as on the spiritual, social, and political condition of humanity over time. We must note, however, that all areas of cultural life, and all modes of symbolic expression, do not necessarily evolve at the same pace within a society. While moral theology and texts in the vernacular concerning dreams deepened what might be called "literary subjectivity,"[26] the figurative arts maintained the traditional images of dreams throughout the Middle Ages. This was characterized by the juxtaposition of a sleeping figure, head resting on folded arm, eyes generally closed, with the object of the dream, Jacob's ladder, for example, to mention one of the more common images.[27] While autobiographical narratives of dreams existed at the time, particularly from the twelfth century on, there were no autobiographical representations of dreams in other art forms until the sixteenth century (Albrecht Dürer).[28] This is easily understood if we consider the difference in the social status of the works themselves (the relative novelty of painting, compared with the antiquity and venerability of the written word in Church tradition) as well as that of the men who created them (painters and sculptors in this period had just won their place in the social hierarchy).

It is thus, above all, in literature, both ecclesiastical and profane, that the figure of the dream, treated as the oneiric casting of an individual, occupied an increasingly central place—as when the *Roman de la Rose* appeared as a unique first-person dream narrative:

> *A la vingtième année de mon âge, à cette époque où l'amour réclame son tribut des jeunes gens, je m'étais couché une nuit comme à l'accoutumée, et je dormais profondément, lorsque je fis un songe très beau et qui me plut fort, mais dans ce songe, il n'y eut rien que les faits n'aient confirmé point par point. Je veux vous le raconter pour vous réjouir le coeur: c'est Amour qui m'en prie et me l'ordonne . . .* [29]

Dreams were, then, clearly perceived as one of the great means of defining and deepening an individual's understanding; but, until the advent of profane literature, this understanding was inconceivable except in the context of the individual's relation to its source: God. This Christian "subject", who would otherwise have discovered his ego in spiritual exercises of penitent introspection, here experiences it in remembering and reflecting upon his own dreams, interpreting the signs God has addressed to him personally in order to inform him of the meaning of his destiny, within the private circle of his soul's awakening, when his body is asleep and, as it were, abandoned.

Notes

1. Augé 1997: 48, notes that dreams create "problematic relationships within themselves" on three levels: dreamer and dream narrator; listener and the interpreter from whom the narrative is heard; and the "subject" of the dream, who might be the dreamer (reflexive dream), or someone else (an ancestor, God, a loved one, etc.). The identity of this last figure however, is anything but clear: I dream of myself, but is it really me? I dream of another, but is it really him?
2. Le Goff 1985: 171–218; reprint 1985: 265–316.
3. Önnerfors: 32–57; Förster 1908, 1910, 1911, 1916 (publication of many of these small works, in Old English or in Latin); Collet-Rosset 1963: 111–198.
4. Dutton 1994: 23.
5. Ibid.: 63.
6. French translation and commentary by Lauwers 1995: 279–317.
7. Guibert de Nogent 1981: 168–169, ed. Labande.
8. Kruger 1992: 21.
9. Le Goff 1985: 190 et seq.
10. Ibid.: 209.
11. Hildegard of Bingen 1978, *Liber Scivias*, ed. Fürkötter, Turnholt, Brepols.
12. Hildegard of Bingen 1903, *Causae et curae*, ed. Kaiser.
13. Le Goff 1977: 299–306 (305).
14. Dinzelbacher 1981; Carozzi 1994.
15. Guillaume de Lorris and Jean de Meung 1984: 310, *Le Roman de la rose*.
16. Ginzburg 1989.
17. Kelchner 1935: 66–72; see chapter 11 of this volume.
18. Fabre 1996: 69–82.
19. *The Waltham Chronicle, An Account of the discovery of our holy cross at Montacute and*

its conveyance to Waltham, ed. and transl. Watkiss and Chibnall 1994: 2–3: "*Denique faber predictus, ille officialis ecclesie, cum nocte quadam membra sopori composuisset, fessus opere fabrili ut assolet, qui scilicet labor indefessus quanto magis ossa concutit, et omnia membrorum liniamenta dissoluit, tanto vehementiorem sompni profundioris quietem incutit. Sompno itaque fatear set per visionem, venerandi decoris effigiem . . .*"

20. Schmitt 1994.

21. Ibid.: 160.

22. Audradus, *Liber revelationum*, ed. Migne: vol. 115 col. 23–30; Dutton 1994: 128 et seq. Note on p. 137 how Audradus almost completely avoids the usual language of dreams and visions, since his revelations belong to the most direct form of communication, that of prophecy.

23. Schmitt 1985: 291–316.

24. Hermann of Cologne 1963, *Hermanus quondam Judaeus. Opusculum de conversione* sua, ed. Niemeyer.

25. Schmitt 1995: vol. 2, 438–452.

26. Zink 1985.

27. Parvacini Bagliani and Stabile (eds.) 1989; on Jacob's ladder see Heck 1997.

28. Schmitt 1997: vol. 1, 3–36 (p. 33 and fig. 10, Dürer's Nightmare).

29. Guillaume de Lorris and Jean de Meung 1984: 20, *Le Roman de la rose*.

References

Audradus. *Liber revelationum*. Ed. J.-P. Migne. Patrologia latina. Vol. 115.

Augé, Marc. 1997. *La guerre des rêves. Exercices d'ethno-fiction*. Paris.

Carozzi, Claude. 1994. *Le voyage de l'âme dans l'au-delà d'après la littérature latine (Ve-XIIIe siècle)*. Ecole Française de Rome, Rome.

Collet-Rosset, Simone. 1963. "Le liber Thesauri Occulti de Pascalis Romanus (Un traité d'interpretation des songes du XIIe siècle)." *Archives d'Histoire Doctrinale et Littéraire du Moyen Age*, 30, 111–198.

Dinzelbacher, Peter. 1981. *Vision und Visionsliteratur im Mittelalter*. Stuttgart.

Dutton, Paul Edward. 1994. *The Politics of Dreaming in the Carolingian Empire*. Lincoln/London.

Fabre, Daniel. 1996. "Rêver." *Terrain*, 26. March.

Förster, Max. 1908, 1910, 1911, 1916. "Beiträge zur mittelalterlichen Volkskunde." *Archiv für das Studium der neueren Sprachen und Literaturen*. Vols. 120, 125, 127, 134.

Ginzburg, Carlo. 1989. *Storia Notturna. Una decifrazione del sabba*. G. Einaudi, Turin. (French translation, Paris, 1992.)

Guibert de Nogent. 1981. *Autobiographie*. Ed. Edmond-René Labande. Paris.

Guillaume de Lorris and Jean de Meung. 1984. *Le roman de la rose*. Trans. into modern French by A. Mary. Paris.

Heck, Christian. 1997. *L'Echelle céleste dans l'art du Moyen Age. Une image de la quête du ciel*. Paris.

Hermann of Cologne. 1963. *Hermanus quondam Judaeus. Opusculum de conversione sua*. Ed. G. Niemeyer. Weimar.

Hildegard of Bingen. 1978. *Liber Scivias*. Ed. Fürkötter. (Corpus Christianorum. Series Latina, 43 and 43a. Vol. 1.) Turnhout.

———. 1903. *Causae et curae*. Ed. Paulus Kaiser. Leipzig.

Kelchner, G. D. 1935. *Dreams in Old Norse Literature and their Affinities in Folklore, with an Appendix Containing the Icelandic Texts and Translations*. Cambridge.

Kruger, Steven F. 1992. *Dreaming in the Middle Ages*. Cambridge.

Lauwers, Michel. 1995. "L'institution et le genre. À propos de l'accès des femmes au sacré dans l'Occident médiéval." *Clio, Histoire, Femmes et Sociétés, 2*, 279–317.

Le Goff, Jacques. 1977. "Les rêves dans la culture et la psychologie collective de l'Occident médiéval." In *Pour un autre Moyen Age. Temps, travail et culture en Occident*. Paris, 299–306.

———. 1985. "Le christianisme et les rêves (IIe–VIIe siècles)." In Tullio Gregory (ed.), *I sogni nel Medioevo*. Rome, 265–316. (Reprinted in *L'imaginaire médiéval. Essais*. Paris, 1985.)

Önnerfors, Alf. "Über die alphabetischen Traumbücher ('Somnialia Danielis') des Mittelalters." *Mediaevalia. Abhandlungen und Aufsätze. Lateinische Sprache und Literatur des Mittelalters*, 6. Frankfurt am Main, Bern, Las Vegas, 33–331.

Parvacini Bagliani, Agostino and Stabile, Giorgio (eds.). 1989. *Traüme im Mittelalter: Ikonologische Studien*. Stuttgart/Zürich.

Schmitt, Jean-Claude. 1985. "Rêver au XIIe siècle." In Tullio Gregory (ed.), *I sogni nel Medioevo*. Rome, 291–316.

———. 1994. *Les revenants: Les vivants et les morts dans la société médiévale*. Paris. English translation, *Ghosts in the Middle Ages. The Living and the Dead in Medieval Society*. Chicago, London, 1998.

———. 1995. "La mémoire des Prémontrés. A propos de l'autobiographie du Prémontré Hermann le Juif." In Marek Derwich (ed.), *La vie quotidienne des moines et des chanoines réguliers au Moyen Age et Temps modernes*. Publications de l'Institut d'Histoire de l'Université de Wroclaw, Wroclaw, 439–452.

———. 1997. "La culture de l'*imago*." *Annales Histoire Sciences Sociales*, 3–36.

Watkiss, Leslie and Chibnall, Marjorie (eds. and trans.). 1994. *The Waltham Chronicle. An Account of the discovery of our holy cross at Montacute and its conveyance to Waltham*. Oxford.

Zink, Michel. 1985. *La subjectivité littéraire. Autour du siècle de saint Louis*. Paris.

15

Engendering Dreams

The Dreams of Adam and Eve in Milton's *Paradise Lost*

Aleida Assmann

Introduction: Dream and Transcendence

In an aphorism titled "the error of dreams" ("Missverständnis des Traumes"), Nietzsche wrote: "In dreaming, people of a primordial and primitive civilization believed they encountered another reality; this is the origin of all metaphysics. Without the evidence of dreams, human beings would not have been led to divide the world into two different realms."[1] Nietzsche, who passionately opposed a two-worlds theory, identifies dreaming as the source of this heresy. In dreams, human beings could come to learn about "a second reality" that significantly differed from the "first reality" of everyday experience. For Nietzsche, the world of every-night experience that transcends, subverts, and perverts the rules accepted in the waking world nourishes the metaphysical fallacy. To associate dreams with metaphysics is an interesting but surprising move. In the wake of Aristotle, metaphysics was supposed to deal with a stable world of order unaffected by contingency. Certainty, regularity, and expectability were considered qualities of the world beyond this world, cleared of the erratic fits of hazard, mutability, and corruptibility, concentrating on "what is valid at all times or at least at most times."

In his aphorism, Nietzsche is interested in the concept of metaphysics only from a structural point of view; for him, the splitting up of one world into two is more important than any features that might be ascribed to the other world. There is no reason why Aristotle's qualification of *this* world as a world of contingency and *that* world as a world of order could not also be reversed. This is apparently the case in tribal societies. The ethnologist Klaus Muller, who compared dominant traits in the worldviews of such societies, has found a similar separation into two worlds. He refers to them as "world" and "antiworld" or "endosphere" and "exosphere." In exact reversal of the Aristotelean pattern, the social life-world or ethnic endosphere is defined as an "ordered system with clear cut boundaries and reliable regularity."[2] Disorder and the sudden ruptures by the unexpected are ascribed to the exosphere in which the endosphere is embedded. Müller describes the exosphere as an "inverted reflection of this world":

> As seen from the oblique terrestrian point of view, this is the realm of absolute anomalies. According to traditional belief, both worlds, however, do not exist in clear separation from one another but interpenetrate each other in many ways. Together, they form a complementary whole; one would be unthinkable without the other.[3]

While the Aristotelian model of metaphysics tended to keep the two worlds in spendid isolation from one another, they are seen in mutual interaction and interdependence in the folk metaphysics of tribal communities. This interaction is achieved through channels that regulate the transfer of information. The flow of information between the two worlds is possible where the inner walls dividing the dual cosmos are thinner than in other places. At such places, "holes appear, . . . through which spiritual powers may easily, as it were, enter and disappear; it is in such places that occult phenomena and portents occur with significantly higher frequency."[4]

This brings us back to our topic, dreams and dreaming in their cultural environments. Dreams in such societies become prominent doors between endo- and exosphere, points of contact between the two worlds through which information may freely circulate, while dreaming becomes a cultural technique in which bodily perception is blocked and spiritual perception activated. In this process, the mobile soul (*Freiseele*) leaves the body without altogether separating from it. This link with the body is responsible for the fact that clarity of vision is not to be achieved by human beings. The vision of dreams remains restricted by terrestrial bonds. The dreamer moving in interspace could obtain, at best, a distorted perception of the other world: "Using a metaphor, one might say that the impulses or 'impressions' from over there were transformed when hitting the realm of this world, which explains why the images appeared 'blurred.'"[5]

Nietzsche's surprisingly scarce and unfavorable remarks on dreams and dreaming reflect the values of a culture that has opted for rational evolution and discarded dreams as irrelevant, misleading, and even dangerous. Dreaming, for Nietzsche, is a relapse into a primitive state: "To be sure, in sleeping and dreaming we re-enact the earliest stage in the history of mankind."[6] For him, the logic of dreams was the same as that of primitive people. Instead of inferring from cause to effect, this logic worked backward, inferring from effect to cause. Our habitual relapse in dreams can remind us not only of the long and arduous path of acute logical thinking but also of its precarious instability.[7] When the context of his discussion of dreams is not epistemology and cognition but the history of religions, however, Nietzsche casts his reflections in a slightly more nostalgic light. In a rationalistic culture that has discarded the vision of dreams, qualifying them as a regressive phenomenon, something is felt to be missing. The progess in rationality necessarily involved a disenchantment of the world:

> In that the ancients believed in their dreams, their waking life was illumined with another glow. . . . Another light was shed on everyday experiences which could reveal the ways of a god; the same holds true for all decisions and resolutions for the far future: there was the oracle and there were the hidden hints to be deciphered by divination. "Truth" was seen in a different light as long as the madman could qualify as its mouthpiece—which is something that makes us shudder or laugh.[8]

The "other world" as constructed by Western metaphysics is not the opposite but the apex of rationalism. Symptomatic as it may be of the unconscious anxieties and desires of the metaphysicians, it provides no link to dreams. It has cut its bonds with dreams, rendering them insignificant and relegating them to the margins of culture. The metaphysics of tribal societies, on the other hand, as they are reconstructed in ethnographic description, are immediately related to dreaming, and therefore present a more appropriate case for Nietzsche's aphorism. From this ethnographic description, we may extract three points of interest for our further investigation of dreams in culture. Dreams are deemed relevant in cultures that are built on the following hypotheses:

1. A dual cosmology (a two-world model) is taken for granted.
2. Dreams create an important transitional passage between these two worlds.
3. The images of dreams are acknowledged as signs encoding messages from another world; these signs, however, are received in a blurred form and call for an art of decoding.

In myths all over the world, the splitting up of the world into two worlds is generally considered to be a consequence of some kind of fall. Gods and men lived happily together before a fatal rift occurred, separating their realms. Either the gods withdrew from direct commerce and interaction with men, leaving them in a dismal place devoid of their presence, or human beings were expelled from the site of a happy community into a land of toil, pain, and death. The vision of the world as a homogenous unity precedes the status quo of a dual cosmos. If these assumptions are correct, paradise would not be a fit place for dreams, because here estrangement or distance have not yet been experienced. In paradise—a world of perfect presence and direct communion with the gods—dreams are not necessary as a projection of desire or a vehicle of communication. Prior to the experience of death, the very prototype of alterity, a counterworld of inverse order could not have been imagined. And prior to the experience of lack and absence there was no stimulus for dreams and their compelling and infinitely productive flow of images.

In other words: there were no dreams in paradise. The biblical account of Genesis refers to the sleep of Adam while his rib was removed, but it does not mention any dreams of the first human couple. When in the seventeenth century John Milton composed his version of the fall in an ambitious biblical epic, he took the poetic liberty to include two dreams into the prelapsarian account of Eve and Adam in paradise. To invent the first dreams of humankind, and to invent them in a gendered way, is surely a remarkable project. In the following I shall argue that Milton's dreams of Adam and Eve are touchstones of his gendered anthropology. Their significance, in other words, by far surpasses their narrative convenience or dramatic effects and deserves careful attention.

Eve's Dream

Eve, as we learn from Milton, had been habitually dreaming in paradise, but these dreams were considered unremarkable. They were concerned with three topics in particular—first of all with her sole companion, Adam, as well as with events of the past and anticipations of the future. But this was a world of uneventful regularity, in which the experience of time did not yet exist in the sense of severing the present from an irrevocable past, or from the open possibilities of the future. Under such cirumstances it is not easy to see how memory or significance may be developed. Milton bypasses these unremarkable dreams to highlight Eve's one and only remarkable dream. Before we hear anything about the content of this dream, we are informed about its circumstances. And these circumstances are truly alarming. Without great effort, Satan had managed to overcome the protecting walls of paradise. It was beyond the power of the patrolling angels to prevent this event, as it is beyond their power to protect the sleep of Eve in her bower. Before Milton's Satan eventually attacks Eve under the tree of knowledge, which leads to the Fall, he attacks her in a dream vision. Milton uses his poetic license to double Satan's temptation, dramatizing it in two steps, the first directed at Eve's imagination in the shape of a toad, the second directed at her reason in the shape of a snake. The competence of the guardian angels on duty is severely restricted; all they are able to do is to discover and expel the fiend after he has performed his task:

> Him there they found
> Squat like a toad, close at the ear of Eve,
> Assaying by his develish art to reach
> The organs of her fancy, and with them forge
> Illusions as he list, phantasms and dreams;
> Or if, inspiring venom, he might taint
> Th'animals spirits, that from pure blood arise
> Like gentle breaths from rivers pure, thence raise

> At least distempered, disconnected thoughts,
> Vain hopes, vain aims, inordinate desires,
> Blown up with high conceits engendering pride.[9]

Demonic Dreams and Puritan Ethic

Milton's epic narrative constructs a direct temporal and causal link between the intrusion of Satan into the garden of paradise and Eve's dream. This means that the dream has an external source; it is inspired by a demon who tries to corrupt the mind of the dreamer. The seemingly medieval or folkloristic notion of the demonic dream was revived by writers of the sixteenth and seventeenth centuries within the frame of Puritan ethics. To illustrate the importance of this motif, I want to refer to another demonic dream on which Milton could have drawn as a possible source for Eve's dream. Spenser's national and moral epic *The Fairie Queene* (1589) is designed to fashion the Puritan prince, dramatizing the virtues and vices of the Christian soldier. In this psychomachia inspired by a Manichean anthropology, humankind is represented by a male prototype depicted as the battleground of rather gender-specific vices and virtues. As the human constitution is considered to be frail and radically deficient, a fierce armor of virtues is needed to fend off lurking temptations. There are two breaches in the human frame, in particular, through which the fiend was considered to launch his continuous attacks: the senses and the imagination.

The imagination was considered a highly problematic faculty. With few but significant exceptions, this feature of the anthropological constitution was treated by medieval philosophers with utmost suspicion.[10] The image-producing faculty of the imagination was discussed in terms of idols and simulacra, doubling reality with appearances and thereby polluting the sense of plain truth. It is easy to see how this polemical discourse could be revived under the circumstances of Puritanism and welded into a weapon for Puritan politics. In Spenser's epic, Satan appears in the shape of a figure called Archimago, who hides under the mask of a pious monk and hermit. This deceitful villain offers shelter to the knight and a lady in whose company and on whose behalf the former is performing his errand. As soon as they have fallen asleep, the pious monk assumes the shape of a magician, conversing with spirits and the demons of the night. Out of a host of spirits "he chose out two, the falsest two, / And fittest for to forge true-seeming lyes."[11] One of them he sends as a messenger to the cave of Morpheus, which is situated in the dark depth of the earth, commanding him to return thence with "a fit false dreame, that can delude the sleepers sent [=sense]."[12] The messenger issues with the false dream through the ivory door and returns to his master who, in the meantime, has fashioned the other spirit into the alluring shape of the lady. In sinister cooperation, the dream and the false spirit try to delude the fancy of the sleeping knight. The dream, which is presented as a spirit in human shape, is sent to oppress the sleep of the knight:

Now when that ydle dreame was to him brought
Vnto that Elfin knight he bad him fly,
Where he slept soundly void of euill thought
And with false shewes abuse his fantasy . . .
The one vpon his hardy head him plast,
And made him dreame of loues and lustfull play
That nigh his manly hart did melt away,
Bathed in wanton blis and wicked joy (I, 1, 46–47)

Awaking in his dream, he cannot break the magic spell of Archimago but is confronted with another simulacrum—the false spirit in the shape of his lady. But in spite of their concerted efforts and the possible effect of a wet dream, they fail to conquer the mind of the exposed knight. The enraged Archimago, who has to consult his magic books once more, now uses the two false spirits to present to the sleeping knight the spectacle of his lady engaged in amorous play with another squire. Jealousy achieves what lust could not do: it prompts the knight to leave abruptly early the next morning, thus abandoning the lady and, in separating his path from hers, exposing her to danger and distress.

Milton was acquainted with this episode of a false dream induced by Satan. Although in his own version of Eve's demonic dream he deviated from the more obvious intertexts of Ovid, Chaucer, and Spenser, he drew on Spenser in elaborating the assault on the soul via fantasy and in the figure of the devil as Archimago or chief dissembler and dealer in human and animal shapes:

For by his mightie science he could take
As many formes and shapes in seeming wise,
As euer Proteus to himselfe could make (I, 2, 10)

In Spenser as in Milton, fantasy is closely linked with dissimulation, the first principle of dramatic irony and strategic guile, and is highly suspect in Puritan ethics. Puritan thinkers, favoring unity, detest duplicity, dissembling and dissimulation. As the complex art of self-fashioning is incompatible with sincerity and plain truth, so images are highly suspect that tend to double and obscure truth rather than reveal it. While Catholic writers of the sixteenth and seventeenth centuries such as Castiglione and Gracian developed a positive code of indirection and dissimulation, the Puritans committed themselves to unambiguous truth. In doing so, they became particularly vulnerable to the effects of an art they abhorred. In *Paradise Lost*, there is a brief episode in which Satan in the shape of an angel converses with another one, after which the epic narrator inserts the following passage on hypocrisy:

So spake the false dissembler unperceived;
For neither man nor angel can discern
Hypocrisy—the only evil that walks

Invisible, except to God alone,
By his permissive will, through Heaven and Earth;
And oft, though Wisdom wake, Suspicion sleeps
At Wisdon's gate, and to Simplicity
Resigns her charge, while Goodness thinks no ill
Where ill seems. (III, 681–689)

Eve's Dream Narrative

When the angelic guard finally discovers Satan, "Squat like a toad, close at the ear of Eve" (IV, 800), his mission has been successfully completed. The next morning, Adam discovers unusual features in his mate:

His wonder was to find unwakened Eve,
With tresses discomposed, and glowing cheek,
As through unquiet rest. (V, 8–10)

Temperance, the balanced harmony of body and soul, has been violated. The unprecedented singularity of this night is stressed by Eve after her awakening. In creating this dream episode, Milton has doubled the Fall. Its first stage occurs at midnight, affecting her with the experienc of a *prima nox*. For the first time, she has dreamt of offense and trouble which, as she claims, "my mind / Knew never till this irksome night" (V, 54–55). The dream, which echoes parts of her evening's conversation with Adam, breaks up their bodily and mental alliance, revealing her hidden desires for sovereignty, and thus foreshadows the central motive of the Fall. Satan, who has projected himself into her dream, plays the register of her unacknowledged narcissistic desire. She is tempted with idolatry, and she herself is to be the idol, the center and core of creation. Instead of being the helpmate and submissive partner of man, she is lured with the promise of becoming the pagan goddess of creation. Immediately after her creation, she had already experienced a first fit of this heresy when, upon seeing her image reflected in the water, she considered herself to be superior to man, choosing her independence. When tasting the fruit that she is offered in her dream, she experiences an ascension, an elated state tinged with erotic and mystic flavor. As in the case of the Fall itself, the experience of transcendence is followed by a fit of depression.

Adam as Eve's Analyst

Milton does not only give us Eve's dream, he also gives us an analysis of it. This, however, is not the evaluation of a psychoanalyst but the rather tedious instruction of a Renaissance medical doctor.[13] Adam does not interpret the dream—this task is left to the reader; rather, he explains it away. In the tone of his complacent superiority in matters of science, he tries to account for an experience that clearly surpasses the limits of his knowledge. His instruction is permeated with personal reflections and questions, showing that in spite of his ostentatious knowledge, he is really at his wit's end:

> . . . nor can I like
> This uncouth dream—of evil sprung, I fear;
> Yet evil whence? (V, 97–99)

Unde malum? Milton traces evil back to Satan, and in conformity with medieval and Renaissance anthropology, he defines imagination as the gate through which evil enters into the human mind. In a section on the inner senses in his *Anatomy of Melancholy*, Robert Burton expounded the received knowledge of the time on the topic from a medical point of view:

> Inner senses are three in number, so called because they be within the brain-pan, as common sense, phantasy, memory. Their objects are not only things present, but they perceive the sensible species of things to come, past, absent, such as were before the sense. This common sense is the judge or moderator of the rest, by whom we discern all differences of objects; for by mine eye I do not know what I see, or by mine ear that I hear, but by my common sense, who judgeth of sounds and colours. . . .
>
> Phantasy, or imagination . . . is an inner sense which doth more fully examine the species perceived by common sense, of things present or absent, and keeps them longer, recalling them to mind again, or making new of his own. In time of sleep this faculty is free, and many times conceives strange, stupend, absurd shapes, as in sick men we commonly observe. . . . In poets and painters imagination forcibly works, as appears by their several fictions, antics, images: as Ovid's house of sleep, Psyche's palace in Apuleius, etc. In man it is subject and governed by reason, or at least should be; but in brutes it hath no superior, and is *ratio brutorum*, all the reason they have. . . .
>
> Sleep is a rest or binding of the outward senses, and of the common sense, for the preservation of body and soul . . . ; for when the common sense resteth, the outward senses rest also. The phantasy alone is free, and his commander, reason: as appears by those imaginary dreams, which are of divers kinds, natural, divine, demoniacal, etc., which vary according to humours, diet, actions, objects, etc.[14]

What Burton unfolds in digressive scientific discourse, Milton condensed in epic pentameters some forty years later:

> But know that in the soul
> Are many lesser faculties, that serve
> Reason as chief. Among these Fancy next
> Her office holds; of all external things
> Which the five watchful senses represent,
> She forms imaginations, aery shapes,
> Which Reason, joining or disjoining, frames
> All what we affirm or what deny, and call
> Our knowledge or opinion; then retires

Into her private cell when Nature rests.
Oft, in her absence, mimic Fancy wakes
To imitate her; but, misjoining shapes,
Wild work produces oft, and most in dreams,
Ill matching words and deeds long past or late. (V, 100–114)

While Burton distinguishes the inner senses with the help of a line drawn between human beings and animals—he associates common sense with higher reason and defines fantasy as *ratio brutorum*—Milton distinguishes them by an implied gender difference. The operations of the faculty of reason are exemplified by Adam, while Eve's dream is the product of unbridled ramblings of her reason when she parts from her partner and sponsor to explore the world on her own. In Milton, the state of sleep allegorically presents the case of female reason: unguided and unguarded by male censure. According to Burton, fancy, or female reason, is subject and governed by [male] reason, or at least should be—Eve's demonic dream and, later on, the Fall show the catastrophic results when woman lacks the support and control of man as the higher form of rationality. Without Adam as her superior, Eve is confined to fancy; just as women without men, as Milton is suggesting, are defined by *ratio brutorum*, which is "all the reason they have."

Adam's Dream

Milton has invented in his biblical epic not only a female but also a male dream. Scholarly attention has been paid to each dream individually, but seldom to the pair. It is, however, just this gendered configuration and polarization that gives a specific meaning to both of them. A remarkable distinction occurs already in the setting of the dream narratives: Eve tells her dream to Adam, Adam tells his to Raphael. The movement goes upward, showing that just as woman finds her rational counterpart in man, so man finds his rational counterpart in the archangel. Adam's dream is embedded in a narrative of his first memories as a human being. This account begins with his awakening into life which, in its imagery, recalls the birth of an animal:

As new-waked from soundest sleep,
Soft on the flowery herb I found me laid,
In balmy sweat, which with his beams the Sun
Soon dried, and on the reeking moisture fed. (VIII, 253–256)

Adam, who is not born of woman into a family, is created by God into nature, where he is fostered and nurtured by the sun. He immediately springs onto his feet and stretches heavenward, instinctively knowing his origin and destination. At this point his anthropological evolution begins, a sequence of phases through which Adam swiftly passes. After having taken in the new surroundings through his various senses, and after having learned the mechanism of his body by moving freely about, he proceeds to more self-conscious forms of cognition. This new stage begins with wonder, questioning, and the discovery of a lack of knowledge.

> But who I was, or where, or from what cause,
> Knew not. (VIII, 270–271)

Language is born in this stage. It helps Adam to interact with the creation and to communicate his problem, which is the conscious ignorance (as opposed to the instinctive knowledge) of his origin. With the command of language, however, he also experiences an alienation from nature. A rift between speaking man and mute nature becomes more and more obvious. *Natura loquitur* is certainly not the principle of the creation as Milton presents it. The world of nature can be named by articulate man, but it cannot respond to his existential questions. The silence of nature is the beginning of Jewish and Puritan religious experience. At this point, the *educatio generis humani* as exemplified by Milton's Adam comes to a full stop. Metaphysical knowledge is to be obtained neither by sensuous experience nor by rational investigation, but only by revelation. Adam tells the archangel that he is exhausted and frustrated from his quest for higher knowledge, the knowledge of his Maker,

> Pensive I sat me down. There gentle sleep
> First found me, and with soft oppression seized
> My drowsed sense, untroubled, though I thought
> I then was passing to my former state
> Insensible, and forthwith to dissolve: (VIII, 287–291)

This is Adam's first experience of sleep, which he cannot immediately distinguish from a regression into his former state of nothingness. The difference between sleep and death, the general dissolution of identity, is marked by yet another phenomenon experienced by Adam for the first time: a dream.

> When suddenly stood at my head a dream,
> Whose inward apparition gently moved
> My fancy to believe I yet had being,
> And lived. (VIII, 292–294)

While Eve, accustomed to the habit of dreaming, experiences for the first time a subversive dream "of offence and trouble," Adam's account presents the very first dream given to mankind. This dream is a gift of God's, not Satan's, and is part of the divine education of man. In the tradition of Greek and Roman literature, the dream is personified as a shape that stands at the head of the dreamer. The quality of the dream is already indicated by the position of the dream; if it is oppressive, it squats heavily on the dreamer almost in the manner of a Fuselian nightmare—Spenser had indicated that "The one vpon his hardy head him plast"—but if the dream is illuminating, it assumes the position of a guardian angel. Again, fancy is mentioned as the faculty through which dreams are communicated; but this time, all devaluating associations are carefully eliminated. We come to learn that fancy, the image-producing faculty, is not only an organ of depravation but also one of mystic illumination. In Adam's dream, fancy is not attacked by devilish art but "gently moved"; in these lines, there is an element of friendly communication and even caressing communion, a far cry from the fancy that has to be fortified and harnessed against the strategic assaults of evil.

Like Satan in Eve's dream, God (or one of his messengers) projects himself into Adam's dream. The answer that mute nature would not yield comes from a "shape divine" who responds to Adam's yearning and addresses him directly. After having named the creation, he is given a name himself along with a place and a first command:

> One came, methought, of shape divine,
> And said, "Thy mansion wants thee, Adam; rise,
> First Man, of men innumerable ordained
> First father! called by thee, I come thy guide
> To the garden of bliss, thy seat prepared." (VIII, 295–299)

Milton uses the dream as a mode of divine communication but not of divine revelation. What is revealed in the dream is the identity and destiny of Adam as master of paradise, not of God as the creator of the universe. The self-revelation of God ("Whom thou sought'st I am / . . . Author of all this thou seest / Above, or round about thee, or beneath." VIII, 316–318) does not occur in the dream but happens only after Adam's awakening in paradise. The same holds true for the first covenant of Eden, which combines an internal restriction of power with an external extension of power: the prohibition to touch the forbidden fruit and the commandment to assume dominion over Eden and "all the Earth."[15] The function of Adam's dream, then, is restricted to a poetic device facilitating his translocation into paradise. In the biblical account, the creation of man precedes the creation of paradise, thus necessitating a local transfer of Adam: "And the Lord God planted a garden east-ward in Eden; and there he put the man whom he had formed."[16] The function of the dream, then, is played down from a theological point of view, but it is highlighted from a poetic point of view. The point and content of the dream is a translocation:

> So saying, by the hand he took me, raised,
> And over fields and waters, as in air
> Smooth sliding without step (VIII 300–302)

that is similar to what Eve experiences in her dream. The meticulously parallel construction of both dreams highlights their contrast: both dreamers are called and led away by a divine shape, one in order to forget her true self in a state of precarious regression, the other to discover and assume his true self in his own destined domain. Both experience flight and a view of the world from above, Eve in a narcotic and delusive experience of ascension, Adam in an empowering act of surveillance and control over his new dominion. Both are confronted in their dreams with the crucial motif of the epic, the forbidden fruit, and both are tempted in their dreams "with sudden appetite / To pluck and eat" (VIII, 308–309). But while Eve transgresses and tastes the fruit in her dream, Adam is spared a similar shameful experience by waking up just in time:

> Each tree
> Loaden with fairest fruit, that hung to the eye
> Tempting, stirred in me sudden appetite
> To pluck and eat; whereat I waked, and found
> Before mine eyes all real, as the dream
> Had lively shadowed. (VIII, 306–311)

The last and perhaps the most significant contrast between the dreams is the manner of awakening. At the end of her dream, Eve experiences a loss; she is left alone, her guide is gone, she sinks down in her sleep into a deadly depression from which Adam luckily liberates her in waking her up:

> but O, how glad I waked
> To find this but a dream! (V, 92–93)

The opposite is true for Adam; he does not experience a relapse—on the contrary, he steps out of his elated state right over into a new world. The dream is a preparation for a higher state of being; as Adam is "translated" into paradise, the dream "translates" him into a higher state of identity and consciousness. There is no break, no gap, no breach between dream and reality, but rather a creative transition from one to the other.

Imagination and Fancy—the Romantic Engendering of Anthropology

This smooth transition between dream and reality did not fail to impress Romantic readers. The notion that dreams can prefigure and even create reality greatly appealed to their idealism. They had turned the principle of sensualist philosophy—according to which nothing exists in the intellect that did not earlier pass through the senses—upside down. Quite the contrary, thought the Romantics. It was their firm conviction that everything, including physical reality, depended on a prior, constructive act of the mind. Among these readers, Keats was the one to choose Adam's dream as presented by Milton, transforming the epic episode into a paradigm of poetic creativity. In a famous letter to Benjamin Bailey on "the holiness of the Heart's affections and the truth of Imagination," he wrote:

> The Imagination may be compared to Adam's dream,—he awoke and found it truth. . . . And yet such a fate can only befall those who delight in Sensation,

> rather than hunger as you do after Truth. Adam's dream will do here, and seems to be a conviction that Imagination and its empyreal reflection is the same as human Life and its Spiritual repetition.[17]

In reshaping the terms "fancy" and "imagination," Keats translates the (gendered) anthropological discourse of the seventeenth century into a (gendered) discourse of aesthetics. In a last step, I want to trace this shift from seventeenth-century anthropology to nineteenth-century art theory. We shall see that as the same terms reappear with new definitions in new contexts, their gendered implications are elaborated and made ever more explicit.

So far, the terms "imagination," "fancy," and "fantasy" had been used interchangeably. This indifference in terminological distinction prevailed in the eighteenth century. When in the beginning of that century Joseph Addsion wrote one of his Spectator essays on "the Pleasures of the Imagination or Fancy" he added the notice in brackets: "(which I shall use promiscuously)."[18] The same is still true for Dr. Johnson's dictionary, in which "fancy" is rendered by "imagination" and vice versa.[19] The situation changes with the Romantic poets, who take up these terms, turning them into key words of their poetic theory. They tranform "imagination" and "fancy" into gendered concepts. It is significant that Keats, in referring to Adam's dream, speaks of the "imagination" rather than of "fancy." His concept of the imagination is similar to that of Coleridge, who in his theoretical writings created a hierarchy between the two terms. Coleridge was influenced by Kant and had studied German idealistic philosophy in Göttingen; he disengaged the faculty of the imagination from the the derogatory associations of whim and simulacrum, elevating it to a paradigmatic anthropological prerogative. Among the Romantics, who considered creativity to be the foremost human potential, the artist was man writ large; he was considered the prototype of humankind.

As usual, the elevation of one quality implies the sinking or debunking of another, a dialectic process that in this case is implicitly substantiated by a clear hierarchy of gender. The aesthetics of the Romantic age that developed the notion of genius defined the latter by the imagination, separating creative originality from unoriginal and repetitive production. The way that imagination and fancy were defined made it impossible for women to qualify for the higher forms of creativity:

> It dissolves, diffuses, dissipates, in order to recreate; or where this process is rendered impossible, yet still at all events it struggles to idealize and to unify. It is essentially vital, even as all objects (as objects) are essentially fixed and dead.
>
> Fancy, on the contrary, has no other counters to play with, but fixities and definites. The Fancy is indeed no other than a mode of Memory emanicipated from the order of time and space.[20]

"In poets and painters imagination forcibly works, as appears by their several fictions, antics, images," Burton had written. Two centuries later, to redefine imagination and claim it as a male prerogative meant to deprive women, who in the meantime had entered the platform or art, of their most important resource, namely genius and original creativity. They were thrown back on natural reproduction, on one hand, and mimetic repetition, on the other, as their specific modes of creativity. Moreover, the Romantic artists privileged dreaming—the projecting of a world—as a paradigmatic form of creativity. Some of them, such as Keats, Coleridge, or DeQuincey, were self-trained and self-conscious dreamers. Having cut the bonds of tradition in a thrust toward originality, they discovered the dream as a primal source and energy of art. The ideal of the creative dream, however, was clearly gendered; Keats found its prototype not in Eve's but in Adam's dream.

Conclusion

Even in Milton's paradise, experience is not unified and whole but opens up into higher and lower worlds. Adam and Eve show how dreaming extends the range of human experience for better and worse. Dreams are the privileged medium in which—to use the words of the ethnographer—human beings communicate with the powers of the exosphere.[21] Induced by a demonic or divine source, the dreamer is initiated into a new realm. The directions upward and downward mark the scale on which humankind can rise or sink in its notoriously unstable status. Milton exemplifies this fundamental anthropological situation in terms of gender; he makes it quite clear who is chosen to rise beyond and who is liable to sink below the level of common humanity.

I hope to have shown that the dreams of our first parents as invented by Milton in his biblical epic merit critical analysis. In analyzing these dreams today, we are less interested in the psychic symptoms of the dreamers than in those of Milton and his age. The gendered dreams of Adam and Eve show how the universal human potential tends to be split up by culture into complementary male and female components. The possible range of social action ascribed to men and women is defined and confined by cultural discourses—in this case, by definitions and distinctions of anthropology. Although the focus had shifted from theology and anthropology in the seventeenth century to poetological concerns in the nineteenth century, certain tenacious patterns of thought survived—or were reestablished on new grounds.

Notes

1. Nietzsche 1962: I, 450. For the context of Nietzsche's dream reflections in the history of *Wissenschaft* compare Treiber 1994.
2. Müller 1992: 35.
3. Müller 1992: 36.
4. Müller 1992: 39.
5. Müller 1992: 37.
6. Nietzsche 1962: I, 12, 454.
7. Nietzsche 1962: I, 13, 456.

8. Nietzsche 1962: II, 139.

9. Milton 1968 [=1667–74] in the edition of Beeching and Williams 1968: 201. Hunter (1946: 255–265) provides extensive background information to this topic ranging from St. Thomas to Joseph Glanvill.

10. In *De anima*, Aristotle gives an account of the various operations of the mind, later on referred to as "faculty psychology." In his long Arabic commentary on *De anima* in the early eleventh century, Avicenna systematized this knowledge, which became part of the scholastic tradition after it was translated into Latin in the twelfth century. A concise account of this history is to found in Wolfson 1935. See also Bundy 1927.

11. Spenser I, canto I, 38 in Smith and Selincourt 1959: 7.

12. Spenser I, canto I, 43. He writes this episode in a clear-cut literary tradition, exchanging, however, the true prophetic dream of his source for a false dream. The motif of the messenger sent to the cave of Morpheus to procure from him a dream is vividly described by Ovid, *Metaporphoses*, book 11 in the story of Ceyx and Halcyone, which Chaucer adapted in a rather burlesque version in his allegorical poem *Hous of Fame*. A constant feature in the rendering of this episode is the sleep of Morpheus, from which to awake him for a moment in order to deliver the message proves to be a major task.

13. As an expert in Renaissance dream lore, Adam may know that there are four types of dreams: natural, oracular, divine, and demonic, and that only the oracular and the divinely inspired dream are fit objects of hermeneutic exegesis.

14. In Jackson 1972: 159–160 (I, 1, 7).

15. Into the covenant of Eden as presented by Milton in VIII, 321–341 can be read the principle of Puritan colonial rule; discipline, a conscious restriction of the self, legitimizes the expansion of rule into foregn domains.

16. Gen. 2:8 (King James version).

17. The letter from November 22, 1817 can be found in Rollins 1958: 185.

18. *The Spectator* No. 411 (June 21, 1712) in Bond 1965: III, 536.

19. Johnson 1799, I.

20. Coleridge in Shawcross 1979: I, 202 (chapter 13).

21. Compare Ludwig Strümpell 1874: 38, "The dream became a bridge across which higher powers communicated with human beings and vice versa."

References

Beeching H. C. and Charles Williams (eds.). 1968. *The English Poems of John Milton*, London

Bond, Donald F. (ed.). 1965. *The Spectator.* Oxford.

Bundy, Murry Wright. 1927. *The Theory of the Imagination in Classical and Medieval Thought* (University of Illinois Studies in Language and Literature 12) Urbana, Illinois.

Hunter, William B. 1946. "Eve's Demonic Dream," *English Literary History* 13, 255–265.

Jackson, Holbrook (ed.). 1972. *Burton, Robert. The Anatomy of Melancholy (1621).* London.

Johnson, Samuel. 1799. *A Dictionary of the English Language*, 2 vols., London.

Müller, Klaus E. 1992. "Reguläre Anomalien im Schnittbereich zweier Welten," *Zeitschrift für Parapsychologie und Grenzgebiete der Psychologie* 34, 1/2, 33–50.

Nietzsche, Friedrich. 1962. *Werke in drei Bänden*, Edited by Karl Schlechta. Munich.

Rollins, Hyder E. (ed.). 1958. *The Letters of John Keats.* Cambridge, MA.

Shawcross, J. (ed.). 1979. *Samuel T. Coleridge, Biographia Litteraria.* Oxford.

Smith, J. C. and E. de Selincourt (eds.). 1959. *The Poetical Works of Edmund Spenser.* London.

Strümpell, Ludwig. 1874. *Die Natur und Entstehung der Träume.* Leipzig.

Treiber, Hubert. 1994. "Zur 'Logik des Traumes' bei Nietzsche," *Nietzsche Studien* 23, 1–41.

Wolfson, Harry A. 1935. "The Internal Senses," *Harvard Theological Review* 28, 69–133.

16

The Cultural Index of Freud's *Interpretation of Dreams*

Stéphane Moses

1

In his book on the interpretation of dreams (*Die Traumdeutung*, 1900), Freud begins by comparing his own theory of dreams to ancient doctrines concerning the nature of dreams and their interpretation, yet juxtaposes it, as well, with modern scientific theories, especially that of psychiatry. In doing so, he places his research in the continuity of a long tradition while demonstrating, at the same time, the radical innovation of his own discoveries. They are opposed both to the positivist theses of the psychiatric school, according to which "a dream is not a mental act at all, but a somatic process,"[1] and to the conceptions of ancient cultures that saw dreams as supernatural revelations. These two conflicting views of the nature of dreams necessarily lead to two opposite conceptions of how they may be interpreted: if dreams are pure physiological processes, the very question of their meaning is irrelevant, and the attempt to interpret them will forever be "a purely fanciful task;"[2] on the other hand, if dreams are messages coming from another realm, they must be decipherable—provided the interpreter has the keys that can unlock their code.

Based on observation of his own dreams and those of his patients, Freud, for his part, reached the conclusion that dreams, far from being pure physiological phenomena, are rather part of the texture of psychic life and for that reason bear meaning. The meaning they hold, however, is not that of a message coming from some supernatural world, but expresses, rather, the mental life of the dreamer. This linking of the dream to the subject's own spontaneous activity—in contrast to antique conceptions, in which the dream, coming from without, visits a completely passive dreamer—is clear testimony that Freudian theory belongs fully to Western modernity: that is, to a cultural paradigm characterized, since Decartes and Kant, by the preeminence of the subject. Indeed, it is precisely because the dream is the expression of a subject's activity that it is, for Freud, essentially interpretable. Conversely, by postulating that dreams belong not to the subject's world but to the body as an object, late nineteenth-century psychiatry held them to be devoid of all meaning and impervious to all interpretation.

In affirming that dreams have meaning and are interpretable, Freud seems, somewhat paradoxically, to return to the ancient conception of dreams that survives in our own day in folklore and popular beliefs. "Here once more," wrote Freud, "we have one of these not infrequent cases in which an ancient and jealously held popular belief seems to be nearer the truth than the judgment of the prevalent science of today."[3] Freud often remarked that psychoanalytic theory goes back to certain intuitions central to archaic thought, myth, and folklore rather than voicing the positivist prejudices of contemporary science. For him, though, this did not imply a naive return to prerational forms of thought, but rather to their integration, somewhat like citations, in his own scientific discourse. This analogy or parallel between ontogenesis and phylogenesis is one of the fundamental axioms of Freudian thought, and his dream theory is clearly marked by it as well. The parallel between the antique view of the dream and the Freudian conception of dreams as an expression of the individual unconscious comes to light in a particularly striking way in Freud's theory of dream symbolism. It appeared relatively late in the process of elaborating on his *Traumdeutung* (in the editions of 1909, 1911, and above all 1914) and was no more than "auxiliary" in his technique of interpretation.[4] Its theoretical importance, though, is nonetheless considerable for, in Freud's eyes, it grants his doctrine of dreams a cultural, that is, objective, legitimacy. "This symbolism," he wrote, "is not peculiar to dreams, but is characteristic of unconscious ideation, in particular among the people, and it is to be found in folklore, and in popular myths, legends, linguistic idioms, proverbial wisdom and current jokes to a more complete extent than in dreams."[5]

This principle of symbolism, Freud held, was the basis on which the technique of dream interpretation was founded in antiquity. We must point out that Freud applies the term "symbolism" here in two different senses, one specific and the other generic. The first designates one of the two methods of dream interpretation used in antiquity, as opposed to the method Freud calls "cryptographic." The second sense refers in a global manner to these two methods as a whole. Taken in this most general sense, the ancient conception of dream symbolism rests upon a theory (explicit or implicit) of the dream as a deformed reflection of reality. Freud cites, in this connection, a definition offered by Aristotle (in the treatise *De divinatione per somnium*) according to which "dream-pictures, like pictures on water, are pulled out of shape by movement, and the most successful interpreter is the man who can detect the truth from the misshapen picture."[6] The metaphor of a reflection suggests both a theory of analogy and a theory of truth: it implies, on one hand, that certain correspondences exist between different aspects of reality, but on the other hand, that these aspects of reality are organized in a hierarchy, that their degree of intelligibility depends on their proximity to or distance from an archetypal truth. To say the images of dreams are like reflections in water is thus, first of all, to translate one image by another, to express the theory of analogy by an analogy. It is, second, to affirm that the images of dreams are not arbitrary, that they correspond to a truth and therefore have meaning. But, above all, it implies that in dreams this meaning appears deformed, and that in order to understand it, all disturbances engendered by the surrounding environment—that of the dream (and it is thanks to these disturbances that there are images)—must be eliminated to restore them to the truth from which they originated. The task of the interpreter, then, is both to discover the analogies between the dream images and the ideas to which they refer, and to translate the imaged dream language into intelligible form.

We can easily understand to what extent Freud must have seen an anticipation of his own theories in Aristotle's thesis. The notion that the "images" of dreams are the disguised expression of certain realities that, relative to them, represent "truths," and that interpretation consists of leading its images back to their true meaning, corresponds perfectly to Freudian theories of the "manifest dream" and "latent dream," to the process of deformation set in motion by the "dream-work," and to interpretation as the deciphering of meaning. In the same context, Freud also refers to another author of antiquity, Artemidorus of Daldis, for whom the art of dream interpretation is founded (as in magic) on the principle of association; in his view, writes Freud, "a thing in a dream means what it recalls to the mind."[7] Clearly, for Freud this principle seems to presage the psychoanalytical technique of free association, a condition as indispensable for analytical dialogue as for the interpretation of dreams. Nonetheless, Freud objects, symbolic interpretation as it appears in both of these authors' thought is always based on the interpreter's skills, intuition, and imagination. For that reason it remains essentially arbitrary and makes no guarantee of being "scientific." In other words, it cannot be made the object of a theory and is thus not generalizable.

The other technique of interpretation practiced in antiquity is the "cryptographic" method. Unlike the symbolic method proper, this technique is founded on a precise code in which each symbol corresponds with the "key," that is, the meaning appropriate to it. "The dream," Freud wrote, "is treated as a kind of cryptography in which each sign can be translated into another sign having a known meaning, in accordance with a fixed key."[8] Here, once again, to interpret thus means to translate one system of signs into another system of signs, but this time with the aid of a lexicon. Western culture has known a host of "dream keys," each one based on a system of analogies—more or less elaborate—between the dream images and their presumed meaning. What is interesting about this cryptographic method is that it presupposes the existence of recurrent symbols, and thus of a sort of universal dream language. In the first edition of the *Traumdeutung*, Freud for his part had already affirmed the existence of "typical dreams," that is, "dreams which almost everyone has dreamt alike."[9] It was not until 1914, however, that he added a special chapter to his book, titled "Symbolic Representation in the Dream: Other Typical Dreams," in which he attempted to develop a theory of universal dream symbolism and its presuppositions. This theory, founded on the hypothesis of an original human ability to perceive networks of analogies in nature, an ability lost in the course of history and whose last remaining trace is the existence of universal symbols in the individual unconscious, was meant to confer some scientific legitimacy on the Freudian symbolic code, differentiating it from the arbitrary codes proposed by the various dream keys.

2

Freudian interpretation of dreams, however, is based only partially on the symbolic method. That method is actually secondary to what we could call "rhetorical" analysis of the dream, founded on the minute description of figures or tropes used by the subject of the unconscious in its work of elaborating the dream. It is here that the difference between Freudian method and that of antiquity is most clearly apparent. Nonetheless, the great principles of Freudian hermeneutics apply equally, though in a less evident way, to his use of the symbolic method. The first difference concerns the way the interpreter views his object of study: while the seers of antiquity saw the dream as a whole, Freud separates it immediately into a series of elements that he interprets one by one, each independently from the others. Dreams, he writes, are "conglomerates of psychic formations"; they should be analyzed "en detail" rather than "en masse."[10] This primary difference, though, Freud remarks, has more to do with the symbolic method proper than the cryptographic method, which also isolates the diverse symbols within the dream. The second difference is much more essential: it concerns the nature of the associative method as it is implemented by psychoanalysis, which differs radically from the associative processes used in archaic techniques of interpretation. The latter follow the associations of ideas the dream suggests to the interpreter, while for Freud the meaning of the dream becomes clear through associations evoked in the dreamer personally. In antiquity (and to a great extent in European romanticism) dreams were conceived as the reflection, in the soul of the dreamer, of a web of cosmic, that is, objective, analogies. But although the interpreter may have taken the dreamer's personal situation into account (like Joseph in the biblical story, when he interprets the dreams of the two ministers or Pharaoh's two dreams), the dream was still seen as bearing a general meaning based on a system of objective correspondences between the images that constituted them and certain external realities. For Freud, on the contrary, the meaning of a dream is a strict function of the personal history (both recent and distant) of the dreamer. He held each dream to be a unique constellation that translates an absolutely singular moment in the psychic biography of the subject. Hence a third difference between the Freudian and the antique conceptions of dreams: while for the ancients dreams had a prophetic character and were thus oriented toward the future, in Freud's eyes they refer to the dreamer's past. In them, immediate memories related to events that occurred the day preceding the dream crystallize with memory traces (*Gedächtnisspuren*) inscribed in the unconscious by much earlier events, dating perhaps to the subject's earliest stages of childhood. In that sense, every dream is a link in a "psychic chain" the subject will be asked to "trace backwards in his memory."[11] For Freud, the dream is not a sign announcing the future but rather the "symptom" of a history.[12]

Relative to traditional conceptions of dreams, Freudian theory represents a kind of Copernican revolution comparable to what Kant had accomplished in his theory of knowledge. The ancient doctrines held a dream to be an objective entity, the eruption of a mysterious reality into the soul that the intellect could not apprehend alone. Dream images were understood as symbols referring to secret aspects of reality. Freud was the first to conceive a theory of dream as something produced by the subject, as a creation comparable to an artist's work of art. As such, Freudian theory fits quite clearly into the dominant paradigm of European culture since Decartes and Kant, marked by the preeminence of the subject, whose intellectual activity gives form and sense to the world. But within that paradigm, Freudian theory incites a new revolution that shakes the philosophy of the subject to its very foundations. The transcendental subject of Kantian and post-Kantian philosophy was in its essence the subject of knowledge. Its noetic horizon was that of knowledge, its substance merging with that of consciousness. The Freudian discovery of the unconscious completely subverted the identity of the subject and of conscious life by transporting the subject outside himself and toward a space where he no longer knows himself. Freud's division of the psychic apparatus into a conscious and unconscious system explodes the classical notion of subject and scatters its fragments in multiple psychic instances that may no longer be reassembled, as in classical psychology, into one original synthesis. Hence the paradoxical nature of an idea such as the "subject of the unconscious" forged by Jacques Lacan and critiqued by Jacques Derrida, for after the concept of subject as an original source of mental activity was radically called into question, neither the conscious nor the unconscious—all the more so—could still be considered subjects of themselves.[13]

Nonetheless, for Freud it is the subject of the unconscious that remains at the root of dreams. This metaphor, which does not appear explicitly in Freud's text, designates the psychic instance that, behind the unconscious, is supposed to direct its activity. That instance is in reality none other than a function whose existence is postulated by the play of psychic economy. In effect, the unconscious is presented in Freudian thought as the concept of a space where elementary psychic realities dwell (affects, drives, memory traces, etc.) and where they will begin to manifest themselves in a series of "primary processes." When these unconscious forces collide with barriers imposed by the ego (censorship, reality principle) they must, in order to find expression, agree to a series of compromises that manifest themselves as symptoms; one of these compromises is the dream. The whole of these processes is described, in Freud's discourse, through impersonal metaphors, the terms of which are borrowed, most essentially, from the language of classical mechanics and physics of energy. This impersonal model of psychic activity, however, collides with another implicit demand of Freudian theory—a finality that will influence how the psychic apparatus functions. Hence the Lacanian hypothesis of a "subject of the unconscious," an originating instance of Desire that can regulate its dynamic and carry out, in its name, the compromises essential for its manifestation.

Although the concept of the "subject of the unconscious" is absent from Freud's texts, most notably from the *Traumdeutung*, it seems the elaboration of dreams is due, in Freud's eyes, to just such an originating instance, with the dream work comparable to the way an artist creates a work of art. Freud often emphasized the role of the unconscious in artistic creation (as, for example, in his 1908 essay on "The Writer and Dreaming"), sometimes going so far as to see a literary work as a projection of the author's conflicts and neuroses. (The most extreme case of such a reduction of literature to pathology is the study on "Dostoevsky and Parricide" of 1927). The analogy, though, functions in reverse as well; for example, at one point in the *Traumdeutung*, Freud illustrates a description of the mechanism of the free association of ideas in psychoanalytical treatment using a passage from a letter by Schiller describing the unconscious appearance of images and ideas in the process of his literary creation.[14] Reading the *Traumdeutung* or the case reports in his case stories, it is always striking to see to what extent certain people, who seem so thoroughly prosaic in their daily lives, manifest such an extraordinary literary talent in their dreams, as if great poets were concealed deep in their unconscious minds. This mysterious element, capable of liberating unsuspected imaginative forces in the depths of the psyche, then of creating scenarios from them of extraordinary richness and complexity, seems to function, in effect, as a poetic instance. We might note that this metaphor is absolutely reversible; each of its terms could function either as signifier or as signified: if a poet is able to draw inspiration from the depths of the unconscious, that is because the unconscious has always functioned as a poet does.

Although we experience dreams in the form of images, Freud studied them not as visual structures but as texts. Or rather, the images of the dream are transposed in Freud's presentation to verbal signs. The reasons for this, of course, are evidently pragmatic: while the dream is experienced in a visual form, it can only be communicated in verbal terms (through speech or writing). Yet aside from that formal constraint, Freudian analysis is always presented, in the *Traumdeutung*, as a textual analysis. If the dream—composed of a series of images—may be compared to a film, the narrative Freud makes of it would be analogous to a scenario, or rather to the script of that film. The analysis of a dream, for its part, follows not the film but its script (provided, that is, we consider the script as a particularly developed literary text). Most striking, in the Freudian process, is the transformation of images into words. One of many examples may be found in a brief passage from the very beginning of Freud's account of his dream "The Count Thun":

> A crowd of people, a meeting of students.—A count (Thun or Taaffe) was speaking. He was challenged to say something about the Germans, and declared

> with a contemptuous gesture that their favorite flower was colt's foot, and put some sort of dilapidated leaf—or rather the crumpled skeleton of a leaf—into his buttonhole. I fired up—so I fired up [*Ich fahre auf, fahre also auf*] though I was surprised at my taking such an attitude.[15]

Freud comments on the phrase "I fired up—so I fired up" in the following note: "This repetition crept into the dream-text, apparently through inadvertence. I have let it stand, since the analysis showed that it was significant."[16] In this note, the expression "dream-text" clearly relates to Freud's transcription of the dream after awakening. The "inadvertence" in question betrays that the text itself took place in a semi–dream state, so that the "dream-text" that Freud transmits to the reader represents a sort of osmosis between the dream itself and its transcription. Indeed, as Freud suggests in his note, the analysis of the dream reveals that its central significance turns upon the repeated phrase "*Ich fahre auf.*" But before reaching that point, let us note that the verb *fahren* (travel, move) and its grammatical variations are repeatedly invoked in the narrative of this remarkably long and complex dream whose central theme is movement in space (by walking, train, carriage, or tram) and in time. Just as the different compounds based on the word *Bahn* (road) such as *Eisenbahn* (railroad), *Strassenbahn* (streetcar), *Bahnhof* (station), and *Bahnstrecke* (train journey), which also appear repeatedly in the dream, may reflect the Freudian concept of *Bahnung* (facilitation), formed of the same root and designating the way sensations must go to reach the unconscious and register there in the form of "memory traces,"[17] so the recurrence of the verb *fahren* and its derivatives may refer, in the context of the dream, to the concept of displacement (*Verschiebung*). In effect, the analysis of the dream concludes by showing that spatial displacements (journeys) themselves appear in this dream as temporal displacements (*Verschiebungen*). Freud's interpretation actually ends by recalling two riddles based on two puns: in one, the verb *vorfahren* (drive a car up) is read as the substantive plural *Vorfahren* (ancestry); in the other, the verb *nachkommen* (follow after) is understood as the substantive plural *Nachkommen* (successors). The meaning of the dream, according to Freud, may be summarized in the following formula: "It is absurd to be proud of one's ancestry; it is better to be an ancestor oneself," which one could translate as: "Better to be a father than a son," or "it is the son who is the true father." The paradox of the son who, in turn, becomes a father nullifies the mechanistic conception of linear and irreversible time and institutes the notion of a temporality of the unconscious in which "before" and "after" seem to be reversible. This dechronologization of time is translated in the dream into its spatialization: temporal "before" and "after" in the latent dream are substituted in the manifest dream by spatial "behind" and "before," and the principle of their reversibility is suggested: "It was as if," said the dreamer (Freud himself) in the dream of "Count Thun," I had already driven with him for some of the distance."[18]

Clearly, the transition, in the dream's analysis, from the spatial dimension in the manifest dream to the temporal (and, in its elaboration, from the temporal dimension to the spatial) in the latent dream is only possible when images of different journeys appearing in the manifest dream are substituted with words corresponding to them, along with the entire halo of linguistic associations that surround them (the verb *fahren* and its derivatives). The analysis, which replaces the images with words, returns the spatial scenario of the dream to its temporal meaning, while in the work of the dream's elaboration, which translates time to space, the original words are transformed into images. In essence, using Freudian terms, the content of a latent dream consists of ideas, but these are perceptible only through words. The Freudian unconscious is a fabric of words woven together by a nearly limitless network of associations. It is "considerations of representability" (*Die Rücksicht auf Darstellbarkeit*) that compels the unconscious to translate them into visual images.[19] The fundamental difference between Freudian interpretation and traditional interpretation of the symbolic sort may thus be summarized in the following manner: while the symbolic method translates each image of the dream into an external reality supposed to correspond to it, Freudian method restores the images to the endless network of verbal associations from which they originated.

3

There is, though, one case in which interpretation is essentially independent of the dreamer's own associations, and that is when symbolic elements play a part in the dream. For Freud, the symbols of dreams disclose a universal lexicon whose validity is supposedly immutable, regardless of the psychic biography of the dreamer and of the specific constellation that each of his dreams uniquely expresses. In addition, we know that for Freud dream symbolism is almost always sexual in nature. Compared to the nearly infinite proliferation of associative chains and their boundless multiplicity of meanings, here we find a relatively poor and nearly always one-dimensional interpretative technique. And, in fact, the coexistence of two such different hermeneutical approaches seems to have presented Freud with a difficult theoretical problem. In principle, the dominant method of interpretation in the *Traumdeutung*, which is rhetorical, does not allow for the simultaneous presence of a symbolic method. The dream, in effect, is elaborated segment by segment through a process of distortion (*Entstellung*) in which unconscious ideas, under the pressure of censorship, decompose and recompose in altered form, change places and enter new configurations—in short, disguise themselves to reappear in hardly recognizable form within the manifest dream. We know that in order to achieve this distortion, the dream uses two processes: displacement (*Verschiebung*) and condensation (*Verdichtung*). Displacement is a clearly metonymic process; in it, one signifier is replaced by another similar one in a chain of associations based simply on contiguity—that is, with no resemblance between the different signifiers (for example, in the analysis of the dream "Count Thun," the chain "Wachau—England—fifty years ago—fifteen years ago—my fifteen years—the conspiracy—Henry VIII—the giraffe—the professor of German"). Condensation, which indicates the fusion of a number of heterogeneous signifiers, may indeed imply a certain element of resemblance between those signifiers (the figure of Irma, for example, in the dream of "Irma's injection" is a "montage" of many women in Freud's life), but it, too, is based first and foremost on the principle of contiguous metonymy. Symbol, in contrast, functions according to the principle of resemblance, in the manner of metaphor (in Pharaoh's dreams, the fatted cows and the sheaves of ripe wheat symbolize fertility; similarly, in chapter 7 of the book of Daniel, the four beasts that appear in the prophet's dream symbolize the four empires whose qualities they incarnate). This principle of resemblance, which does not imply any proximity between the symbol's signifier and what it signifies, very clearly underlies Freudian interpretation of sexual symbolism, in which hollow objects represent, almost automatically, female sexual organs and pointed objects male ones. The principle of resemblance, which implies that the symbol image faithfully reflects the thing it symbolizes thus excludes, on principle, any kind of radical distortion. Indeed, according to the citation from Aristotle Freud presents, the dream image may be blurred or disturbed in relation to the truth it represents, but the resemblance between them remains no less evident. We must ask, then, how a symbolic representation might correspond with the distortions the dream creates.

This is the solution Freud proposes: the symbols themselves, despite their unchanging meaning, are integrated like all the other elements of psychic life into the dream work. They, too, are a part of "the peculiar plasticity of the psychic material."[20] A symbol may, for example, appear in a dream without referring to its canonical meaning, exhibiting only its pure reality as an object (an umbrella, then, would signify nothing more than an umbrella). On the other hand, new sexual symbols may be invented from the subject's individual history. Furthermore, "if a dreamer has a choice open to him between a number of symbols, he will decide in favor of the one which is connected in its subject-matter with the rest of the material of his thought—which, that is to say, has individual grounds for its acceptance in addition to the typical ones."[21] What defines these different cases is the suppression of a necessary link between the signifier and signified, which characterizes the traditional conception of symbol. Once pulled into the endless play of psychic forces, the symbol acts as one signifier among many, to the extent that it may be mobilized by the unconscious to take part in the various processes of displacement and condensation by which the dream is elaborated. Yet even if, in the case of the dream symbol, the connection between signifier and signified may be suspended (as in the example of the umbrella) and even though new signifiers may be invented for the same signified, or, alternately, the same symbolic signifier may refer to more than one signified, the original meaning of the symbol nonetheless cannot be changed: as Freud remarked, "The imagination does not admit of long, stiff objects and weapons being used as symbols of the female genitals, or of hollow objects, such as chests, cases, boxes, etc., being used as symbols for the male ones."[22] Dream symbols, for Freud, are thus open to a certain—but by no means unlimited—multiplicity of meaning: a single symbol may simultaneously refer to many significations, but not indiscriminately. Such symbols, then, do not have the almost limitless plasticity of other elements in the dream. Yet, unlike archaic conceptions of the dream, Freudian theory does not assign them univocal meaning; submerged in a psychic space where, as in the system of language, all meaning is differential, the symbols of dreams are also part of an essential ambiguity. "They frequently have more than one or even several meanings," Freud writes, "and, as with Chinese script, the correct interpretation can only be arrived at on each occasion from the context."[23]

4

To conclude, I would like to relate to this "open" conception of Freudian dream symbolism in order to suggest a comparison of psychoanalytical and religious symbolism. To do so, let us take a concrete example, that of "dreams of ascension": Freud analyzes them in his *Traumdeutung* and Mircea Eliade devoted a number of studies to them.[24] Freud, particularly interested in the symbol of the staircase one ascends or descends, proposed two very different interpretations of the theme, one strictly sexual, the other a great deal more ambiguous. On one hand, we find the following definition: "Steps, ladders or staircases, or, as the case may be, walking up or down them, are representations of the sexual act."[25] This one-dimensional explanation, though, in which the symbol leads to only one of its possible meanings, stands in sharp constrast to the multiplicity of interpretations given for "A lovely dream" (*Ein schoener Traum*), in which the same symbol refers both to the theme of ascension and of social decline,[26] and more generally the antithesis between "up" and "down."[27] Here, once again, it is the integration of the symbol in its psychic context that gives it such polyvalence.

For Mircea Eliade, who faults Freud for his "reductive" conception of the theme of ascension, that theme represents a universal symbol which appears in all religions to illustrate the idea of interior movement toward transcendence, the soul's aspiration to struggle free of its own boundedness and rise toward the absolute: "Upon the different but interconnected planes of the oneiric, of active imagination, of mythological creation and folklore, of ritual and of experience, the symbolism of ascension always refers to a breaking-out from a situation that has become 'blocked' or 'petrified,' a rupture of the plane which makes it possible to pass from one mode of being into another—in short, liberty 'of movement,' freedom to change the situation, to abolish a conditioning system."[28] In other words, the symbolism of ascension "delivers its 'true message' upon the planes of metaphysics and mysticism."[29]

We note straight away, however, that this religious reading of the symbol is just as one-sided as Freud's sexual reading. In both cases, the symbol is conceived as a signifier whose relationship with its signified is one of equivalence both necessary and exclusive. It matters little, from this point of view, whether the reading of the symbol is sexual or religious: in either case, its meaning is inscribed in an immutable and predetermined code. As for Aristotle, at issue is a quasi-ontological conception of symbolism, assumed to reflect the very essence of reality. Freud, incidentally, was aware of this essentialist implication of his theory of symbolism; as he suggests in the *Traumdeutung*, the existence of sexual symbolism may be understood phylogenetically as the residue or trace of a sense of cosmic identity (fundamentally sexual) that was intrinsic in prehistoric times.[30] Is this sense of cosmic identity, for Freud, no more than a simple "conceptual and linguistic" representation, or does it express the actual nature of things? Or is the nature itself of things actually of a conceptual and linguistic order? Whatever the case, the hypothesis of a sense of cosmic identification with archaic stages of humanity, and the belief in a universal symbolism that continues to express it even in the dreams of modern people, seems to bring Freudian theory quite close to the conception of religious symbolism propounded by Mircea Eliade or by Jung.

On the other hand, we have seen that Freud strives, with ever-renewed insistence, to relativize this dogmatic vision of symbolism by showing that oneiric symbols are not changeless substances but that their meaning varies continually as a function of the mental context in which they appear.

Symbols are marked, "like all other psycho-pathological structures, by the usual ambivalence of dreams."[31] In effect, "any dream-element may be taken in a positive or negative sense (as an antithetic relation)."[32] Even sexual symbols may often (but not always) bear bisexual signification.[33] In general, all the elements of a manifest dream are overdetermined: in other words, they express a relatively large number of unconscious ideas.[34] The main reason for this multiplicity of meaning for dream elements, and oneiric symbols among them, stems from the fact that, for Freud, the materials from which the dream is made (the "dream-ideas") are linguistic in nature. The dream is constructed from a substance of words, and each of these words refers to a nearly limitless series of associations. Thus "words, since they are the nodal points of numerous ideas, may be regarded as predestined to ambiguity."[35] The Freudian method of interpretation dissolves the diverse components of the dream—including symbols—in an indefinitely extendable system of associations of ideas and images, but above all verbal associations (paronomasia, puns), in which each element is always defined solely in relation to the elements contiguous to it.

It is this linguistic approach to oneiric symbols that truly distinguishes Freudian theory from essentialist conceptions (whether archaic or modern). The difference between them concerns not their content but the form of thought (or, if you wish, the implicit philosophy) they profess. The sexual interpretation of symbolism is not more reductive (or less reductive) than metaphysical interpretation. The real opposition is between a closed vision of symbolism, in which the symbol is conceived as an entity endowed with a permanently fixed meaning, and an open vision, in which the symbols of the dream are given to an endless process of interpretation. "It is only with the greatest difficulty," writes Freud, "that the beginner in the business of interpreting dreams can be persuaded that his task is not at an end when he has a complete interpretation in his hands—an interpretation which makes sense, is coherent and throws light upon every element of the dream's content. For the same dream may perhaps have another interpretation as well, an 'over-interpretation,' which has escaped him. It is, indeed, not easy to form any conception of the abundance of the unconscious trains of thought, all striving to find expression, which are active in our minds. Nor is it easy to credit the skill shown by the dream-work in always hitting upon forms of expression that can bear several meanings—like the Little Tailor in the fairy story who hit seven flies at one blow."[36]

Notes

1. Freud 1953: 169.
2. Freud 1953: 173.
3. Freud 1953: 174.
4. Freud 1953: 339.
5. Freud 1953: 467.
6. Freud 1953: 171.
7. Ibid.
8. Ibid.
9. Freud 1953: 339.
10. Freud 1953: 178.
11. Freud 1953: 174.
12. Ibid.
13. Derrida 1978.
14. Freud 1953: 177.
15. Freud 1953: 301.
16. Ibid.
17. Jacques Derrida (1978) made a classic analysis of the concept of *Bahnung*.
18. Freud 1953: 561.
19. Freud 1953: 459.
20. Freud 1953: 469.
21. Ibid.
22. Freud 1953: 476.
23. Freud 1953: 470. See Derrida 1978.
24. Those essays have been collected in the chapter "Symbolisms of Ascension and 'Waking Dreams'" in Eliade 1960.
25. Freud 1953: 472.
26. Freud 1953: 393.
27. Freud 1953: 439.
28. Eliade 1960: 118.
29. Eliade 1960: 119.
30. Freud 1953: 468.
31. Freud 1953: 231.
32. Freud 1953: 456.
33. Freud 1953: 476.
34. Freud 1953: 389.
35. Freud 1953: 456.
36. Freud 1953: 669.

References

Derrida, Jacques. 1978. "Freud and the Scene of Writing." In *Writing and Difference* (trans. by A. Bass). Chicago.

Eliade, Mircea. 1960. *Myths, Dreams, and Mysteries*, New York (trans. from *Mythes, Rèves et Mystères*, Paris, 1957).

Freud, Sigmund. 1953. *The Interpretation of Dreams*, London (*Die Traumdeutung* 1900, trans. by James Strachey).

Ricoeur, Paul. 1965. *De l'interprétation. Essai sur Freud*, Paris.

Index